G.K.Chesterton

Michael Ffinch

G.K.CHESTERTON

1817

HARPER & ROW, PUBLISHERS, SAN FRANCISCO

Cambridge, Hagerstown, New York, Philadelphia, Washington
London, Mexico City, São Paulo, Singapore, Sydney

FIRST U.S. EDITION

Library of Congress Cataloging-in-Publication Data

Ffinch, Michael.
  G.K. Chesterton.

  Bibliography: p.
  Includes index.
    1. Chesterton, G. K. (Gilbert Keith), 1874-1936—Biography.
2. Authors, English—20th century—Biography.
I. Title.   II. Title: GK Chesterton.
PR4453.C4Z63   1987   828'.91209 [B]   86-45805
ISBN 0-06-252576-X

86 87 88 89 90 RRD 10 9 8 7 6 5 4 3 2 1

Contents

Illustrations

For Dorothy Collins

C.S.Lewis once admitted to Charles Gilmore that it was Chesterton's *The Everlasting Man* that had helped him to a logical view of the outline of Christian history, and advised a closer study of the book, for Chesterton, like most of the great writers, would be rediscovered and revalued about fifty years after his death. On 14 June 1986 it was the fiftieth anniversary of Chesterton's death.

Acknowledgements

I should like to thank Miss Dorothy Collins and her agent A.P.Watt, for their kindness in allowing me to quote freely from the published and unpublished work of G.K.Chesterton. I should also like to thank Dorothy Collins and Judith Lea for their kindness to me while I carried out my research at Top Meadow Cottage. I also thank the Warden of Top Meadow and Mrs Reed for their kindness while I was in Beaconsfield.

My thanks are due to A.D.Peters and Company Ltd for permission to quote from the work of Hilaire Belloc; to Chapman and Hall Ltd for permission to quote from *The Chestertons* by Mrs Cecil Chesterton; The Bodley Head for permission to quote from *Orthodoxy* by G.K.Chesterton; Hodder and Stoughton for *The Everlasting Man*; the Estate of Canon Percy Dearmer, care of Oxford University Press, for permission to quote the hymn 'O God of Earth and Altar'.

I should like to thank Mrs Jean Farrant for her permission to quote from the G.K.Chesterton memorabilia, now in her keeping, once devotedly preserved by Hilary Gray (the late Hilary Broderick); Mrs Chris Budden, the Records Officer of University College, London; Mrs Eleanor Denton, the Archivist of St Paul's School; and Mr Aidan Mackey, for most valuable help. I should like to thank Mr Roy Brewer; Mr Lawrence James; Dr Carl Hallam; and Dr Ranald Campbell for their help. I should also like to thank Fr Jeremy Davies; Mr Shaun Maclaughlin; Mr Rex Mawby; Mr Peter George; Sr Gemma Duffy; the late Hugh Burden, and many others who have helped me in different ways to come to a deeper understanding of Chesterton's life and work.

Lastly I should like to thank my wife, Patricia, for her support during such a long period of writing and research.

Foreword

The life of G.K.Chesterton spans almost exactly the years between the beginning of the rapid growth of Empire in Queen Victoria's reign and the rise of National Socialism in Germany. In the year after Chesterton's birth Disraeli bought the Khedive of Egypt's shares in the Suez Canal Company, and two years after Chesterton's death Hitler marched into Austria. Thus his life began and ended in the gloom of movements whose aim Chesterton would have considered to have been much the same, a self-interested expansionism, seeking to deprive others of their rights, property and land. Had Chesterton lived another three years it is certain that he would have supported the Allies in the war, but it would have been for the same reason that he had supported the Boers in 1898, and in 1914 had been convinced that the evil of what he called Prussianism had to be defeated, because Chesterton was above all things a great champion of Liberty.

This being so, it has often come as a surprise that in religion Chesterton should have moved away from the Liberal Unitarianism of his childhood towards Catholicism. At first the move had been gentle, and, largely through the influence of his wife, Frances, he had become an Anglo-Catholic; but in later years he converted to Roman Catholicism, and to a kind of Roman Catholicism that perhaps very few people today are able to remember, except vaguely, so dramatic have seemed the changes brought about by the Second Vatican Council. Yet Chesterton knew that it was only by loving and serving God through his Church that perfect freedom may be found, so it was inevitable that in the cause of Liberty he also became a defender of the Faith.

The understanding of this seeming paradox must be the chief concern of any biography of Chesterton, for the expounding of it was the chief concern of his life.

Writing the life of someone is in many ways like being washed up on an island with them. Certainly one hopes to come to know them better, but also one hopes not to fall out with them. When Chesterton was once asked which book he would most like to take with him if he knew he was going to be wrecked on a desert island, his inner answer was no doubt to the effect that he would prefer not to make the journey at all, but his given answer was immediate: 'I think I should like to take Thomas's "Guide to Practical Shipbuilding".' In my case I made the journey willingly, and the island on which I found myself was a Chestertonian Paradise, for it was the attic of Top Meadow Cottage, in Beaconsfield, where Miss Dorothy Collins, who had been Chesterton's secretary for the last ten years of his life and his Literary Executor, had generously allowed me to look at anything I wished. I remained happily stranded in the attic for twelve hours a day for several weeks.

As each chest, trunk, suitcase or box revealed its treasures in the form of letters, articles, drawings and notebooks (in one box I found some thirty notebooks), I felt as if I had discovered Ben Gunn's gold. In a suitcase there were many of the characters and scenery from Chesterton's Toy Theatre, which he said was 'as philosophical as the drama of Athens'; in another the early drafts of his great book, 'The Everlasting Man'; while in a drawer I found more personal things: Chesterton's passport, his pen, his spectacles, a Papal Medal, and his rosary.

If ever I had time to glance out of the attic window – and my attention was sometimes distracted by the jets that seemed to expand like giants down towards Heathrow – it was to look down on to the small garden, now lively with flowers, but once the kitchen garden that Chesterton knew so well. Of such he said love poems might be written – why should a poet not say that in a lady's cheek the turnip and the carrot fought for supremacy? Such a description, he said, is far truer to the mellow and tawny quality in the human complexion than the violent similes of the rose and the lily.

One day it rained so heavily that I felt like Noah in the Ark as I closed the attic window; but Chesterton was again at my side, as 'the seven heavens came roaring down for the throats of hell to drink', and his voice of encouragement came to me through the years: 'I don't care where the water goes if it doesn't get into the wine.'

Michael Ffinch
Newbiggin-on-Lune
1985.

PART ONE
The Early Years

I

Starry Streets that Point to God

1874–1880

A prophet is one whose inspired vision of the world enables him to speak out accurately against the errors of his time. By reminding his people of past faults and pointing out the follies of the present he may predict that, if his promptings go unheeded, an inevitably disastrous future will follow. Thus it is only through a true interpretation of the present that a prophet may be said to foretell the future, and those who come after him are able to see with the benefit of hindsight whether his prophecy was true or false.

Now G.K.Chesterton was considered by many in his lifetime to be a prophet. It seems clear enough that he had certain prophetic qualities but, unlike the great prophets of old, most of whom were utterly rejected and brutally done to death, Chesterton was avidly listened to and, it appears, was one of the few men who never made an enemy. The reason was that everything he said was said with such good humour. Even those whose opinions he attacked felt confident that it was only their opinions that were under attack. What would have been the effect on the audiences of Isaiah and Jeremiah, one cannot help wondering, had the prophets chuckled ecstatically to themselves as they delivered their forebodings of doom, punctured their messages with puns, or tossed ideas into the air with the agility of a juggler at the circus? At least they might have been listened to: but the great prophets were more intent on speaking truth than in delighting an audience. Chesterton was intent on both truth and delight. For Chesterton, who in the opinion of the poet, Alfred Noyes, had one of the most original minds of his day in Europe, nothing was more pitiful than the common objection to a man laughing at his own jokes. 'If a man may not laugh at his own jokes,' he once asked, 'at whose jokes may be laugh? May not an architect pray in his own cathedral?'

In his youth Chesterton had taken his ideas seriously, though he soon came to realize they were, strictly speaking, not his ideas at all. 'I am the man', he admitted, 'who with the utmost daring discovered what had been discovered before.' However, at no time did he take himself seriously in the sense of believing in himself. As far as he was concerned, 'the men who really believe in themselves are all in lunatic asylums'. So it was that for the sake of the truth as he saw it, Chesterton was prepared to play the buffoon in the spirit of St Francis who called his followers the *Jongleurs de Dieu* (God's jugglers). Even the renowned loose-fitting Inverness cape, the wide-brimmed slouch hat and the swordstick began as a pose, a conscious decision on the part of his wife Frances, who, realizing she had failed in all attempts to make him tidy, decided at least to make him decorative. One who saw him in Fleet Street in the early 1900s, the years before he left London for the country, remembers

> ... a form novel, and huge and wide, and altogether satisfying to the vague sense of the expectant wonder that never quite dies out in the mind of whoever walks the streets of London. The figure advances, and what is seen is a wild mane of hair, a wide, open face, the expression benign in the way a child's is, though the eyes behind the glasses frown a little after the manner of persons of short sight; a flattish nose which perhaps contains part of the secret of the child expression; a moustache which grows wildly like an ill-tended but luxuriant elderberry bush; chubby cheeks that would be more in keeping with the child note if their dead whiteness could take on a rosy tint; a restless mouth, and under all this such a huge long-as-broad swaying body as only one man carries. In a map of Mr Chesterton the lines of latitude would have to be drawn as carefully as the lines of longitude.

Here is the traditional view of Chesterton, the Chesterton of legend, the Chesterton that Shaw described as 'a large, abounding, gigantically cherubic person who is not only large in body and mind beyond all decency, but seems to be growing larger as you look at him, "swellin' wisibly", as Tony Weller puts it'. Chesterton enjoyed playing the part of Tony Weller, just as he enjoyed dressing up as Dr Johnson or Old King Cole; he seemed to the world to be enjoying his physical greatness. 'I am six foot two,' he informed a reporter in America, 'and my weight has never been calculated.' On another occasion he remarked, 'I always enjoy myself more than most, there's such a lot of me having a good time.' When during the First World War a woman accosted him with 'Mr Chesterton, why are you not out at the Front?' he replied calmly, 'Madam, if you go round to my side you will see that I am.' Such stories seem endless, since Chesterton was continually drawing attention to his size as though he saw it in a distorted mirror. A man who had grown gross through self-indulgence would hardly laugh at himself so, but one who was embarrassed might; it was not something he could very well hide. When the motley was hung back in the wardrobe, the jolly mask removed and the face of the jester in repose, what was he like, this 'World-Famous Literary Genius, G.K.Chesterton, the World renowned Essayist, Dramatist, Romancist, Poet, Brilliant Epigrammist, Wit, Phrase-maker, the Inspiring Philosopher whose ideas attract, fascinate, impress – make people think'? 'It is always easy to let the age have its head', he wrote, 'The difficult thing is to keep one's own.' 'I am only human', he once told another American reporter. One of his closest friends, the famous Dominican Fr Vincent McNabb, said he believed Chesterton had died of a broken heart.

Chesterton's first novel, *The Napoleon of Notting Hill*, published in 1904, includes among its several illustrations a map of the 'Seat of War' which on closer inspection turns out to be a map of a small part of Kensington. This was the Chesterton family's home ground, for it was in the centre of his imaginary battlefield, in a house in Sheffield Terrace, a secluded street situated between Holland Park and Kensington Palace Gardens, that Gilbert Keith Chesterton was born on 29 May 1874, close to the 'great grey water-tower/That strikes the stars of Campden Hill'. He was, no doubt, early to appreciate the humour in the fact that the house next door was the home of Prebendary Wilson Carlile, the founder of the Church Army.

Sheffield Terrace is one of several small streets that lie parallel with Notting Hill Gate to the north and Kensington High Street to the south, linking Campden Hill Road with Kensington Church Street, and a little less than four hundred yards from Notting Hill Gate underground station. Any walker intent on visiting the birthplace, No. 32, which is marked with a square brass plaque, is likely to be heralded, not to say hounded, by the giant name of 'Chesterton' backed by garish yellow, boarded on portico and porch roof, or slung from upper-storey windows, since the family firm of Chesterton and Son is still one of the largest estate agents in London. The business had been founded by Gilbert

Chesterton's great-grandfather, Charles Chesterton, who began by running a poulterer's shop in Kensington High Street but, turning to house-agency and surveying, had been fortunate to obtain the management of the extensive Phillimore interests in the Kensington area.

Chesterton gives very little of his family's early history in his *Autobiography*, published posthumously, and it is almost certain that he did not know much of it. He never took seriously the family's claim to be descended from the Lords of the Manor of Chesterton, a small village once on the outskirts of Cambridge, but long since swallowed up by the town. He was to make fun on one occasion of the dangers of a man named Chesterton going to Chesterton, for 'the steeple might crack and the market cross fall down'. The matter is of little consequence, though it is perfectly reasonable to suppose that the family tradition really was a tradition and that the Chestertons had originated from that Cambridgeshire 'village of the camp', in spite of the fact that there are no records of the family in the Cambridge County Record Office, or that there are several other Chestertons in the country to choose from (there is even one near Oxford). Chesterton himself was indifferent to such things, and after his mother died he destroyed 'without examination' all the family records which she had kept safely and intact since her husband's death. At the same time he almost destroyed the entire collection of press cuttings his father had collected, as Dorothy Collins, Chesterton's secretary for the last ten years of his life remembers:

> Gilbert's father had a wonderful collection in his study, which was closed at his death. Gilbert threw everything out on his mother's death. The Council had taken three loads away for destruction and were coming back for a final load. Luckily I went with the car to fetch him one evening and I saw a pile on the floor. Rather against Gilbert's will, I was very anxious to save these things and brought them back in the car.

All Chesterton's admirers are exceedingly grateful to Miss Collins for her swift action and the saved papers form the nucleus of the remarkable collection of Chesterton papers at Beaconsfield.

However, the family papers had already left in the Council cart, so that little is known beyond the fact that at the time of the Regency, the head of the family was said to have been one of the Prince's cronies who 'dissipated his fortune in riotous living and incurred various terms of imprisonment for debt'. Whether or not this unfortunate member of the family had been of the Prince's circle had never been established, but it gave a certain respectability to his folly. His letters written in custody were handed down in the family, and Chesterton's father relished them and enjoyed reading them out to the children.

More interesting were the autobiographical observations of Captain George Laval Chesterton, who had served in the Peninsular War, though 'supinely occupied' at the garrison at Cartagena which debarred him from receiving the Peninsular Medal. Later he saw a certain amount of action in America, and was among those who hoped 'for further adventure and hope of personal advancement' when Napoleon escaped from Elba. The Captain's autobiography leaves little to the imagination, and is worth reading for its eyewitness accounts of the harsh barbarities of British military life, when officers could be 'made ill by the sight of a private receiving five hundred strokes of the lash'. On his return to England he was appointed governor of the Cold Bath Fields Prison, and became a friend of Elizabeth Fry and Charles Dickens. In his *Revelations of Prison Life* he records that his reforms, if his testimony may be believed, achieved 'a triumph fraught with civilizing influences'.

Of his immediate family Gilbert Chesterton was more forthcoming. He recalled that his paternal grandfather, Arthur Chesterton, was 'a fine-looking old man with white hair and beard and manners that had something of that rounded solemnity that went with the old-fashioned custom of proposing toasts and sentiments'. He would break into song at the dinner table, giving renditions of 'old and pompous patriotic songs of Waterloo and Trafalgar'. No doubt he had learnt such songs when he had gone to sea as a boy, sailing from Gravesend to the West Indies in 1829, in a ship called the *Lune*. Just five letters sent to the 'dear little sailor boy' on his trial voyage have survived. His mother informed him that 'Kensington as usual is quite out of this world'. She was concerned for his cleanliness:

> Do not forget to let your things be washed before you leave Jamaica. Do not think what the cost is, it is better not to let them lay in the dirt, it spoils the colour and rots them, and I will repay you what you expend upon the occasion.

Such attention to dress and cleanliness did not remain a family characteristic in the 1870s. Gilbert's grandmother continued:

> Neither do you suppose because you are a sailor, that you should

not be polite and attentive to your manners to everyone, look at the
universal good conduct of your father and you will perceive he is
generally respected and beloved, if you follow in his steps, you will
gain friends and be a comfort to us in our latter days.

Her final admonition was, 'Tell the truth that we may not be afraid
of repeating what you tell us.'

Chesterton's father, Edward Chesterton, known affectionately by the
family as 'Mister', or 'Mr Ed' – a child having first given the name
– was described by his son as 'serene, humorous and full of hobbies',
and by his daughter-in-law, Ada Jones, as 'a man of many small and
endearing talents'. He was a Liberal of the school that existed before
the rise of socialism, who 'took it for granted that all sane people believed
in private property; but did not trouble to translate it into private enterprise'. He had been expected after 'a sound education' to enter the
family firm and to become, as his father exhorted him by letter, 'an
active, steady and honourable man of business'. In the event Edward
Chesterton did not enjoy the best of health and early in life showed
signs of the heart trouble which resulted in his retiring from the firm
early. This was a considerable relief to him since he had never really
settled down and lacked any interest in the firm's affairs. As the eldest
son and nominal head of the firm he had already tended to leave the
day-to-day running of the business to his brother Sidney, which enabled
him to devote himself more fully to his many pastimes, of which water-
colour painting, making models, photography, collecting stained glass,
fretwork, magic lanterns and medieval illuminations were but a few.
Above all was a passion for toy theatre, something Gilbert was to inherit.

'The old-fashioned Englishman, like my father,' wrote Chesterton,
without referring to his ill health, 'sold houses for a living but filled
his own house with his life.' Nevertheless his son expressed gladness
that, although undoubtedly artistic, his father had never taken up art
as a profession. 'It might have stood in his way in becoming an amateur.
It might have spoilt his career, his private career. He could never have
made a vulgar success of all the thousand things he did so successfully.'

Above all, Edward Chesterton was particularly well read and knew
English literature backwards, passing his love of it on to his son, who
knew a great deal of it by heart, long before he could really get it into
his head. Gilbert Chesterton could remember knowing 'pages of Shakespeare's blank verse without a notion of the meaning of most of it',

which, he suggested, is perhaps the right way to begin to appreciate verse. Edward Chesterton was 'universal in his interests and very moderate in his opinions' and a man who really listened to an argument. Although of a quiet disposition, he enjoyed taking the rise out of people; often his victims were unaware that this was happening as was the case on the occasion he gave some 'grave ladies' a tour round his garden 'dwelling especially on the rustic names given in certain localities'.

'The country people call them Sailor's Pen-knives,' he would say in an offhand manner, after affecting to provide them with the full scientific name, or, 'They call them Baker's Bootlaces down in Lincolnshire, I believe'; and it is a fine example of human simplicity to note how far he found he could safely go in such instructive discourse. They followed him without revulsion when he said lightly: 'Merely a sprig of wild bigamy.' It was only when he added that there was a local variety known as Bishop's Bigamy, that the full depravity of his character began to dawn on their minds.

Chesterton certainly shared his father's teasing quality, but his ready and very sharp wit, for which he is renowned, seems to have come not from his father but his mother, who in comparison receives little notice in the autobiography. By all other accounts Mrs Edward Chesterton emerges as a much stronger and more positive character than her husband; to her other son, Cecil, she was quite simply 'the cleverest woman in London'.

Marie Louise Grosjean was of Swiss-Scottish descent. The Grosjeans had left Neuchâtel in the French-speaking part of Switzerland where they had owned 'large property' two generations earlier, and Marie Louise's father was a Wesleyan lay preacher and an early member of the temperance movement, 'who divided his leisure between his ministrations and attendance at the Covent Garden Opera'. Her mother was a member of the Keith family of Aberdeen, which is how Gilbert came by his second Christian name. His Scottish blood, he admitted, 'appealed strongly to his affections and made a sort of Scottish romance of his childhood'. Marie Louise was one of twenty-three children. Gilbert never knew his maternal grandfather (though he came to know many of his aunts and uncles), but he always felt that he shared his grandfather's love for and involvement in public controversy.

After their marriage the Edward Chestertons settled at Sheffield Terrace. Their first child had been a girl, christened Beatrice and known to the family as 'Birdie'. Sadly, the little girl died when she was eight and when Gilbert, aged three, was only just beginning to talk. It is with regard to Beatrice's death that the idealized portrayal of the father's character built up by his son is seen to have been inadequate. To forget his own thoughts, Edward Chesterton forbade Marie Louise to mention Beatrice's name, and he faced her portrait towards the wall. It was 'as though Beatrice had disgraced her name and been thrust Victorian fashion out of the home'. This puritanical attitude meant that the Chesterton boys were never allowed to attend, or even witness, a funeral; and should a funeral procession pass down the street, they would be bustled away from the front window and made to stay in one of the back rooms of the house.

This odd, though perhaps not unusual, attitude to death was matched by a most unusual attitude to health. Sickness was taboo; not only would Edward Chesterton never refer to his own illness, but he attempted to ignore it in others, so that 'a queer atmosphere of silence concerning physical ailments prevailed'. Knowing how it might distress her husband, Marie Louise kept the fact from him that she had broken her arm when a suitcase had fallen from the luggage rack on the express train from Scotland. When they reached home she made her own arrangements to go to hospital to have the bone set.

Gilbert Chesterton inherited, or rather imitated, these phobias. A childhood friend, Annie Firmin, remembered how if his brother, Cecil, gave the slightest sign of choking at dinner, Gilbert would 'throw down his spoon and fork and rush from the room. I have seen him do it many times.' When, many years later, his father lay on his death-bed 'it was only with real pain and difficulty that he summoned sufficient fortitude to see the dying man'.

'I *was* the mother of three children and I had a beautiful girl,' Mrs Chesterton once confided to a friend. For Gilbert his sister was only a vague memory.

I do not remember her dying; but I remember her falling off a rocking horse. I know from experience of bereavements only a little later, that children feel with exactitude, without a word of explanation, the emotional tone or tint of a house in mourning. But in this case, the greater catastrophe must somehow have become confused and identified with the smaller one. I always felt it as a tragic memory, as if she had been thrown by a real horse and killed.

It was very soon after his daughter's death and largely because of it that Edward Chesterton decided to move house, though not to move away from Kensington. No. 11 Warwick Gardens was situated south of Kensington High Street in a less sought-after part of the borough. This was to be the Chestertons' home from then on, and Gilbert lived there until his marriage in 1901. It was at this new home that a second son, Cecil Edward, was born on 12 November 1879. Gilbert was five and, on hearing the news that he now had a brother, he is reputed to have said, 'That's all right; now I shall have an audience' – an ironic remark as it turned out, for as the years went by Cecil proved to have if anything the sharper intellect and Gilbert was usually the one who did the listening. As Fr Vincent McNabb was to put it, 'God had given Gilbert Chesterton a brother whose intellect was so granite-like that on it he was able to sharpen his own more slowly-tempered mind.'

Cecil was always his mother's favourite, and in many respects he was more like her: fearless, stoical, 'with the same sunny temperament and enjoyment of simple things'. Gilbert on the other hand had more of his father's unworldliness and was all his life notoriously absent-minded, although both had inherited 'something of his mildly bohemian ways'.

Puritanical attitudes to death and health were not reflected in their attitude to cleanliness. If cleanliness was next to godliness, then the Chesterton boys were pagans. They had a reputation for looking unkempt and Gilbert was noted when he went to school for his grubby, well-bitten finger-nails. 'I always noticed his hands,' recalled his school friend Digby d'Avigdor, 'long and soft, usually dirty.' Cecil he remembered as having a 'really filthy appearance'; his nose was usually running. 'Why do you go about with that awful fellow Chesterton?' a fellow pupil at St Paul's once asked, yet d'Avigdor continued to consider it to be a real honour to have Gilbert for a friend.

There were times, however, when the boys did look smart, on visits to the photographers or if guests came to the house; and Gilbert's long golden locks were so admired by the Italian artist Baccani that he begged permission to paint the boy's portrait when he met Edward Chesterton and his six-year-old son walking in the park. The quarter-length portrait which once hung in the dining room at Warwick Gardens is now in the hall at Top Meadow Cottage; it shows Gilbert in his sailor suit with hair that reminds one of the younger of Millais's Princes in the Tower.

We have a glimpse of the inside of the house at Warwick Gardens
through the eyes of Mrs Cecil Chesterton:

> The setting of the home never altered. The walls of the dining room
> renewed their original shade of bronze green year after year. The
> mantelpiece was perennially wine colour, and the tiles of the hearth,
> Edward Chesterton's own design, grew more and more mellow.
>
>   Books lined as much of the wall space as was feasible and the
> shelves reached from floor to ceiling in a phalanx of leather. The
> furniture was graceful, a slim mahogany dining table, a small side-
> board, generously stocked with admirable bottles, and deep chairs.

A description, surely, of a fairly typical middle-class home of the period,
apart from a greater quantity of books. Chesterton was to speak of his
family as middle-class in the days when 'it really was a class and it
really was in the middle'. Of a family such as his own he wrote:

> It attached rather too much importance to spelling correctly; it attached
> enormous importance to speaking correctly. And it did spell and speak
> correctly. There was a whole world in which nobody was any more
> likely to drop an 'h' than pick up a title.

He had discovered early how to shock his parents.

> What my parents were really afraid of was any imitation of the intona-
> tion and diction of the servants. I am told that at about the age of
> three or four, I screamed for a hat hanging on a peg, and at last
> in convulsions of fury uttered the awful words, 'If you don't give
> it me, I'll say "at".' I felt sure that would lay all my relations prostrate
> for miles around.

This false gentility is interesting, since it shows that the Chestertons
were very much in the middle; they were not of, nor had they family
connections with, the gentry; neither would they have 'dreamed of knowing the aristocracy except in business'. Gilbert and Cecil and their cou-
sins, Sidney Chesterton's children, were the first generation to be
'educated', in the sense that they were the first to attend a public school.
   The Chesterton parents believed in complete freedom of thought,
no pressure of any kind being put upon the boys' development intellectually or, as time progressed, spiritually. The Chestertons were the 'best
sort of middle-Victorian Liberals'. All theories and creeds were tried
on their merits and, although sceptical in all supernatural aspects of

religion they played lip-service, at least, to a Unitarian form of worship. According to Cecil they believed in 'The Fatherhood of God, the Brotherhood of Man, the non-eternity of evil, the final salvation of souls'. Such revolt from Calvinism created by a free method of thought Cecil described as a 'vague but noble theo-philanthropy'. A belief in the 'non-eternity of evil' had not prevented both boys from being baptized 'according to the formularies of the Church of England'. Gilbert had received the name of his godfather, Tom Gilbert, and the family name Keith at the small church, St George's, opposite the large waterworks tower. 'I do not allege any significance in the relation of the two buildings,' wrote Chesterton, 'and I indignantly deny that the church was chosen because it needed the whole water-power of West London to turn me into a Christian.'

When they did attend services it was to hear the Reverend Stopford Augustus Brooke, a notable Irish preacher, who left the Church of England in 1880, 'unable to believe in miracles'. As Chesterton was to put it in one of his early clerihews,

> The Rev. Stopford Brooke
> The Church forsook.
> He preached about an apple
> In Bedford Chapel.

Chesterton for his part remained unaffected. He had accepted the supernatural intuitively. For him the miraculous was an integral part of living, and when after his death his friends tried to express this indelible part of his character, it was to use only clumsy phrases such as 'he never grew up' or 'he was always a child', as though he was some kind of Peter Pan. It was another way of stating the truth that Chesterton had kept his sense of wonder. There was nothing childish about it, but rather that childlike quality exhorted in the Gospels. Chesterton knew intuitively that 'a little child shall lead them'. Far from childishness it was a matter of intellect, integrity, and above all a humility that comes from the acceptance of the gifts of the Holy Spirit, for Chesterton, as he came to acknowledge, was greatly blessed. As William Titterton (one of Chesterton's Fleet Street colleagues), said of him, 'As a very small child he knew God.'

'What was wonderful about childhood is that everything in it was a wonder,' wrote Chesterton in a well-known passage in the autobiography. 'It was not merely a world full of miracles; it was a miraculous

world.' What he had earlier called his 'first and last philosophy' he
had learnt in his nursery.

> The things I believed most then, the things I most believe now, are
> the things called fairy tales. They seem to me to be the entirely reason-
> able things. They are not fantasies: compared with them other things
> are fantastic. Compared with them religion and rationalism are both
> abnormal, though religion is abnormally right and rationalism abnor-
> mally wrong. Fairyland is nothing but the sunny country of common
> sense.

Such a statement either whets one's appetite to read on, or prompts
one to dismiss this as one of the Chestertonian paradoxes of which
he has so often been accused. Although Chesterton would have argued,
'It is always easy to let the age have its head, the difficult thing is to
keep one's own.'

The premise on which Chesterton's philosophical development was
founded was deeply impressed on his mind at a very early age, not
least by the plays performed in Edward Chesterton's toy theatre for
the children to watch. 'The very first thing I can ever remember seeing
with my own eyes was a young man walking across a bridge. He had
a curly moustache and an attitude of confidence verging on swagger.'
The figure described here, as large as life, was one of the puppets
that appeared in the fairy tales which were performed. In these plays,
where the word 'law' was avoided, the boy Chesterton learnt that giants
should be killed because they are gigantic, for as he wrote in 1907,
'the Titans never scaled heaven, but they laid waste the earth', and
from *Cinderella*, he learnt the lesson which he later came to see as being
the same as the Magnificat – *exaltavit humiles*.

A hint may be seen here as to how fairyland and the faith might
be drawn together; but the whole spirit of fairyland or, as Chesterton
so often termed it, 'Elfland', was learnt before he could speak and would
be retained for the rest of his life. 'I am concerned with a certain way
of looking at life, which was created in me by fairy tales, but has since
been meekly ratified by the mere facts.'

Such stimulus to the imagination emanated from Edward Chesterton's
den or study 'piled high with the stratified layers of about ten or twelve
creative amusements'. The boys too were encouraged to have their dens
in out-of-the-way corners of the house.

In Cecil's cubbyhole were kept several cockroaches which were fed on bread and butter. Unlike Gilbert at this stage, Cecil was very fond of animals and had a cat named Faustine, because he wanted her to be abandoned and wicked, but Faustine turned out to be a Tom! Also there were 'stacks of copybooks containing juvenile notes for novels, political theses and economic systems – the outline of a Cecilian form of government, which covered every phase of national life'.

Warwick Gardens was seen by the Chestertons' friends as 'ideally happy'. Children came and went freely. The Firmin girls, Annie and Lizzie, were friends from childhood and remained close until eventually Annie married and went to live in Canada, where Lizzie followed her. It was no secret that Mrs Chesterton had hoped that Annie would marry Gilbert. 'One of my first memories,' wrote Chesterton, remembering Annie, 'is playing in the garden under the care of a girl with ropes of golden hair; to whom my mother afterwards called from the house, "You are an angel", which I was disposed to accept without metaphor.' As he said, 'The two Firmin girls had more to do with enlivening my early years than most.'

For her part Annie remembered that neither of the boys was demonstrative, and she never saw either of them kiss his mother.

Aunt Marie [as she called Mrs Chesterton] was a bit of a tyrant in her own family! I have been many times at dinner, when there might be a joint, say, and a chicken – and she would say positively to Mr Ed, 'Which will you have, Edward?' Edward: 'I think I'd like a bit of chicken!' Aunt M, fiercely: 'No, you won't, you'll have mutton!' That happened so often. Sometimes, Alice Grosjean, the youngest of Aunt M's family, familiarly known as 'Sloper', was there. When asked her preference she would say diffidently, 'I think I'll have a little mutton!' 'Don't be a fool, Alice, you know you like chicken' – and chicken she got.

Another friend, Lucian Oldershaw, whom Chesterton met at school, remembered that Mrs Chesterton had no thought for her personal tidiness, and her decayed front teeth, visible when she grinned, and her untidy dress gave her a witch-like appearance that used to terrify young children.

Summing up the period of his early childhood, Chesterton made these four statements which are important to an understanding of his development.

First; my life unfolded itself in the epoch of evolution, which really only means unfolding. But many of the evolutionists of that epoch really seemed to mean by evolution the unfolding of what is not there. I have since, in a special sense, come to believe in development; which means the unfolding of what is there. Now it may seem both a daring and a doubtful boast, if I claim that in my childhood I was all there. At least, many of those who knew me best were quite doubtful about it. But I mean that the distinctions I made here were all there; I was not conscious of them but I contained them. In short, they existed in infancy in the condition called implicit; though they certainly did not then express themselves in what is commonly called implicit obedience.

Second; I knew, for instance, that pretending is not deceiving. I could not have defined the distinction if it had been questioned; but that was because it had never occurred to me that it could be questioned. It was merely because a child understands the nature of argument. Now it is still not uncommon to say that images are idols and that idols are dolls. I am content to say here that even dolls are not idols, but in the true sense images. The very word images means things necessary to imagination. But not things contrary to reason; no, not even in a child. For imagination is almost the opposite of illusion.

Third; I have noted that I enjoyed Punch and Judy as a drama and not a dream; and indeed the whole extraordinary state of mind I strive to recapture was really the very reverse of a dream. It was rather as if I was more wideawake then than I am now, and moving in broader daylight, which was to our broad daylight what daylight is to dusk. Only, of course, to those seeing the last gleam of it through the dusk, the light looks more uncanny than any darkness. Anyhow, it looks quite different; of that I am absolutely and solidly certain; though in such a subjective matter of sensation there can be no demonstration. What was the real meaning of that difference? I have some sort of notion now; but I will not mention it at this stage in the story.

Fourth; it will be quite natural, it will also be quite wrong, to infer from all this that I passed a quite exceptionally comfortable childhood in complete contentment; or else that my memory is merely a sundial that has only marked the sunny hours. But that is not in the least what I mean; that is quite a different question. I was often unhappy in childhood like other children; but happiness and unhappiness seemed of a different texture or held on a different tenure. I was very often naughty in childhood like other children; and I have never doubted for a moment the moral of all the moral tales; that, as a general principle, people ought to be unhappy when they have been naughty. That is, I held the whole idea of repentance and absolution implicit but not unfolded in my mind. To add to all this, I was by no means unacquainted with pain, which is a pretty unanswerable thing; I had a fair amount of toothache and especially earache; and few can bemuse themselves into regarding earache as a form of epicurean hedonism. And here again there is a difference. For some unaccountable reason, and in some indescribable way, the pain did not leave on my memory the sort of stain of the intolerable or mysterious that it leaves on the mature mind. To all these four facts I can testify; exactly as if they were facts like loving a toy gun or climbing a tree. Their meaning, in the murder or other mystery, will appear later.

For I fear I have prolonged preposterously this note on the nursery; as if I had been an unconscionable time, not dying but being born, or at least being brought up.

Chesterton believed in prolonging childhood, and he was never sorry that he was a backward child.

2

Fide et Literis

1880–1892

Chesterton's early education was received at a preparatory school which eventually became Colet Court, today the junior department of St Paul's School.

The decision to move St Paul's away from the City to a site in Hammersmith had been taken, and the High Master, Dr F.W.Walker, anticipating that the numbers at the school would increase, decided that a preparatory school situated nearby would be greatly to the school's advantage, besides being convenient for the parents.

The task of starting this new venture was given to one of the assistant masters who had also acted as Walker's secretary, Samuel Bewsher. Bewsher and his wife lived at No. 33 Edith Road in West Kensington, and had for several years accommodated several Pauline boarders. He was trusted greatly by Walker, and had arrived at St Paul's with him from Manchester Grammar School, where Walker had also been High Master.

Originally known as 'Bewsher's', the new school began in the basement of No. 33 Edith Road on a Tuesday during the third week of January 1881, a day known as 'Black Tuesday' because the school's opening had been heralded by a fierce blizzard. To begin with there were only six pupils, but by the following September it had become necessary to take over another house on the opposite side of the road. From the outset 'the teaching was sound and thorough and methods were systematic', with the result that a waiting list built up and it became obvious that the premises in Edith Street would be insufficient. Bewsher commissioned the firm of Gibbs and Flew to design and build a school building at the corner of the playground of the new St Paul's School; this was opened for the autumn term of 1883, and named Colet House. When the main school was officially opened a year later, Colet House had some two hundred pupils of whom fifty-six entered St Paul's that year.

Once at West Kensington, Samuel Bewsher was appointed Bursar of St Paul's, so that he now had less time to devote to Colet House; but his younger brother, James Bewsher, who had recently gained a first at Oxford in Mathematics and Natural Science, was appointed Second Master, and three years later became Head Master. Another member of the family involved in the school was Mary Bewsher, who taught the very small boys; but the staff as a whole were very highly qualified and most were graduates of Oxford or Cambridge. Numbers continued to increase, so that three more houses were rented in Talgarth Road, near the school; and early in 1886 a new playground was laid out and an iron building put up which was large enough to make three classrooms, and at the weekends was used as a chapel. Eventually, with forty boarders and four hundred day boys, it became necessary to build yet another school, and in 1889 work began on the future buildings of Colet Court. This opened in September 1890, by which time Chesterton had been in the senior school for four years.

Chesterton recorded nothing of his time at Colet House, and the school records give no precise information as to when he entered the school. It is possible that he was one of the very first pupils with which the school opened in 1881, but it seems more likely that he was among those who began at Colet House in the autumn of 1883 when he was nine, for he had only just learnt to read at that age. Although Chesterton did not recall his days at the school there were others who remembered him there: E.C.Bentley, his greatest friend at school, remembers him as an 'unusually tall, lanky boy with a serious, even brooding, expression that gave way very easily to one of laughing happiness'.

His home being so close to the school, it was an easy walk from Warwick Gardens. Chesterton often made the short journey in the company of Stafford Aston, a boy of about his own age, who lived in Pembroke Gardens. It was Aston who was to remember the withering remark of one of the masters: 'You know, Chesterton, if we could open your head, we should not find any brain but only a lump of white fat!' – the kind of remark from a master calculated to make a boy 'switch off' school work for good. It is perhaps worth noting also that at the time Chesterton was slim. Aston also recalled how Chesterton generously offered to give him ten shillings that he did not want, so that he could purchase something from the toyshop the pair passed on their way to and from school. Such was Chesterton's notorious vagueness about money; he never came to know the value of it, and as Dorothy Collins has verified, whenever he had any he usually gave it away. The story shows also his remarkable generosity of spirit, something which also remained.

All through his school days Chesterton was the type of pupil which school masters know only too well: a dreamer. He was shortsighted and his chief occupation was to draw all over his books. As we have seen, he was slow at learning to read, and his companions considered him odd. Although he was, as Bentley put it, 'as tall as most men' he was still wearing sailor suits as though he was a little boy. His height was the principal reason why he was not bullied, but what teasing came his way was accepted 'with such unfailing good temper that there soon ceased to be any fun in it'. Lucian Oldershaw recalled that 'at physical gym everyone turned out to watch Chesterton being pushed over a horse'. He was always considered something of a butt, yet he never lost dignity and he was one for whom others had respect.

Chesterton was twelve when he moved up into the senior school in January 1887, to be placed in the second form. Edward Fordham, one of his friends, recalled:

> He sat at the back of the room and never distinguished himself. We thought him the most curious thing that ever was. I can see him now very tall and lanky, striding untidily along Kensington High Street, smiling and sometimes scowling as he talked to himself, apparently oblivious of everything he passed; but in fact a far closer observer than most, and one who not only observed but remembered what he had seen.

This view of Chesterton's memory was not shared by the staff. His report, written in December 1887, records his form master's sense of bewilderment in his assessment of his eccentric pupil:

> Too much for me: means well by me, I believe, but has an inconceivable knack of forgetting at the shortest notice, is consequently always in trouble, though some of his work is well done, when he does remember to do it. He ought to be in a studio not at school. Never troublesome, but for his lack of memory and absence of mind.

Two terms later he was still 'wildly inaccurate in everything, never thinks for two consecutive moments to judge by his work'. However, from now on there appear frequent hints as to his ability. After he had been at the school for a year his neatness was improved and his stock of general knowledge noticed. At the end of the summer term of 1889 he was described as 'a great blunderer with much intelligence'. The truth was that Chesterton was not in the least interested in classics, and the Greek letters seemed to him 'quite nastly little things like a swarm of gnats'. As for the Greek accents, he 'triumphantly succeeded, through a long series of school terms, in avoiding learning them at all'. He was later to describe his education as 'the period during which I was being instructed by somebody I did not know, about something I did not want to know'.

Looking back on his schooldays, Chesterton considered that he had probably been wiser at the age of six than at the age of sixteen.

Boyhood is a most complex and incomprehensible thing. Even when one has been through it, one does not understand what it was. A man can never quite understand a boy, even when he has been the boy. There grows all over what was once the child a sort of prickly protection like hair; a callousness, a carelessness, a curious combination of random and quite objectless energy with a readiness to accept conventions. I have blindly begun a lark which involved carrying on literally like a lunatic; and known all the time that I did not know why I was doing it.

Chesterton considered that the chief impression he had produced on both staff and boys was that he was asleep, but that if he was asleep, he was also dreaming. His mind was already occupied though he himself was idle. It was not to be long, however, before this dreaming idler was noticed by Dr Walker, the High Master. Chesterton was exceedingly fortunate to have been at St Paul's at a time when the school had a High Master of genius, anxious to see the school flourish on its new site and to achieve academic excellence.

Frederick William Walker had been appointed from Manchester Grammar School in 1876 on the resignation of Dr Kynaston. He had himself been educated first, for a short spell, at the Grammar School of St Saviour's, Southwark, and then at Rugby when the future Archbishop Tait was Head Master. At Corpus Christi College, Oxford, he took a first in Classical Moderations and Literae Humaniores, besides taking honours in Mathematics. After his finals he remained at Oxford,

gaining the Boden Sanskrit Scholarship and the Vinerian Law Scholarship. As a fellow and tutor of his college, Walker's vigour and originality
'made a deep impression on his contemporaries'. It was at this time
that his lifelong friendship began with Dr Jowett, the great Master of
Balliol. Walker moved to Manchester Grammar School in 1859, where
he remained until he moved to St Paul's.

The High Master Chesterton knew was a formidable-looking figure,
not unlike the aged Tennyson in a mortarboard. As Chesterton said,
he was a man who may live in anecdotes, like Dr Johnson. Chesterton
remembered 'the startling volume of his voice' and his heavy face and
figure, and 'a certain tendency to explode at what did not seem to be
exactly the appropriate moment.'

> He was never angry without just cause; but no one entered the School
> who did not fear his anger. The boys who knew him best, and who
> had seen most of the gentle and affectionate side of his nature, would
> have undergone anything rather than a rebuke from him. To say
> he ruled by fear would be wholly untrue; but fear was always in
> the background.

This fear was not that of the cane or of other impositions; but simply
of the force of Walker's personality. He knew every boy in the school,
hated humbug of any sort, and was insistent that St Paul's, being a
day school, could not and should not pretend to fulfil the conditions
of a boarding school. He made this clear in his last speech to the school:
'We strive,' he said, 'not without success, to make our boys intellectually
strong, industrious, loyal, and, as far as man can do so, morally pure
and upright. The rest we are forced to leave – and I do not regret
it – to fathers and mothers and the influence of home.'

It was the High Master who, to use Chesterton's own words, dragged
Chesterton 'out of the comfortable and protected atmosphere of obscurity
and failure' in which he had been perfectly content to remain; but
the influence of home was always to be the stronger. Edward Chesterton
continued to play an important part in his son's education, taking him
to museums and art galleries, and above all extending his knowledge
of literature. He encouraged the various friendships Gilbert had made
at school, and was actively involved in the many productions of plays
that were performed at Warwick Gardens. The friendships that were
established at St Paul's, though few, were to have a great influence

on Chesterton's later life, particularly those with Edmund Bentley and
with Lucian Oldershaw, who would one day become his brother-in-law.

Edmund Clerihew Bentley was two years Chesterton's junior, yet
the two had become friends at Colet House. The version Chesterton
later gave of their first encounter, in which they supposedly fought
for three-quarters of an hour in the school playground, not, it seems,
having noticed each other previously, is reminiscent of the fight between
Pip and Herbert Pocket, and indeed Dickens had been brought into
it, 'when exhausted Bentley had quoted Dickens or the *Bab Ballads*'
and the two 'plunged into friendly discussion on literature'. The episode
was not denied by Bentley, but he 'wished his memory of the occasion
had been so good'. The meeting was to be the beginning of an intense
friendship; and a 'conversation that was to last, with the minimum of
interruption, for seven or eight years, and thereafter to be resumed
at short or long intervals' until Chesterton's death.

'Three is certainly the symbolic number for friendship,' wrote Chesterton, remembering his other close friend Lucian Oldershaw, a dark,
very thin youth who 'brought into our secrets the breath of ambition
and the air of the great world'. Oldershaw's father was an actor, and
the unpredictable nature of the theatrical profession had meant that
the boy had travelled about a great deal and attended several schools
before he arrived at St Paul's, where he and Chesterton were to be
in the same form from then on. He was understandably older for his
age than Chesterton, and was possessed with the 'vast, amazing and
devastating idea of *doing* something'. Oldershaw's influence over Chesterton would be profound during the remaining years at school; and
afterwards, as it was through Oldershaw that he met the girl he married.
It was Oldershaw's powers of organization and highly developed business sense that made the venture of the Junior Debating Club and its
mouthpiece, *The Debater*, such a remarkable success.

As the boys lived within easy walking distance of each other it was
inevitable that they visited each other's homes at weekends and during
the holidays; but it was Oldershaw who suggested that meetings should
take place on a more formal and regular basis. The inaugural meeting
of the Junior Debating Club was held at his house in Talgarth Road
on 1 July 1890. The Club's Minute Book, written in Oldershaw's mature
hand though with occasional lapses in spelling, is preserved in the
archives of St Paul's School. However, it is important to remember
that the Junior Debating Club was run entirely by the boys, although

one of the Masters, Robert Cholmeley, encouraged the venture once it had got going. The minutes of the first meeting stated:

> The object of the above Club is to get a few friends together to amuse one another with a literary or something approaching a literary subject. It was thought best to have someone to manage it, so a Chairman and Secretary have been elected, and the rules given below have been framed. It was thought at first to confine it only to Shakespeare, but it was decided to let it be any literary subject.

Chesterton had been 'chosen' Chairman and Oldershaw Secretary 'by the unanimous consent of the Club'. The two had proposed each other and found willing seconders in two of their contemporaries: Langdon-Davies and Fordham. They were to remain in office throughout the Club's existence, though the formality required by Rule 3 of the Club, 'That the Chairman be elected at the beginning of every term, also the Secretary', was strictly adhered to.

The Club was restricted to twelve members, who would take it in turn to present a paper or get up a debate on some literary subject. If any member failed to read a paper he was liable to the statutory fine of sixpence; a similar fine was imposed on anyone who was absent twice running without an excuse accepted by the Chairman. In the printed list of Club rules one cannot help noticing that the name of the Secretary appears before that of the Chairman. The names of the founding members of the Club were: Chesterton, Oldershaw, Bentley, Fordham, Langdon-Davies, Turner (another contemporary), Digby d'Avigdor and Lawrence Solomon (later a very good friend of Gilbert's), and several boys joined at a later date, including Salter (eventually Gilbert's solicitor) and the poet Robert Venède. Later that month, Chesterton presented the first paper in his own home on 'The Opening of Shakespeare's Plays compared with other authors'; the members had been informed that the only books required for the occasion were copies of Shakespeare's plays.

There was nothing unusual about the Club's proceedings to begin with. It had been founded by younger boys as a rival to the Senior Debating Club at St Paul's, which was restricted to members of the top form, known as 'the Eighth'. Such ventures were, and still are, common to most schools; but in the way the Junior Debating Club developed it was unusual. It was again Oldershaw's organization that brought into being *The Debater*, the Club's magazine which in eighteen issues between March 1891 and February 1893 revealed Chesterton's remarkable literary gift to the public. Perhaps more importantly, it attracted the attention of the High Master, who on the Apposition Day mentioned at the top of his voice that the periodical 'showed some glimmerings of talent; adding that he was not sure that he would have given it his imprimatur if he had been consulted in the matter'. Of course, Dr Walker would not have been consulted; for apart from the fact that all the members of the Club were boys at the shool, the running of the Club and the publication of the magazine were carried on at home entirely outside the school's jurisdiction.

The Debater was assembled and written out in longhand and then typed by the 'Typewriting Studio' run by a Miss Davidson at 13 Charleville Road, West Kensington. A hundred copies were run off, and Oldershaw had organized its distribution so efficiently that 'by night-fall we had disposed of all our copies'. The magazine's first number began with 'some explanation of the causes for which it had been published': 'It is patent to an awe-struck universe that this paper is the offspring of that illustrious Society, the Junior Debating Club, whose fame has reached so many remote out-posts of the Empire, and whose ranks contain so many of the most able and distinguished men of the day.' How true this last statement was is borne out by the subsequent careers of the members.

After the editorial came an account of the various meetings held in the members' houses. For instance, at the meeting held on 30 January at d'Avigdor's house Bentley had 'made a humorous speech to the effect that the members should assume the names of celebrated political personages', a proposition which was objected to on the grounds that politics were barred. On 4 February at Fordham's house proposals were put forward for the Club's motto. Chesterton had suggested two possibilities: 'Words are the only things that live for ever', and 'Reading maketh a full man, conference a ready man, and writing an exact man.' Neither of these came to the vote, and eventually Digby d'Avigdor's suggestion of 'Hence, loathèd melancholy' was chosen, a fitting compliment to one of St Paul's many famous pupils. From then on the motto was to appear on the cover of the magazine. The literary contributions published in the first number were 'Dragons: A Sketch' and a poem 'Sunset and Dawn' by Chesterton; 'Chaucer', the first of a series on 'the Great English' continued in subsequent numbers, by Oldershaw; and 'Misinterpretation of Design' (which began: 'The man who invented class

examinations in public schools very likely thought he had struck a rather
good idea') and a poem, by Bentley. As these were the only contributors
at the start it is hardly surprising to read in the July number that 'Chesterton, Bentley and Oldershaw are described as among the most earnest
and well-read members of the Club.'

Chesterton's style in both prose and verse is recognizable from the
start:

> The dragon is certainly the most cosmopolitan of impossibilities. His
> eccentric figure has walked through the romances of all ages and
> of all nations ... this scaly intruder has appeared from the earliest
> times, and appeared apparently with the sole object of being killed,
> whether by the lance of St George, the club of Herakles, the sword
> of Siegfried, or the arrows of Hiawatha. We have even seen a dragon,
> together with some dubious-looking quadrupeds, in the arabesques
> of Mohammedans ....

Even a short passage reveals an amazingly wide range of reading for
a boy of seventeen. The note of humour is there from the start which
all admirers of Chesterton will recognize immediately, and through the
author came to make many of his most serious points.

> [The dragon] doesn't see the good of going about as a roaring lion,
> but seeks what he may devour in a quiet and respectable way, behind
> many illustrious names and many imposing disguises. Behind the
> scarlet coat and epaulettes, behind the star and mantle of the garter,
> behind the ermine tippet and the councellor's robe, behind, alas,
> the black coat and white tie, behind many a respectable exterior in
> public and in private life, we fear that the dragon's flaming eyes and
> grinning jaws, his tyrannous power, and his infernal cruelty, some-
> times lurk.
>
> Reader, when you or I meet him, under whatever disguise, may
> we face him boldly, and perhaps rescue a few captives from his black
> cavern; may we bear a brave lance and a spotless shield through
> the crashing mêlée of life's narrow lists, and may our wearied swords
> have struck fiercely on the painted crests of Imposture and Injustice
> when the Dark Herald comes to lead us to the pavilion of the King.

As the months passed *The Debater* went from strength to strength,
not only because of the high standard of the contributions but also
because of its presentation. After the first number's immediate success

Oldershaw had decided on having the April number professionally printed, and what was to become the magazine's format was established. The printer trusted with the task was J.W.Wakeham, whose premises were in Bedford Terrace, Kensington. It was hardly surprising that the author of 'Poetry and Science' and 'The Happiness of Genius', who could write: 'The Philistine is not displeased to console himself for the absence of literary tastes by the theory that the life of men of letters is invariably a career of despair and misery, varied by vice and terminated by suicide', became recognized as having 'decided literary aptitude' on his form report, although this also said, 'He does not trouble himself enough about school work'. The fact was that he never did; and never would.

The JDC meetings had become more ritualistic, and specially composed songs were sung. The theme song, which Mrs Chesterton thought quite fatuous, was sung to the tune of 'Clementine' and went:

> I'm a Member, I'm a Member, Member of the JDC
> I'll belong to it for ever,
> Don't you wish that you were me?

Tea was the chief refreshment, and another chant included the lines:

> The hissing of the holy urn
> Makes better songs than I.

and a rousing last verse:

> Then pass the cup, debaters all
> And fill the tea-pot high,
> And o'er the joy of wild debate
> May hours like moments fly.
> As critics quiet and composed,
> As brothers kind and free,
> Join hand in hand the tea-pot round
> Joy to the JDC

In as much as the members held political opinions they were ardently socialistic. In one of his notebooks Chesterton began a letter to Lawrence Solomon: 'With what you say about Socialism I most cordially assent. It is utterly impracticable as things stand: that is why I am so fond of it. It is almost as impracticable as Christianity.' Some few years later, he wrote to Solomon on the same subject:

Those early Christians were the only true socialists, with the first fresh glory of the gospel teaching around them they could not be otherwise, for democracy is an essentially spiritual idea, a contradiction of the modern materialism which would encourage the brute-tendency to an aristocracy of the physically 'fittest'. There is no doubt that the eagle is much larger and stronger and handsome than the sparrow: there is no room for equality in the question, save from the spiritual point of view, 'For not one sparrow falls to the earth ...' you know the rest. No, nor man either and I think that he who sees them fall will call society to account for them and will not be answered by the survival of the fittest or the law of individual success or any other modern paraphrase of the good old formula 'Am I my brother's keeper?'

Chesterton's verse contributions to *The Debater*, which he described as 'bad imitations of Swinburne ... so exactly balanced with worse imitations of the Lays of Ancient Rome', set the tone also for much that was to follow in the years to come. The rhythms may be imitations, but the manner of 'Lepanto' is easily seen in such lines as these in 'Danton' printed in the fourth number:

On the grim and crowded tumbrils high he reared his giant frame,
While the doubtful crowd seemed awe-struck at the murmuring of
    his name;
'Sight most strange,' he muttered, 'strangest e'en these blood-stained
    streets have seen;
I, the fiercest of the tribunes, passing to the guillotine.'

Such was the popularity of Chesterton's historical soliloquies that the Editor of the magazine soon announced 'We have arranged with G.K.C. to publish every now and then historical soliloquies to form a series.' 'Simon de Montfort' and 'Algernon Sydney' were to follow in later issues. Then the July number announced some staggering news: 'As we go to press we hear the pleasant news that our Chairman, Mr Chesterton, has gained the Milton Prize for English verse at St Paul's School, the subject for treatment being St Francis Xavier, the apostle of the Indies.'

The prize poem, written in Spenserian stanzas, is limp compared with the historical soliloquies in *The Debater*. Perhaps Chesterton knew who was judging the competition and that energy and exuberance might have fallen on deaf ears. Instead the poised and polished Spenserian stanzas would be more likely to find appreciation:

> He left his name, a murmur in the East
>   That dies to silence amid older creeds,
> With which he strove in vain ...'

Bentley remembered the sight of his friend, 'tall, gawky and untidy' as he wiped the sweat from his brow and read the poem to a great audience of parents as well as boys at the end of the school year.

As far as the school was concerned, Chesterton's success was a surprise, if not a scandal, for the Milton Prize had until then always been won by a member of the Eighth. Dr Walker was quick to recognize the possible friction that might follow and pinned up on the school notice board the simple directive: 'G.K.Chesterton to rank with the Eighth.' Chesterton, however, was well known already to several members of the Eighth, and two of them, V.M.C.Trotter and S.P.Bunting, had judged *The Debater*'s essay prize, awarding the first place to his essay 'Boy's Literature'. Academically, Chesterton was never to rise higher than form 6B, two years behind the average achievement of boys of his age.

Chesterton's late success at school was endorsed more publicly when he heard *The Speaker* had accepted his poem 'The Song of Labour'. The poem ended with thoughts that would become even more familiar to him in the future:

> For the High God heareth for ever the voice of the work we have
>   done:
> He knows who have striven with Nature, and claimed and conquered
>   the earth,
> He knows who have stood to a manhood where work is the title of
>   worth.

The poem appeared in the magazine the week before Christmas that year, but it was to be many more years, more than Chesterton must have wished, before God appeared to have heard the voice of the work he had done.

3

How to be a Lunatic

1892–1895

Chesterton had left St Paul's at the end of the summer term of 1892, with the reputation of being the only poet of his generation; but in spite of his undoubted literary promise shown so magnificently in the pages of *The Debater* his parents were, as Bentley put it, 'mistrustful of writing regarded as a means of livelihood'. Chesterton for his part lacked any confidence in his powers as a writer and so was willing to be guided by his father who, recognizing Gilbert's talent for drawing, was prepared to support his future as an artist and to pay the fees at an art school.

Chesterton's school notebooks, many of which have survived, give ample testimony to his amazing skill as a draughtsman, and particularly to a cartoonist's ability to give a character in a few lines. The style is recognizable immediately and remained almost exactly the same as Chesterton grew up. The notebooks and exercise books abound in busy battle scenes, grotesque faces, devils, politicians, generals in all their finery, and many angels. Often the figures seem vaguely androgynous and only occasionally do those of women appear, with the exception of the Virgin Mary, who is depicted several times and in one instance is the last figure to appear in a book which begins with a figure of Satan. There are several examples of illustrated short stories often with an elaborately designed title page.

It is easy to see from all this how Edward Chesterton was persuaded that Gilbert's future might best be served by his attending drawing classes. He remembered all too vividly how his own artistic hopes had been set aside in favour of his expected early entry into the family business. He advised Gilbert that he would be happy to see his skill developed, but that he should, besides attending art classes, continue to study more widely, for a year at any rate, at home. If all went well he could consider a Fine Arts course at University College, London, the following year. With this course of action decided upon, and as some recognition of Gilbert's recent success at school, Edward Chesterton arranged to take him to France for a few weeks. The family had been used to spending holidays at the seaside each year, but this would be Gilbert's first trip abroad.

The two travelled by rail with no definite itinerary in mind beyond the intention of seeing several towns in Normandy before spending some time in Paris. From their various stopping places Chesterton scribbled notes to Bentley, who heard how they had visited Rouen and then moved on to Arromanches. Travelling by horse-drawn coach from the station into the town, Edward Chesterton had struck up a conversation with two young boys sitting in front of them. Gilbert, feeling his French to be unequal to a lengthy conversation, proceeded to draw a picture of Napoleon, 'hat, chin, attitude, all complete'. The success of this first moment of communication resulted in his dashing off a large number of goblins. In this there was nothing unusual, for, as already mentioned, goblins and demons had made regular appearances in Chesterton's drawings at school and one book in particular, compiled when he was about sixteen, had shown a series of illustrations for his own 'Half-Hours in Hades, an elementary handbook of demonology'. Neither was it, for that matter, the first appearance of Bonaparte.

A foreign town is a very funny sight with solemn old abbés in their broad brims and black robes and sashes and fiery bronzed little French soldiers staring right and left under their red caps, dotted everywhere among the blue blouses of the labourers and the white caps of the women. The people are most rapid, obliging and polite, but talk too much.

Such observations were set out for Bentley. Chesterton was glad to consider himself a traveller and not a tripper, although his father engaged a guide to show them round Notre Dame. Among the cathedral's many treasures they were shown the cross given by Louis XIV to Louise de La Vallière, whom the guide out of consideration for his English party referred to as 'Mees La Vallière'. Chesterton thought that 'concession to the British system of titles was indeed touching. I also thought, when reflecting what the present was, and then to whom it was given, that this showed pretty well what the religion of the Bourbon régime was and why it has become impossible since the Revolution.'

He returned to England feeling that he had begun to understand a little of 'the nation that is nearest ... and yet is the furthest away'. He saw France as a 'square fortress of equal citizens and Roman soldiers; full of family councils and *patria potestas* and private property under Roman Law; and keep and citadel of Christendom'. It was the first of several visits, and his experience in the coach at Arromanches may have prompted his decision to include French as one of the subjects he would come to study at University College.

There is no record of what exactly happened during the following months, beyond the minutes of the JDC meetings, which carried on as usual during the autumn and up to the middle of December. At d'Avigdor's house a meeting was held on 16 December at which 'a constitutional discussion was held regarding the future of the Club. This was opened by the Secretary, who remarked on the necessity for holding such a discussion, as members were already beginning to leave St Paul's School, and in a year or so more would be scattered over different parts of the world.' It was decided that *The Debater* should be discontinued, and Chesterton especially urged that other friends made later in life might be admitted, but that the Club should remain as it was except that the rule limiting the number to twelve should be abolished.

The following day there was a visit to the Tower, and some members went over the Mint, by the kind permission of the Constable. 'We saw all over the Tower, and some parts that are not open to the public'. The visit had been a follow-up from a meeting of JDC Antiquarian Society held at Chesterton's house on 14 December at which someone had read a paper on 'The Tower of London', and after which both Gilbert and Cecil Chesterton had spoken, for by this time Cecil had become one of the more vociferous members of the Club. The Tower visit was the final meeting of the Club to be recorded in the last full issue of *The Debater*, which came out in February 1893.

> With this number *The Debater* ceases to exist. Regretful though we may be at losing our Magazine, we may still claim that enthusiasm which prompted us to start it, and a belief that the idea which it was intended to embody, has been helped rather than hindered by its championship.

The end of *The Debater* came as a great blow to Chesterton. It had been very much the centre of his life, and for the moment there was

nothing to replace it. The magazine had been losing money, and there
was no alternative but to bring the venture to a close. Another fact
that Chesterton had to face was his isolation from his friends, for
although he still saw them regularly at the weekends and during the
school holidays, he no longer shared in their daily life at school. Gradually he began to close in upon himself, and found himself prone
to fits of depression which for the next few years would plague his
life. It was the beginning, as he was to put it, of 'the period of youth
which is full of doubts, morbidities and temptations'. What Chesterton
called his 'period of madness' coincided with a period of drifting and
doing little. What was he doing? Lawrence Solomon thought that Chesterton had studied at an art school in St John's Wood called 'Calderon's'.
If this was so it was not an art school in the accepted sense, for Calderon's
was a group of artists known as the 'St John's Wood Clique', whose
chief unifying bond seems to have been a fondness for practical jokes.
It was led by the son of a 'spoiled' Spanish priest, Philip Hermogenes
Calderon, whose first successful painting, *Broken Vows*, is described
as 'a sharp essay in Pre-Raphaelitism'. Chesterton himself mentions
that he studied for a while at Wood's Art School, but nothing is known
beyond the fact the he had been offered a place at University College,
London, for the autumn.

The notebooks from this period show that he was as industrious
as ever as a cartoonist, though there is nothing to suggest any formal
art tuition; rather, they resemble the notebooks of his time at school.

During the summer of 1893 the family spent some weeks in North
Berwick. Chesterton was writing yet another novel and, somewhat out
of character, tried his hand at golf. 'I did not play it well,' he recalled
some years later; 'on the contrary I enjoyed it very much ... my friends
in North Berwick played with more levity and friendliness than is now
fashionable in England.' Towards the end of the holiday he informed
Bentley:

I am enjoying myself very much down here, though our time is drawing
to a close. One of the nicest things about it is the way you mix with
strangers and the absence of the cursed class feeling which makes
me feel as if we were all humbugs. Whenever I feel tired of writing
the novel, I sally out in the evenings and play with children on the
sands: coastguards' and visitors' children alike, except that the coastguards' are rather the more refined. Our Christian names are known

all over the sands, and we behave generally like the inhabitants of one sandy nursery.

Early in September Bentley and Oldershaw returned to St Paul's for the beginning of their last year, leaving Chesterton to wait the three weeks or so before beginning at University College in the first week of October. The two were among the first pupils to grace the History Eighth, a class created specially for them with Robert Cholmeley, now also Bentley's house master, as form master. Among the first members of this new form was a particularly shy boy, Edward Thomas, 'who kept a rat or so, and a few snakes in his desk'.

It was during this same September that Chesterton completed his series of drawings for Bentley's *Dictionary of Biography*, a collection of short four-line verses which later came to be known as clerihews, taking their name from Bentley's second Christian name. The clerihews had been written over a period of many months, and some of them may have been several years old, but it is strange that there was no sign of them in the pages of *The Debater*. The verses collected together in a notebook were the work of several hands, though Bentley himself had provided the lion's share, but there were several by Chesterton, either wholly or in part, and others owed their origins to ideas suggested by Oldershaw, Digby d'Avigdor's younger brother Waldo, and Maurice, Lawrence Solomon's younger brother to whom the whole collection was dedicated. Perhaps not surprisingly, since he took such a keen interest in all the boys' ventures, there were several clerihews to which Edward Chesterton had contributed lines.

Bentley was later on in life a little vague about the sequence of events leading up to the compilation of the notebook, but there seems no reason to doubt that the very first clerihew was the one about Sir Humphrey Davy, though the second line was to undergo at least three revisions. It appears in the collection as:

> Sir Humphrey Davy
> Was not fond of gravy.
> He lived in the odium
> Of having discovered sodium.

In the collection three clerihews appear on each page in Bentley's handwriting, illustrated or embellished by Chesterton's cartoons with a pictorial signature denoting the author, or in some cases, the group of authors. A dodo represented Bentley, a gavel Chesterton, and so

on. As befitted an older generation, Edward Chesterton was allotted
a pipe.

Of the verses supplied by the illustrator the best is:

> The Spanish people think Cervantes
> Equal to half a dozen Dantes;
> An opinion resented most bitterly
> By the people of Italy.

The little volume, dated September 1893, remained in Solomon's possession until his death in 1954, when his widow presented it to the St
Paul's School Library.

Chesterton matriculated into University College, London, on 6
October. He had chosen to read four subjects: Latin, English, French,
and Fine Art. He studied Latin under A.E.Housman, who had been
appointed Latin Professor at the beginning of the previous academic
year. Housman bemoaned the fact that he 'seldom had pupils who possessed a native aptitude for classical studies or intended to pursue them
far'. In this Chesterton seems to have proved to be no exception, since
after a year he was persuaded to give the subject up; but it is strange
to think that until now it was not known that the author of the delicately
polished verses of *A Shropshire Lad* had spent time giving 'individual
attention' to the almost certainly 'indelicate' unseen translations of the
author of 'Lepanto'. In the spring of 1884 Housman delivered a course
of nine lectures on Latin literature which Chesterton should have
attended, but, unlike the lectures of his English professor, W.P.Ker,
which Chesterton does admit to attending, there is a hollow silence
upon the matter.

Chesterton studied English under W.P.Ker for two years. In the
same class was Ernest Hodder Williams, who afterwards became the
head of the well-known publishing house. He became Chesterton's particular friend and proved to be a considerable help to him later when
Chesterton went down from the college. In his autobiography Chesterton
mentions that Williams 'was attending Latin and English lectures at
University College while I was attending, or not attending, to the art
instructions of the Slade School. I joined him in following the English
course.' Here Chesterton's memory has deceived him. Williams did
not, in fact, study Latin at all, though he did attend Professor Lalle-
mand's French lectures with Chesterton, and during Chesterton's first

year attended Ker's English lectures; but it is irrefutable that Chesterton was in the class from the start.

I am able to boast myself among the many pupils who are grateful to the extraordinarily lively and stimulating learning of Professor W.P.Ker. Most of the other students were studying for examinations; but I had not even that object in this objectless period of my life. The result was that I gained the entirely undeserved reputation for disinterested devotion to culture for its own sake; and I once had the honour of constituting the whole of Professor Ker's audience. But he gave as thorough and thoughtful a lecture as I have ever heard given, in a slightly more colloquial style; asked me some questions about my reading; and, on my mentioning something from the poetry of Pope, said with great satisfaction: 'Ah, I see you have been well brought up.'

It is true that Chesterton had no examinations in mind, and it is likely that his performance at St Paul's had meant that he was not considered to be up to the standard. The forms he filled in at the beginning of each academic year show a blank where students were invited to state which examinations they had in view. The fees for his first year amounted to £29 18s. 6d.; and for the year following, although he took on two extra subjects, by dropping Latin and Fine Art they were reduced to £14 3s. 6d.

For his Fine Art classes Chesterton studied at the Slade, a department of University College, which took its name from the philanthropist Felix Slade. This was the beginning of what Bentley was to call Chesterton's 'quite fruitless enterprise of study at the Slade'. 'Fruitless' indeed, for after one year Chesterton was asked to leave, as the professors found they could not teach him anything, for, as Bentley put it, 'he did not learn the slightest shade of technical improvement on his natural gift for decorative and grotesque drawing'.

Chesterton gave no description of his tutors or teachers. 'There is nothing harder to learn than painting and nothing which most people take less trouble about learning,' he said. 'An art school is a place where about three people work with feverish energy and everybody else idles to a degree that I should have conceived unattainable by human nature.'

He was by his own admission 'a very idle person'; but at the time the Slade School was entering one of its great periods: the days of Brown and Tonks, as they came to be known. The Professor of Fine

Art was Frederick Brown, 'a gruff, hard-bitten man, of great feeling, with something of the Victorian military man about him'. In 1893 he had been at the Slade for a year having previously been the professor at the Westminster School of Art. Among the students who had followed him from Westminster was Henry Tonks, a Fellow of the Royal College of Surgeons who had become a part-time artist and was 'very eloquent in persuading patients to pose as models, and, when obliged to fall back on the dead, seized every opportunity to draw corpses that were dissected'. Tonks was a tall, lean man with 'a fierce expression, vehement tongue and opinions most tenaciously held'. In the term that Chesterton entered the schools Tonks had taken up the appointment of Assistant Professor. 'I cannot teach you anything new,' he had told his students; 'you must find that out for yourselves. But I can tell you something of the methods of the Old Masters – if that will be of any use to you.'

Students at the Slade normally began by drawing in the Antique Room where they were 'purified and elevated' by Greek and Roman sculpture before they were considered fit to move on to the life class. Augustus John, who entered the school a year after Chesterton, described his first visit to the life class, where 'seated on the "throne" a girl, Italian and completely naked, gave him a strange sensation of weakness at the knees as he seated himself and with trembling hand began to draw, or pretend to draw this dazzling apparition'.

There was nothing like that to come from the pen of Chesterton at the time; rather, it was the period of his life that left on his mind for ever 'a certitude upon the objective solidity of Sin'. While his fellow students did not want to be discursive and philosophical, Chesterton's mind was moving at an amazing pace, but in the wrong direction. The 'idle philosophy' he began to pursue was 'a very negative and even nihilistic philosophy'. Although, as he said, he had never accepted it altogether, it threw a shadow over his mind and made him feel that most profitable and worthy ideas were, as it were, on the defensive. Chesterton must explain the situation for himself:

I am not proud of believing in the Devil. To put it more correctly, I am not proud of knowing the Devil. I made his acquaintance by my own fault; and followed it up along lines which, had they been followed further, might have led me to devil-worship or the devil knows what....

I dabbled in Spiritualism without having even the decision to be a Spiritualist. Indeed I was, in a rather unusual manner, not only detached but indifferent. My brother and I used to play with planchette, or what the Americans call the ouija board; but were among the few, I imagine, who played in a mere spirit of play. Nevertheless I would not altogether rule out the suggestion of some that we were playing with fire; or even with hell-fire. In the words that were written for us there was nothing ostensibly degrading, but any amount that was deceiving. I saw quite enough of the thing to be able to testify, with complete certainty, that something happens which is not in the ordinary sense natural, or produced by the normal and conscious human will. Whether it is produced by some subconscious but still human force, or by some powers, good, bad or indifferent, which are external to humanity, I would not myself attempt to decide. The only thing I will say with complete confidence, about that mystic and invisible power, is that it tells lies. The lies may be larks or they may be lures to the imperilled soul or they may be a thousand other things; but whatever they are, they are not truths about the other world; or for that matter about this world.

Chesterton goes on to mention instances of his use of the planchette and the weird answers it provided. On one occasion it was asked what advice should be given to 'rather a dull Member of Parliament who had the misfortune to be an authority on education'. The planchette with brazen promptitude wrote down the simple words 'Get a divorce'. Chesterton continues:

The wife of the politician was so respectable, and I will add so hideous, that the materials of a scandalous romance seemed to be lacking. So we sternly enquired of our familiar spirit what the devil he meant; possibly an appropriate invocation. The result was rather curious. It wrote down very rapidly an immensely and indeed incredibly long word, which was at first quite illegible. It wrote it again; it wrote it four or five times; it was always quite obviously the same word; and towards the end it was apparent that it began with the three letters 'O.R.R.'. I said, 'This is all nonsense; there is no word in the English language beginning O.R.R., let alone a word as long as that.' Finally it tried again and wrote the word out quite clearly; and it ran: 'Orriblerevelationsinighlife.'

The absurdity of all this filled Chesterton with wonder and a faint alarm when he considered the number of people 'who seem to be taking spirit communications seriously, and founding religions and moral philosophies upon them'. Many years later Chesterton told his friend Father O'Connor that he had to give up using the planchette because his sessions were always followed by splitting headaches; 'after the headaches came a horrid feeling as if one were trying to get over a bad spree, with what I can best describe as a bad smell in the mind'.

Chesterton's obsession with evil at this period was exacerbated by, though not entirely owing to, the fact that he was going through an unusually late puberty. It seems his pituitary gland was not functioning normally: his voice had barely broken, and his laugh, particularly, remained a high treble throughout his life. Edward Fordham, recalling the voice, remembered it as 'rather cracked and creaking, which gave the impression of adenoids'. However, at the age of twenty there was no sign of the gross overweight that assailed Chesterton in his early thirties. In fact, as the photographs taken at about this time reveal, he was surprisingly slim. What seems certain is that the sexual awareness usually associated with a child's early teens did not begin in Chesterton until he had left school. His fits of depression became more and more frequent, he filled his notebooks with grotesque and often sadistic figures, and there appeared for the first time a woman in what might be called an 'inviting position'. Seeing some of his wild drawings at this time, two of his closest friends thought Gilbert might be going mad. That he was passing through a critical time is obvious, but apart from the lateness of it there was nothing particularly unusual about his fantasies. Few boys express their fantasies so graphically, and the fact that he was able to hurl them outside himself and on to paper was always for him an important release.

There is something truly menacing in the thought of how quickly I could imagine the maddest, when I had never committed the mildest crime. Something may have been due to the atmosphere of the Decadents, and their perpetual hints of the luxurious horrors of paganism; but I am not disposed to dwell much on that defence, I suspect I manufactured most of my morbidities for myself. But anyhow, it is true that there was a time when I had reached that condition of moral anarchy within, in which a man says, in the words of Wilde, that 'Atys with the blood-stained knife were better than the thing I am.'

I have never indeed felt the faintest temptation to the particular madness of Wilde; but I could at this time imagine the worst and the
wildest disproportions of more normal passion; the point is that the
whole mood was overpowered and oppressed with a sort of congestion
of imagination. As Bunyan, in his morbid period, described himself
as prompted to utter blasphemies, I had an overpowering impulse
to record or draw horrible ideas and images; plunging deeper and
deeper as in a blind spiritual suicide.

Chesterton's denial of any homosexual tendency is supported by all
the evidence, and only worth mentioning because he has occasionally
been accused of it. However, there are throughout his school days not
only continual references to girls in the boys' letters to each other during
the holidays, but also ample evidence that girls, such as the Firmin
and Vivien sisters (also neighbours in Kensington), as well as several
of the boys' sisters, were involved in their games of charades and other
dramatic performances. Even in his friendship with Bentley, which was
certainly intense, Chesterton often saw his friend as a hero and con-
queror of women's affections. One long story written in one of the
notebooks describes how Bentley woos one of the Vivien sisters. Once
his friends had gone up to Oxford in the October of 1894 Chesterton's
almost daily letters to one or another of them abound with references
to women, though it is true that he had not as yet found a girl for
himself, and some of his comments smack of envy. 'It is with deep
pain,' he informed Lawrence Solomon, 'that I hear of your "carryings
on". You too, my poor friend, are being driven on the rock of the
sirens (I allude to the fascinating Miss . . .).'
    Besides another family holiday in North Berwick, Chesterton visited
Florence, Verona and Venice with some of his fellow university students
during the summer of 1894. Professor Brown seems to have made up
his mind that there was nothing the Slade could teach Chesterton without
destroying his natural style of drawing. He told Lawrence Solomon
some years later that whenever Chesterton should have been drawing
he was usually reading, and when he should have been reading he
was drawing. Anxious about Gilbert's general lack of progress, his
mother sought the advice of Dr Walker at St Paul's, a visit which
prompted the remark: 'Six foot of genius. Cherish him, Mrs Chesterton,
cherish him.'
    So it was that Chesterton ceased to study at the Slade in the autumn,

but returned to University College on 23 October to continue with his English and French classes; he dropped Latin and took on two extra subjects, History and Political Economy. Later in the year he decided to attend French Literature classes as well. Both Chesterton and his brother were particularly vague about this period of his life, which is understandable as there must have been some feeling of shame involved. Cecil was to admit with reference to the art training that 'the experiment was not wholly a success'. With the benefit of hindsight he could see 'It was not in that direction that his deepest impulses led. He proved this by the fact that he shrank from the technical toils of art as he never shrank from the toils of writing.' What Cecil called the 'silent years' were full of reading and writing, a period he had entered 'crude and unformed' and which he left 'almost mature'.

Chesterton himself in later life naturally attempted to conceal the extent of his 'failure'. With his school friends all doing so excellently in their schools at Oxford, it was natural that he should come to view his time at the Slade as in some way equivalent to their time at Oxford, which in the long run, of course, it was.

The autumn of 1894 was a difficult time. Although he was to make a good friend of Hodder Williams at his college, he could not but feel envious of his closest friends remaining together. Letters such as the one he received from a friend, written on 1 November, must have hurt him deeply. 'We have kept every Friday evening so far, and intend to do so in future, my rooms are the "holy of holies" tomorrow evening.' However, the depression of the previous year was kept at bay. During the summer he had been able to talk freely about it in a letter to Bentley:

> Inwardly speaking I have had a funny time. A meaningless fit of depression, taking the form of certain absurd psychological worries, came upon me, and instead of dismissing it and talking to people, I had it out and went very far into the abysses, indeed. The result was that I found that things, when examined, necessarily spelt such a mystically satisfactory state of things, that without getting back to earth, I saw lots that made me certain it is all right. The vision is fading into common day now, and I am glad. It is embarrassing talking to God face to face, as a man speaketh to a friend.

Throughout the Michaelmas term, letters continued to speed between Oxford and Warwick Gardens, but although at first his friends attempted to include him (albeit at a distance) in their various pursuits, it was bound to be a diminishing involvement, especially when he heard they had founded the Human Club, an Oxford version of the JDC. 'I went to breakfast with Bentley yesterday,' wrote Salter. 'You ought to come up, if only to see his new rooms. He had just had them packed full overnight with some twenty-two men come to hear a paper of his on Chaucer.' It was hardly bearable.

Chesterton's notebook begun at this time, however, gives a very good idea of his philosophical and spiritual development, his 'talking to God face to face'. The difficulties of the previous year – the deep scepticism, the despair – have given way to a more positive wrestling between two opposites. He wrote:

> I live in an age of varied powers and knowledge,
> Of steam, science, democracy, journalism, art;
> But when my love rises like the sea,
> I have to go back to an obscure tribe and a slain man
> To formulate a blessing.

But of Christmas Day he wrote: 'Good news: but if you ask me what it is, I know not.'

In the same notebook appears a short passage, which may possibly be of a slightly later date, but it is important to any understanding of the premise on which Chesterton's thinking rests. It is entitled 'Two Strands'.

> Man is a spark flying upwards. God is everlasting.
>
> Who are we, to whom this cup of human life has been given, to ask for more? Let us love mercy and walk humbly. What is man, that thou regardest him?
>
> Man is a star unquenchable. God is in him incarnate.
>
> His life is planned upon a scale colossal, of which he sees glimpses. Let him dare all things, claim all things: he is the son of Man, who shall come in clouds of glory.
>
> I saw these two strands mingling to make the religion of man.

The 'spark flying upwards' is in juxtaposition to another spark, the spark that 'will be less bright' which figured in a strange encounter Chesterton had had with a fellow student at University College, and a grim conversation that filled him with alarm.

> It was strange, perhaps, that I liked his dirty, drunken society; it was stranger still, perhaps, that he liked my society. For hours of

the day he would talk with me about Milton or Gothic architecture; for hours of the night he would go where I have no wish to follow him, even in speculation.

He was a man with a long, ironical face, and close red hair; he was by class a gentleman, and could walk like one, but preferred, for some reason, to walk like a groom carrying two pails. He looked like a super-jockey; as if some archangel had gone on the Turf. And I shall never forget the half hour in which he and I argued about real things for the first and last time.

He had a horrible fairness of the intellect that made me despair of his soul. A common, harmless atheist would have denied that religion produced humility or humility a simple joy; but he admitted both. He only said, 'But shall I not find in evil a life of its own?'

The man had asked Chesterton why he was becoming more and more orthodox, and he had replied by pointing to the fire that was burning in front of them. Using the sparkling flames as a symbol, Chesterton had argued the case for religion and humility: 'Seduce a woman, and the spark will be less bright. Shed blood, and that spark will be less red.'

The other replied, 'Granted that for every woman I ruin one of those red sparks will go out; will not the expanding pleasure of ruin...'

'Do you see that fire?' Chesterton asked. 'If we had a real fighting democracy, somcone would burn you in it; like the devil-worshipper that you are.'

'Perhaps,' he said, in his tired, fair way. 'Only what you call evil I call good.'

He went down the great steps alone, and I felt as if I wanted the steps swept and cleaned. I followed later, and I went to find my hat in the low, dark passage where it hung. I suddenly heard his voice again, but the words were inaudible. I stopped startled; then I heard the voice of one of the vilest of his associates saying, 'Nobody can possibly know.' And then I heard those two or three words which I remember in every syllable and cannot forget. I heard the Diabolist say, 'I tell you I have done everything else. If I do that I shan't know the difference between right and wrong.' I rushed out without daring to pause; and as I passed the fire I did not know whether it was hell or the furious love of God.

In May 1895 Chesterton came of age. His mother wrote him a note from Warwick Gardens to Oxford where he was staying:

My heart is full of thanks to God for the day that you were born and for the day on which you attain your manhood. Words will not express my pride and joy in your boyhood which has been without stain and a source of pleasure and good to so many – I wish you a long happy useful life. May God grant it. Nothing I can say or give would express my love and pleasure in having such a son. The enclosed is for Oxford expenses or books.

On his return to London Chesterton informed Bentley:

Being twenty-one years old is really rather good fun. It is one of those occasions when you remember the existence of all sorts of miscellaneous people. A cousin of mine, Alice Chesterton, daughter of my Uncle Arthur, writes me a delightfully cordial letter from Berlin, where she is a governess; and better still, my mother has received a most amusing letter from an old nurse of mine, an exceptionally nice and intelligent nurse, who writes on hearing that it is my twenty-first birthday ... Yes, it is not bad being twenty-one, in a world so full of kind people.

The letter continues in his more usual vein with images drawn from his reading, but it is interesting to discover Chesterton's attitude to the weather:

I have just been out and got soaking and dripping wet; one of my favourite dissipations. I never enjoy weather so much as when it is driving, drenching, rattling, washing rain. As Mr Meredith says in the book you gave me, 'Rain, O the glad refresher of the grain, and welcome water-spouts of blessed rain.' (It is in a poem called 'Earth and a Wedded Woman', which is fat.) Seldom have I enjoyed a walk so much. My sister water was all there and most affectionate. Everything I passed was lovely, a little boy pickabacking another little boy home, two little girls taking shelter with a gigantic umbrella, the gutters boiling like rivers and the hedges glittering with rain. And when I came to the corner the shower was over, and there was a great watery sunset right over No. 80, what Mr Ruskin calls an 'opening into Eternity'. Eternity is pink and gold. This may seem a very strange rant, but it is one of my 'specimen days'. I suppose you would really

prefer me to write as I feel, and I am so constituted that these daily
incidents get me that way. Yes, I like rain. It means something, I
am not sure what; something freshening, cleaning, washing out, taking in hand, not caring-a-damn-what-you-think, doing-its-duty,
robust, noisy, moral, wet. It is the Baptism of the Church of the
Future.

Yesterday afternoon (Sunday) Lawrence and Maurice came here.
We were merely infants at play, had skipping races round the garden
and otherwise raced. ('Runner, run thy race,' said Confucius, 'and
in the running find strength and reward.') After that we tried talking
about Magnus [a schoolfriend], and came to some hopeful conclu-
sions. Magnus is all right. As for Lawrence and Grey [Maurice],
if there is anything righter than all right, they are that.

There is an expression in Meredith's book which struck me immensely: 'the largeness of the evening earth'. The sensation that the
Cosmos has all its windows open is very characteristic of evening,
just as it is at this moment. I feel very good. Everything out of the
window looks very, very flat and yellow: I do not know how else
to describe it.

It is like the benediction at the end of the service.

There is something absurd, to say the least, at the thought of the
six-foot-two Chesterton and the two smaller Solomon brothers galumph-
ing about the little patch behind No. 11 Warwick Gardens; but in spite
of their remarkable intellectual maturity they were as often as not, as
Chesterton said, 'merely infants at play'. No doubt such antics continued
when Chesterton joined the Solomon family at Broadstairs during the
summer. It was not so much that Chesterton was young for his age,
but that he always considered such antics perfectly adult, just as he
enjoyed playing with his toy theatre. 'Toys are not childish,' he said,
'they are human.' His parents though found him unreliable and tended
to treat him as if he were quite incapable of organizing his own affairs.
How many twenty-one-year-olds would be likely to receive a letter such
as the one Edward Chesterton wrote from Southwold on 9 September?
Its tone is more like a letter to a small boy about to cross London for
the first time.

Your mother has wired you that you can stay till Thursday morning,
and, as there is no one at Warwick Gardens to get you bed and board,
and no one else in town you could go to, it is decided you should

come down here for the remaining few days. You will have to come up from Broadstairs to London early on Thursday morning, taking a place in that part of the train that goes to Ludgate Hill. Mind that the train you come by allows ample time (after allowance for its being possibly half an hour late in arrival) to get to Liverpool Street for the 3.20 train thence to Halesworth, arriving here at 6.50. Of course you will want also time to get something to eat. No doubt the Solomons will not be coming up to town by so early a train as you will, but don't let anything prevent your carrying out the foregoing arrangement, as we shall expect your arrival at 6.50.

We expected you to turn up yesterday, not having heard otherwise. Take what they call 'third class fornightly' ticket 15/-.

Whether he arrived or not we shall never know. Chesterton used to say that the only way to catch a train was to miss the one before, and he was once seen to queue up at the booking office and ask for a cup of coffee.

4

Vision in Bedford Park

1895–1898

Chesterton left University College without a degree at the end of the summer term, 1895, and towards the end of September began work for the small publishing house of Redway which specialized in books on spiritualism and the occult. It was as though the demons were still keeping tabs on him. Situated close to the British Museum, the office was in familiar territory: 'I am beastly busy, but there is something exciting about it', he informed Bentley. With a hundred different things to attend to, he felt better employed than 'with one blank day of monotonous "study"' before him. He outlined in some detail a typical day in which he had been engaged in three different tiring occupations and enjoyed them all.

> Redway says: 'We've got too many MSS.; read through them, will you, and send back those that are too bad at once.' I go slap through a room full of MSS., criticising deuced conscientiously, with the result that I post back some years of MSS. to addresses, which I should imagine, must be private asylums. But one feels worried somehow. . . .

Chesterton was placed in charge of the entire press department. He sent out review copies of books, a task which required a knowledge of all the magazines and an inkling as to 'what sort of books they'd crack up'. 'I used to think I hated responsibility,' he told Bentley; 'I am positively getting to enjoy it.'

However, the main task of the day as far as he was concerned was his writing in the evenings. 'Now that I have tried other kinds of hurry and bustle,' he said, 'I solemnly pledge myself to the opinion that there is no work so tiring as writing, that is, not for fun, but for publication.'

He had received further encouragement during the year when the
Clarion had published his poem 'Easter Sunday' in its issue of 20 April;
and his first review, of *The Ruskin Reader*, had been printed unsigned
in *The Academy*. 'It is by this event that the beginning of my friend's
career as a writer may be dated,' noted Bentley, although, as we have
seen, it was not Chesterton's first publication. However, it was by reviewing books on art that he would in a few years become known.

> Other work has a reputation, a machinery, a reflex action about it
> somewhere, but to be on the stretch inventing things, making them
> out of nothing, making them as good as you can for a matter of
> four hours leaves me more inclined to lie down and read Dickens
> than I ever feel after nine hours' ramp at Redway's. The worst of
> it is that you always think the thing so bad, too, when you're in
> that state. I can't imagine anything more idiotic than what I've just
> finished.

Bentley and the rest had returned to Oxford at the start of their second
year. 'What an idiotically long time 8 weeks is,' Chesterton wrote. On
12 October he was pleased to receive a post card from Waldo d'Avigdor:
'I shall come to see you tomorrow evening so get back from Redway's
early, if you can.'

It is not known exactly how long Chesterton remained at Redway's,
but it was probably for only a few months before he moved to T.Fisher
Unwin, a larger and more prosperous firm, whose offices were in the
City at 11 Paternoster Buildings. This publishing house, which was
later taken over by Ernest Benn, launched the careers of several well-
known authors including Somerset Maugham, whose *Liza of Lambeth*
it brought out in 1897. It is possible that Chesterton was the reader
who recommended the novel, for, as Frances Chesterton told Fr
O'Connor (who became the Chestertons' closest friend), he had read
some ten thousand novels for Fisher Unwin, and could remember the
plots and most of the characters for the rest of his life. Fr O'Connor
tested Chesterton's power of memory one day at Beaconsfield by asking
if he remembered passing for publication a novel by Dr William Barry,
called *The Two Standards*. Chesterton thought for a moment: 'Let me
see ... Oh yes! that's where the Rector's daughter goes atheist through
reading the Book of Job, isn't it?' It was.

Chesterton was to remain at Fisher Unwin until 1901, by which time
he was already the author of two books of verse and one of essays,

and recognized as a promising young journalist. It is important to remember that throughout the romantic period of his life that he was now about to enter he was in regular employment. Many letters were to be written from Paternoster Buildings, and numerous drawings and fragments of verse, now at Beaconsfield, are on Fisher Unwin letterhead. However, at no time did he relax in his resolve to be a writer, and on most evenings he worked away at his writing after work.

Although he was fully occupied by all this, Chesterton managed to see something of his old school friends during their vacations from Oxford and sometimes at weekends during the term. Both Bentley and Oldershaw continued to play a major part in his life, and they were destined to take an even greater part in the future. As Oldershaw said of Chesterton 'He did nothing for himself till we came down from Oxford and pushed him.' In 1896 both he and Bentley were becoming increasingly well known at the university and each in turn would reach the highest office in the Union, becoming over the next two years successively Librarian and then President. From the start the Union had played an important part in their Oxford careers, and many an early letter to Chesterton in the first days of the Michaelmas term of 1894 had been written on Union writing paper. All this was to prove of moment to Chesterton, since it was through their brilliance at debating, something he had done so much to encourage, that they came to know and greatly admire the man who was President of the Union during their second term, Hilaire Belloc; but it would be several years before they effected a meeting between their two mentors.

It was through debating and Oldershaw's affection for a girl whose family lived in Bedford Park, that Chesterton came to meet his future wife some time during the autumn of 1896. That summer he had spent a week at Margate followed by a short trip to France. He was evidently ripe for romance. He wrote to Bentley from the Hotel St Pierre at Ault: 'Judging by the first day at Ault, I shall be getting horribly fond of those Cowton [family friends] girls here before the fortnight is out. I will give you a series of portraits some day. As soon as we got near the place we found them in white dresses and red berets, dotting the town like scarlet poppies.'

As to the French girls, he did not think he had much of a chance with them. 'The little French girls with black pigtails in red ribbons run after and take care of the little French boys in cropped hair and oblique eyebrows whether I had ever been born or no.'

At the same time he was becoming more and more intrigued by the French way of life. 'The capacity of joy is one of the great qualities of this odd people. In one way travelling in France is good for the soul. It accentuates strongly, by the difference of type and language, that sense of being outside, unnecessary, a privileged spectator of the great glory of human life.'

Chesterton's remarks about the Cowton girls and his observations of the little French girls seem more like those of a sixteen-year-old rather than a young man of twenty-two. They would hardly lead anyone to suppose that within a few months he would be falling deeply in love with a woman five years older than himself and that his love would be reciprocated.

Auspiciously, he met Frances Blogg at a debate held at her home. It was the second time he had visited No. 6 Bath Road, but on the first occasion Frances was away, although Oldershaw had introduced him to her younger sister, Ethel, of whom Oldershaw was growing increasingly fond, and would eventually marry. On the subsequent meeting Chesterton found himself sitting next to Frances, a pale, rather sad-looking girl with dreamy blue eyes, a particularly strong, determined mouth, and light brown hair swept back from her face according to the fashion of the time. She was wearing a green velvet dress barred with green fur. She appeared to Chesterton to be 'artistic', a 'queer card', but she gave him such a straight look as they sat side by side on the sofa that he said to himself plainly as if he had read it in a book:

> If I had anything to do with this girl I should go down on my knees to her: if I spoke with her she would never deceive me: if I depended on her she would never deny me: if I loved her she would never play with me: if I trusted her she would never go back on me: if I remembered her she would never forget me. I may never see her again. Goodbye. It was all said in a flash: but it was all said. . . .

So it was that the two fell in love at first sight, but they were so shy of each other that it would be months before they could speak to each other about their feelings openly; after that there would never by anyone else for either of them.

Frances was elvish and petite, five feet two and a half inches tall; she would always look tiny and frail beside Gilbert. Perhaps on that first meeting he failed to notice her surprisingly large, almost masculine hands. 'She had a sort of hungry appetite,' he said, 'for all the fruitful things like fields and gardens and anything connected with production; about which she was quite practical. She practised gardening; in that curious Cockney culture she would have been quite ready to practise farming; and on the same perverse principles she practised a religion.'

Unlike most of the inhabitants of Bedford Park Frances was an ardent Anglo-Catholic, having been educated at a local convent, and, as Chesterton noted, her quiet practise of her faith was something 'utterly unaccountable ... to the whole fussy culture in which she lived'. To the whole agnostic or mystic world of Bedford Park 'practising a religion was much more puzzling than professing it'.

Bedford Park was the first garden suburb. Situated at Chiswick, it had been founded by Jonathan Comyns-Carr, who had employed the architect Norman Shaw to design well-ordered red-brick buildings round a 'village' green, dominated by St Michael and All Angels church and The Tabard, an inn whose name was intended to remind the inhabitants of the 'happy days' of Chaucer. From this centre, roads led off with rows of detached 'Queen Anne' houses which had pretentious names like 'Asgard' – one wag on seeing this suggested that the next-door house should have been called 'Horse Guard'. In 1881 the *St James's Gazette* published an atrocious rhyme about the place:

> This was a village builded
> For all who are aesthete
> Whose precious souls it fill did
> With utter joy complete.

In fact, Bedford Park was 'bohemian' in the most self-conscious way; the inhabitants were predominantly middle-class and what in the 1960s would have been called 'trendies'. They were mostly doctors, lawyers, retired naval and army officers, besides the expected smattering of actors, playwrights, artists and poets. Yeats, who had once cast Frances's horoscope, lived at No. 3, Blenheim Road. 'The inhabitants had a partiality for fancy-dress balls, walked about in bedroom slippers, and met on Sunday mornings for a drink at the Tabard.' The whole venture bankrupted its founder, and it represented everything that Chesterton's mother scorned. Since he was, of course, still living at home, it was a long time before Chesterton plucked up the courage to tell her he had ever been there.

Although he was to make fun of the place as 'Saffron Park' in his
oınovel *The Man Who Was Thursday*, Chesterton enjoyed the kind of
life lived there. 'It was described with some justice as an artistic colony,'
he wrote, 'though it never in any definable way produced any art. But
although its pretensions to be an intellectual centre were a little vague,
its pretensions to be a pleasant place were quite indisputable.' In one way
and another it came to dominate his life for the next five and a half years.

Many people, it seems, had come to live in Bedford Park because
it was relatively cheap. Blanche Blogg was the widow of a diamond
merchant. Her husband, whose family was of Huguenot descent, had
died when the four children were still very young. The family name
de Blogue had been anglicized somewhat unfortunately to Blogg, though
it was hardly the Bloggs' fault that the name (with that of Gubbins)
should be used so freely by the English upper class to denote people
who had pretensions to gentility. The family was quite poor, so that
all three girls went out to work as secretaries. Frances, the eldest, worked
for the Parents' National Educational Union, better known by its initials
as the PNEU. Gertrude was, at the time Chesterton came on the scene,
Rudyard Kipling's secretary, so that during the week she was usually
away at Rottingdean, but she would often return for the weekends;
she was engaged to Rex Brimley Johnson, who would later become
one of Chesterton's first publishers. Ethel, who would eventually marry
Lucian Oldershaw, worked for a group of women doctors at the Royal
Free Hospital. The girls were used to travelling on the new Underground
to work, and Chesterton took a particular delight in calling at Frances's
office at Westminster on his way to Fisher Unwin's to leave either a
letter or a poem, sometimes both, or scribble a message on her blotter
before she arrived.

When she met Chesterton, Frances was twenty-seven; she was not
then, nor would she ever be, physically strong. She found the journey
to and from Westminster each day exhausting; but she was sensitive
and mentally alert. Although not at this time notably well read, she
enjoyed controversy, readily agreeing to become secretary of the debating
club she founded for her brother Knollys, but she did not ever take
part in the debates herself. She recognized Chesterton's brilliance immediately, noticing how in a debate he could remember every point
another speaker had made and could deal with them in order. The
combination of an ordered mind and a totally disordered appearance
appealed to her, and although like him she had been very late in reaching

maturity, she felt motherly and protective towards him. He was quite unlike anyone she had met before, and she was impressed that he had already had several poems published. Her own poems were kept neatly in a notebook which she had begun three years earlier, in 1893. She would continue to write poems for the rest of her life, and from 1909, when her first poem appeared in the *Westminster Gazette*, she would occasionally have them published. Her well-known carol 'How Far is it to Bethlehem?', written in 1917, won a prize in 1922, and is today included in the *Oxford Book of Carols*.

Chesterton saw Frances as

...a harmony in green and brown. There is some gold in it some-where, but cannot be located on examination. Probably the golden crown. Harp not yet arrived. Physically there is not quite enough of her to carry all that temperament: she looks slight, fiery and wasted, with a face that would be a Burne Jones if it were not brave: it has the asceticism of cheerfulness, not the easier asceticism of melancholy. Devouring appetite for sensations; very fond of the Bible; very fond of dancing. When she is enjoying herself thoroughly, one has a sense that it would be well for her to go to sleep for a hundred years. It would be jolly fine for some prince too.

One of the few girls, with all their spiritual superiority, who have souls, i.e. intellect and emotion pulling the same way. That all women are supernatural is obvious to the meanest capacity. But she is espe-cially so. She dresses nicely and looks all green and furry.

This was Chesterton's entry on Frances's character in what he called 'An Encyclopaedia of Bloggs', written in the early days of his relationship with the family. Of Ethel, he wrote that when Christ was made every-body's brother, Miss Ethel Blogg was made everybody's sister. She did, of course, become his sister-in-law, and remain a close and loyal friend.

The courtship was long, but in the true sense it was courtly. Like a knight of the *Roman de la Rose* Chesterton wooed his lady, cajoled her, teased her, tumbled for her, and attempted to inspire her in turn. The sadness, not to say madness, of any romatic lover is that all too often he attempts to make a woman fit into his preconceived idea of her. Chesterton had already written verses to 'Her whom I have not yet met' in one of his notebooks. Sadly, many of his letters to Frances have been lost or intentionally destroyed, but those that do remain are magnificent. Predictably, he described the journey on which he had

embarked as a journey to fairyland. Years later Frances confessed that
the courtship had lasted so long she began to wish Chesterton would
come to the point.

The two wrote to each other almost daily, and Chesterton considered
his letter to Frances 'the only thing worth doing' in the day. 'I suppose
it is selfish to simply starve for words from you, but it is a form of
selfishness we probably do not dislike in each other,' he told her when
he had not heard from her for two days, 'I suppose because of Sunday
and Bank Holiday.'

When he was away from London, particularly during the summer
– for both Cecil and he continued to join their parents at either Felixstowe
or Southwold – his letters were understandably longer and more carefully planned. One such letter sets out an inventory of the equipment
with which he had set out on his romantic journey:

> 1st. A Straw Hat. The oldest part of this admirable relic shows traces
> of pure Norman work. The vandalism of Cromwell's soldiers has
> left us little of the original hat-band.
> 2nd. A Walking Stick, very knobby and heavy: admirably fitted to
> break the head of any denizen of Suffolk who denies that you are
> the noblest of ladies, but of no other manifest use....

The list continues to inform Frances that Cecil and he were teaching
each other to play tennis, but generally he was having a pretty idle
time. A body 'absorbing tea, coffee, claret, sea-water, and oxygen, to
its own satisfaction. It is happiest swimming, I think, the sea being about
a convenient size.' The last item on the inventory was 'A heart – mislaid
somewhere', but one of the important items was 'A number of letters
from a young lady, containing everything good and generous and loyal
and holy and wise that isn't in Whitman's poems'.

Chesterton was quite incapable of handling legal or financial matters.
When he and Frances were buying a piece of land from the Burkes'
Estate at Beaconsfield on which they eventually built Top Meadow,
the solicitor corresponded with Frances and used phrases such as: 'Get
Gilbert to sign where I have marked a cross.' Some of their friends
were embarrassed for him, in the days when he was becoming the most
celebrated man in Fleet Street, that he had to ask Frances for even
the smallest sums of money. However, Frances's practicality was most
necessary. Once on hearing that he had lost his pyjamas on one of
his lecture tours to the north Frances asked him why on earth he had

not bought himself a new pair, he looked puzzled, and expressed some surprise that pyjamas were something one could buy. It is convenient here to mention the most frequently told Chesterton anecdote of all, although the name of the place tends to change with each telling, of how Frances received the cryptic telegram: 'Am at Market Harborough. Where should I be?'. Frances's reply was 'Home', but the place to which her reply was sent was Market Harborough, to settle the matter once for all.

A letter, written from 1 Rosebury Villas, Granville Road, Felixstowe, teases Frances about their future life together.

There will be a sofa for you, for example, but no chairs, for I prefer the floor.... We will each retain a suit of evening dress for great occasions, and at other times clothe ourselves in the skins of wild beasts (how pretty you would look) which would fit your taste for furs and so economical.

The letter ends with a short paragraph in which Chesterton tells Frances how very much he loves her.

Reading such a letter one cannot help feeling sorry, to say the least, that Frances Chesterton felt it necessary to destroy all the correspondence she had had with Gilbert during their courtship, and it is only by chance that a few letters have survived. It is impossible, therefore, to trace the progress, smooth or otherwise, of their affections.

In the summer of 1898 Chesterton had suddenly proposed to Frances in St James's Park. At last he came to the point during the lunch hour on a sunny day when he had walked across from Fisher Unwin's to spend a little time with Frances, and she accepted him immediately.

That same evening, feeling himself 'recently appointed to the post of Emperor of Creation', he wrote:

...Little as you may suppose it at the first glance, I have discovered that my existence until today has been, in truth, passed in the most intense gloom. Comparatively speaking, Pain, Hatred, Despair and Madness have been the companions of my days and nights. Nothing could woo a smile from my sombre and forbidding visage. Such (comparatively speaking) had been my previous condition. Intrinsically speaking it has been very jolly. But I never knew what being happy meant before tonight. Happiness is not at all smug: it is not peaceful or contented, as I have always been till today. Happiness brings not

peace but a sword: it shakes you like rattling dice; it breaks your
speech and darkens your sight. Happiness is stronger than oneself
and sets its palpable foot upon one's neck.

The letter ends by giving Frances a chance to change her mind if she
wished, when they met the next day. 'Should you then be inclined to
spurn me, pray do so. I can't think why you don't, but I suppose you
know your own business best.'

It was in many respects the beginning of many trials. There was
no hope whatsoever of an early marriage. Chesterton was earning about
twenty-five shillings a week at Fisher Unwin, and according to the custom
of the time Frances would be obliged to give up work as soon as she
married. They could not have possibly lived on his small income. Then
there was the matter of their families, neither of which really approved
of the relationship. Mrs Blogg considered Chesterton to be a 'self-
opinionated scarecrow' and she advised that the engagement should
remain private for the time being, although it was all right for members
of the family to know, and a few very close friends. Frances's cousin,
Margaret Heaton, was one of the family who wrote to Gilbert. 'I wish
you both the most perfect union and God's blessing. I have known
you pretty intimately for some time now, and I have never heard you
say an unkind word of anyone and have often observed how you championed the cause of the weak, this makes me feel more confident than
anything of my dear cousin's happiness with you.' She went on to say,
'I think Francesca needs a great deal of looking after. She is often
very foolish and unkind to herself, and overworks shockingly (and
underfeeds!)' Gertrude wrote from the Kiplings' house at Rottingdean:
'Please don't be afraid of me any more. I confess I have occasionally
expressed the desire to shake you, at which Rex has unkindly laughed,
but the impulse will no longer seize me now.... Of course, you are
quite unworthy of Frances but the sooner you forget it the better!...'
'I feel just centuries older than you two now!' she added, referring
to the fact that she and Rex Brimley Johnson were already engaged.

Both girls knew instinctively that Frances was unlikely to receive the
kind of practical support she really needed, though with some reservations they liked Chesterton well enough. When these two letters were
written in the July of 1898 Chesterton himself had not summoned up
sufficient courage to break the news to his parents. This unsatisfactory
situation, which continued for many weeks, began to cause Frances

anxiety. 'Please tell your mother soon,' she begged him. 'Tell her I am not so silly as to expect her to think me good enough, but really I will try to be.' Marie Louise, who had quite made up her mind that Gilbert should marry Annie Firmin, was unlikely to look with favour on anyone with the name of Blogg who lived in Bedford Park.

During that summer Chesterton joined his brother and parents on their usual holiday in Suffolk and, finding it quite beyond his power to face his parents outright on the subject, decided on the more cowardly course of writing his mother a letter. She saw nothing unusual in the sight of Gilbert writing away at the table, but she may have been surprised when he handed her a letter as he said goodnight to her, requesting her to read it in private. After suggesting in the letter that she might possibly think it 'a somewhat eccentric proceeding' as she had been sitting opposite him when he wrote it, he tells her his reason: 'because it occurs to me that you might possibly wish to turn the matter over in your mind before writing or speaking to me about it'.

Chesterton then reminds his mother that some eight years ago she had once said that when he eventually fell in love, if the girl was good, she would not mind who she was. 'I don't know how many times I have said this over to myself in the last two or three days in which I have decided on this letter,' he continues.

Then the letter comes to the point, though his mother's hold over him meant that he had to lie.

Do not be frightened: or suppose that anything sensational or final has occurred. I am not married, my dear mother, neither am I engaged. You are called to the council of chiefs very early in the deliberations. If you don't mind I will tell you, briefly, the whole story.

You are, I think, the shrewdest person for seeing things whom I ever knew: consequently I imagine that you do not think I go down to Bedford Park every Sunday for the sake of the scenery... The first half of my time of acquaintance with the Bloggs was spent in enjoying a very intimate, but quite breezy and Platonic friendship with Frances Blogg, reading, talking and enjoying life together, having great sympathies on all subjects; and the second half in making the thrilling, but painfully responsible discovery that Platonism, on my side, had not the field by any means to itself... I will not say that you are sure to like Frances, for all young men say that to their mothers, quite naturally, and their mothers never believe them, also

quite naturally. Besides, I am so confident, I should like you to find
out for yourself. She is, in reality, very much the sort of woman
you like, what is called, I believe, 'a Woman's Woman', very humorous, inconsequent and sympathetic and defiled with no offensive exuberance of good health.... Here you give me a cup of cocoa. Thank
you.

    Believe me, my dearest mother, always your very affectionate son,
                                   Gilbert.

His mother's immediate reaction is not known but, as Annie Firmin
told Maisie Ward (Chesterton's biographer), she was a woman of strong
likes and dislikes, and she 'always disliked Frances'. Mr Ed however,
liked Frances from the start and grew very fond of her; he was used
to his wife's trenchant dislikes, and had long endured her irrational
hatred of Kate Chesterton, his brother Sidney's wife. However, neither
Cecil, nor later his wife, liked Frances, so the poor girl would in many
ways have to pay for accepting Gilbert's proposal; but she was right
to do so. Fr O'Connor went so far as to say 'We owe Gilbert to Frances:
she fostered his genius and kept away disturbing elements'; and Fr
Vincent McNabb thought that Chesterton's physical dependence on
Frances was part of an all-round dependence, moral and intellectual
also.

5
Pride and a Little Scratching Pen

1898–1900

Whatever difficulties Chesterton might have faced with his mother and future mother-in-law at the outset of his engagement, he considered these quite insignificant, and they faded in the light of the confidence his love gave him. He was obsessed by the 'honour of the house of Eve' and the girl, who, by his antics and humour, he was able to raise to a state of happiness and laughter. Mrs Blogg took Lucian Oldershaw aside and asked whether he could possibly prevail upon Gilbert to smarten himself up a bit. The result was a weekend when the two men went off together, but when Oldershaw broached the subject, Chesterton indignantly exclaimed that Frances had accepted him exactly as he was, and he would not change for anyone but her. However, many of his letters to her have sly references to tidiness, and it seems she too was a little worried what the neighbours might think, who evidently took more care over their tidiness. 'I am clean,' Chesterton told her, 'I am wearing a frock coat, which from a superficial survey seems to have no end of buttons. It must be admitted that I am wearing a bow-tie; but on careful research I find that these were constantly worn by the Vikings.' He goes on to produce a mock translation from some 'as yet unknown' Norse saga:

> Frockcoat Folding then
> Haken Hardrada
> Bow-tie Buckled
> Waited for war.'

I resume. My appearance, as I have suggested, is singularly exemplary.

When in 1900 the members of the JDC invited their 'ladies' to attend
the annual dinner, Chesterton drew a special menu for each guest;
for Miss Blogg, who was offered 'Crocodile de Nile Rôti Dhabea' and
'Poisson extraordinaire à la société naturaliste P.N.E.U.' he drew two
hands; one was holding a hairbrush and furiously brushing the wild
hair of a head which is an obvious self-portrait, while the other is turning
the pages of a book. Although Frances might be failing in the matter
of his hair, he had managed to increase her range of reading. He even
persuaded her to read Herodotus. 'So glad that you want to read that
fascinating old liar, the Father of History,' he told her, 'I don't know
why he was called the Father of History, except that he didn't pay
much attention to it: may be said to have cut it off with a shilling.'
Then, listing the various translations she might try, including
Bohn's, he added: 'But as the prophet Ezechiel said, "The Bohn's, very
dry."'

Frances most likely remained ignorant of her mother's attempts
through Oldershaw on her behalf, not that she would have necessarily
blamed her mother had she known. She could hardly have forgotten
the first time she took Gilbert to Bath Road after she had accepted
his proposal. Mrs Blogg, in an attempt to put Gilbert at his ease, asked
him how he liked her new wallpaper. Nervously he advanced to the
wall and, producing a coloured chalk from his pocket, proceeded to
draw a lightning sketch of Frances! Drawing on walls seemed quite
natural to him, and once when he was ill in bed as a boy he had asked
for a long cane to which he tied a pencil and drew all over his bedroom
ceiling; after his marriage, at his second home, in Battersea, he lined
his small study with brown paper so that he might draw on the wall
when he felt like it.

It was as though Chesterton had no concept of time or space, and
yet, blessed with a prodigious memory, his mind was becoming more
and more orderly. He might have been absent-minded, but he was not
scatterbrained. The sense of order which Frances had admired when
he was in debate was equally, if not more highly, developed in his
writing. This would be perhaps his greatest asset in the years to come,
when he would have to produce article after article and meet various
deadlines for the many magazines to which he had become a regular
contributor. Once established, he was able to employ secretaries, and
the first thing they noticed was his amazing ability to dictate a whole
article, beautifully structured and often grammatically complicated,

JUNIOR DEBATING CLUB. DINNER.

If you would like to grow as fat
And imperturbable as that
Know this is what he may have been
Before he had a Magazine

L.R.
OLDERSHAW
Esq. —
from Memory

MENU.-

Hors d'œuvres Variés.

- Soup -

Turbot.

Lamb Cutlets Réforme.
— . — Peas & Potatoes

Macaroni Italienne.

Roast Chicken &Chips.
— Salade

Ice Pudding.

Cheese
— Dessert

Oldershaw's personal menu drawn by Chesterton for a Junior Debating Club Dinner without having to make more than the most simple punctuation changes. Dorothy Collins has described how he dictated to her his book on St Thomas Aquinas amid much other work. 'Shall we do a bit of Tommy?' he would say, and produced whole paragraphs without having to look anything up or make alterations.

His life too, in the early months of 1899, had become ordered. The daily train journey from Kensington to the City, which he often broke at Westminster to mount the long flight of stairs that led to the PNEU offices in order to leave a message for Frances; the day at Fisher Unwin's, reading, editing, sometimes discussing with his superior, Edward Garnett, the books under consideration, and occasionally talking over his own writing with him. On one occasion Garnett insisted on taking him out to lunch, and 'over a gorgeous repast at a restaurant, succeeded in plucking the secret of a novel he was working on from his bosom', and made him promise to send him some chapters of it. Chesterton could not help wondering where the 'jealous, spiteful, depreciating men of letters we read of in books' had got to, so much sympathetic treatment was he receiving from the literary men he knew.

When he returned to Kensington in the evenings he would have dinner with the family and then continue with his writing until about eleven o'clock, after which he would pen a quick letter to Frances.

He was seldom alone with Frances; as was the custom then with engaged couples, they met in their parent's or friend's houses. The debating club at the Bloggs' house was a regular meeting place. On 10 March Ethel Blogg, who had taken over the post of secretary from Frances, wrote to Chesterton. 'I am sorry that I worried you about this debate, but it was awfully nice of you to take it so seriously, and to take so much trouble.' She went on to add: 'I still think you are the most good-natured soul alive.'

Both Bentley and Oldershaw were frequent speakers at the Bath Road debating club, known as the 'IDK', because whenever anyone was asked what the club was called the answer had invariably been, 'I don't know.' The name stuck. Another regular speaker was Cecil Chesterton, who had now left St Paul's and was training to be a surveyor, and 'sent to value libraries, attend sales, and study the techniques of auctioneering' before entering the family firm. He had been 'converted to socialism' at the age of sixteen and, instead of working for Chestertons', went into journalism after he had gained his surveyor's qualifications, and became a leading member of the Fabian Society. Cecil had none of

Gilbert's hesitancy, and seemed to know exactly where he wanted to be from the start.

Chesterton's letters to Frances kept up the same teasing tone. References to his appearance were constant, but also remarks about money, which was a sore point, for while he continued to be earning so little there remained no prospect whatsoever of marriage. 'As long as one hasn't by some oversight got too much money,' he joked, 'there is a deal of poetry in a penny. Particularly the one that stamps this letter.' 'How charming these simple limitations are,' he told Frances, referring to his lack of money. Frances saw them as far less charming. When someone asked Gilbert to look out for a house for a couple about to be married, presumably thinking that with his family connections he might be in the know, Frances is reported to have said somewhat bitterly, 'I wish you'd look out for one for us.' Gilbert answered, 'Good idea.' However, in spite of all his industry in the evenings, there was as yet little prospect of publication. It was as though he was perfectly content with the situation: he had no responsibilities, he had time to write, and he had a girl who loved him. The future did not seem to matter.

Then, during the first week of July, everything changed suddenly and tragically, when Gertrude, who was home for a few days from Sussex, was knocked off her bicycle by an omnibus and fatally injured. She died a few days later. Frances, who had always felt a closer affinity with Gertrude than she had with Ethel, was for a while inconsolable, and went into a deep depression. At the funeral, amid the mass of white flowers piled on the coffin, was a wreath of orange and scarlet blooms from Gilbert, with the inscription: 'He that maketh His angels spirits and His ministers a flame of fire'.

He hardly knew what to do. To begin with his letters continued very much in the same tone; he considered it best to be constant, but the humour seems peculiarly inappropriate. A few days after the death Frances received a letter which began:

> I am black but comely at this moment: because the cyclostyle has blacked me. Fear not. I shall wash myself. But I think it my duty to render an accurate account of my physical appearance every time I write: and I shall be glad of any advice and assistance.

Conscious that his 'rambling levity' might be thought inappropriate, he attempted to explain:

> I, for one, have sworn, I do not hesitate to say it, by the sword of

God that has struck us, and before the beautiful face of the dead, that the first joke that occurred to me I would make, the first nonsense poem I thought of I would write, that I would begin again *at once* with a heavy heart at times, as to other duties, to the duty of being perfectly silly, perhaps extravagant, perfectly trivial, and as far as possible, amusing. I have sworn that Gertrude should *not* feel, wherever she is, that the comedy has gone out of our theatre. This, I am well aware, will be misunderstood. But I have long grasped that whatever we do we are misunderstood – small blame to other people: for, we know ourselves, our best motives are things we could neither explain nor defend. And I would rather hurt those who can shout than her who is silent.

On 11 July he wrote:

I have made a discovery: or I should say seen a vision. I saw it between two cups of black coffee in a Gallic restaurant in Soho: but I could not express it if I tried.

But this was one thing that it said – that all good things are one thing. There is no conflict between the gravestone of Gertrude and a comic-opera tune played by Mildred Wain. But there is everlasting conflict between the gravestone of Gertrude and the obscene pomposity of the hired mute: and there is everlasting conflict between the comic-opera tune and any mean or vulgar words to which it may be set. These, which man hath joined together, God shall most surely sunder. That is what I am feeling ... now every hour of the day. All good things are one thing. Sunsets, schools of philosophy, babies, constellations, cathedrals, operas, mountains, horses, poems – all these are merely disguises. One thing is always walking among us in fancy-dress, in the grey cloak of the church or the green cloak of the meadow. He is always behind, His form makes the folds fall so superbly. And that is what the savage old Hebrews, alone among the nations, guessed, and why their rude tribal god has been erected on the ruins of all polytheistic civilisations. For the Greeks and Norsemen and Romans saw the superficial wars of nature and made the sun one god, the sea another, the wind a third. They were not thrilled, as some rude Israelite was, one night in the wastes, alone, by the sudden blazing idea of all being the same God: an idea worthy of a detective story.

To begin with Frances tried to accept her grief in the spirit of the

Gospels; she had suggested to Gilbert that, as God had allowed Gertrude's death, they must say, like the disciples on the mountain of the Transfiguration, 'It is good for us to be here.' Chesterton in his reply wrote:

> It has always been one of my unclerical sermons to myself, that that remark which Peter made on seeing the vision of a single hour, ought to be made by us all, in contemplating every panoramic change in the long Vision we call life – other things superficially, but this always in our depths. 'It is good for us to be here,' repeating itself eternally. And if, after many joys and festivals and frivolities, it should be our fate to have to look on while one of us is, in a most awful sense of the words, 'transfigured before our eyes': shining with the whiteness of death – at least, I think, we cannot easily fancy ourselves wishing not to be at our post. Not I, certainly. It was good for me to be there.

Gertrude's death served to strengthen Chesterton's faith. It was something 'precious', he told Frances a few weeks later; yet by September he was asking further questions.

> I do not know on what principle the Universe is run, I know or feel that it is *good* or spiritual. I do not know what Gertrude's death was – I know that it was beautiful, for I saw it. We do not feel that it is so beautiful now – why? Because we do not *see* it now. What we see now is her absence: but her Death is not her absence, but her Presence somewhere else. That is what we *knew* was beautiful, as long as we could see it. Do not be frightened, dearest, by the slow inevitable laws of human nature, we shall climb back into the mountain of vision: we shall be able to use the words, with the accent of Whitman. 'Disembodied, triumphant, dead.'

At the same time he wrote several verses in his notebook 'In Memoriam', in which he spoke of 'the sisters' broken trinity'.

> But when she fell, the hot and young –
>   Whose plans were laid, whose road was clear
> – the very glaring mystery –
>   whispered wild gospels in my ear.

Frances later pinned a prayer into the same notebook: 'If in aught I can minister to her peace, be pleased of thy Love to let this be ....'

In all his letters to Frances he had tried to keep up her spirits, refusing to give in to 'the sumptuous humbug of the mortuary sentiment'. The word 'reverence' had had 'a cartload of nonsense' talked about it. As far as he was concerned, 'If there occurs to anyone a really good joke about the look of my coffin, I command him by all the thunders to make it. If he doesn't I'll kick the lid up and make it myself.'

He had been consoling in the best way he knew, yet in his own mind he was tortured, not so much by the death itself, but by the appalling violence of it. Knowing how in the past he had found he could lay 'horrors' to rest, and finding a quiet moment at the office, he took a sheet of Fisher Unwin notepaper, picked up his pen and drew a gruesome picture of a fiend whipping forward a chariot whose gigantic nearside wheel was trundling over and squashing a young woman to death.

In the autumn of the same year two seemingly unconnected events came together which would profoundly affect Chesterton's career and ultimately make it possible for him to give up publishing and make some kind of living by his pen. First of all, the *Speaker*, the Liberal magazine that had published several of his poems, was taken over by a group of Oldershaw's Oxford friends; and then, as those friends had predicted, came the outbreak of the Second Boer War.

The *Speaker*, for long the mouthpiece of moderate Liberal opinion, became, under its new management, the bugle call of anti-imperialism, and was, as Bentley put it, 'vigorously, even ferociously, pro-Boer'. The fact that the magazine was now in the hands of people with whom he had some connection would surely make a difference, Chesterton thought. It did not prove to be as easy as he had hoped when he informed Frances on 3 October that 'the *Speaker* for this week – the first of the *New Speaker*, is coming out soon, and may contain something of mine though I cannot be quite sure'. He was bitterly disappointed, for his contribution had been turned down for the most absurd of reasons. F.Y.Eccles, the literary editor, thought Chesterton's handwriting looked Jewish and, as the policy of the magazine was that the war was largely being fought to satisfy the greed of international bankers, many of whom were foreigners and Jews, Chesterton's article was turned down, and for at least a year little of his was accepted. It was indeed ironic in view of the strong charge of anti-Semitism which is so often laid at Chesterton's door, and which I will deal with at some length later on.

Goodness knows what Eccles had meant, but it is true that Chesterton's handwriting was distinctive, a beautifully formed Gothic script, remarkably neat and orderly on the page. He had spent much time perfecting it, as his notebooks testify, just as he had perfected his famous signature, which is more like a drawing than writing. At Beaconsfield there is a notebook which has page after page of the signature in the course of creation, in all sorts and sizes.

It is difficult to understand why Oldershaw did not make a stand against Eccles's absurd prejudice; but Eccles continued to reject everything Chesterton submitted until October of the following year and, according to Oldershaw, even when Chesterton had become a regular contributor, attempted to persuade Belloc against reading anything written by Oldershaw's 'Jewish friend'.

The group that had taken over the magazine were nearly all well-known Oxford personalities of the middle 1890s. J.L. le B.Hammond, who had been Secretary of the Union in 1895, when Belloc had been President, became editor. Another Union past President, John Simon, worked for the *Speaker* for a while, but left when he thought his association with it might damage his legal career. Then there were Philip Comyns Carr, F.W.Hirst, and Eccles, who were on the staff of the magazine, and Bentley and Oldershaw, who were frequent contributors. It was, as Bentley put it, as though the committee of the Russell Club, as he had known it in his first year at Oxford, had moved up to Bouverie Street.

Towards the end of the year, at about the same time as he began reading in barrister's chambers, Bentley's first article appeared in the *Speaker*, and some months later Hammond asked him to join the staff. Once again Chesterton's hopes were raised, but it was his friend from University College, Ernest Hodder Williams, whose family owned the *Bookman*, a magazine that specialized in art and artists, who gave him an opening into book reviewing. On 26 October he sent a letter to Frances, who was abroad.

You see, I am developing into a sort of art critic, under the persistent delusion which possesses the Editor of the *Bookman*. And I think an article attacking the theories that every sane man has held about classic art for a thousand years would be the sort of thing I should enjoy writing. You will come back next week probably just in time to see my first experiment in art criticism in the *Bookman*. The two reviews do not join on well together having been written separately. Otherwise I think they will do.

Again he was disappointed. The review did not appear in the November number as he had expected, but it was included in the December issue with no mention of the reviewer's name.

The two books he had been given to review were about Velazquez and Poussin. From the outset his tone is commanding and, as in the case of his first article on the dragon for *The Debater*, his style is immediately recognizable.

> Diego Rodriguez de Silva Velasquez, the living man, was a court-painter, polished, stately and serene. The trouble is that three centuries after his entombment, the dead man has suddenly become a demagogue, a controversialist, a party leader. He is the captain of the Impressionists. Fortunately for himself, Velasquez lived in an age which did not call upon him to be any sort of 'ist', except an Artist. He was impressional, decorative or realistic, as he felt inclined, and had no new critic looking over his shoulder to weep when he lapsed into lucidity. One of the very few virtues we are really losing is the virtue of inconsistency.

Chesterton's attitude to Impressionism seems peculiarly quaint today, but he saw it at the time as an expression of scepticism. 'The philosophy of Impressionism', he wrote many years later, 'is necessarily close to the philosophy of Illusion.' It was, of course, the most radical art-form at the time Chesterton spent his few months at the Slade, a time when 'nobody dared to dream there could be such a thing as Post-Impressionism or Post-Post-Impressionism'. What shocked the nineteenth-century bourgeois consciences of France, and yet charms us so today, Chesterton attacked on philosophical grounds.

> I think there was a spiritual significance in Impressionism, in connection with this age as the age of scepticism. I mean that it illustrated scepticism in the sense of subjectivism. Its principle was that if all that could be seen of a cow was a white line and a purple shadow, we should only render the line and the shadow; in a sense we should only believe in the line and the shadow, rather than the cow. In one sense the Impressionist sceptic contradicted the poet who said he had never seen a purple cow. He tended rather to say that he had only seen a purple cow; or rather that he had not seen the cow but only the purple. Whatever may be the merits of this as a method of art, there is obviously something highly subjective and sceptical

about it as a method of thought. It naturally lends itself to the meta-physical suggestion that things only exist as we perceive them, or that things do not exist at all.

He felt that the closeness of Impressionism to Illusion had tended to contribute, however indirectly, 'to a certain mood of unreality and sterile isolation' that had dogged him and exacerbated his deep depression experienced at the university.

His attitude to Poussin was equally illuminating. Poussin he saw as uninteresting because of his merits, 'because he is the most perfect exponent of the matured school of classicism and of classic mythology, and of classic mythology the world is sick with a deadly sickness'. It was a theme he would develop more fully over the next few years, for the New Paganism or Neo-paganism as preached by Swinburne and Walter Pater, and later by Lowes Dickenson, he did not see as new or as bearing any resemblance to Paganism. It would appear as one of the heresies to come under attack in his book *Heretics*, which he would bring out six years later. In the Poussin review, he wrote:

> When paganism was re-throned at the Renaissance, it proved itself for the first time a religion by the sign that only its own worshippers could slay it. It has taken them three centuries, but they have thrashed it threadbare. Just as poets invoked Mars and Venus, for every trivial flirtation, so Poussin and his school multiplied nymphs and satyrs with the recurrence of an endless wall-paper, till a bacchanal has become as respectable as a bishop and the god of love is too vulgar for a valentine.

This last sentence alone should have alerted the readers of the *Bookman* that a great writer had emerged on the scene, but there was more to come.

> This is the root of the strange feeling of sadness evoked by the groups and landscapes of Poussin. We are looking at one of the dead loves of the world. Never were men born so much out of the time as the modern neo-pagans. For this is the second death of the gods – a death after resurrection. And when a ghost dies, it dies eternally.

One may see clearly here how much more interested Chesterton was in the 'modern neo-pagans' than he was in Poussin. The ease with which he could turn any subject to his own use was something his readers, and more particularly the audiences who heard his lectures,

became accustomed to. It never mattered what the official title was –
lectures on a wide range of subjects, anything from Unitarianism to
Umbrellas – would all end up, after a short preamble (which might
be to the point), as a springboard from which an exposition of Chestertonian philosophy might begin.

At about this time Edward Chesterton decided that he would like
to help Gilbert. He could easily have afforded to give him a small allowance to enable him to marry; instead he chose to negotiate on Gilbert's
behalf with Fisher Unwin for a rise in salary. After all Gilbert had
spent some time now with the firm, and he had heard that Fisher Unwin
was considering asking Gilbert to write a book about Paris. Gilbert
informed Frances:

> My father again is engaged in the critical correspondence with Fisher
> Unwin, at least it has begun by T.F.U. stating his proposal terms
> – a rise of 5/- from October, another rise possible but undefined
> in January, 10 per cent royalty for the Paris book and expenses for
> a fortnight in Paris. These, as I got my father to heartily agree, are
> vitiated to the bone as terms by the absence of any assurance that
> I shall not have to write *Paris*, for which I am really paid nothing,
> *outside* the hours of work for which I am paid 25/-. In short, the
> net result would be that instead of gaining more liberty to rise in
> the literary world, I should be selling the small liberty of rising that
> I have now for five more shillings. This my father is declining and
> asking for a better settlement. The diplomacy is worrying, yet I enjoy
> it: I feel like Mr Chamberlain on the eve of the war. I would stop
> with T.F.U. for £100 a year – but not for less. Which means, I think,
> that I shall not stop at all.

Besides his correspondence with Fisher Unwin, Edward Chesterton
had advanced a sum of money to the publisher Grant Richards towards
the expense of bringing out a collection of Gilbert's poems. Few fathers
could have done more, but it would be another twelve months before
the book would appear.

Early in April 1900, Chesterton spent a night at the Bloggs' house,
so that he could attend a pro-Boer meeting at the Bedford Park studio
of the artist, Archie MacGregor. As the meeting was likely to last until
very late, Ethel had taken the advantage of Frances's absence in the
Lake District to suggest that Chesterton should stay at 6 Bath Road.

Archie MacGregor was a friend of Yeats's, whom Chesterton considered to be a 'virile and valiant ... fighting atheist', but saw that his atheism was not really revolutionary in the matter of morals. It was very decidedly the 'old morality' that MacGregor was defending against imperialism, merely on the ground that it was murder and theft. As Chesterton put it, in the kind of sentence that would soon be called 'Chestertonian', 'He was defending against the new ethic of Nietzsche the old ethic of Naboth.'

The meeting was important because it seems to have been the first occasion that Chesterton and Hilaire Belloc were in the same room; and each spoke during the debate, although the two were not introduced.

On hearing Belloc speak, Chesterton was 'lifted out of the stuffy fumes of forty-times repeated arguments into really thoughtful and noble and original reflections on history and character'. It was the kind of speech that Frances would have hated, he thought. Belloc talked for half an hour and introduced his speech with a variety of subjects, leaving little time for the motion before the house. He talked about (1) the English aristocracy, (2) the effects of agricultural depression on their morality, (3) his dog, (4) the Battle of Sadowa, (5) the Puritan Revolution in England, (6) the luxury of the Roman Antonines, (7) a particular friend of his who had by an infamous job received a political post he was utterly unfit for, (8) the comic papers of Australia, (9) the mortal sins in the Roman Catholic Church. When Belloc ended Chesterton felt as though the half-hour had been only five minutes. He had, no doubt, expected something exceptional after hearing from his friends how brilliant Belloc was as a speaker, but perhaps even he was surprised how engrossed he had become.

Among those who spoke from the floor, he informed Frances, who was staying at Ambleside, was 'what looked like an uncultivated mopstick in a frock-coat and was that remarkable figure, the Art Critic of the *Bookman* and the most divinely blessed of all the sons of men'. ... 'His sleevelinks were, by a stroke of recollection, in their right place, his coat, as he had been fighting with Johnnie for the recovery of his sword-stick, was not perhaps all that you might desire – but about his abstract and speculative wrath there could be no doubt.'

This may have been the first evening Chesterton had spent at Archie MacGregor's studio, though it is unlikely; if so, it was to be the first of many. The place was obviously ideal, and could hold quite a gathering of people, and was the venue for plays, debates and charades, organized principally to entertain MacGregor's sons and to bring them into contact with like-minded people of both sexes. On one occasion it was announced that a Professor Pumperdinkel was to lecture on heathen mythology.

Mr MacGregor, dressed to look the part, began a discourse to the effect that the heathen gods had never existed. Suddenly with a flash of fire Lucian Oldershaw appeared as Mephistopheles and called up the gods. Gilbert came in as Bacchus and two young people holding out their hands as in Egyptian carvings declared themselves to be Isis and Osiris. In came Thor with his hammer and he and Bacchus began to knock the professor about, Bacchus especially roaring with laughter, enjoying his own part and everybody else's.

There is a photograph of Chesterton dressed as Bacchus; it was just one of the many parts he would play for, like Dickens, whom he so admired and in some respects resembled, he loved to act and dress up as often as occasion allowed. He particularly enjoyed playing the part of a judge, and he presided over several of the mock trials he and his friends organized. The most remembered of these took place on 7 January 1914, at the King's Hall, in King Street, Covent Garden, when, under the auspices of the Dickens Fellowship, Chesterton presided at 'A Trial of John Jasper for the Murder of Edwin Drood', and Cecil Chesterton led for the defence. The evening, described by the editor of the *Dickensian* as 'the most exhilarating, most enjoyable, and distinguished and historic evenings that London had had the opportunity of taking part in for many years', was somewhat wrecked when after the judge had summed up and the jury had been directed to retire to consider the verdict. The jury's foreman, Bernard Shaw, declared that there was no need because the jury had decided the verdict during the luncheon interval.

A less celebrated trial took place some years later in the early days of 1925, at what Chesterton's friends called the Garret Club, a 'big attic among the roof tops over Warren Street Tube Station', where Cecil Palmer, the publisher who brought out the first collected edition of Chesterton's poems, was charged with being sober on the premises.

Hilaire Belloc was conspicuously absent from such proceedings and, although he had an equally lively sense of humour, there seems to be no record of his joining in any of Chesterton's theatrical performances. Be that as it may, Belloc was destined to play a major part in Chesterton's life, and the friendship, which began almost immediately after their first meeting at a Soho restaurant some weeks after the debate at MacGregor's studio, was to be the most important of both their lives.

It was on an evening in early summer. Belloc, whose pockets were stuffed with French nationalist and French atheist newspapers, was wearing a straw hat to shade his eyes. He would wear such a hat when in the following year he walked from the French town of Toul to Rome. Oldershaw, Bentley, and Eccles who, like Belloc, was half French, had assembled at the Mont Blanc Restaurant in Gerrard Street, which had become a regular meeting place for those sympathetic to the pro-Boer cause in the war. Belloc, they informed Chesterton, was in low spirits, though Chesterton noted that Belloc's low spirits were 'much more uproarious and enlivening than anybody else's high spirits'. Calling for a bottle of Moulin-à-Vent, Belloc complimented Chesterton on his writing; exactly what writing he had seen is not known, though it is likely Oldershaw had shown Belloc some of Chesterton's poems. Belloc then proceeded to launch into a long monologue, beginning with an enquiry as to whether King John had been the finest English king, but quickly turned the subject to the state of the war. Chesterton later recalled that on that first meeting, just as he had experienced at the debate, he was conscious of an undercurrent of sympathy with Belloc's ideas running through his own mind. 'What he brought into our dream', he wrote, 'was this Roman appetite for reality and for reason in action, and when he came into the door there entered with him the smell of danger.'

Neither men could possibly have realized on this first meeting what a significant occasion it was. As Chesterton put it later, 'it was from that dingy little Soho cafe that there emerged the quadruped, the twin-formed monster Mr Shaw has nicknamed the Chesterbelloc'. Yet each could see that their attitudes to the war were similar, and each, although ardently pro-Boer, tended to dislike those pro-Boers they had met. Chesterton remained pro-Boer, but he would come to give up socialism as much through meeting socialists as through the influence of Belloc, who would at this time still have called himself a Republican. There was four years' difference in age between the two men. Chesterton at twenty-six was decidedly young for his age, while Belloc was an unusually worldly-wise thirty; and their backgrounds were totally different.

Belloc was born in 1870 at La Celle St Cloud on the outskirts of

Paris. His father, Louis Belloc, was half French and half Irish, and married Bessie Parkes, an English girl from Birmingham who after a visit to Ireland had decided to become a Catholic – a move which her Unitarian father was convinced showed signs of insanity. She gave birth to Hilaire when she was forty-one.

After her husband's early death, Madame Belloc decided to settle in Sussex, so that Hilaire, known to the family and friends as Hilary, was by upbringing and education English, and his home was the county with which he will always be associated. Leaving the Oratory School, Birmingham, with a sound classical background and already certain he could write, Belloc served briefly in the French army as a gunner before going up to Balliol College, Oxford, where he took a First in History and became President of the Union.

In 1896, after he had been refused a fellowship at one of the Oxford Colleges, as he thought – quite wrongly – because of his Catholicism, Belloc made a second trip to America to marry an Irish-American girl, Elodie Hogan, whom he had met some five years previously in England, and who had for a very short time tried her vocation with the Sisters of Charity. On their return to England he had taken his wife to Oxford where he worked for the University Extension, and by teaching and writing attempted to make a living, while still in the back of his mind remained the hope of a fellowship.

Towards the end of the same year Belloc's book of comic verse, *The Bad Child's Book of Beasts*, illustrated by his friend Basil Blackwood, was published. This was the first of four similar books which over the next few years would make Belloc popular, the public finding in him a worthy successor to Lewis Carroll. Among the new friends he made at this time was Maurice Baring, who was in Oxford being coached in Latin for the Diplomatic Service. On the first meeting Belloc had told him that he would most certainly go to hell, so that Baring had not thought it likely that they should ever make friends; but the two were to remain close friends for life, and it would not be long after Belloc met Chesterton that he was introduced to Baring.

By the time Belloc met Chesterton he was also the successful author of a biography of Danton, and a prose satire, *Lambkin's Remains*. He had spent most of the summer of 1899 in Paris working on a life of Robespierre, and early in 1900 with Elodie and their two youngest children he had moved to London and was living at 104 Cheyne Walk.

The creation by Shaw of the formidable monster, the Chesterbelloc,

has tended to be misleading, and the term should really be restricted
to the ten novels by Belloc which Chesterton illustrated. To speak of
a Chestertbelloc novel makes sense, but to apply the term otherwise
is to suggest that in some way the two thought with one mind. It is
true that on most major issues they were largely in agreement; but this
is common, surely, to most close and lasting friendships. Each learned
much from the other, but temperamentally they were very different.

Chesterton was a natural romantic, seeing things in the highlights
of his imagination, inclined to be impatient of reality. 'Belloc', he once
wrote, 'suggests a classic temple, while I am only a sort of Gothic gargoyle.' His imagination was stronger than Belloc's, just as his philosophical intuitions were more profound. But they needed the Attic salt of
Belloc's realism; Chesterton's fantasy required Belloc's fact. Both men
were enviably well-read in their own fields of interest: Belloc had an
extraordinarily wide range of historical knowledge, while Chesterton
had a much more intimate understanding of English literature. However,
Belloc's influence on Chesterton's political thinking and, as the years
went by, on his awareness of the place of the Catholic Church in history,
was formative and lasting; but he saw in Chesterton a 'profusion of
active genius', and at the end declared that it had been a benediction
to know him.

6

The Wild Knight

1900–1901

In his *G.K. Chesterton: A Criticism*, published in 1908, Cecil Chesterton, who presumably should have known the facts of his brother's career as well as anybody, wrote: 'In the autumn of the year 1899 no one outside his own circle had ever heard of G.K. Chesterton. In the spring of 1900 every one was asking every one else, "Who is G.K.C.?"'

On Good Friday Gilbert had informed Frances he had an important job in reviewing a book on Ruskin for the *Speaker*. 'As I have precisely 73 theories about Ruskin it will be brilliant and condensed. I am also reviewing the *Life of the Kendals*, a book on the Renaissance and one on Correggio for the *Bookman*.' More to the point, as far as Frances was concerned, was another matter that the letter mentioned. 'I have been making some money calculations with the kind assistance of Rex, and as far as I can see we could live in the country on quite a small amount of literary work.' This was in answer to a letter from her in which she had set out a series of questions 'with such alarming precision' that he felt bound to answer them categorically. As might have been expected, the answer to another of her questions was:

> Does my hair want cutting? My hair seems pretty happy. You are the only person who seems to have any fixed theory on this. For all I know it may be at that fugitive perfection which has moved you to enthusiasm. Three minutes after this perfection, I understand, a horrible degeneration sets in: the hair becomes too long, the figure disreputable and profligate: and the individual is unrecognised by all his friends. It is he that wants cutting then, not his hair.

He even went on to suggest that they might marry almost immediately, 'in April if not before', a plan that failed to materialize.

The review of the Ruskin book appeared in the *Speaker* on 28 April, and in June the first of three monthly articles, one of them in collaboration with Hodder Williams, appeared in the *Bookman*, with the other two in the July and August issues. His first article, as opposed to book reviews, to be published in the *Speaker* was entitled 'An Election Echo' and came out on 20 October. Then in December he wrote for the *Bookman* on 'The Literary Portraits of G.W.Watts, RA', and for the *Speaker* two articles, 'St Francis of Assisi' and 'William Morris and his School'; these alone would hardly have led to 'every one asking every one else, "Who is G.K.C.?"'; but the autumn of 1900 had also seen the publication of two books of verse, *Greybeards at Play* and *The Wild Knight and Other Poems*. The publication of the two books was all something of a homespun business. *Greybeards at Play*, illustrated by the author, had been published by Rex Brimley Johnson, and on 6 October it was reviewed at considerable length in the *Speaker* by the author's father. Edward Chesterton, immensely proud of the author, was determined to see the book well launched.

This little book [he wrote] marks a stage in the development of a kind of literature which has grown up in the last century – that of nonsense. Slight thing as it is, it is not too much to say that that development means a change in thought, a loosening of certain bonds which used to be considered the proper trammels of reverence, earnestness and dignity. Mr Chesterton and those like him would consider that in throwing off those bonds they ran no risk of dissipating those virtues, but rather stood to practise them with better insight. I hope he and they will succeed in making it clear.

It will probably be admitted on all hands that Mr Chesterton's drawings are much superior to anything usually associated with this sort of work, and they should go far toward winning him recognition from a very large public.

The reviewer had concentrated largely on the illustrations for, as he had said earlier, the verses without the drawings 'would be much in the same position as Mr W.S.Gilbert's librettos without Sir Arthur's music: they would delight a few and puzzle the multitude'. But he had been careful also to praise the book's originality: 'throughout all the mass of creative work that is yearly thrust upon the world we come very rarely upon one which owes neither its plan, nor its subject, nor its spirit to the example set by some fortunate pioneer'.

The book which, in the opinion of W.H.Auden, contained some of the best pure nonsense verse in English, consisted of three poems: 'The Oneness of the Philosopher with Nature', 'Of the Dangers Attending Altruism on the High Seas', and 'On the Disastrous Spread of Aestheticism in All Classes'. There was a poem of dedication to Bentley, who 'through boyhood's storm and shower' had been the author's 'best, my nearest friend'.

> We wore one hat, smoked one cigar,
> One standing at each end.

The idea, it seems, had originated in what Chesterton referred to as the 'fish poem', the second poem in the book, in which a pirate ship rescues a fish because 'he will be wet if he remains much longer in the sea'. This he had written and illustrated for Frances's young cousin, Rhoda Bastable, who over the years would be the recipient of many such offerings. With a touch of inverted pride Chesterton informed Frances: 'To publish a book of my nonsense verses seems to me exactly like summoning the whole of the people of Kensington to see me smoke cigarettes.' He ignored the three poems in later life, excluding them from his *Collected Poems*, and failing to mention the publication of the book in his autobiography. Instead, he referred to *The Wild Knight* as his 'introduction to literature'.

The Wild Knight and Other Poems was published on 20 November by Grant Richards. It contained some of the poems that had appeared in the *Speaker*, and one poem, 'A Chord of Colour', had been published by *Outlook* early in March 1899; but the majority of the poems were appearing in print for the first time. In comparison with *Greybeards at Play* it received considerable notice from the critics, and it must be remembered that at the time much more interest was shown in books of poetry than is shown today. 'The main note, then, of this book is the manly acceptance of the world and a revelation of the hidden glory in it; to look not away, but within, for beauty is its burden. A daisy, the love of a friend, or King's Cross Station seem equally able to move Mr Chesterton', wrote the reviewer in *Black and White*.

The poems had been written over a period of about ten years, so it was not surprising that the collection was considered by nearly all the critics to be uneven. 'It is scarcely an exaggeration to say that Mr Gilbert Chesterton's *The Wild Knight* pleases and displeases upon alternate pages', wrote the reviewer in *Literary World*. However, the general feeling was that here was the 'stuff of poetry' though touched by 'rash sincerity and a quite juvenile earnestness'. The reviewer of the book in *Literature*, who had only a month before reviewed *Greybeards at Play*, welcomed the 'quiet strength and brilliant expression among Mr Chesterton's poems' but, remembering the previous book, added, 'If it were not for the haunting fear of losing a humorist, we should welcome the author of *The Wild Knight* to a high place among the poets.'

Rex Brimley Johnson sent a copy of the book to Kipling, who replied from Rottingdean:

> Many thanks for *The Wild Knight*. Of course I knew some of the poems before, notably 'The Donkey' which stuck in my mind at the time I read it.
>
> I agree with you that there is any amount of promise in the work – and I think marriage will teach him a good deal too. It will be curious to see how he'll develop in a few years. We all begin with arranging and elaborating all the Heavens and Hells and stars and tragedies we can lay our hands on – later we see folk – just common people under the heavens.

The letter ends recalling Rex's recent loss, and it is obvious from the reference to his having seen some of the poems before that Gertrude had shown Kipling some of her prospective brother-in-law's work.

> Meantime I wish him all the happiness that there can be and for yourself such comfort as men say time brings after loss. It's apt to be a weary while coming but one goes the right way to get it if one interests oneself in the happiness of other folk. Even though the sight of this happiness is like a knife turning in a wound.

In a postscript Kipling added his only criticism, what he called 'a matter of loathsome detail'.

> Chesterton has a bad attack of 'aureoles'. They are spotted all over the book. I think everyone is bound in each book to employ unconsciously some pet word but that was Rossetti's.
>
> Likewise I notice 'wan waste' and many 'wans' and things that 'catch and cling'. He is too good not to be jolted out of that. What do you say of a severe course of Walt Whitman – or will marriage make him see people?

Chesterton had, in fact, long been a devotee of Whitman, ever since an afternoon soon after he had left St Paul's when Oldershaw introduced him to *Leaves of Grass*, and the two had entertained each other for some three hours, taking it in turn to read aloud in Oldershaw's study in his house in Talgarth Road. It had been Whitman who had lifted him out of the mood of pessimism into which Wilde and the Decadents had sunk him. Yet Kipling too had noticed the 'juvenile earnestness' of most of the poems, and although Whitman had influenced Chesterton's life, he was not recognizable as a major influence in the poems.

The most surprising reaction of all was that of F.Y.Eccles, who had come to terms with the handwriting of Oldershaw's 'Jewish friend' sufficiently to review his book at some length for the *Speaker*:

> Mr Chesterton is a poet whose sincerity is, so to speak, in the first degree; who speaks directly, from soul to soul, of the things that preoccupy all men, who applies a spontaneous and cultivated lyrical talent not to the adornment of given themes, but to the representation of the world he sees, divines and desires.

It had been a creditable beginning. A few of the poems remain among the best he wrote: 'By the Babe Unborn', 'The Donkey' and 'The Pessimist'. The title poem, it must be admitted, is a pretty tedious melodrama, in which the Wild Knight, who rides for ever seeking God, 'burning for ever in consuming fire', meets his end by mistaking the villainous Lord Orm for God. The plot, which introduces the reader to Captain Redfeather, who sees his life behind him as one of 'drink, duels, madness, beggary, and pride', and Lady Olive, who has often prayed to Satan, is trivial; but the short play is important to an understanding of Chesterton's spiritual development, for 'The Wild Knight' was written soon after his encounter with the diabolist student on the steps of University College, and is obviously influenced by it. Lord Orm, like the student, is interested only in experiencing different sensations, one who says, 'Evil be my good; let the sun blacken and the moon be blood.' Yet in Captain Redfeather's final killing of Orm, Chesterton leaves his readers in no doubt that the resolution lies in the facts that truth is bound up with faith, and that good will ultimately triumph over evil. He put it more succinctly later when he wrote, 'He who does not believe in God will believe in anything.'

Before leaving the subject of 'The Wild Knight' it is amusing to note that James Douglas, reviewing the book for the *Star*, was quite convinced that 'Gilbert Chesterton' was a pseudonym for the much more celebrated poet at the time, John Davidson. 'I could quote', he wrote, 'poem after poem to prove that Mr John Davidson's voice betrays him, and that in this volume he has given us better than his very best.' Few critics can have fallen flatter on their faces than that!

That Christmas Eve Chesterton accompanied the Bellocs to Midnight Mass; as far as is known, it was the first Catholic service he had attended. As a present for Frances he had chosen a copy of his new book and written a poem on the flyleaf. It was the last Christmas they would have to celebrate apart.

On 22 January 1901, Queen Victoria died at Osborne House; for weeks the press had carried bulletins regarding her health. Chesterton, happily entering the most exciting year of his life, broke down and wept when he heard the news of the Queen's death, though as a rule he seldom wept and then only 'with extreme difficulty'. On the day of the funeral, 2 February, he informed Frances:

I did not see the procession, first because I had an appointment with Hammond ... and secondly because I think I felt the matter too genu-inely. I like a crowd when I am triumphant or excited: for a crowd is the only thing that can *cheer*, as much as a cock is the only thing that can crow. Can anything be more absurd than the idea of a man cheering alone in his back bedroom? But I think that reverence is better expressed by one man than a million. There is something un-natural and impossible, even grotesque, in the idea of a vast crowd of human beings all assuming an air of delicacy. All the same, my dear, this is a great and serious hour and it is felt so completely by all England that I cannot deny the enduring wish I have, quite apart from certain more private sentiments, that the noblest English-woman I have ever known was here with me to renew, as I do, private vows of a very real character to do my best for this country of mine which I love with a love passing the love of Jingoes. It is sometimes easy to give one's country blood and easier to give her money. Some-times the hardest thing of all is to give her truth.

Judging by this last sentence, it seems Chesterton was already aware that his moment might have come at last, and his campaign in the cause of truth, as he saw it, had commenced. He was certainly aware of the cut and thrust of the journalist's life. On 19 February he told Frances:

I am, for the first time in my life, thoroughly *worried*, and I find
it a rather exciting and not entirely unpleasant sensation. But everything depends just now, not only on my sticking hard to work and
doing a lot of my very best, but on my thinking about it, keeping
wide awake to the turn of the market, being ready to do things not
in half a week, but in half an hour; getting the feelings and tendencies
of other men and generally living in work.

On the following day he had arranged to see Rudolph Lehmann, the
editor of the *Daily News*, and he felt many things might come of the
meeting. He continued:

I cannot express to you what it is to feel the grip of the great wheel
of real life on you for the first time. For the first time I know what
is meant by the word 'enemies' – men who deliberately dislike you
and oppose your career – and the funny thing is that I don't dislike
them at all myself. Poor devils – very likely they want to be married
in June too.

The result of his visit to the *Daily News* office was more reviewing.
His first review for the paper had appeared unsigned on 6 January.
About a month later the first of his 'Defence' articles, on 'Nonsense',
was published in the *Speaker*. His work was being noticed too, for on
3 February a paragraph from this promising new journalist was picked
up by the *Darlington North Star*.

The poet writing his name upon a score of little pages in the silence
of his study, may or may not despise the journalist: but I greatly
doubt whether he would not morally be the better if he saw the light
burning on through darkness into dawn, and heard the roar of the
printing wheels weaving the destinies of another day. Here at least
is a school of labour and of some rough humility, the largest work
ever published anonymously since the great Christian cathedrals.

Chesterton saw his association with the *Daily News* as the 'turning-
point of his journalistic fate'. The paper, like the *Speaker*, had been
bought by a group of pro-Boers including Lloyd George and George
Cadbury who were on its board, Cadbury providing most of the money.
Rudolph Lehmann was editor and principal journalist, and he had
appointed Archibald Marshall as literary editor, who, as Chesterton
put it, had the rashness to appoint him as a regular contributor. When

in 1902, after an interregnum, Lehmann was succeeded by A.G. Gardiner, Chesterton was given a weekly column. His article appeared on a Saturday, and after a time was said to double the paper's circulation on that day. Chesterton's 'Saturday pulpit' made him famous and gave him a form of regular employment for some twelve years, his last article appearing on 1 February 1913.

As Chesterton made his reputation largely through his writing about the Boer War, it is important to look more closely at his attitude to it. In 1900 the Boer commander, General Cronje, had surrendered at Paardeburg, and the British had captured the Boer capital towns of Pretoria and Bloemfontein, but although the British had annexed the Transvaal and the Orange Free State, the Boer resistance had continued and the Boer Kommandos carried out their guerilla tactics for another two years. This persistent hostility resulted in dreadful reprisals; the burning of hundreds of farms and the setting up of blockhouses and of appallingly ill-equipped camps where women and children lived out a miserable existence, and where through disease about one in six inmates died.

Chesterton had always seen the Boer farmers as he might have seen the yeoman farmers of Gloucestershire or Herefordshire, 'mostly educated and civilized men who like President Kruger's style of government as little as we do.' He had expressed his thoughts on Kruger in a short verse which he wrote on a postcard:

> The little sardines of the tin
> Lie calmly side by side within.
> So when our victory is o'er
> Briton shall lie at peace with Boer
> We shall provide the tin, I guess,
> And Kruger will the oiliness.

One thing is clear, he did not, nor did any of his fellow Boer sympathizers, consider for a moment the native population which the Boers had originally dispossessed. In one of his notebooks of this time there is a fragment of an article which, as far as I am able to discover, was not worked up into any publishable form. It contains this striking passage:

Africa has always been called the 'Dark Continent', but step by step civilization has driven that darkness into the interior before the

advance of light, knowledge and communication, the essential spirit
of Africa, the spirit of mystery had made as it were a last stand,
with her strange beasts and strange tribes about her, in the very centre
of the continent – that she might keep her ancient secret intact. Ex
Africa semper aliquid novi.

Chesterton saw the war as purely an intellectual war, and when the
Daily News gave him Canon Rawnsley's *Ballads of the War* to review
he saw his chance to say so:

Nothing in the whole psychology of the present war is so significant
as the fact that it has produced sheafs of speeches, bushels of essays,
and not one good song. There is something heavy and unpoetic about
the task even to those who think it high and just. Englishmen are,
doubtless, for the most part convinced in their minds of the propriety
of the campaign, but they are not convinced in their hearts. To its
wisest and most honourable supporters this is an entirely intellectual
war, and there never was in the history of the globe such a thing
as an intellectual song.

Turning to the limp verses in hand he added:

Rawnsley writes of monstrous confusions of life and death, of instantaneous valour and dazzling destruction, and all the time his lines
have a weary, prosaic beat, as if they were written to celebrate the
erection of a free library or a parish pump.

Such hard hitting was bound to draw notice, and the first three months
of 1901 were intensely active. His contributions to the *Daily News* were
by no means regular yet, but they were fairly frequent. On the 4 March
Chesterton wrote Frances (who was on holiday in Italy) a long letter
in which he set out his financial prospects. As may be seen, things
were still a little tenuous:

I have delayed this letter in a scandalous manner because I hoped
I might have the arrangements with the *Daily News* to tell you; as
that is again put off, I must tell you later. The following, however,
are grounds on which I believe everything will turn out right this
year. It is arithmetic. The *Speaker* has hitherto paid me £70 a year,
that is £6 a month. It has now raised it to £10 a month, which makes
£120 a year.

He went on to list in what he admitted was 'a very dull letter' every conceivable source of income, but he had not as yet 'given a thought to the application and distribution of them in rent, furniture, etc.'. When he had managed to think about such mundane things, he informed her, he would write her another dull letter. Frances by this time was understandably becoming bored with the situation. However, they might now be able to live on the £300 a year, which might be 'on the road to four in a little while'. He asked her to 'speculate and suggest a little as to the form of living and expense'. The letter is interesting for one remark it contained: 'I can keep ten poems and twenty theories in my head at once. But I can only think of one practical thing at a time.'

He was now intent on a summer marriage; but there remained the thorny problem of this mother's reaction. Marie Louise still hoped that somehow the event would never take place, though, as Gilbert was now twenty-seven, she could not reasonably oppose it except on the practical grounds of finance. At about the same time as he wrote the 'dull' letter to Frances he penned a similar one to his mother. It sets out in much the same way to scrape up every possible source of income from his prospects, and Chesterton manages to bump up the final sum to £500. Now *Reynolds News* and the *Manchester Sunday Chronicle* are added to the list of possible sources of income, neither of which seems to have borne much fruit. Yet he was confident.

I have, as I say, what seems to me a sufficient income for a start. That I shall have as good and better I am as certain as that I sit here. I know the clockwork of these papers and among one set of them I might almost say that I am becoming the fashion.

The last part of the letter makes it quite clear that there can be no turning back.

I make all these prosaic statements because I want you to understand the risks I think of running. But it is not any practical question that is distressing me: on that I think I see my way. But I am terribly worried for fear you should be angry or sorry about all this. I am only kept in hope by the remembrance that I had the same fear when I told you of my engagement and that you dispelled it with a directness and generosity that I shall not forget. I think, my dear Mother, that we have always understood each other really. We are neither of us very demonstrative: we come of some queer stock that can always say the least when it means most. But I do think you can trust me when I say that I think a thing really right, and equally honestly admit that I can hardly explain why. To explain why I know it is right would be to communicate the incommunicable, and speak of delicate and sacred things in bald words. The most I can say is that I know Frances like the back of my hand and can tell without a word from her that she has never recovered from a wound and that there is only one kind of peace that will heal it.

I have tried to explain myself in this letter: I can do it better in a letter, somehow, but I do not think I have done it very successfully. However, with you it does not matter and it never will matter, how my thoughts come tumbling out. You at least have always understood what I meant.

Chesterton's remark to his mother about his 'becoming the fashion' is almost certainly a reference to the attention his series of articles was receiving in the *Speaker*. Appearing at almost weekly intervals, these short essays were the finest he had written so far. Among the best was 'A Defence of Skeletons' which was in the issue of 20 April. It contained a passage later to become famous.

A strange idea has infected humanity that the skeleton is typical of death. A man might as well say that a factory chimney is typical of bankruptcy. The factory may be left naked after ruin, the skeleton may be left naked after bodily dissolution; but both of them have had a lively and workmanlike life of their own, all the pulleys creaking, all the wheels turning, in the House of Livelihood as in the House of Life. There is no reason why this creature (new, as I fancy, to art), the living skeleton, should not become the essential symbol of life.

The passage shows two distinctive features of Chesterton's style. Firstly, here is a perfect example of what came to be known as a 'Chestertonian paradox'; but, as Belloc pointed out, it was only those 'half-educated and uncultured' people who used the term to describe what was really an 'illumination through an unexpected juxtaposition'. Those people had done Chesterton a disservice in labelling him with such titles as the 'Master of Paradox', in which the word was used to imply something like 'nonsense through contradiction'.

Chesterton himself saw paradox as the 'mere restoration of reality', and it is easy to see in the particular case of the skeleton that reality has been restored. Touching on the subject of paradox some years later he wrote, albeit humorously:

It means that when there has been a fashion among a few people for about five years of saying that pigs have wings, some lazy prodigal yawning and waking up among the swine happens to look at a pig or two and perceives that they haven't; but the pigs are sometimes quite angry and sometimes become wild boars. The best test is a simple one: when next you hear some attack called an 'idle paradox' ask after the 'dox'; ask how long the 'dox' has been in the world; how many nations or centuries have believed in the 'dox'; how often the 'dox' has proved itself right in practise; how often thoughtful men have returned to the 'dox' in theory. Pursue the 'dox'. Persecute the 'dox'; in short, ask the 'dox' whether it is orthodox.

Towards the end of his life, in his *St Thomas Aquinas*, Chesterton returned to the subject yet again. There is one important passage which shows even more clearly what he considered to be the 'use of paradox'.

The fact that Thomism is the philosophy of common sense is itself a matter of common sense. Yet it wants a word of explanation, because we have so long taken such matters in a very uncommon sense. For good or evil, Europe since the Reformation, and most especially England since the Reformation, has been in a peculiar sense the home of paradox. I mean in the very peculiar sense that paradox was at home; and that men were at home with it. The most familiar example is the English boasting that they are practical *because* they are not logical. To an ancient Greek or a Chinaman this would seem exactly like saying that London clerks excel in adding up their ledgers, because they are not accurate in their arithmetic. But the point is not that it is a paradox; it is that paradoxy has become orthodoxy; that men repose in a paradox as placidly as in a platitude. It is not that the practical man stands on his head, which may sometimes be a stimulating if startling gymnastic; it is that he *rests* on his head; and even sleeps on his head. This is an important point, because the use of paradox is to awaken the mind. Take a good paradox, like that of Oliver Wendell Holmes: 'Give us the luxuries of life and we will dispense with the necessities.' It is amusing and therefore arresting; it has a fine air of defiance; it contains a real romantic truth. It is all part of the fun that is stated almost in the form of a contradiction in terms. But most people would agree that there would be considerable danger in basing a whole social system on the notion that necessaries are not necessary; as some have based the British Constitution on the notion that nonsense will always work out as common sense. Yet even here, it might be said that the invidious example has spread, and that the modern industrial system does really say: 'Give us luxuries like coal-tar soap, and we will dispense with necessities like corn.'

So much is familiar; but what is not even now realised is that not only the practical politics, but the abstract philosophies of the modern world have had this queer twist. Since the modern world began in the sixteenth century, nobody's system of philosophy has really corresponded to everybody's sense of reality; to what, if left to themselves, common men would call common sense.

Secondly, the skeleton passage gives a fine example of what Belloc saw as Chesterton's amazing, almost superhuman, capacity for parallelism, something 'so native to his mind; it was naturally a fruit of his mental character that he had difficulty in understanding why others did not use it with the same lavish facility as himself'. Through this use of parallelism, here exemplified in the sentence, 'A man might as well say that a factory chimney was typical of bankruptcy', Chesterton was able to illustrate an unperceived truth by its exact consonance with the reflection of some truth already known and perceived. 'In whatever manner he launched the parallelism,' wrote Belloc, 'he produced the shock of illumination. He *taught*. He made men see what they had not seen before. He made them *know*. He was an architect of certitude, whenever he practised this art in which he excelled.'

Chesterton's friends knew that he used the same 'invaluable instrument' in his private conversation. 'How well I recall,' wrote Belloc, 'the discussions upon all affairs, of art, of politics, of philosophy, in which this genius of his appeared! All he advanced as argument was lit up by the comparison of an unknown by a known truth; of something half hidden by something fully experienced among us all.'

So it was that the readers of the *Speaker* recognized that something unusual was happening, that a writer of exceptional powers of persuasion and one growing in stature almost weekly, one who had begun by defending nonsense and was now defending almost anything, had arrived in Fleet Street. Chesterton's subjects ranged from China Shepherdesses to Baby-Worship, from Ugly Things to Penny Dreadfuls.

However, it was not by defending but by denouncing that Chesterton was most noticed, and his 'A Denunciation of Patriotism' which the *Speaker* printed in its issue of 26 May made a great impact on many people. The article began provokingly: 'The decay of patriotism in England during the last year or two is a serious and distressing matter. Only in consequence of such a decay could the current lust of territory be confounded with the ancient love of country.'

Taking as his theme the phrase heard on all sides at the time, 'the love of our country', Chesterton argued that the true meaning of love had been ignored. People seemed to mean by 'the love of country' 'not what a mystic might mean by the love of God', but 'something of what a child might mean by a love of jam'. To those who might have used the phrase 'My country right or wrong' Chesterton argued that it was 'a thing no patriot would think of saying save in a desperate case'.

It is like saying, 'My mother, drunk or sober.' No doubt if a decent man's mother took to drink he would share her troubles to the last; but to talk as if he would be in a state of gay indifference as to whether his mother took to drink or not is certainly not the language of men who know the great mystery.

What was really needed, he suggested, for the frustration and overthrow of 'a deaf and raucous Jingoism' was a renascence of the love of the native land.

When that comes, all shrill cries will cease suddenly. For the first of all the marks of love is seriousness: love will not accept sham bulletins or the empty victory of words. It will always esteem the most candid councellor the best. Love is drawn to truth by the unerring magnetism of agony; it gives no pleasure to the lover to see ten doctors dancing with vociferous optimism round a death-bed.

His argument gained strength as it progressed. Why, he asked, had British patriots given their adoration to qualities and circumstances good in themselves, but comparatively material and trivial, such things as 'trade, physical force, a skirmish at a remote frontier, a squabble in a remote continent'? Then, with a touch of brilliance, he continued: 'Colonies are things to be proud of, but for a country to be only proud

of its extremities is like a man being only proud of his legs. Why is
there not a high central intellectual patriotism, a patriotism of the head
and heart of the Empire, and not merely of its fists and its boots?'

The prevailing patriotic sentiments might be honest, but they then
were none the less 'simple-minded, vulgar eulogies upon trivialities
and truisms'. The reason why so many Englishmen fell back on such
gross and frivolous things for their patriotism was, he argued, that the
English were the only people in the world who were not taught in childhood their own literature and their own history. It should be remembered, of course, that at the time the emphasis of all teaching in the
schools was on the study of Latin and Greek.

The English were, he continued, in the truly extraordinary condition
of not knowing their own merits. A vast heritage of intellectual glory
was kept from schoolboys like a heresy, and they were left to die in
the dull and infantile type of patriotism, which they learned from a
box of tin soldiers. 'It would not be in the least extraordinary if a claim
of eating up provinces and pulling down princes were the chief boast
of a Zulu. The extraordinary thing is, that it is the chief boast of a
people who have Shakespeare, Newton, Burke, and Darwin to boast
of.'

Chesterton concluded that the peculiar lack of generosity or delicacy
in the current English nationalism – and it is interesting that he should
have substituted this word for 'patriotism' – appeared to have no other
possible origin but in the fact of a unique neglect in education of the
study of the national literature. To say, as the schoolmasters did say,
that a vast amount of English grammar and literature is picked up in
the course of learning Latin and Greek was like saying

> ... that a baby picks up the art of walking in the course of learning
> to hop, or that a Frenchman may successfully be taught German
> by helping a Prussian to learn Ashanti. Surely the obvious foundation
> of all education is the language in which that education is conveyed;
> if a boy has only time to learn one thing, he had better learn that.

The tone of the article was sustained throughout, and the last paragraph was a *tour de force*:

> We have deliberately neglected this great heritage of high national
> sentiment. We have made our public schools the strongest walls against
> a whisper of the honour of England. And we have had our punishment

in this strange and perverted fact that, while a unifying vision of patriotism can ennoble bands of brutal savages or dingy burghers, and be the best thing in their lives, we, who are – the world being judge – humane, honest, and serious individually, have a patriotism that is the worst thing in ours. What have we done, and where have we wandered, we that have produced sages who could have spoken with Socrates and poets who could walk with Dante, that we should talk as if we have never done anything more intelligent than found colonies and kick niggers? We are the children of light, and it is we that sit in darkness. If we are judged, it will not be for the merely intellectual transgression of failing to appreciate other nations, but for the supreme spiritual transgression of failing to appreciate ourselves.

I have dealt with this article at some length, not only because it shows again the strength of Chesterton's unique style, but also because it was largely by the force of it that he became a talking point. Now, if never before, every one *was* asking every one else, 'Who is G.K.C.?' He would never look back. Chesterton was the only writer of importance to begin the war in complete obscurity and to emerge from it as a national figure.

There was now little to stand in the way of a June wedding, and the date was fixed for the twenty-eighth. As the day drew near and the wedding presents began to arrive, Chesterton declared that he felt like the rich young man in the Gospels: sorrowful because he had 'great possessions'. The ceremony took place not at Bedford Park, but at St Mary Abbots, the Kensington parish church. A close friend of the bride and groom, the Revd Conrad Noel, whom they had met through the Christian Social Union, officiated; and Lucian Oldershaw was the best man. Oldershaw found his task taxing, for Chesterton had forgotten his tie, and when he knelt down during the service it was seen that he still had the price tag on one of his shoes. Nothing much else was recorded about the ceremony. It is not known what kind of a wedding dress Frances was wearing, but her bridesmaids were Rhoda Bastable, and little Doris Child, who was aged eight. In later years Doris could remember how, after the service, Frances had thrown her bouquet for her to carry, though she was 'already holding her own flowers, gloves and a prayer book'. Looking at the tall Gilbert and the tiny, frail Frances, she had remarked, 'They don't match a bit.'

The honeymoon was to be spent on the Norfolk Broads; but the wedding night at the Great White Horse Inn in Ipswich. 'It was like meeting a friend in a fairy-tale to find myself under the sign', Chesterton recalled. After the reception, Oldershaw went on ahead to Liverpool Street Station with the bulk of the luggage; but the bride and bridegroom failed to turn up, and the train left without them.

The reason for the delay had been Chesterton's insistence on taking Frances to a milk bar in Kensington High Street for a 'ritual consumption' of a glass of milk. 'I stopped at that particular dairy', he wrote many years later, 'because I had always drunk a glass of milk there when walking with my mother in my infancy. And it seemed to me a fitting ceremonial to unite the two great relations of a man's life.' Outside was the great figure of a white cow which he saw 'as a sort of pendant to the figure of the White Horse'.

He had also insisted in stopping at a gunsmith's where he purchased a revolver and cartridges, another part of the ritual, with the general notion of protecting his bride 'from the pirates doubtless infesting the Norfolk Broads.' For her part, Frances would have enjoyed the eccentric humour of it all, from the man she loved very deeply, who once said, 'The relations of the sexes are mystical, are and ought to be irrational. Every gentleman should take off his head to a lady.'

They arrived at Ipswich, like David Copperfield, 'very late', by a slow train. At the Great White Horse their luggage was already in their room. Realizing that Frances was exhausted after the journey and general excitement of the day, he encouraged her to share a little wine with him, and then take a rest while he went for a short stroll. He turned out of the door of the hotel into the streets that Dickens knew so well. Cheered by the wine, and feeling ecstatically happy, he walked on through the town until he reached the open country and, lost in thought, he also lost his way. When he returned eventually to the hotel, having had to ask where he was, and the way back, he found himself with Frances 'utterly, unbelievably alone'. He was 'fathoms deep in love'. 'And then his whole world went crash. The woman he worshipped', whom earlier in the day he had vowed he would worship with his body, 'shrank from his touch and screamed when he embraced her'.

PART TWO
G. K. C.

7

Under a Dragon Moon

1901–1903

The honeymoon in Norfolk lasted for six days, a time long enough for God to make the world, as Chesterton put it in verse a week or two later, a poem in which he spoke of the 'fierce future, proud and furled'. From Norfolk he had informed his parents: 'I have a wife, a piece of string, a pencil and a knife, what more can a man want on a honeymoon?' Perhaps only his mother might have seen in this remark that things had not gone very smoothly, for although the bride and bridegroom felt exalted in each other's company, it is fairly certain that when they returned to London on 3 July their marriage had not been consummated.

The Chestertons' first home was a house in Edwardes Square, only a street away from 11 Warwick Gardens. As Chesterton himself had been unsuccessful in finding a suitable place, a Mr Boore, a close friend of Frances's, had generously offered the couple his home to rent on a temporary basis. They were to remain there only for about three months or so before they moved to a flat in Overstrand Mansions, in Battersea, south of the river. Bentley recalled something of their time at Edwardes Square. 'I remember the house well, with its garden of old trees and its general air of Georgian peace.' At the back of the house the outside wall was sheltered by a portico on which Chesterton had amused himself by producing 'flaming frescoes, done in vivid crayons, of knights and heroes and divinities'. Bentley could not help wondering whether the landlord 'charged for them as dilapidations at the end of the tenancy'.

During the rest of July and August the last of the 'Defence' articles were printed in the *Speaker*. After writing one more article, 'The Heroines of Shakespeare' in October, Chesterton concentrated all his energies into reviewing for the *Daily News*. In his Shakespeare article he suggested that to the Elizabethan mind 'Man was natural, but woman

was supernatural' and, speaking of Portia, 'the most splendid and magnanimous woman in literature', he said:

> Shakespeare had conceived, with extraordinary force, humour and
> sympathy, a man to express the ideal of technical justice, formal mor-
> ality, and the claim of a man to his rights: the man was Shylock.
> Over against him he set a figure representing the larger conception
> of generosity and persuasion, the justice that is fused of a score of
> genial passions, the compromise that is born of a hundred worthy
> enthusiasms. Portia had to represent the ideal of magnanimity in law,
> morality, religion, art and politics. And Shakespeare made this figure
> a good woman because, to the mind of his day, to make it a good
> woman was to ring it with a halo and arm it with a sword.

Like Shakespeare Chesterton saw Woman ringed with a halo, and later
in life saw her not armed with a sword, but as the Second Eve, whose
heart seven swords had pierced; and his own woman too, whose soul
he saw 'blue as skies are blue/And red as battlefields are red', he liked
to see ringed with a halo. A friend, Freda Rivière, whose husband,
Hugh, painted Chesterton's portrait, visited the Chestertons when they
had moved away from London. She remembered how Gilbert once
pointed to a small window, unusually placed and high up, and said,
'I like that window. When the light catches her hair, it gives Frances
a halo and makes her look something like what she really is.'

Edwardes Square was so close to his old home, that Chesterton saw
much of his brother at this time, and the bantering discussions that
had always been such a feature of their past continued as fiercely as
ever. In fact, it was noted that the wedding reception had been about
the only occasion the two had been together in the same room without
arguing. Cecil, who had always been referred to in Gilbert's letters
to his friends as 'the Innocent Child', had recently met and fallen head
over heels in love with a lady journalist, Ada Jones, a woman some
years older than himself, and already well established in Fleet Street.
Writing under the name of John Keith Prothero, and known to her
friends as 'Keith', this attractive woman was the only one that Cecil
would ever look at. He wooed her arduously for sixteen years and,
after many refusals, married her in 1917 shortly before he left for France
in uniform.

Gilbert evidently considered his brother worldly-wise enough to be
able to confide in him, and the account of his 'confession' to Cecil

was given by Ada Jones in her book, *The Chestertons*, published in 1941 after the two brothers and Frances were dead. While it may be admitted that she was almost the complete antithesis of her sister-in-law, and was critical of her in many respects, considering her to have been over-protective of Gilbert, Mrs Cecil Chesterton was particularly generous in her praise of Frances's poetry. There is no reason to suppose that she had either the malice or the motive for inventing a story which certainly has a ring of truth about it, even if it cannot be supported by other evidence. After the difficulties Gilbert and Frances had experienced on their wedding night, she said, Gilbert had been haunted by the fear

> ... that his brutality and lust had frightened the woman he would have died to protect. He dared not even contemplate a repetition.

He went to Cecil, quivering with self-reproach and condemnation. His young brother took a completely rationalistic view of the contretemps, and suggested that some citadels must be taken by storm, while others yield only to long siege. Anyway, he insisted, nothing had happened that could not be put right; they could both be happy and have lots of children. But the mischief had been done. Gilbert hated himself for what had happened, and Frances could not reconcile herself to the physical realities of marriage. Temperamentally ascetic, physically sickly through spinal disease, the experience must have shocked her profoundly. Her tragedy was that, desiring children, she shrank from sex. The final adjustment between them seems never to have been made, and Gilbert, young and vital, was condemned to a pseudo-monastic life, in which he lived with a woman but never enjoyed one.

It was true that Frances never really enjoyed good health, and at various times in her life she endured great pain with 'back trouble'; for the last eighteen years of her life she had to wear a support belt which served to ease the pain considerably. The physical difficulties in her sexual relationship with Gilbert, however, were not due to her spinal problems. It would seem, judging by a letter written in 1924 by Dr Harold Gardner Hill of the Clinical Medical Unit at St Thomas's Hospital, that there was a gynaecological reason why she could not enjoy sexual intercourse; this would also explain why Frances, at the suggestion of Dr Joyce, a woman doctor in Battersea, underwent an operation, almost certainly for an imperforate hymen, 'to make it possible for her to have children'. Unfortunately all attempts to solve the problem proved unsuccessful.

It was a deep source of sadness to both her and Gilbert, for they each would dearly have loved to have a family, and Frances ever afterwards felt a sense of failure, but it also bound them more closely together, and provided a well of suffering from which they both were able to draw living water which, with divine grace, enabled them to grow spiritually. Sadly, Chesterton wrote five years later:

> Oh when the bitter wind of longing blows,
> And all between us seems an aching space
> Think that we hold each other close; so close
> We cannot even see each other's face.

Nevertheless, both would have considered themselves to have been happily married. 'Of all human institutions', Chesterton wrote, 'marriage is the one which most depends upon slow development, upon patience, upon long reaches of time, upon magnanimous compromise, upon kindly habit.' On another occasion he wrote of that

> ... dreamy old bachelor notion – that notion that the unity of marriage, the being one flesh, has something to do with being perfectly happy, or being perfectly good, or even with being perfectly and continuously affectionate! I tell you, an ordinary honest man is part of his wife even when he wishes he wasn't. I tell you, an ordinary good woman is part of her husband even when she wishes him at the bottom of the sea. I tell you that, whether the two people are for the moment friendly or angry, happy or unhappy, the Thing marches on, the great four-footed Thing, the quadruped of the home. They are a nation, a society, a machine. I tell you they are one flesh, even when they are not one spirit.

His poem on the 'perfect marriage day' had ended:

> Never again with cloudy talk
> Shall life be tricked or faith undone,
> The world is many and is mad,
> But we are sane and we are one.

By the time *The Defendant* was published by Rex Brimley Johnson in December, the Chestertons had moved to Battersea. Overstrand Mansions was a red-brick block of flats with no lift, overlooking Battersea

Park. It was to be their home for the next eight years, although they occupied two flats in the building at different times. A visitor remembered that on one side of the flat they had a bird's-eye view of Battersea's thickly clustering roofs and from the front windows, including those of the watch-tower-like turret which forms so pleasing a feature of the little drawing room, a wide view of 'the green glories of the adjacent Battersea Park'. Remembering the innumerable stairs up to the flat, and the relief at eventually arriving at the Chestertons' home, the same visitor described the study:

> It would be difficult, indeed, to find either in town or country a better miniature 'temple of peace' than the plainly equipped little study in which Mr Chesterton docs his work – and upon which Mrs Chesterton, as she will laughingly tell you, finds it necessary to make occasio nal raids in the interests of 'Heaven's first law'.
>
> There is certainly nothing formal in the arrangement of the contents of this elevated literary workshop, one wall of which is decorated with a quaint reminder of its tenant's versatility of talent, in the form of a still unfinished crayon frieze, drolly depicting a procession of knightly figures of history and legend, following the lead of a grotesquely impish-looking child – a piece of pictorial symbolism of which the visitor has permission to supply any interpretation that pleases him best.
>
> You are startled at first to observe on the opposite wall, inscribed in bold and arresting characters of chalk: 'Lest we forget', an appropriate heading for casual memoranda relating to projected articles and pending literary and other engagements.

Needless to say, the walls of Chesterton's study had been lined with brown paper in anticipation of his bursts of inspiration, and the engagements board was an idea of Frances's in an endeavour to bring some order into Gilbert's life. Fr O'Connor could remember a cartoon by Max Beerbohm, in which he had depicted Belloc in the act of converting Chesterton 'from the errors of Calvinism', hanging in the flat, and Belloc himself had penned an ode, which was pinned up next to the engagements board.

> Frances and Gilbert have a little flat
> At eighty pounds a year, and cheap at that,
> Where Frances, who is Gilbert's only wife,

A cartoon that Chesterton drew for Hilary Gray

> Leads an unhappy and complaining life:
> While Gilbert, who is Frances' only man,
> Puts up with it as gamely as he can.

Chesterton wrote in 1904,

There's something that is especially jolly about Battersea. In the first place, Battersea exists. It is an entity. Chelsea, and Kensington, and Finsbury, and Clapham are mere geographical expressions; but Battersea has a real corporate life and individuality of its own, and revels in it. If you want to catch something of the genuine 'civis Romanus sum' feeling, you can't do better than become a Battersea resident, and share the strenuous life of the Borough in which portraits of John Burns [the local MP] are sold in every street for a penny.

The autumn of 1901 also saw the third annual dinner of the JDC held, as in the previous years, at Pagani's. Although Chesterton had designed the menu card, this year it had been professionally printed with a seating plan on the back. The plan shows that besides himself both of the d'Avigdor brothers and Fordham were now married. The evening was a lively affair, and after the toasts there seems to have been some sort of an entertainment at which Waldo d'Avigdor, now married to Mildred Wain, played a banjo solo and sang a duet with his wife. The proceedings ended up very much in the manner of the two previous years with a raucous rendering of the JDC Anthem sung to the tune of 'Clementine', and then, 'borrowing each other's arms and legs in an inextricable tangle', the singing of 'Auld Lang Syne'.

The highlight of the last weeks of the year was the publication of *The Defendant*, which did much to enhance Chesterton's reputation. It received much more attention than the two books of verse had done; the *Whitehall Review* described it as 'one of the most delightful companions possible for a man to have with him, and if it does not run through two or three editions rapidly then there is no virtue of honour left in these decadent days'. The book went into three editions, but it took six years to do so.

Sir Arthur Quiller-Couch spoke in the *Bookman* of Chesterton's 'courageous innocence', and said that 'the most ordinary occurrences in the world are marvellous in his eyes, and his optimism proceeds from a blessed contentment with a planet which provides so many daily miracles'. The book of essays also prompted a fairly lengthy article by

Charles Masterman in the *Speaker*. It was time, he suggested, for some dull person 'to raise the banner of protest, however sober and grave, against the philosophy of life which Mr Chesterton is slowly indurating into the respectable brain of the English householder'. He predicted that essays on '"Chesterton as a religious teacher" would soon be utilised in the older universities'.

But what was Chesterton's religion at this time? His marriage to a devout Christian was certainly making a difference to his attitude to the Church. He was living with a wife who was a practising Anglo-Catholic and a regular communicant. For his part he attended no church, although he occasionally accompanied Frances to Mass. He had, as he put it, 'hung on to religion by one thin thread of thanks'. In fact, at no time in his life would he have admitted to enjoying church services, and even after his conversion to Roman Catholicism attendance at Mass was very much of an obligation for him. Dorothy Collins has told how

... on the occasions when the Catholic Church demanded attendance at Mass on a weekday, as it was a small parish there would be only an early morning Mass and he would drag himself from bed. As he got fasting into the car, I have heard him say, 'What but religion would bring us to such a pass.' But never did I know him miss a Day of Obligation either at home or abroad.

In the early days of his marriage the chief religious influence in Chesterton's life was the priest who had presided at his wedding, the Revd Conrad Noel. He was the son of a poet and the grandson of a peer; for some years he had been curate at St Mary's, Paddington Green, an Anglo-Catholic church, which meant that the services were closely modelled on the Roman rite, with all the ritual associated with Roman Catholicism; and the church decorated and furnished with such ornaments as Catholics find comforting and Cromwell had swept away. Noel who had, according to Chesterton, 'all the incalculable elements of the eccentric aristocrat', was not only a high churchman; he was also a radical socialist and a leading member of the Christian Social Union. Later, when he had been appointed Vicar of Thaxted in Essex, he organized a communist crusade and 'flew the Red Flag from his church'. Chesterton remembered that Noel 'delighted in making the quaintest combination of costume made up of the clerical, the artistic and the proletarian. He took great pleasure in appearing in correct clerical clothes, surmounted with a sort of hairy or furry cap, making him look like a aesthetic rat-catcher.'

It was Noel's unusual appearance as much as anything else that had made him an attractive figure to both Gilbert and Cecil Chesterton, and it was Cecil who had met him first at one of the Fabian Society meetings. Gilbert wrote:

> This fringe of eccentricity, even of eccentricity in dress, upon the border of the Anglo-Catholic party in the Anglican Church, really had a great deal to do with the beginning of the process by which Bohemian journalists, like my brother and myself, were drawn towards the serious consideration of the theory of a Church. I was considerably influenced by Conrad Noel; and my brother, I think, even more so.

In 1902 Chesterton still claimed to have 'the interests and honour of the Liberal party at heart'. In the September of that year he wrote that some of the best Liberals he had ever known were Anglo-Catholics, although at the same time he insisted that he himself was not one. It was during the autumn too that he became embroiled in the first of the public debates that he was to conduct through the correspondence columns of the *Daily News*. The matter was in general concerned with Balfour's Education Bill, which was then before Parliament; but in particular Chesterton chose to 'do battle' with Dr Clifford, a Baptist Minister of militant Protestant views, who was the leader outside Parliament of the Nonconformist opposition to the Bill on the grounds that it would provide 'the Church on the Rates' and be, as was perfectly true, particularly beneficial to both the Established and the Roman Catholic Churches. However, it was quite clear from much that Dr Clifford said that his main objection was that the Bill might further the cause of Romanism in the country. '"Popery" in politics we will not have,' he declared, 'the capture of the machinery and resources of the whole State for sectarian ends we cannot endure; the creation out of public funds of sectarian and denominational "atmospheres" we must resist, for the sake of the country, for the sake of the children, for the sake of education and of commerce, of progress, and of liberty.' Balfour, noting the extremism of Clifford, wrote: 'According to Dr Clifford, Parliament would be going beyond its function in teaching, at the cost of public funds, that man *has* a Maker.'

Chesterton entered the controversy in the third week in September under the heading 'Dr Clifford and the "No Popery" Cry'. The whole correspondence on both sides makes unexciting reading, but it is interesting to see how, although he had not committed himself to any particular denomination, he was familiar with the 'atmosphere' of Anglo-Catholicism, and to a lesser extent of Roman Catholicism also. In defending the Anglo-Catholic position he was at pains to make it clear that Anglo-Catholic priests were not 'gyrating in Roman robes', as Dr Clifford had suggested, but that in their reverence for the Blessed Sacrament they were 'invoking and inducing in the stillness of a human building the presence of the Living Christ'.

'Let us attack the Education Bill as Liberals,' he exhorted in another letter, 'without binding the living body of Liberalism to the slimy corpse of the Protestant Truth Society.' In his last letter he asked:

> Surely we are, as a party, blundering badly if we tie ourselves to any theological or any ecclesiastical section. Our case against the Government Bill is that it violates an elementary liberal principle in not equalising contribution and control. It is, I conceive, an elementary rule of controversy that it is tactically bad to base a case on disputed principles when we could base it on undisputed principles. The principle of taxation and representation is an undisputed principle. The principle that the English Church Union is Popish, or the principle that it ought to be Protestant, are not only disputed, but are, pace Dr Clifford, highly disputable propositions. They are historical propositions about which we most of us know little or nothing. To decide whether the English Church is Catholic, as Bishop Gore says, or Protestant, as Prebendary Webb-Peploe says, we ought to be familiar with Bulls and judgments, with Councils of the Fourth Century, with Statutes of the Sixteenth Century, with the controversies about the Sarum Rite and the Statute of Praemunire. Most of us, as a matter of fact, have not read even the introduction to the Prayer Book. It is one of the hardest things in human history to say exactly what happened in England at the Reformation.

As he grew older and came under Belloc's forceful influence Chesterton came to a much deeper awareness of what had happened in England at the Reformation; but the Clifford correspondence shows that at the time he was undecided.

The reaction of the editor of the *Daily News* to this the first of his protégé's wrangles in print is unrecorded; but A.G.Gardiner is known to have ranked Dr Clifford very highly, and wrote of him: 'No nation was ever kept sweet and vital by moral opiates, and it is because he is a bracing tonic in a time of moral slackness that John Cifford ranks among the chief assets of our day.' He saw Clifford as the last of the Puritans, who was happiest when the battle was fiercest. 'Had he lived in the great days of the Puritans, how joyously would he have had his ears cropped, with what hymns and psalms and spiritual songs he would have rushed to battle, and, when the victory was won, what sermons he would have preached as the sun went down on the carnage of the battle-field!'

Gardiner was equally enthusiastic about Chesterton. 'I can conceive him standing on his head in Fleet Street in sheer joy at the sight of St Paul's', he wrote. He saw Chesterton as some survivor 'of the childhood of the world.'

Most of us are creatures of our time, thinking its thoughts, wearing its clothes, rejoicing in its chains. If we try to escape from the temporal tyranny, it is through the gate of revolt that we go. Some take to asceticism or to some fantastic foppery of the moment. Some invent Utopias, lunch on nuts and proteid at Eustace Miles', and flaunt red ties defiantly in the face of men and angels. The world is bound, but they are free. But in all this they are still the children of our time, fleeting and self-conscious. Mr Chesterton's extravagances have none of this quality. He is not a rebel. He is a wayfarer from the ages, stopping at the inn of life, warming himself at the fire and making the rafters ring with his jolly laughter.

Whereas time and place were accidents, Gardiner saw Chesterton as 'elemental and primitive'. He was not of our time, he said, 'but for all times'. While never doubting his sincerity, Gardiner knew that Chesterton loved an argument for its own sake, and was 'indifferent to the text'. There was no subject in which Chesterton could not find a theme 'on which to hang all the mystery of time and eternity'. Chesterton was, Gardiner thought, free from the tyranny of things. 'Though he lived in a tub he would be rich beyond the dreams of avarice, for he would still have the universe for his intellectual inheritance.'

For his part Chesterton knew Gardiner as a 'well-read and sympathetic editor', and he owed a great debt to him, for it was Gardiner who employed him to write the Saturday articles, which, as his colleague on the paper remembered, 'began a controversy, continued by Chesterton in many newspapers, reviews, and books until his death, which has had, and is having, more effect on thought and even on affairs than any other journalism of our time'.

After he had been writing his weekly articles for a little more than a year, even unlikely periodicals and newspapers were quoting from the articles or providing titbits about their author. The *Sunday School Chronicle*, for instance, was saying, 'If there is a more popular journalist just now than Mr G. K. Chesterton, I should like to know him'; and the *Christian World* noted that 'Mr Chesterton, to use his own words, has as his principal amusement "kicking up a row".' 'I like getting into hot water,' Chesterton once said, 'it helps to keep me clean.'

The Chestertons found life in Battersea convivial, and the fact that the cost of living was considerably lower south of the river was a help in their present circumstances, for although Gilbert was fast acquiring fame, he was still by the standards of the middle class, all of whom kept servants, decidedly poor. 'We were very poor in those days,' remembered a neighbour and close friend, Mrs Saxon Mills. 'When we were short, they used to feed us. When they were short, we used to feed them.' The Millses, who had known Cecil first, remained friends for life, as did the Kennedys. Rann Kennedy was an avid reader and possessed a sizeable library, largely of classical literature. He used to read Chesterton 'great chunks of Plato' aloud, and Chesterton would often emerge from the Kennedys' flat with his pockets bulging. Invariably he would forget to return the books, so that Frances would periodically gather them together and return them for him with a note: 'Apologies as usual for my thief of a husband.'

Kennedy has told how astonished he was by Chesterton's 'reach into the interiorities of something he had just heard of. He knew what the great authorities know – only they don't. In three hours lolling against a bookcase he would have left aside all unnecessary, absorbed all vital elements. He had the daemonic spirit of Socrates.' It was, he thought, as if Chesterton had been taught by the Holy Ghost.

There is an amusing story told by the Kennedys about the Battersea days. Chesterton on one of his many visits accidentally upset a bottle of glue. When the Kennedys' little cockney maid was next cleaning out the flat she was heard to say: 'Great big oaf, that Mr Chesterton, throws the gum abaht.'

It was not a very long walk across the river from Battersea to Chelsea and to Cheyne Walk where, except for the odd summer letting, the Bellocs lived until they moved to King's Land, their final home, at

Shipley in Sussex, in 1906. Belloc's daughter, Eleanor, who later married Rex Jebb, recalled her 'Uncle Gilbert' and 'Auntie Frances'.

> When he was in Battersea, a young journalist, and we were in Chelsea in a nursery, he would come over the river with Auntie Frances and give us absorbing displays of phantasy through puppets with plaster heads and appropriate gowns. The heads were detached, lifeless and mournful in a box. They came to life by the gowns and the heads being slipped on to those gifted hands of Uncle Gilbert – by the use of his fingers – by the accompanying antics and whims which enlivened them. They appeared to need no stage or scenery. They came to life immediately as Uncle Gilbert sat perilously on the edge of a nursery chair and rumbled off into the story of action! Oh that delightful rumble! Oh that groaning joy that carried us with it into long since vanished and forgotten lands! We have still treasured a little sword of gilt and mosaic handle here at King's Land, with which he made the hero wield many a thrust in the cause of Right and gallantly cause the death of many a villain – much to our satisfaction. Gilbert could always murder without malice, savagery or hate!

In the October of 1902 the publisher Arthur L. Humphrey brought out Chesterton's second book of essays. *Twelve Types*, like *The Defendant*, was a collection made up from pieces which had already been published in the *Daily News* and the *Speaker*. The book, which went into several impressions, enhanced Chesterton's reputation but seemed to alarm some reviewers, such as the one in the *Academy and Literature*, who wrote:

> For sheer cleverness there is probably no one at the present moment to compare with Mr Chesterton. His gift of brilliant improvisation is amazing. But we must confess to being a little appalled by his new book: it is so confident, so assertive, its rhetoric is so breathless. The spectacle of a young man putting Savonarola and Scott, St Francis and Tolstoy each in his place with the assurance and familiarity that Mr Chesterton exerts strikes us as a little uncanny.

The other eight 'types' included in the book were Charlotte Brontë, William Morris, Byron, Pope, Rostand, Charles II, Stevenson, and Carlyle. Chesterton would at a later date write more fully about Stevenson and St Francis, and at one time considered writing a life of Savonarola, which was advertised once or twice as 'in the course of preparation'.

'Men like Savonarola', he wrote, 'are the witnesses to the tremendous psychological fact at the back of all our brains, but for which no name has ever been found, that ease is the worst enemy of happiness, and civilisation potentially the end of man.' Savonarola was making war against no trivial human sins, he argued, but against 'godless and thankless quiescence, against getting used to happiness, the mystic sin by which all creation falls. He was preaching that severity which is the sign-manual of youth and hope.'

As Louis McQuilland noted in his review for the *New Age*, Chesterton did not regard Savonarola so much as a great religious reformer thundering against the sins of the world, as a great social deliverer intent on saving his century from the hedonistic coma of the Italian Renaissance, 'drugging the spirits of men with the lotus-brew of a degenerate luxury'.

Once again Charles Masterman found himself reviewing Chesterton, this time for the *Bookman*. His comments are of interest because in the course of them he reveals that Chesterton had been commissioned by John Morley, the editor of the 'English Men of Letters' series, to write the life of Browning. As Masterman put it, Morley had 'entrusted to this unknown poet the biography of Robert Browning in that series which is compiled by men of three-score years, knighted, and with unchallenged literary supremacy'.

It was impossible to forecast Chesterton's future, Masterman concluded; but he was engaged on so many projects that his friends asserted that he was writing too much. Masterman remained doubtful if a man with ideas could write too much: '... the ephemeral perishes, the permanent survives.' He felt that Chesterton had faith in himself and confidence in his message. Besides the 'Browning', he had a volume of poems, a volume of prose essays, a fantastic novel, and a play 'bearing the title of the "Devil amongst the Cattle"'. The novel, although it did not yet bear the name, was *The Napoleon of Notting Hill*, but the play seems never to have been written. Finally, Masterman suggested,

He may find that laughing at the Devil and protesting the vanity of sin will have to yield to the sterner and more traditional methods of warfare. At present he is one of the few interesting writers in contemporary literature, with something to say, and a future of golden possibility, and the power of compelling a jaded and tired age to listen to his voice.

Chesterton's work was receiving such notice that it was not surprising that other writers sought his company. Earlier in the year he had opened a note from Max Beerbohm written on Savile Club writing paper. 'I have seldom wished to meet anyone in particular,' the note read; 'but you I should very much like to meet.' It seems that Beerbohm's mother had been a friend of Chesterton's grandmother, Mrs Grosjean, and knew Marie Louise. Through Beerbohm Chesterton was introduced to Edmund Gosse and his wife. Beerbohm, of whom Chesterton wrote:

> ... Max's queer crystalline sense
> Lit, like a sea beneath a sea,
> Shines through a shameless impudence
> As shameless a humility,

remained a lifelong friend, and in his house in Italy painted a fresco on one of the walls of his many friends: leading them was Chesterton.

On their first meeting Chesterton had been surprised to find Beerbohm 'a remarkably humble man', in fact, the very opposite of 'the undergraduate who exhibited the cheek of a guttersnipe in the garb of a dandy', he had expected. 'I have never known him', he wrote later, 'by a single phrase or intonation, claim to know more or judge better than he does.' Above all, Chesterton noted, Beerbohm did not indulge in the base idolatry of believing in himself. Chesterton had recently heard that he had been offered the chance of writing his book on Browning: Beerbohm had said, 'A man ought to write on Browning while he is young.' At the time Chesterton had been unsure what he had meant since 'no man knows he is young while he is young', but later he realized Max had been right, 'as he generally is'.

Chesterton's *Robert Browning*, which was published by Macmillan in May 1903, and retailed at 2s., marked a progression in many people's minds, though not in Chesterton's own, from journalism to literature. In his own estimation he was very much still 'a jolly journalist'.

I will not say I wrote a book on Browning; but I wrote a book on love, liberty, poetry, my own views of God and religion (highly developed), and various theories of my own about optimism and pessimism and the hope of the world; a book in which the name of Browning was introduced from time to time, I might almost say with considerable art, or at any rate with some decent appearance of regularity. There were very few biographical facts in the book, and those were nearly all wrong.

Indeed, there were many inaccuracies in the manuscript that arrived at Macmillan's office, particularly in the matter of quotations from Browning, and a selection from a Scots ballad had three or four lines misquoted. Stephen Gwynn, who worked for Macmillan's at the time, remembered how old Mr Craik, the senior partner, had sent for him 'in white fury', with Chesterton's proof corrected – or rather not corrected – there were thirteen errors on one page. Gwynn wrote to Chesterton saying that the firm thought the book was going to 'disgrace' them. His reply was 'like the trumpeting of a crushed elephant. But the book was a huge success.'

The charge of innaccuracy would often be made against Chesterton in his writing; but he insisted on quoting from memory 'both by temper and on principle. That is what literature is for, it ought to be part of a man.' Later, he took to using phrases like 'if my memory serves me right'; he never bothered to look anything up.

Chesterton had worked particularly hard on the 'Browning' book, spending much time in the British Museum Reading Room. There was a story bandied about at the time that on one occasion finding himself famished and without a penny in his pocket, he had hastily sketched a figure shaking with hunger, which he passed around the desks with the plea for a sixpenny loan. Succeeding with several of the people with whom he had a nodding acquaintance, he gathered up his sixpences and went off to the pub. The story was typical, and might have been true.

'Robert Browning', Maisie Ward said, 'created a sensation and established G.K. in the front rank'; a rank which included Sir Leslie Stephen, Sidney Colvin, and the many other eminent authors of the 'English Men of Letters' series. The *Athenaeum* welcomed 'one of the most refreshing in an admirable series'.

'Browning strikes Mr Chesterton on that part of his soul which is most resonant, and the reverberating clang is deep and full and clear,' wrote James Douglas in *The Bookman*. 'The explanation of this is an explanation of Browning, on the one hand, and of Mr Chesterton on the other.' Chesterton made the 'true Browning fully visible.' He went on,

The only difference between the Browningite and the anti-Browningite is that the second says he is not a poet, but a mere philosopher, and the first says he was a philosopher and not a mere poet. The admirer disparages poetry in order to exalt Browning; the opponent exalts poetry in order to disparage Browning; and all the time Browning himself exalted poetry above all earthly things, served it with single-hearted intensity, and stands among the few poets who hardly wrote a line of anything else.

Chesterton saw Browning's love poetry as of the finest sort of love poetry in the world, 'because it does not talk about raptures and ideals and gates of heaven, but about window-panes and gloves and garden walls. It does not deal much with abstraction; it is the truest of all love poetry, because it does not speak much about love.'

Alfred Noyes found in *Robert Browning* 'a weird fascination that it is almost impossible to define or exaggerate'. He felt that Chesterton had 'wrought the old miracle anew', and that 'we have the wild joy of looking upon the world once more for the first time'. The book, he said, revealed something of 'the strange issues that await the twentieth century.... how after long grief and bitter doubt and all the hesitant pain of human hearts that yearn for hope or faith, men are slowly beginning to postulate the Eternal as the first mad need of life and the only explanation of death.' How wrong he was about men. Chesterton was never so deceived, though he would have shared Noyes's hope, for he knew it was no flock of sheep the Christian shepherd was leading, 'but a herd of bulls and tigers, of terrible ideals and devouring doctrine, each one of them strong enough to turn to a false religion and lay waste the world'.

8

Enter Father Brown

1904–1905

In the summer of 1903 Chesterton, 'that clear-sighted and virile new-comer', was being heralded as 'Fleet Street's only author'. How he ever managed to fall on his feet in Fleet Street remained a mystery to him. He belonged, as he said, to the 'old Bohemian life of Fleet Street', to the life of taverns and ragged pressmen where work and recreation came at all hours of the night, a life destroyed, not by the idealism of detachment, 'but by the materialism of machinery'. When he was once asked by George Cadbury, the proprietor of the *Daily News*, what his inspiration was, and where he wrote his articles, Chesterton replied that he wrote them on beer, and 'in the little pubs in Fleet Street'. As Titterton recalled, such news was 'hard for a teetotal proprietor to hear'.

It is true that Chesterton began to enjoy wine and beer at about this time, but only after several years of increasingly immoderate drinking did his physical appearance change dramatically, and his body tend to retain fluid, giving his face, and particularly his hands, a puffy look. People began to talk of Chesterton's 'Gargantuan debauch'; but, as Titterton realized, such jibes were usually uttered by men 'who drank more in a week than Chesterton did in a year of Sundays'. Chesterton looked upon pubs and wine bars as much as anything as convenient places of work for, like his brother, he had an extraordinary power of concentration which enabled him to write almost anywhere, on buses, trains, or inside a hansom cab, which was his favourite form of travel. The stories of unpaid hansoms waiting for hours outside the pubs of Fleet Street are many, and Chesterton, who 'never moved with the quickness and decision of his brother physically', would frequently hire a hansom to take him a hundred yards down the road. Ada Jones remembered,

If you wanted to get hold of Gilbert you could generally locate his whereabouts by the attendant hansom faithfully waiting for his disposal. He quite forgot it was there, and would chuckle delightedly when he realized it had been stationary for hours. He would pull out a handful of money and invite the cabby to take his fare and a tip, and, generally speaking, he was by no means robbed.

His favourite haunts were El Vino, the George, and the Bodega, but he also frequented the Cheshire Cheese and Peel's for beer and sandwiches. At El Vino he would usually sit at the same mahogany table 'under the shelter of a vast cask of sherry'. His friends made a point of looking in at about six in the hopes of seeing him. It was at El Vino one evening that Chesterton suddenly announced: 'I oughtn't to be here. I'm supposed to be speaking to the Literary Society at Bletchley – I should be speaking now.' He looked incredulously at the clock, ordered himself another glass of port and 'then with an effort heaved himself up'.

Titterton said that Chesterton went to the tavern as he later went to the church, for spiritual refreshment. Like Johnson, for whom a tavern stool was the 'throne of human felicity', Chesterton relished a 'masculine period of hard thinking and hard drinking', Fleet Street was a 'recrudescence of old Grub Street, with in those early days G.K. as the presiding figure'.

Frances, on the other hand, loathed the whole Fleet Street atmosphere, and kept away from it as far as possible. She had just cause to resent Gilbert's late arrivals home, for he would often remain out until closing time, which in Fleet Street was midnight. However, she almost always accompanied him when he attended dinners or was lecturing; sometimes she would miss the eating and slip in to hear the speeches. 'Gilbert and I meet all sorts of queer, well-known, attractive, unattractive people', she recorded in her diary.

In 1903 she went with Gilbert to the North, where he lectured in Bradford, and in Keighley, to the Keighley Scientific and Literary Society, on 'The Shyness of the Journalist'. The audience must have noticed that there was nothing in the least shy about Chesterton. During the Northern lecture tours, the Chestertons often stayed with a family called Steinthal at their house, St John's, Wharfemead, near Ilkley. In the summer of 1904 the Steinthal children, with several friends, including Rhoda Bastable, performed a masque in the garden of St

John's written by Chesterton to celebrate their father's fiftieth birthday. The characters in the masque were Robin Hood and Maid Marian, with three English Kings, Stephen, John and Henry, involved in the plot. The verse was rich in topical allusions. For instance, when Robin Hood seized King Henry he proclaimed:

> Upon this place in after time shall stand
> A splendid house that shall be called St John's.
> This glade of which I am king, this Yorkshire vale
> Of this hereafter Steinthal shall be King
> Here, on this barren glade on which we tread,
> Steinthal shall have a garden; possibly
> Children of Steinthal may herein enact
> The very battle between you and me . . .

With the children of the house playing major parts, there was more than a touch of Milton's 'Comus' in the proceedings.

In the audience that August evening was the man who was already beginning to play an important part in the lives of both Gilbert and Frances Chesterton, although they had only known each other for a few months. On 9 February 1903 Chesterton had received a letter written from the presbytery of St Anne's, Keighley. It read:

> I like you, and advised by the Autocrat of the Breakfast Table I make bold to tell you so. . . . I am a Catholic priest, and though I may not find you quite orthodox in details, I first wish to thank you very heartily, or shall I say, to thank God for having gifted you with the spirituality which alone makes literature immortal, as I think.

Fr John O'Connor had been impressed by Chesterton's poetry, and what he had read in both the *Speaker* and the *Daily News*. There is some confusion with regard to the date the two men actually met. In his book *Father Brown on Chesterton*, O'Connor states that he met Chesterton for the first time at Keighley in the spring of 1904, at the house of Mr Herbert Hugill. The pair then walked home together over the moors the following day. However, there is at Beaconsfield a letter dated 6 December 1903, from O'Connor to Frances, which relates how he and Chesterton 'walked together over the moor to Ilkley, favoured by the only two hours of sunshine in three days'.

It all remains a bit of a mystery but what does seem certain is that O'Connor had known Chesterton before the famous walk across the moors, which was described both in his book and in Chesterton's autobiography. That walk took place in March 1904. Chesterton, taking Frances with him, travelled to the West Riding to spend a few days with the Steinthals at Ilkley. From there it was easy to get to Keighley where he had been booked to deliver a lecture. Fr O'Connor was in the audience. He remembered how Chesterton had spoken on one of his favourite aspects of Modern Thought, the guileless pretence of getting everything both ways: liberty without justice, ease without vigilance, Peace alongside of Push, the Palm without the Pang; and how 'folk would shout hooray, if you kept talking like this: "Whilst avoiding the manifest difficulty of institutional religion, let us cultivate the broader atheism which allows for a personal God."'

After the lecture the priest was among the few selected members of the audience invited to Herbert Hugill's house to meet the lecturer. He was, Chesterton recalled, 'a small man with a smooth face and a demure elvish complexion', and he was struck by the tact and humour with which Fr O'Connor mingled with his very Yorkshire and very Protestant company; but soon he realized that the local people had learnt to appreciate the small parish priest as something of a Character. He recalled,

> Somebody gave me the very amusing account of how two gigantic Yorkshire farmers, of that district, had been deputed to go the rounds of various religious centres, and how they had wavered, with nameless terrors, before entering the little presbytery of the little priest. With many sinkings of the heart, they seem to have come finally to the conclusion that he would hardly do them any serious harm; and that if he did, they could send for the police. They really thought, I suppose, that he had the house fitted up with all the torture engines of the Spanish Inquisition.

Chesterton learned that even these farmers had since accepted the priest as a neighbour, and as the evening wore on other neighbours decidedly encouraged his powers of entertainment.

It seems that Frances had remained at Ilkley with the Steinthals, for on the following day Fr O'Connor and Chesterton crossed the moors alone. The two walked, or rather strolled, over Keighley Gate, the wide bank of moorland that separates Keighley from Wharfedale, and on towards Ilkley Moor. The conversation ranged widely over a variety of subjects, including lunacy, the problem of vagrancy, and the burning

of heretics. The priest told the story of how a French beggar woman
bandaged a walnut shell over her baby's eye; inside the shell was a
spider, which had eaten a large hole in the little eyelid.

As they crossed over the canal before ascending the steps of Morton
Bank, Zola was the subject discussed. Fr O'Connor mentioned that
Zola had once offered money to a woman miraculously cured at Lourdes
to induce her denial of the miracle. Chesterton interjected that Gardiner
had recently blue-pencilled his recent reference to Zola as an 'Obscene
Nonconformist'. 'Not', he went on, 'that I ever thought Nonconformists
obscene, only Zola! He would like to turn civilization into a drowsy
Sunday afternoon, which is, I think a Nonconformist ideal.'

Approaching Ilkley, they talked of confession and of *The Awful Confes-
sions of Maria Monk*, the bitterly anticlerical account of a young girl's
experiences in a convent in Canada, the author of which Chesterton
was to brand later as 'a dirty half-wit'. They recited ballads and sang
songs, for 'there is a point on the high moorland where everyone breaks
into song'. Fr O'Connor could not help noticing that Chesterton was
tone-deaf, though 'most sensitive to musical rhythm and tempo'. When
they arrived finally at St John's, they found it full of visitors, including
two Cambridge undergraduates who, while admitting that the priest
was a remarkable man, showed their 'breezy contempt for the fugitive
and cloistered virtue of a parish priest'. However, after his morning
with his companion, Chesterton was well aware that as regards all the
'solid Satanism' which the priest knew and warred with all his life,
these two Cambridge gentlemen knew as much about 'real evil as two
babies in the same perambulator'.

Chesterton felt strongly by now that it was an important friendship
that was developing, though how deep that friendship was to become
for both him and Frances none of them knew, nor could it have been
foreseen that Chesterton would soon be allowing himself the 'grave
liberty' of taking his friend, a man who through his hours spent in
the confessional knew more about crime than the criminals, and, as
he put it, 'knocking him about; beating his hat and umbrella shapeless,
untidying his clothes, punching his intelligent countenance into a condition of pudding-faced fatuity, and generally disguising Father
O'Connor as Father Brown'.

It would be some years, however, before the Father Brown stories
came to be written. The first, 'The Blue Cross', was published by the
Storyteller in September 1910, by which time Fr O'Connor's friendship

with the Chestertons was one of long standing, and he had been their guest both in London and, later, in Beaconsfield.

March 1904 was an exciting time in other ways. Not only were two more of Chesterton's books published, *G.F.Watts* and *The Napoleon of Notting Hill*; but he was also deeply embroiled in a controversy with Robert Blatchford, the editor of the *Clarion*, which had more far-reaching results than his earlier skirmish with Dr Clifford. The controversy had begun towards the end of 1903 when Blatchford and his friends had published a rationalist credo, which they entitled *God and My Neighbour*; this Chesterton had called his 'favourite text-book of theology'. He had mentioned Blatchford in his *Daily News* article on 12 December. He wrote:

> The problem is what is normal in man or, to put it more simply, what is human in him. Now, there are some who maintain, like Mr Blatchford, that the religious experience of the ages was abnormal, a youthful morbidity, a nightmare from which he is gradually waking. There are others like myself who think that on the contrary it is the modern rationalist civilization which is abnormal, a loss of ancient human powers of perception of ecstacy in the feverish cynicism of cities and empire. We maintain that man is not only part of God, but that God is part of man; a thing essential, like sex. We say that (in the light of actual history) if you cut off the supernatural what remains is the unnatural. We say that it is in believing ages that you get men living in the open and dancing and telling tales by the fire. We say that it is in ages of unbelief, that you get emperors dressing up as women, and gladiators or minor poets wearing green carnations and praising unnamable things. We say that, taking ages as a whole, the wildest fantasies of superstition are nothing to the fantasies of rationalism.
>
> Mr Blatchford and others have an odd picture of human history in their minds which represents it as having been a gradual emergence from extreme belief or superstition to extreme scepticism. The truth is that history is chaotic, and man so varied, that by judicious selection you can represent social evolution as having tended to anything you choose.

This is followed by a brilliant paragraph in which Chesterton gives numerous examples of just how history may be so manipulated to suit any argument.

Take the north of Europe from the landing of Augustine to the *Origin of Species*, the theology seems to have been cut down and simplified. Take the south of Europe from the Epistle to the Romans to the Council on Infallibility and it seems to have been vastly increased. Put Actium at the beginning of history and Mr Blatchford at the end, and we have grown materialists; put Topsy at the beginning and Sir William Crookes at the end and we have become occultists. You can make history a march towards materialism by saying that the savage had never heard of Haeckel, and foolishly believed that spirits lived in matter. But you can make it a march away from materialism by saying that the savage had never heard of Berkeley and foolishly supposed in the existence of his own legs.

Blatchford then threw down the gauntlet and challenged Chesterton to state his beliefs categorically. 'Are you a Christian?' he asked.

'Certainly', Chesterton replied. 'If I gave each of my reasons for being a Christian', he said, 'a vast number of them would be Mr Blatchford's reasons for not being one.'

Chesterton was not alone in counter-attacking Blatchford's rationalistic attack on faith, but he was the most outstanding figure and by far the most eloquent. It is evident too from Chesterton's arguments that he was now fully convinced of the truth of the Incarnation. He answered every proposition put forward by the rationalists: that there are many myths parallel with the Christian story, Pagan Christs, Patagonian Crucifixions, and so on. Chesterton replied,

> If the Christian God really made the human race, would not the human race tend to rumours and perversions of the Christian God? If the centre of our life is a certain fact, would not people far from the centre have a muddled version of that fact? If we are so made that a Son of God must deliver us, is it odd that Patagonians should dream of the Son of God?

The Blatchfordian position, as he called it, amounted to the idea that because a certain thing has impressed millions of different people as likely or necessary, therefore it cannot be true. 'When learned sceptics come to me and say, "Are you aware that the Kaffirs have a sort of Incarnation?"' Chesterton asserted that his reply would be: 'Speaking as an unlearned person, I don't know. But speaking as a Christian, I should be very much astonished if they hadn't.'

The second arm of the secularist attack was that Christianity has been 'a gloomy and ascetic thing', it pointed, the secularists argued, to a procession of austere and ferocious saints who had given up home and happiness and macerated health and sex. Chesterton replied that it never seemed to have occurred to the secularists

> that the very oddity and completeness of these men's surrender make it look very much as if there were really something actual and solid in the thing for which they sold themselves. They gave up all pleasures for one pleasure. They gave up all human experiences for the sake of one superhuman experience. They may have been wicked, but it looks as if there were such an experience.

There then follows a typical Chestertonian parallelism.

> It is perfectly tenable that this experience is as dangerous and selfish a thing as drink. A man who goes ragged and homeless in order to see visions may be as repellent and immoral as a man who goes ragged and homeless to drink brandy. That is a quite reasonable position. But what is manifestly not a reasonable position, what would be, in fact, not far from being an insane position, would be to say that the raggedness of the man, and the stupefied degradation of the man, proved that there was no such thing as brandy.
>
> That is precisely what the Secularist tries to say. He tries to prove that there is no such thing as supernatural experience by pointing at the people who have given up everything for it. He tries to prove that there is no such thing by proving that there are people who live on nothing else.

Then the secularist argued that Christianity produced tumult and cruelty. This argument was used, Chesterton said, in an attempt to prove that it was therefore bad. 'But,' he argued, 'it might prove it to be very good. For men commit crimes not only for bad things, far more often for good things. For no bad things can be desired quite so passionately and persistently as good things can be desired, and only very exceptional men desire very bad and unnatural things.' Most crime was committed, Chesterton thought, because, owing to some peculiar complication, very beautiful or necessary things were in some danger. 'When something is set before mankind that is not only enormously valuable, but also quite new,' he said, 'the sudden vision, the chance of winning it, the chance of losing it, drive them mad. It has the same effect in the moral world that the finding of gold has in the economic world. It upsets values, and creates a kind of cruel rush.'

Chesterton then took the example of the modern doctrines of brotherhood and liberality and showed how during the French Revolution, although the educated classes everywhere had been growing towards them, and the world to a very considerable extent welcomed them, all the preparation and openness were

> unable to prevent the burst of anger and agony which greets anything good. And if the slow and polite preaching of rational fraternity in a rational age ended in the massacres of September, what an a fortiori is here! What would be likely to be the effect of the sudden dropping into a dreadfully evil century of a dreadfully perfect truth? What would happen if a world baser than the world of Sade were confronted with a gospel purer than the gospel of Rousseau?
>
> The mere flinging of the polished pebble of Republican Idealism into the artificial lake of eighteenth century Europe produced a splash that seemed to splash the heavens, and a storm that drowned ten thousand men. What would happen if a star from heaven really fell into the slimy and bloody pool of a hopeless and decaying humanity? Men swept a city with a guillotine, a continent with a sabre, because Liberty, Equality, and Fraternity were too precious to be lost. How if Christianity was yet more maddening because it was yet more precious?
>
> But why should we labour the point when One who knew human nature as it can really be learnt, from fishermen and women and natural people, saw from his quiet village the track of his truth across history, and, in saying that He came to bring not peace but a sword, set up eternally His colossal realism against the eternal sentimentality of the Secularist?

So it was, Chesterton argued, that when the learned sceptic says, 'Christianity produced wars and persecutions', the immediate answer should be: 'Naturally.'

The fourth and last contention Blatchford had put forward was that the Hebrew and Christian religions began as local things; that their god was a tribal god; that they gave him material form, and attached him to particular places. This gave Chesterton the chance to produce one of his strongest arguments.

This is an excellent example of one of the things that if I were conducting a detailed campaign I should use as an argument for the validity of Biblical experience. For if there really are some other and higher beings than ourselves, and if they, in some strange way, at some emotional crisis, really revealed themselves to rude poets or dreamers in very simple times, that these rude people should regard revelation as local, and connect it with the particular hill or river where it happened, seems to be exactly what any reasonable human being would expect. It has a far more credible look than if they had talked cosmic philosophy from the beginning. If they had, I should have suspected 'priestcraft' and forgeries and third-century Gnosticism.

If there be such a being as God, and He can speak to a child, and if God spoke to a child in the garden, the child would, of course, say that God lived in a garden. I should not think it less likely to be true for that. If the child said: 'God is everywhere; an impalpable essence pervading and supporting all constituents of the Cosmos alike' – if, I say the infant addressed me in the above terms, I should think he was much more likely to have been with the governess than with God.

So if Moses had said God was an Infinite Energy, I should be certain he had seen nothing extraordinary. As he said he was a Burning Bush, I think it very likely that he did see something extraordinary. For whatever be the Divine Secret, and whether or no it has (as all peoples have believed) sometimes broken bounds and surged into our world, at least it lies on the side furthest away from pedants and their definitions, and nearest to the silver souls of quiet people, to the beauty of bushes, and the love of one's native place.

Thus, then, in our last instance (out of hundreds that might be taken), we conclude in the same way. When the learned sceptic says: 'The visions of the Old Testament were local, and rustic, and grotesque', we shall answer: 'Of course. They were genuine.'

Chesterton's 'very pugnacious public argument with Mr Blatchford' continued over a period of many months, but the two always remained on friendly terms when they met. In his autobiography Chesterton paused to salute Blatchford across the ages, hoping he would not count him less friendly if he recalled 'battles of the distant past'. He cheerfully admitted that there may have been a good deal of real and culpable digression and shapelessness in his articles against Mr Blatchford; they were written for the most part in a great hurry, and generally in 'a condition of some hilarity'. Nevertheless, the articles contained some of the best writing he had produced so far. His discursive manner, he explained, arose out of necessity, out of a very ample and satisfied conviction. Christianity, Chesterton now claimed, was so generally and solidly true that he did not care at what end one took hold of it, or by what path one approached it, or how one turned it upside down or inside out. It was a solid statue that could be 'seen from all points of the compass'. If Blatchford thought that Chesterton did not believe in Christianity because he played with it, he was 'falling into an almost bottomless error'.

It was not his fault that existence was a strange and dim affair. What was really the matter with Mr Blatchford was that he could not even put to himself for a moment that the materialistic philosophy might be false. He could not even make a picture of it in his head. Chesterton towards the end of the controversy turned to a defence of the doctrine of free will against Blatchford's determinism; an understanding of the Fall of Man was necessary to an understanding of free will, Chesterton argued, and here he produced another striking parallelism.

If you wanted to dissuade a man from drinking his tenth whisky, you would slap him on the back and say, 'Be a man.' No one who wished to dissuade a crocodile from eating his tenth explorer would slap it on the back and say, 'Be a crocodile.' For we have no notion of a perfect crocodile; no allegory of a whale expelled from a whaley Eden.

Chesterton argued most strongly against Blatchford's denial of all miracles.

He does not question them. He does not pretend to be agnostic about them. He does not suspend his judgment until they shall be proved. He denies them. Faced with this astounding dogma I asked Mr Blatchford why he thought miracles would not occur. He replied that the Universe was governed by laws. Obviously this answer is of no use whatever, for we cannot call a thing impossible because the world is governed by laws unless we know what laws. Does Mr Blatchford know all about all the laws in the Universe? And if he does not know about the laws, how can he possibly know anything about the exceptions? For obviously the mere fact that a thing happens seldom, under odd circumstances, and with no explanation within our knowledge, is no proof that it is against natural law. That would apply to the Siamese twins or to a new comet or to radium three years ago. The question of miracles is merely this. Do you know why a pumpkin goes on being a pumpkin? If you do not you cannot possibly tell whether a pumpkin could turn into a coach or couldn't, that is all. All the other scientific expressions you are in the habit of using at breakfast are words and wind. You say 'It is a law of nature that pumpkins should remain pumpkins.' That only means that pumpkins generally do remain pumpkins, which is obvious. It does not say why they do. You say, 'Experience is against it.' That only means 'I have known many pumpkins intimately and none of them turned into coaches.' There was a great Irish rationalist of this school, possibly related to Mr Leckey, who when he was told that a witness had seen him commit murder, said that he could bring a hundred witnesses who had not seen him commit it. You say, the modern world is against it. That means that a mob of men in London and Birmingham and Chicago in a thoroughly pumpkiny state of mind cannot work miracles by faith. You say, 'Science is against it.' That means that so long as pumpkins are pumpkins their conduct is pumpkiny, and bears no resemblance to the behaviour of a coach. That is fairly obvious. What Christianity says is merely this: that this repetition in nature has its origin not in a thing resembling a law, but a thing resembling a will. Of course its phrase of a heavenly Father is drawn from an earthly father. Quite equally Mr Blatchford's phrase of a universal law is a metaphor from an Act of Parliament. But Christianity holds that the world and its repetition came by will or love, as children are begotten by a father, and therefore that other and different things might come by it. Briefly, he believes that a God who could do anything so extraordinary as making pumpkins go on being pumpkins is like the prophet Habbakuk capable de touts. If you do not think it extraordinary that a pumpkin is always a pumpkin think again. You have not even begun philosophy, you have not even seen a pumpkin.

Chesterton's use of fairy-tale imagery, perhaps understandably, puzzled Blatchford, who complained that his antagonist was 'making brilliant efforts to evade the issues in debate', and the ease with which Chesterton brought in references to 'Zulus, and gardening, and butcher's shops, and lunatic asylums, and the French Revolution', positively irritated him; but 'Faith,' said Chesterton, 'breeds of its nature a kind of frivolity.'

However, it was on Blatchford's own ground of socialism that Chesterton was hardest on him. Blatchford had asserted that 'bad surroundings inevitably produced bad men', that men should be given better conditions, and then they would be good. Chesterton found this proposition almost incredible. 'He cannot, surely, mean that mere conditions of physical comfort and mental culture produce good men, because manifestly they do not.' Chesterton argued that in the British Isles there existed every conceivable degree of riches and poverty, 'from insane opulence to insane hunger'. 'Is any of those classes morally exquisite or glaringly any better than the rest', he asked. Where so many modes of education had failed, by what right, he asked, had Mr Blatchford to assume that his remedy was infallible?

As for the great part of the talk of Mr Blatchford about sin arising from vile and filthy environments, I do not wish to introduce into this discussion anything of personal emotion, but I am bound to say that I have great difficulty in enduring that talk with patience. Who in the world is it who thus speaks as if wickedness and folly rage only among the unfortunate? Is it Mr Blatchford who falls back on the old contemptible impertinence that represents virtue to be something of the upper classes, like a visiting card or a silk hat?

Chesterton, who always praised 'the eternal heroism of the slums', then made his strongest attack.

The association of vice with poverty [is] the vilest and the oldest and the dirtiest of all the stones that insolence has ever flung at the poor. Man that is born of a woman has short days and full of trouble, but he is a nobler and a happier being than this world makes him out. I will not deign to answer even Mr Blatchford when he askes how a man born in filth and sin can live a noble life. I know so many who are doing it within a stone's throw of my own house in Battersea, that I care little how it is done. Man has something in him always which is not conquered by conditions. Yes, there is a liberty that has never been chained. There is a liberty that has made men happy in dungeons, as it may make them happy in slums. It is the liberty of the mind, that is to say, it is the one liberty on which Mr Blatchford makes war.

The Blatchford controversy continued intermittently until the summer of 1904. Chesterton found almost no ground for agreement. Blatchford thought the materialism of nineteenth-century westerners one of their noble discoveries: Chesterton thought it 'as dull as their coats, as dirty as their streets, as ugly as their trousers, and as stupid as their industrial system'. The last paragraph he wrote in the matter came at the end of his article entitled 'Mr Blatchford's Religion', which appeared in the *Clarion* on 5 August.

Mr Blatchford's philosophy will never be endured among sane men. But if ever it is, I will very easily predict what will happen: man, the machine, will stand up in those flowery meadows and cry aloud. 'Was there once a thing, a Church, that taught us we were free in our souls? Did it not surround itself with tortures and dungeons in order to force men to believe that their souls were free? If there was, let it return, tortures, dungeons and all. Put me in those dungeons, rack me with those tortures, if by that means I may possibly believe it again.'

Chesterton's claim to know the poor of Battersea was no exaggeration, for both he and perhaps even more so Frances were actively involved in social reform and municipal affairs. Working men's and working women's movements found the Chestertons sympathetic allies, who were 'instant with help and goodwill'. Their own flat was described as 'austerely furnished with a restrained taste that expressed itself in blues and greens, and a simplicity of line in the old furniture'. Battersea would never fire Chesterton's imagination as Kensington had done; but were he to meet anyone who had been born in Battersea, who was, as it were, a Battersea patriot, he would have hoped to find him proud of Battersea, and not like the journalist from Clapham he once met who was 'ashamed of Clapham'.

This man had glowered at him, and became, Chesterton said, the problem of his life. 'He has haunted me at every turn and corner like a shadow, as if he were a blackmailer or a murderer.' It was against him that he had 'marshalled the silly pantomime of halberdiers of Notting Hill and all the rest'. The problem, as Chesterton saw it, was how to make men realize the wonder and splendour of being alive 'in environments which their own daily criticism treated as dead-alive, and which their imaginations had left for dead'. Such men, he said, were citizens of no mean city, who had resigned themselves to being citizens of mean cities. He wanted Englishmen to want English things that nobody else could import and that were too much enjoyed to export.

The 'fantastic romance' *The Napoleon of Notting Hill* had been written in an attempt 'to make men realise the fullness and power of one of their most deeply-rooted sentiments: the sentiment of local patriotism'. Bentley reviewed the novel for the *Bystander*.

> The story is one of a cynically humorous Autocrat of England who, a century hence, has the idea of reviving in the swarming parochial divisions of London the old mediaeval pomps and prides of municipal patriotism. Thus, King Auberon endows Notting Hill, West Kensington, Hammersmith, Bayswater, and all the other recognised neighbourhoods (including Battersea) with town charters, coats of arms, and mottoes, together with funny privileges and immemorial rights, invented on the spur of the moment. Also, it is the story of a splendid visionary, Adam Wayne, who alone of all men takes the King's freak quite seriously, and as provost of Notting Hill, infects all his fellow Notting Hillers with his own ardour – the story, in fact, of the triumph of a spiritual idea over the multitude of common-minded men, a possibility of which Mr Chesterton is, to his great honour, one of the resolute maintainers.

> The situation has a bizarre outcome. Notting Hill is moved to a 'passion of resentment' at the proposal to demolish Pump Street in order to run a road nearby, and resorts to arms in an attempt to prevent the threat. At length Notting Hill becomes the inspiration of the other boroughs with her ideals of local patriotism, and so regenerates the city; but in so doing has to learn that those who took up the sword must perish by it.

Chesterton had had the idea for the novel in his mind for some time, at least since the early days of the war; but the bulk of the writing was done at Battersea, and typed by Mrs Saxon Mills 'in rather a two-fingered way'. The title had not been the author's original choice. 'I now write in a violent hurry just to say that the name of the book can be either "The Lion of Notting Hill' or "The King and the Madman"', he wrote to his publisher, John Lane. The book was illustrated with seven drawings by William Graham Robertson, who was nothing like as good an illustrator as Chesterton himself. Together with *The Flying Inn*, *The Napoleon of Notting Hill* seems likely to remain among Chesterton's more popular books.

Clement Shorter was among those few who found the book 'tiresome'.

I do not think Mr Chesterton has the faintest talent either as a novelist, a literary critic, or a literary biographer, but I do credit him with a talent in the direction of art. Perhaps his real achievement in the future, when this curious, and to me absolutely incomprehensible enthusiasm has subsided, will be as an art critic. I have just read a very pretty little book by him on George Frederick Watts. Mr Chesterton's *Watts*, published in a little series issued by Mr Duckworth, seems to be a very clever book, written with genuine sympathy and insight.

Watts was admittedly one of Chesterton's less memorable books, but it contained much 'vintage Chesterton', including such passages as:

There is no more remarkable psychological element in history than the way in which a period can suddenly become unintelligible. To the early Victorian period we have in a moment lost the key: the Crystal Palace is the temple of a forgotten creed. The thing always happens sharply: a whisper runs through the salons, Mr Max Beerbohm waves a wand and a whole generation of great men and great achievement suddenly looks mildewed and unmeaning.

Another example of his insight was:

Now Watts, with all his marvellous spirituality, or rather because of his peculiar type of marvellous spirituality, has the Platonic, the philosophic, rather than the Catholic order of mysticism. And it can scarcely be a coincidence that here again we feel it to be something that could be deduced from the colours if they were splashed at random about a canvas. The colours are mystical, but they are not transparent; that is, not transparent in the very curious but unmistakable sense in which the colours of Botticelli or Rossetti are transparent. What they are can only be described as iridescent. A curious lustre or glitter, conveyed chiefly by a singular and individual brush-work, lies over all his great pictures. It is the dawn of things: it is the glow of the primal sense of wonder; it is the sun of the childhood of the world; it is the light that never was on sea or land; but still it is a light shining on things, not shining through them. It is a light which exhibits and does honour to this world, not a light that breaks in upon this world to bring it terror or comfort, like the light that suddenly peers round the corner of some Gothic chapel with its green or its golden or blood-red eyes. The Gothic artists, as I say, would have liked men's bodies to become like burning glass (as the figures in their windows do), that the light might pass through them. There is no fear of light passing through Watts's *Cain*.

As in his book on Browning, Chesterton tended to go off at what one might call a relevant tangent.

There is nothing that is not relevant to these ancient studies. There is no detail from buttons to kangaroos, that does not enter into the gay confusion of philosophy. There is no fact of life, from the death of a donkey to the General Post Office, which has not its place to dance and sing in, in the glorious Carnival of theology. Therefore I make no apology if I have asked the reader, in the course of these remarks, to think about things in general.

Then, as something of an excuse, he added: 'It is not I, but George Frederick Watts, who asks the reader to think about things in general.'

It was hardly surprising that some of Chesterton's friends felt he might be doing too much, for it was hardly possible to open a newspaper without seeing some reference to him. One journalist noted that his name was now better known to compositors than that of Bernard Shaw. 'At the present rate of production he must either wear or tear' was one opinion, and these fears were even expressed across the Atlantic where Chesterton was also becoming increasingly well known. On 9 April 1904 the *Chicago Evening Post* commented.

No man born can keep so many irons in the fire and not himself come between the hammer and the anvil. It is a pitiable thing to have a good man spend himself recklessly; and I repeat once more that if he and his friends have not the will or power to restrain him, then there should be a conspiracy of editors and publishers in his favour. Not often is a man like Chesterton born. He should have his full chance. And that can only come by study and meditation, and by slow, steady accumulation of knowledge and wisdom.

Those wise words unfortunately remained unheeded, and even Bullock admitted that both physically and mentally Chesterton was a Hercules, and from what he had heard of his methods of work he was capable of a great output without much physical strain; but his words would have been substantiated by Frances, who tended to think that Gilbert had mistaken his vocation, which she saw as that of a poet or even a preacher. 'He considered himself nothing beyond a jolly journalist, who wanted to paint the town red,' she told Fr O'Connor, 'and was always wanting more buckets of red paint.'

One of the best moments had come for her when on 16 March Chesterton had preached at St Paul's, Covent Garden for the Christian Social Union. 'One of the proudest days in my life', she recorded in her diary. 'A crammed church – he was very eloquent and restrained. Sermons will be published afterwards.' Chesterton, in fact, preached twice in the same month. Frances wrote on 30 March: 'The second sermon: "The Citizen, the Gentleman, and the Savage". Even better than last week. "Where there is no vision the people perish."' Both sermons were published later in *Preachers from the Pew*.

Frances would have been happy had Gilbert agreed to accept Sir Oliver Lodge's invitation to stand as a candidate for the chair of English Literature at Birmingham University; but it was the last thing he himself would have wanted. Her diary for the early months of 1904 shows that they were heavily engaged in both literary and religious circles. On 17 February, for instance, she wrote: 'We went together to Mr and Mrs Sidney Colvin's "At home". It was rather jolly but too many clever people there to be really nice. The clever people were Mr Joseph Conrad, Mr Henry James, Mr Laurence Binyon, Mr Maurice Hewlett, and a great many more. Mr and Mrs Colvin looked so happy.' Frances was much happier entertaining at home herself. On 27 April the Bellocs and the Noels had dinner at Overstrand Mansions. 'Hilaire in great form', she remembered; [he] recited his own poetry with great enthusiasm the whole evening.' However, she found the Literary Fund Dinner they attended on 8 May about the greatest treat she had ever had in her life. 'After the formal dinner,' she recorded, 'was a reception at which everyone was very friendly. It is wonderful the way in which they all accept Gilbert, and one well-known man told me he was the biggest man present. Anyhow there was the feeling of brotherhood and fellowship in the wielding of "the lovely and loathly pen".'

The last phrase was one of J.M.Barrie's, who had made a speech as President, and had been 'so complimentary'. Frances thought Mrs Barrrie 'very pretty', but 'the most beautiful woman there was Mrs Anthony Hope – copper-coloured hair, masses, with a wreath of gardenias – grey eyes – and a long neck, very beautiful figure'. The Chestertons were to become particular friends of the Barries; it was later while they were staying as guests of the Barries that one of the more amusing incidents concerning Chesterton's size occurred. The Barries had rented one of the Asquith houses in the Cotswolds, and Michael Asquith's butler was met on the stairs carrying Chesterton's dinner jacket which he had just pressed. 'Mr Chesterton's evening trousers', he remarked. 'It reminds you of going down the Underground.'

We also learn from Frances's diary that during the summer Chesterton visited Swinburne at Putney Hill. He was, Chesterton recalled, 'a sort of god in a temple, who could only be approached through a high priest'; but he found him quite jolly and skittish, though his manner affected Chesterton strangely as 'spinsterish'. However, Swinburne had charming manners and especially 'the courtesy of a consistent cheerfulness'. Theodore Watts-Dunton, who played the high priest or, rather, the Grand Vizier to the 'Prophet of Putney', had been introduced to the Chestertons on an earlier occasion, when Frances had had a 'nice little conversation' with him. She had noticed how his 'walrusy appearance', which made the bottom of his face look fierce, was counteracted by the kindness of his eyes. It had been Watts-Dunton who had written to Frances suggesting that a visit to Putney should take place. 'Until quite recently,' he had said, 'I used to ask friends to luncheon as being the most convenient hour for both Mr Swinburne and me, but I am sorry to say that of late his deafness has somewhat increased, and he prefers to see friends after the clatter of feeding time is over.'

Watts-Dunton struck Chesterton as 'very serious indeed'. 'It is said,' he wrote, 'that he made the poet a religion; but what struck me as odd, even at that time, was that his religion seemed to consist largely of preserving and protecting the poet's irreligion. He thought it essential that no great man should be contaminated with Christianity.' Chesterton, of course, knew Swinburne's poetry, as he said, 'backwards', just as he knew that of Meredith, another literary celebrity whom he made a special journey to visit. Frances seems to have been unable to accompany Chesterton to Putney, and she was not able to gather much from him about the visit. 'I think he found it rather hard to reconcile the idea with the man,' she noted in her diary, 'but he was interested. He was amused by the compliments which Watts-Dunton and Swinburne paid to each other unceasingly.'

September 1904 saw the publication by Methuen of Hilaire Belloc's first novel, *Emmanuel Burden*; it contained thirty-four illustrations by Chesterton, making it the first of the 'Chesterbellocs'. Later in life, after they had collaborated on several such ventures, Belloc came to regard the illustrations as the more important part of the books. He would travel down to Beaconsfield with an idea in his head, insisting that he could not produce a word until Gilbert had produced the drawings. Stories are told of how the two would disappear into Chesterton's study for an afternoon and emerge with all the drawings completed; Chesterton having produced lightning sketches as Belloc had outlined the plot. Belloc considered Chesterton's ability to delineate character so quickly 'an unexpected but most striking example of his power of perception which was the head of his genius'. The drawing was in his view more living, more real, more the human being itself, 'than anything called character-drawing by the literary method'.

> He would, with a soft pencil capable of giving every gradation in emphasis from the lightest touch to the dead black point and line, set down, in gestures that were like caresses sometimes, sometimes like commands, sometimes like rapier-thrusts, the whole of what a man or woman was; and he would get the thing down on paper with the rapidity which only comes from complete possession.

No one among the few writers who had attempted to illustrate their own work – and Belloc immediately thought of Thackeray – had been able to match up to Chesterton; the thing was unique 'not only through its miraculous exuberance, but through its perception of reality'. In Chesterton's drawings, he said, generations to come would know exactly what 'our modern money-dealer, our modern English woman of the world, our modern, honest, well-founded merchants (such as remain), our poor, our middle class, our boobies, even, occasionally, our heroes' were like. 'All our humanity in procession, with the alien type called, I think, "Imperialist" – or so called in Gilbert Chesterton's youth and mine. That very characteristic figure – both as cause and effect of modern England – is recurrent through the whole.'

During the first week of March in the following year Chesterton published a book of his own which he had illustrated. *The Club of Queer Trades* is a series of stories with a vaguely related theme, which had been serialized in *The Idler* with the author's drawings during 1904, and the first story, 'The Tremendous Adventures of Major Brown', had been issued in brown-paper wrappers in a limited edition in December 1903. It is perhaps worth noting that when in April 1905 the publishers, Harper and Brothers, brought out their American edition they jettisoned Chesterton's drawings in favour of those by W.E.Mears, for it must be admitted Chesterton's drawings, except for two or three good ones, were far below his usual standard – the figures tending to have peculiarly shaped shoulders, as though most of the characters were hunchbacked. As Maisie Ward pointed out, *The Club of Queer Trades* was 'the least good of the fantasia', and it made even more of Chesterton's admirers wonder if he was trying too many fields, since 'instead of slowly winning a reputation Mr Chesterton had shot into fame with a rapidity as remarkable as the growth of one of Mr H.G.Wells's Boom-food fed babies'. However, the book was his first essay into the realm of detective fiction, the literary form for which he is best known in his own country, although abroad he has long been valued as an important philosopher.

Chesterton was also at this time accepting more and more lecture engagements. On 16 February he delivered a Sunday afternoon lecture amid considerable opposition in the unlikely premises of Hengler's Circus. Some six hundred people crowded into the big top to hear him speak on 'Religion and Liberty'. Chesterton enjoyed the humour of the situation, for although it was a day of rest for the circus, throughout the lecture 'there could be heard the low howling of the animals in the menagerie behind the scenes'. Combining this animal theme with his more familiar theme of drink Chesterton declared:

> Some people have declared that the great sin of the English people is drunkenness. To that I reply that the most dangerous things and the chief evils of the world are spiritual things. It is only because drink is very nearly a spiritual pleasure that it is so highly dangerous. Drink is not an animal pleasure; it belongs to the intellectual and emotional world. If materialism were true, people would be as intemperate over ham sandwiches and pork pies as they are now over drink. It is because man has a soul that he drinks and because animals have no souls that they do not drink.

The point to which the lecture led up was that of social equality. 'There can be no true equality,' Chesterton argued, 'except that which is founded on religion. Faith alone makes man forget the mighty external differences and fix his heart on the things in which all are brothers.'

On 24 May Chesterton took Frances to visit George Meredith. Frances wrote in her diary: 'I suppose many people have seen him in his little Surrey cottage; Flint Cottage, Boxhill. He has a wonderful face and a frail old body. He talks without stopping except to drink ginger-beer.

He told us many stories, mostly about society scandals of some time back.' Frances also remembered how Meredith had asked Gilbert if he liked babies, and when Gilbert answered that he did, Meredith had commented, 'So do I, especially in the comet stage.' Chesterton remembered that Meredith had a white pointed beard and a puff of white hair, 'like thistle-down'. He was, like Swinburne, deaf, but 'not in the least dumb'. 'He was not humble,' Chesterton wrote, 'but I should never call him proud. He still managed to be a third thing, which is almost as much the opposite of being proud; he was vain. He was a very old man; and he was still magnificently vain.' According to Chesterton Meredith had talked to, or rather at, Frances and not to him, for 'he preferred to dazzle women rather than men'. Meredith also assured him that he had come to enjoy ginger-beer 'quite as much as champagne'.

Chesterton was surprised to discover in the course of his monologue that Meredith had 'swallowed the current racial theory of dividing the nations by the Teuton and the Celt'; but the general impression Chesterton took away with him was that Meredith 'had exactly the shock and shining radiation of a fountain'.

The highlight of the summer of 1905 was the publication by John Lane on 6 June of Chesterton's *Heretics*, a book which 'aroused animosity in many minds', and remains among Chesterton's best. Taking as his standpoint his earlier theme of the importance of orthodoxy, Chesterton had proceeded to attack the creeds of many of his contemporaries, showing how important literary or political figures like Kipling, Shaw, and Wells, and lesser figures like Lowes Dickinson and Joseph McCabe were 'heretics' according to his definition of the word. 'A heretic,' he said, 'is a man whose view of things has the hardihood to differ from mine.' As Christopher Hollis pointed out in his *The Mind of Chesterton*, *Heretics* considerably enhanced Chesterton's reputation. Although this remains an amusing book, it was 'more amusing at the time of its publication when the heretics attacked were all men in the public eye than it would be today when some of them are somewhat forgotten'.

Chesterton said that he had reverted to the doctrinal methods of the thirteenth century, 'inspired by the general hope of getting something done'.

Suppose that a great commotion arises in the street about something, let us say a lamp-post, which many influential persons desire to pull down. A grey-clad monk, who is the spirit of the Middle Ages, is approached upon the matter, and begins to say, in the arid manner of the Schoolmen, 'Let us first of all consider, my brethren, the value of Light. If Light be good in itself ——' At this point he is somewhat excusably knocked down. All the people make a rush for the lamp-post, the lamp-post is down in ten minutes, and they go about congratulating each other on their mediaeval practicality. But as things go on they do not work out so easily. Some people have pulled the lamp-post down because they wanted the electric light; some because they wanted old iron; some because they wanted darkness, because their deeds were evil. Some thought it not enough of a lamp-post, some too much; some acted because they wanted to smash municipal machinery; some because they wanted to smash something. And there is war in the night, no man knowing whom he strikes. So, gradually and inevitably, today, tomorrow, or the next day, there comes back the conviction that the monk was right after all, and that all depends on what is the philosophy of Light. Only what we might have discussed under the gas-lamp, we now discuss in the dark.

The modern student of ethics, Chesterton argued in a chapter on the 'Negative Spirit', even if he remains sane, remains sane from an insane dread of insanity. The advantage of the old 'mystic morality' was that it was always so much jollier. 'A young man may keep himself from vice by continually thinking of disease,' he said. 'He may keep himself from it also by continually thinking of the Virgin Mary. There may be question about which method is the more reasonable, or even about which is the more efficient. But surely there can be no question about which is the more wholesome.'

To those who spoke of 'progress' he would say that the word as commonly enunciated was 'simply a comparative of which we have not yet settled the superlative'. So far from it being true that the ideal of progress was to be set against that of ethical or religious finality, the reverse was the truth.

Nobody has any business to use the word 'progress' unless he has a definite creed and a cast-iron code of morals. Nobody can be progressive without being infallible – at any rate, without believing in some infallibility. For progress by its very name indicates a direction; and the moment we are in the least doubtful about the direction, we become in the same degree doubtful about the progress. Never perhaps since the beginning of the world has there been an age that had less right to use the word 'progress' than we.

It was about direction that modern men disagreed. Whether the future excellence lay in more law or less law, Chesterton argued, or in more liberty or less liberty; whether property would be finally concentrated or finally cut up; whether sexual passion would reach its sanest in an almost virgin intellectualism or in a full animal freedom; whether men should love everybody with Tolstoy, or spare nobody with Nietszche – those were the things about which men were actually fighting most. The word 'progress' was not unmeaning, but it was unmeaning without the previous definition of a moral doctrine, and it could only be applied to groups of persons who held that doctrine in common. 'Progress is not an illegitimate word,' Chesterton concluded, 'but it is logically evident that it is illegitimate for us. It is a sacred word, a word which could only rightly be used by rigid believers and in the ages of faith.'

Chesterton was at his best in *Heretics* not so much when he was attacking the ideas of men like Shaw, 'one of the most brilliant and most honest men alive', though a heretic whose philosophy was 'quite solid, quite coherent, and quite wrong', but more when he was attacking some of the fads of the time, and in as much as some of these have remained fads until our time, Chesterton's comments are still relevant. Chesterton felt that no Englishman could be proud of being simple and direct, and still remain simple and direct. 'In the matter of these strange virtues, to know them is to kill them,' he said. Speaking about the 'simple life', which he said he could not afford, Chesterton had this important comment to make:

> The only kind of simplicity worth preserving is the simplicity of the heart, the simplicity which accepts and enjoys. There may be a reasonable doubt as to what system preserves this; there can surely be no doubt that a system of simplicity destroys it. There is more simplicity in the man who eats caviar on impulse than in the one who eats grape-nuts on principle.

In this matter, as in all the other matters treated in the book, Chesterton's main conclusion was that it was 'a fundamental point of view, a philosophy or a religion' that was needed, and not any change in habit or social routine. The things that were needed for immediate practical purposes were all abstractions, a right view of the human lot, a right view of human society; and if people were living eagerly and angrily in the enthusiasm of these things they would, *ipso facto*, be living simply in the genuine and spiritual sense.

The critic who reviewed the book in *Black and White* accused Chesterton of casuistry, but allowed that he was a casuist, if such a thing were possible, 'on the side of the angels'. 'If he would only take the trouble to be a literary artist as well, what a boon he would be to contemporary letters,' he added. Another reviewer noted, 'The whole book is based on the theory that the only thing about a man that really matters is his philosophy of life, his attitude to the cosmos.'

It was hardly surprising that Shaw, Wells and one or two others attacked in the book were asking themselves: if they were heretics, what were they heretics from? What was this orthodoxy which Chesterton opposed to them? They issued Chesterton with a challenge, which he answered only later. Nevertheless, *Heretics* marked another point from which there could be no turning back. It was, incidentally, the book that contained one of Chesterton's most famous observations, the one concerning blasphemy.

Blasphemy is an artistic effect, because blasphemy depends upon a philosophical conviction. Blasphemy depends upon belief, and is fading with it. If anyone doubts this, let him sit down seriously and try to think blasphemous thoughts about Thor. I think his family will find him at the end of the day in a state of some exhaustion.

In her diary Frances Chesterton recorded that the Bishop of Southwark had told her at a garden party how impressed the Prime Minister had been by *Heretics*. A little over a month later Chesterton met Balfour in person and found him interesting to talk to, but said he looked bored. We also learn from the diary that Granville Barker had visited Gilbert 'touching the possibility of a play', and that Gilbert had dined at the Asquiths' and hated it. However, earlier in the year the diary had contained another sort of entry, since it shows how she was becoming worried about Gilbert's state of mind. She wrote: 'Very puzzled at Gilbert's conduct, which on this particular occasion was peculiarly eccentric.'

At about the same time it was reported that Chesterton had been seen 'walking the streets of Battersea laughing continually to himself, and for ever jotting down in his notebook the funny things that occurred to him'. Such behaviour might have been thought odd, but it did not mean that Chesterton's mind was becoming unbalanced. Those who knew him had seen such sights many times before. Masterman has told how the head waiter of a Fleet Street café had noticed Chesterton working away furiously at one of the tables, and had whispered to Masterman: 'Your friend, he very clever man. He sit and laugh. And then he write. And then he laugh at what he write.' The truth was that as Chesterton took on more work in order to solve his financial problems, he had more to produce; and he tended to drink more heavily. Naturally abstracted from his surroundings, he became at this time even more so. The Chestertons' maid, who used to try to get to the bathroom as soon as he had finished because 'he would flood the floor to the imminent danger of the ceiling below', once heard him get out of the tub, and she was 'hovering around waiting for her moment when a tremendous splash assailed her ears. Then came a deep groan and the words, "Dammit, I've been in here before."'

Other stories from about this time, and also supplied by Mrs Saxon Mills, give a similar picture of Chesterton's totally abstracted state of mind. Mrs Mills could remember how on many occasions she had heard a 'blood-curdling yell' coming from Chesterton's bedroom. 'It sounded like a werewolf', she said. At this, Frances would say: 'Oh, that's Gilbert, he wants his tie tied.' Once, when he had failed to appear from his room, Frances explained, 'Gilbert dropped one of his garters. He went down on the floor to look for it, and found a book there, so he began to read it.' Mrs Mills was 'struck by the placidity with which Frances accepted her husband's oddities in daily life'. She had been surprised, for instance, when Frances had suddenly said to her: 'Oh, do go out and get Gilbert a few pretty ties.'

However, the autumn of 1905 was to bring considerable relief to the Chestertons' financial worries. Sir Bruce Ingram offered Gilbert the well-known 'Our Notebook' column in the *Illustrated London News* on the death of L. F. Austin. This column, which had achieved a world-wide reputation during the time it was written by George Sala, gave Chesterton a regular weekly income for life, since he wrote it with hardly any interruption for the next thirty-one years until he died. The editor suggested a payment of £350 a year, which virtually doubled his income. Although it meant an even greater commitment, Chesterton accepted the offer right away, for it also meant that an even greater weight was now off his mind.

9

The Dust-Heaps of Humanity

1906–1907

In December 1905 the Prime Minister, Mr Balfour, unable to govern with a party divided against itself, resigned. Sir Henry Campbell-Bannerman hastily formed a Liberal Government and just as hastily dissolved Parliament. The result was the famous Liberal landslide victory in the general election of January 1906. Belloc, in the hope of seeing a lively Radical presence in the House of Commons, stood as member for South Salford and was elected. 'This is a great day for the British Empire, but a bad one for the little Bellocs,' he sent in a telegram inviting his friends to meet him at Euston Station. Masterman was elected member for North West Ham; he had been helped in his canvassing by several of his friends, including Chesterton. Chesterton was not a successful canvasser, for instead of moving quickly from house to house, he would remain at the first door that opened and keep the occupier held with his glittering eye, like the Ancient Mariner. Masterman recalled that he himself had moved up both sides of a street while Chesterton was still talking away at his first house.

Cecil Chesterton did not stand for Parliament, but he was on the executive committee of the Fabian Society. However, he was beginning to lose popularity, having 'antagonised a good many of the Society's members' by his habit of speaking his mind bluntly, 'careless of the feelings of members who were pacifists, feminists, vegetarians, and other things that he disapproved of'. He eventually lost his place on the committee early in 1907, largely over the question of women's suffrage, a matter that would soon be occupying much of his brother's time. In 1907 also, Cecil Chesterton became a regular contributor to *The New Age*, the independent socialist review edited by A.R.Orage. This brought him into close contact with Bernard Shaw, who in one way or another came to play an important part in both brothers' lives.

There has been as much speculation as to when Chesterton first met Shaw as there has been over his first meeting with Belloc. Shaw had introduced himself by letter during the summer of 1901, but Chesterton had been 'too shy or too lazy to reply'. The older man had been struck by Chesterton's review of Scott's *Ivanhoe* which had appeared in the *Daily News* on 10 August, and had written to tell him so. 'I wrote to him asking who he was and where he came from, as he was evidently a new star in literature.' Recalling his 'new star's' lack of response, Shaw thought that the next thing he could remember was Chesterton coming to lunch 'on quite intimate terms accompanied by Belloc'. Now it seems unlikely that five years had elapsed between the letter and the lunch, so that an occasion on which both men were together at Rodin's studio in Paris in 1906 was almost certainly not their first meeting, although it was the first to be fully recorded. Oldershaw had taken Chesterton to visit the great sculptor, who was at the time working on a bust of Shaw. The model had proved to be obstreperous, and would not remain still. He was, on the occasion Chesterton was there, delivering a long monologue in moderate French on the merits of the Salvation Army, with the result that Rodin's secretary had to explain to him in broken English; 'The master says you have not much French but you impose yourself.' According to Oldershaw, after he had made Shaw aware of Chesterton's presence, Shaw had 'talked Chesterton down'. This was hardly surprising, as Shaw had been trying to impress, and was in an excitable mood while, stripped to the waist, he was being scrutinized by the man he called 'Rodin the Great'. Rodin, for his part, considered Shaw 'a fraud and a poseur', and it had only been because he saw in Shaw's face 'an authentic Christ mask' that he had allowed Mrs Shaw to persuade him to undertake the task at all.

Shaw was eighteen years older than Chesterton, whom he recognized as 'a man of colossal genius', and one whose literary career he wished to direct on 'a commanding paternal basis'. He was quite convinced that Belloc's influence on Chesterton was damaging and ultimately disastrous, and that Chesterton's genius would be best served in the writing of plays. Most of the letters he sent to both Gilbert and Frances Chesterton during the following years constantly harped on this hope, and he even worked out the plot of a play for Chesterton to write in which St Augustine returned to the island he had converted. It was to be of little avail, and Chesterton's first play, *Magic*, did not materialize until 1913. Much was to happen before then.

However, Shaw was to become a close friend, though never on such an intimate basis as Chesterton's friendship with Belloc, Baring or Fr O'Connor; and it is by no means certain that they were ever on Christian name terms. When, many years later, an American reporter asked Chesterton if he still found Bernard Shaw a coming peril, he replied that on the contrary he found him 'a disappearing pleasure'.

Nevertheless, Shaw was the most illustrious, besides being the most intelligent, of Chesterton's antagonists, and their public debates in the column or on the platform in the years immediately leading up to the First World War, and afterwards, until their last debate, 'Do We Agree?', in 1927, provided some of the most stimulating and amusing entertainment of its kind to be found in London. The first encounter in print was in April 1905, when Chesterton devoted his column for three weeks running to answering Shaw's claim that Shakespeare had written many inferior plays to gain popularity and make ready money. 'The Great Shawkspear Mystery' and 'Sorry, I'm Shaw' were two of the less inspiring titles that Shaw's 'favourite foe' dreamed up in Shakespeare's defence.

Chesterton claimed that it was necessary to disagree with Shaw as much as he did in order to admire him. 'I am proud of him as a foe even more than as a friend,' he said.

By the summer of 1906 Chesterton was settled into his new routine of producing two regular articles a week; his columns continued to reiterate in many different guises his chief concern at the time, which was to assert the truth that 'a man's philosophy of the cosmos is directly concerned in every act of his life'. In his attempt to put this across he used every possible pose that his often tired imagination could devise. The function of the imagination, he had reminded his readers, was not to make strange things settled so much as to make settled things strange; not to make wonders facts but facts wonders. One of his readers had noted that his vision of the things about him was so grotesque that one forgot how commonplace the things themselves were, as Chesterton was summoning up a host of tumbling metaphors from a side-street or a grocer's shop. He was caricaturing the truth in order that his readers might see it more memorably and more clearly. It was as though a man were to giggle out the Beatitudes, so as to impress them firmly upon his audience. On 10 April he had written in the *Daily News*: 'Mankind is not a tribe of animals to which we owe compassion. Mankind is a club to which we owe a subscription.' In July for the *Open Review* he wrote on 'The Necessity of Luxury':

> The great number of abuses peculiar to our present social state work back to that one great heresy which is the perversion of Darwin; I mean the heresy that man is an animal first and a spirit afterwards. The truth is that man is an animal and a spirit simultaneously, and the spiritual life is no more a luxury than his physical; except in the sense that he cannot rationally explain why he denies either of them.

A humane and civilized happiness is one of man's needs, not merely one of his pleasures, he argued. Luxury was itself a necessity, since 'Man does not live by bread alone but, at the very lowest level, by bread and butter.' All arguments about the treatment of the poor which were based on the idea that we could make them first into contented animals and then go on to their souls, he said, were false down to the roots. 'By giving a man just enough air, just enough oatmeal, just enough exercise, just enough cocoa, you cannot make him a contented beast; but only a discontented man', he said.

Chesterton's hostility was not directed towards the theory but to the kind of popular evolutionism that had 'substituted the Beast for the Devil' and made men feel that the real enemy was their 'lower nature'. To equate fallen human nature with animal nature was to degrade animals. The thing wrong in us is not, as the evolutionists say, the brute, he argued. The thing wrong in us is the devil, the 'austere, intellectual virgin devil of the mediaeval story'. He will suffer for evil. He will perform heroic acts of evil. The worst sins were not animal, lusts and appetites were 'things entirely innocent in themselves'; the worst sins were the purely human sins.

In his parody of Hood's poem Chesterton expressed his thoughts on evolution in a more light-hearted manner. He called the poem 'Race-Memory, by a dazed Darwinian'.

> I remember, I remember,
>   Long before I was born,
> The tree-tops where my racial self
>   Went dancing round at morn.
>
> Green wavering archipelagos,
>   Great gusty bursts of blue,
> In my race-memory I recall
>   (Or I am told to do).

In that green-turreted Monkeyville
  (So I have often heard)
It seemed as if a Blue Baboon
  Might soar like a Blue Bird.

Low crawling Fundamentalists
  Glared up through the green mist,
I hung upon my tail in heaven
  A Firmamentalist.

  . . .

I am too fat to climb a tree,
  There are no trees to climb;
Instead, the factory chimneys rise,
  Unscaleable, sublime.

The past was bestial ignorance:
  But I feel a little funky,
To think I'm further off from heaven
  Than when I was a monkey.

As far as Chesterton was concerned the theory of evolution may have been true as a biological fact; he did not know one way or the other, although he always insisted that the 'missing link' was still missing, and it was certainly true that many people argued either as though it had been found or that it did not matter that it was lost. Chesterton also insisted that man was a creature of a different order from the beasts, a spiritual creature, who possessed a fallen nature. The difference between man and the beasts, in spite of obvious similarities, was not one of degree. Man was the only creature subject to evil. In fact, Chesterton saw rightly that 'the less beastly you may grow, the more bad you may grow'. To those who made taunts about the Fall of Man, and asked 'where was the Garden of Eden?', or questions of the sort, he replied that it was like asking a philosophical Buddhist, 'When were you last a donkey?'

Darwinism was a subject to which Chesterton constantly returned, and it was even occupying his mind towards the end of his life. In 1935 he wrote in the *Illustrated London News* of how Darwinism had provoked a 'curious atmosphere of brand-new prejudice and premature pugnacity'. Early disciples of Darwin, men like Huxley and Herbert

Spencer, had really valued Darwinism as an argument for agnosticism. 'It would have been much better if they had cultivated a little more agnosticism towards Darwinism,' he said. 'If hypothesis had not been allowed to harden into a habit of thought, we might by this time have really taken stock of what is actually known about the variation of species and what can only be plausibly guessed and what is quite random guesswork.'

Perhaps it was in *The Everlasting Man*, the book published in 1925 in which 'all Chesterton's random thoughts were concentrated and refined', that the best exposition of the evil effect of Darwinism on faith is set out. Most modern histories of mankind, Chesterton said, began with the word 'evolution', and with a rather wordy exposition of evolution. 'There is something slow and soothing and gradual about the word and even about the idea.' However, Chesterton thought that evolution was not a practical word or a very profitable idea.

Nobody can get an inch nearer to it by explaining how something could turn into something else. It is really far more logical to start by saying 'In the beginning God created heaven and earth' even if you only mean 'In the beginning some unthinkable power began some unthinkable process.' For God is by its nature a name of mystery, and nobody ever supposed that man could imagine how a world was created any more than he could create one. But evolution really is mistaken for explanation. It had the fatal quality of leaving in many minds the impression that they do understand it and everything else; just as many of them live under a sort of illusion that they have read the *Origin of Species*.

The notion of something smooth and slow, like the ascent of a slope, was a great part of the illusion, Chesterton said; but it was an illogicality as well as an illusion; for slowness had really nothing to do with the question. An event was no more intrinsically intelligible or unintelligible because of the pace at which it moved. 'For a man who does not believe in a miracle, a slow miracle would be just as incredible as a swift one.'

In the latter part of August 1906 Chesterton was looking forward to the publication by Methuen of his biography of Dickens, due on the thirtieth; his novel *The Ball and the Cross* was being serialized in *The Commonwealth*; his weekly articles were provoking much lively correspondence, and he was already planning his major book on orthodoxy in answer to the challenge set down by Shaw and G.S.Street. It looked as though his affairs were at last becoming more settled, when on 25 August Frances received shattering news from home. Her brother, Knollys, had been washed up dead on a beach in Sussex.

'I have to write in a great trouble,' she informed Fr O'Connor who was now at St James's, Heckmondwike. 'My dear brother was found drowned at Seaford a few days ago. It is a terrible shock to us all – we were so happy about him.' Frances was referring to the fact that Knollys, after suffering from terrible and prolonged depression largely as a result of Gertrude's death from which he had never really recovered, had seemed much better recently and had been received into the Catholic Church. He had gone to Mass on the Sunday morning, and had apparently drowned himself on the same evening. 'He seemed to have quite recovered from his terrible illness,' Frances's letter continued, 'but he sought his own death.'

She hastened immediately down to Newhaven to identify her brother's body and arrange the funeral. Once again she was plunged into grief, and quite naturally needed all the emotional support she could get, for she had only recently undergone the operation already mentioned 'to make it possible for her to have children'. She needed more comfort than Gilbert was really capable of giving. He had once written in a poem to her:

> God knows I would not blame you, dear
> I do not know what thing am I
> How hard a burden on your back
> How stale an eyesore to your eye.

In the same poem he had seen himself as 'an earth-born monster', while Frances was 'of the seraph-bands'. Just as he had attempted to do after Gertrude's death, he tried to console her as best he could, but Frances was so devastated by her brother's death that she implored Gilbert to take her away. Yes, he would take her abroad for a while; but that was not what she wanted; she wanted to move right away from London altogether, away from the life that had begun to alienate him from her, Fleet Street and the interminable taverns. According to Mrs Cecil Chesterton, 'fearful of the effect of a refusal on her state of mind, and because he loved her with a great and unfailing devotion, he consented'.

In one of his early notebooks he had once written:

One thing the marriage ideal did and did alone: it took love seriously: it demanded the payment of the eternal promise of youth. Herein we think, though the trend of today is wholly against such feeling, it inexpressibly increased the vividness, the poetry, the boyish heroism of life. Society associated itself with the worship of the lover, it set on the woman's head a price high enough to satisfy even his imagination. It said 'You shall not have this secret and superhuman happiness, unless you give up all for it, unless you bring your life in your hands.'

Inevitably, the move had to come, but it would not come for two years. If it may be said that Frances made the decision, it was, as events turned out, the wisest she ever made.

Chesterton's knowledge of Dickens's novels was impressive: not only did he know the plots of each of them intimately, but he also could quote large passages, more or less accurately, by heart. His book *Charles Dickens* was what would be called today a 'critical biography', though one reviewer described it as 'a lyrical outcry rather than a criticism'. Some writers, like André Maurois, considered it one of the best biographies ever written; while T.S.Eliot thought that there was no better critic of Dickens than Chesterton, and he had found the book a delight to read. Shaw informed Chesterton on 6 September, a week after the book appeared: 'As I am a supersaturated Dickensite, I pounced on your book and read it, as Wegg read Gibbon and other authors, right through.' He then proceeded to take Chesterton to task for some inaccuracy before launching into his own theory that Dickens was 'at his greatest after the social awakening which produced *Hard Times*'.

It is important to note that when the book appeared in 1906 Dickens did not hold the reputation he holds now, and it is largely due to Shaw and Chesterton that Dickens began to be recognized once again – for he had, of course, been very popular during his own lifetime. In February 1907 J.M.Dent & Son issued *The Old Curiosity Shop* with an introduction by Chesterton, in the 'Everyman Library'. In September the same year this was followed by ten more titles, and by 1911 Chesterton had written introductions to Dickens's complete works in the series.

In *Charles Dickens* Chesterton saw Dickens as 'a mythologist rather than a novelist', as the last of mythologists and perhaps the greatest. Dickens did not always manage to make his characters men, he said, but he always managed at the least to make them gods. 'They are creatures like Punch or Father Christmas.' Mr Pickwick was a 'fairy' in that he was a being who never grew old and was always the same.

However, no man encouraged his characters as much as Dickens, Chesterton said, and to Dickens's claim to have been 'an affectionate father' to every child of his fancy, he had this to say:

He was not only an affectionate father, he was an over-indulgent father. The children of his fancy are spoilt children. They shake the house like heavy and shouting schoolboys; they smash the story to pieces like so much furniture. When we moderns write stories our characters are better controlled. But, alas! our characters are rather easier to control. We are in no danger from the gigantic gambols of creatures like Mantalini and Micawber. We are in no danger of giving our readers too much Weller or Wegg. We have not got it to give. When we experience the ungovernable sense of life which goes along with the old Dickens sense of liberty, we experience the best of the revolution. We are filled with the first of all democratic doctrines, that all men are interesting; Dickens tried to make some of his people appear dull people, but he could not keep them dull. He could not make a monotonous man. The bores in his books are brighter than the wits in other books.

The two primary dispositions of Dickens, Chesterton said, to make the flesh creep and to make the sides ache, were 'a sort of twins of his spirit', and were never far apart. And if he made the flesh creep, he did not, like the decadents, 'make the soul crawl'. Chesterton saw that, unlike other authors, Dickens created characters rather than imitating them.

Dickens is like life in the true sense – in the sense that he is akin to the living principle in us and in the universe: he is like life at least in this detail, that he is alive. His art is like life, because like life it cares for nothing outside itself, and goes on its way rejoicing. Both produce monsters with a kind of carelessness, like enormous by-products: life producing the rhinoceros, and art Mr Bunsby. ... Dickens's art is like life because, like life, it is irresponsible, because, like life, it is incredible.

Chesterton also saw that Dickens's novels had the permanence of poetry; they were not, like those of Thackeray, based on the observation of the manners of a passing period. Dickens's popularity in his own time, Chesterton thought, was because he had a literary taste akin to that of the community, for this kinship was deep and spiritual. 'Dickens was not like our ordinary demagogues and journalists. Dickens did not write what people wanted. Dickens wanted what the people wanted.'

Critics of the book were not slow to point out the obvious similarity between the author and his subject. Chesterton was a critic whose temperament was more exuberantly Dickensian than that of any of his predecessors. 'He is, like Dickens, an imaginative caricaturist, an artist in grotesque humour, an apostle of exaggeration,' wrote James Douglas in *The Throne*. '"Exaggeration," says Mr Chesterton roundly, "is the definition of art." It is certainly the definition of Dickensian art and Chestertonian art.'

Another reviewer thought the book a remarkable piece of work, but strictly speaking not a book at all. 'It is not an organic unity, it is not self-contained, it is not – taken by itself – even coherent. Like most of his other writings, it is – to borrow a figure of his own – simply a length from the flowing and mixed substance called Mr Chesterton.'

Perhaps the most interesting reaction came from Dickens's daughter, Kate Perugini, who wrote Chesterton two enthusiastic letters, saying that the book was the best appreciation of her father since the first biography by John Forster. However, she corrected him over his assertion that Dickens had fallen in love with all the Hogarth girls and had married the wrong one. As Mrs Perugini pointed out, 'At the time of the marriage her mother, the eldest of the sisters, was only eighteen, Mary between fourteen and fifteen, "very young and childish in appearance", Georgina eight and Helen three.' She went on:

My mother had no sister at that time with whom it was possible to fall in love. Or, no doubt, my father, being young and quite likely very impressionable, might have done so. As it was, he sincerely loved my mother, or thought he did, which came to the same thing, for he married her and, as you know, they did not live happy ever after, although I fancy they had several years of very great happiness indeed before my poor father found out his mistake, and before my poor mother suffered from this discovery. They were both to be pitied.

Chesterton was upset to receive the first letter, and he took Frances with him to call on Mrs Perugini, who lived not far from his parents in Kensington, in Victoria Road. He offered to put the error right in any subsequent editions, as well as to correct the impression he had given that Dickens's moods of depression had meant that the family had had to endure his railings. 'In my father's unhappiness there were no railings,' Mrs Perugini had written. 'When he was really sorrowful and he was very quiet, and depression with him never took the form of petulance. For in his unhappy moods he was singularly gentle and thoughtful for those around him.'

She was somewhat overwhelmed by the Chestertons' concern, and informed Frances that it had been chiefly for her mother's sake that she was anxious to see the matter set straight.

> From my own knowledge of her I feel sure that at the time she was engaged to my father she was a very winning and affectionate creature, and although the marriage, like many other marriages, turned out a dismal failure, I am also convinced that my dear father gained much from her refining influence and that of her family, and perhaps would never have been quite what he became without that influence.

Chesterton either remained unconvinced or he forgot all about it, because he seems to have done nothing to set the matter straight. In fact, his visit to Mrs Perugini had been little more than a courtesy visit, since he felt he had upset her by insulting her mother.

Maisie Ward cited the error over the ages of the Hogarth sisters as a typical example of 'the clash between enthusiasm and despair that fills a Chestertonian while reading any of the literary biographies. For so much is built on this theory, which the slightest investigation would have shown to be baseless.' One of the most celebrated examples of Chesterton's lack of concern for detail was the way he allowed King Alfred's left wing to oppose Guthrum's left wing on the field at Ethandune in 'The Ballad of the White Horse'. Chesterton was amused when the error was pointed out to him, 'but never bothered to alter it'.

On 2 February 1907, Chesterton entertained his *Daily News* readers on the subject of his Toy Theatre. The reason why grown-up people did·not play with toys, he said, was because it would take up more time and trouble than anything else. People had enough strength for politics and commerce and art and philosophy, but not enough strength for play. His journalistic work, which earned money, was 'not pursued with such awful persistency as that work which earned nothing'. Giving examples of the degree of concentration needed to play imaginatively, Chesterton draws from his experience of watching the children near his home in Battersea where the little girls 'worshipped their dolls in a way that reminded one not so much of play as idolatry'. It was as difficult to look after a doll, it seemed, as to look after a child. In some cases the love and care of the artistic symbol had actually become more important than the human reality it was originally meant to symbolize. He continued:

> I remember a Battersea little girl who wheeled her large baby sister stuffed into a doll's perambulator. When questioned on this course of conduct, she replied: 'I haven't got a dolly, and Baby is pretending to be my dolly.' Nature was indeed imitating art. First a doll had been a substitute for a child; afterwards a child was a mere substitute for a doll. But that opens up other matters; the point is here that such devotion takes up most of the brain and most of the life; much as if it were really the thing which it is supposed to symbolise. The point is that the man writing on motherhood is merely an educationalist; the child playing with a doll is a mother.

Such concentration of play was tiring, and Chesterton admitted to working much harder at his toy theatre than at 'any tale or article'; but the work seemed too heavy for him. As he worked at his play of *St George and the Dragon* for his theatre he kept having to break off to betake himself to lighter employments, 'such as the biographies of great men'.

If ever he found himself in any other or better world, he said, he hoped that he would have enough time to play with nothing but toy theatres, for the philosophy of toy theatres was worth any one's attention, and all the essential morals which modern men needed to learn could be deduced from this toy. The article, which was later published along with many others in *Tremendous Trifles*, was important for what Chesterton had to say about the main principle of art, as he saw it, of which for him the toy theatre was a constant reminder.

> ... art consists of limitation; ... that art is limitation. Art does not consist in expanding things. Art consists of cutting things down, as I cut down with a pair of scissors my very ugly figures of St George and the Dragon. Plato, who liked definite ideas, would like my dragon; for though the creature has few other artistic merits he is at least dragonish. The modern philosopher, who likes infinity, is quite welcome to a sheet of the plain cardboard. The most artistic thing about the theatrical art is the fact that the spectator looks at the whole thing through a window. This is true even of theatres inferior to my own;

GK's
WEEKLY

EDITED BY G.K.
CHESTERTON

OCTOBER 11 — 1934
VOL. XX.   No. 500
Registered as a Newspaper   SIXPENCE.

THE

500ᵗʰ

DRAGON

Chesterton as St. George, a cover drawn for *GK's Weekly* by Thomas Derrick
(see page 340)

even at the Court Theatre or His Majesty's you are looking through a window; an unusually large window. But the advantage of the small theatre exactly is that you are looking through a small window. Has not every one noticed how sweet and startling any landscape looks when seen through an arch? This strong, square shape, this shutting off of everything else is not only an assistance to beauty. The most beautiful part of every picture is the frame.

By reducing the scale of events it was possible to introduce larger events, Chesterton argued. On his small stage he could represent the earthquake in Jamaica or the Day of Judgement. 'Exactly in so far as it is limited, so far it could play easily with falling cities or with falling stars.'

The vast Greek philosophy could fit more easily into the small city of Athens than into the immense empire of Persia, Chesterton said. In the narrow streets of Florence Dante felt that there was room for Purgatory and Heaven and Hell. He would have been stifled by the British Empire. Great empires were necessarily prosaic; for it was beyond human power to act a great poem upon so great a scale, since you can only represent very big ideas in very small spaces.

In the June of the same year *Girl's Realm* carried an article illustrated with excellent photographs and written by George Knolleys, entitled 'Mr Chesterton and his Toy Theatre'. It included the outline of *St George and the Dragon*, and gave directions 'for those who would enjoy a fascinating pastime'. Typically, Chesterton had called his theatre the 'Battersea Problem Theatre'.

At about the same time one of Chesterton's best-known poems, 'The Secret People', was published in the first number of *The Neolith*. The theme of the poem was that the people of England had remained silent throughout their history:

> Smile at us, pay us, pass us, but do not quite forget,
> For we are the people of England, and we have not spoken yet.

In his brother's opinion, this was the poem in which Chesterton 'touches his high-water mark'. Cecil, meanwhile, having lost his place on the executive committee of the Fabian Society, had decided to leave the CSU and, together with Masterman and Noel, had 'gone over' to the Christian Social League, a far more radical group whose members 'were committed to accepting the principle of socialism'. Besides this interest and involving himself in *The New Age*, the first number of which appeared on 2 May, Cecil was working on a semi-biographical critical book, on his brother. *G.K. Chesterton: A Criticism* was published by Alston Rivers in the following year.

The year 1907 was an active one for Gilbert also, although he published no 'major' titles. He was now in even greater demand for lectures and debates, as his brother put it: 'His lectures are without number. Indeed, such is his activity that he is ever ready to undertake tasks which cannot possibly add either to his fame or his income.' Any Nonconformist minister who needed to amuse his PSA, 'any group of Tooley Street tailors who call themselves the Social Democratic League of the Human Race', according to Cecil, could draw a lecture from G.K.C. for which many reputable societies might be happy to pay more than ten pounds. This extraordinary demand on his brother's time, Cecil said, recalled 'the propagandist fervour of Mr Bernard Shaw in his earlier days'. However, there was a difference between Chesterton and Shaw: Shaw was a socialist, 'a member of a fighting society, trying to help on a practical movement which he really hoped to see succeed'; whereas Cecil saw his brother as standing for no one but himself, and, 'however much he may deny the existence of "the inevitable"', he could hardly hope for the conversion of modern London to Chestertonism through his lectures. 'He is merely a man expressing his opinions, because he enjoys expressing them,' said Cecil. 'He would express them as readily and as well to a man he met in an omnibus.'

He went on to speak of his brother's need for comradeship; it was a 'necessity of life to him'. His energy seemed to be guided by some inner force, which was not ambition or the desire for fame. 'He is, I should say, the last man in the world to be moved powerfully by ambition, and most of his activities are the last upon which a really ambitious man would ever enter. It is sheer pugnacity and the zest of self-exposition that keeps him so constantly to the front, and forbids him to allow any opportunity of displaying and defending his ideas to pass unused.'

Politically, Cecil saw his brother as born out of his time, he was a 'Tory of the seventeenth or early eighteenth century'. In Bolingbroke's cabinet, for example, he would have found an atmosphere to his liking, and found men

... sympathetic with the national aspirations of the native Irish. He

would have found men who disliked Imperialism and foreign complications, and held that our fleets and armies ought to confine their
energies to the defence of the actual soil of England. He would have
found men who hated plutocracy and the power of riches created
by trade, who loved the life of the cornfields and desired a free peasantry. But, alas! he was born two centuries too late, and by dint
of keeping so far behind his time has acquired the reputation of
an advanced Radical.

At this time that other 'advanced Radical', Belloc, was actively engaged
in the House of Commons. His maiden speech was described in *The
Times* as 'dangerous rant', and had been mostly on the subject of Chinese
labour in South Africa. It is likely that Chesterton had been in the
public gallery to hear him, and was, no doubt, excluding his friend
when he wrote, 'The speaking in the House of Commons is not only
worse than speaking was. It is worse than speaking is, in all or almost
all other places in small debating clubs or casual dinners. England
shows us the blind leading the people who can see.'

It is easy to see that over the period between 1907 and 1911 Belloc
came to exercise an ever-increasing influence over Chesterton's thinking; and it was during that period that there developed the political
philosophy which, for want of a better name, came to be known as
Distributism. But Belloc's influence may be seen too in the gradual
fermenting of what is the most serious blemish on Chesterton's character: I mean his attitude to the Jewish people. There should be no getting
away from the fact that Chesterton became, even if he was not already,
strongly anti-semitic during the years after 1907. Chesterton himself
always hotly denied that he was an anti-semite; it was something no
Christian ought to be, he once said, 'But every Christian ought to be
a Zionist.' Nevertheless, the facts are there to show that in spite of
what he would have considered a perfectly rational approach to the
subject, Chesterton became bitterly, not to say absurdly hostile, particularly when later in life he found himself answering questions from the
platform.

The reference to 'a cringing Jew' in 'The Secret People' might be
regarded as merely a stock image of the Jewish money-lender borrowed
from Shakespeare; but in retrospect, beside numerous other such images
in Chesterton's verse, it becomes more noticeable, as do several references to the ghetto, the tribe, and the use of mock-Biblical language

with regard to the Solomon brothers in several of his letters to Bentley while they were all still at school. This passage, for instance:

I may remark that the children of Israel have not gone unto Horeb, neither unto Sittim, but unto the land that is called Shropshire they went, and abode therein. And they came unto a city, even unto the city that is called Shrewsbury, and there they builded themselves an home, where they might abide. And their home was in the land that was called Castle Street and their home was the 25th tabernacle in that land.

In another letter to Bentley, in which he outlines some arrangement for a meeting or perhaps a party, he wrote:

No Jews; that is, if I except the elder tribe coming over on Sunday to take me to see Oldershaw ... I tried an experiment with Lawrence on Friday night, to see if he would accept on its real ground of friendliness our semitic jocularity; so I took the bull by the horns and said that 'I would walk with them to the gates of the Ghetto.' As he laughed with apparent amusement and even M.S. betrayed a favouring smile, I don't think we need fear the misunderstanding which, I must say, would be imminent in the case of less sensible and well-feeling pagans.

The Solomons may well have laughed, just as I have seen my Irish friends laugh at 'Paddy' jokes – that particularly tedious pastime of a certain sort of Englishman – and the Solomons remained Chesterton's friends for life: Lawrence Solomon even moved out to Beaconsfield to be near his friend. No, there is no denying Chesterton had many very close Jewish friends, including Maurice Baring, though Baring had become a Catholic; but in spite of these close friendships there is always noticeable an underlying feeling of superiority in Chesterton's manner, which is probably aroused by a strange fear. Chesterton would have claimed that he liked Jews, but disliked Judaism. When he was interviewed for *The Jewish Chronicle* in April 1911, he attempted to explain his position, but the manner in which he expressed himself reveals this underlying resentment.

Oh, yes, I know they call themselves, for instance, in this country, Englishmen, and they are patriotic and loyal, and hold land and give liberally to English institutions, subsidise party funds, become peers and members of Parliament, entertain, hunt and shoot, and all the rest of it. Still the Jew is not an Englishman, because his nationality is not English. They are something different and in many ways very much better. Still, being better, they cannot be the same. They are allied, and rightly and justifiably, to their own people of their own race who are not English even in point of citizenship – Jews in Germany, Russia, France, everywhere.

Chesterton's answer was the Zionist answer.

Till the Jew discovers he is a separate race, with a history of its own, and a future which to be worthy he must make his own. Till thus finding himself the Jew perceives the necessity for a habitat, a centrum, wherein he can develop that which he now lacks, nationality. You see, I am not an anti-semite, I am a Zionist.

To anyone who suggested that Zionism and anti-semitism were one and the same thing, he would have replied,

It is equivalent to saying that a man who is anxious for the preservation of the supremacy of the English race is an anglophobe, or that a mountain is a valley. ... I want the Jew to form a key that will fit into his own door. I believe Zionism would bring to the Jew territorial patriotism which he now lacks. It would assuredly allow him to develop his own culture in arts, in literature, in science, and it would put an end to his eternal entanglement of mutual wrong of which he is the unhappy cause between himself and the nations with whom he lives.

It is a weak defence to say that Chesterton's attitude was in no way unusual at the time, or that he had accepted too readily Belloc's attitude to the 'Jew question' – the assertion that there was 'an international money-power which was largely Jewish and which attempted to control the policies of European nations'. But he did not go so far as his brother, who was fanatically convinced that 'there was a Jewish conspiracy for the overthrow of Christian civilization and that every calamity that befell a Christian could always be traced back to a Jewish origin'.

Chesterton would have claimed that he was being constructive. He believed Zionism to be right. Otherwise, he said, history would go on repeating itself for the Jew, and his future would be as his past.

My point is this: that the Jews being landless, naturally alternate between too much power and too little, that the Jew millionaire is too safe and the Jew pedlar too harassed. It is not likely that the millionaire amongst you will be otherwise than the very few. Therefore for the many, I am afraid the future will be as the past has been – murder, outrage, persecution, insult, moral and physical torture, wandering unrest, oscillations of comfortless abasing, and uncertain toleration with grinding, evervating, cramping disabilities: in short, the Jew – at least for the most part – always burnt.

The Romance of Orthodoxy

1908–1909

On 4 January 1908 Chesterton's article 'Why I am not a Socialist' appeared in *The New Age*. This was the second article in what has become known as the 'Chesterton-Belloc-Wells-Shaw Controversy', which had begun with Belloc's 'Thoughts about Modern Thought' in the previous month. Chesterton believed strongly in the mass of the common people who were 'caught in the trap of a terrible machinery, harried by a shameful economic cruelty, surrounded by an ugliness and desolation never endured before among men, stunted by a stupid and provincial religion'. They were, he said, 'the sanest, jolliest and most reliable part of the community'. Just as imperialism had been foisted upon them by the interests of commerce and international banking, so socialism would be imposed on them by the interests of intellectuals, 'decorative artists and Oxford dons and journalists and Countesses on the spree'. What both he and Belloc wanted for the people was an organized Christian state.

In answer to Chesterton, H.G.Wells admitted that even an organized Christian state was nearer to the organized state he and Shaw desired than 'our present plutocracy', though he thought their ideals would have to fight some day. He felt, however, that 'to fight now was to let in the enemy'. He agreed with Chesterton that giving '– oneself out of love and fellowship – is the salt of life'.

Chesterton's article had included yet another of his memorable sayings. In his argument that landlordism was the negation of property, he said, 'It is the negation of property that the Duke of Westminster should own whole streets and squares of London; just as it would be the negation of marriage if he had all the women living in one harem.'

The fourth article in the controversy was provided by Shaw. In his *Belloc and Chesterton*, while admitting that his own creation of the

celebrated G.B.S. was 'about as real as a pantomime ostrich', he presented for the first time the four-legged pantomime elephant, the 'Chesterbelloc'. In Shaw's opinion this chimera was made up of two parts
that were ill-matched, and that as Belloc was the forelegs Chesterton
was obliged to follow. 'For Belloc's sake he says he is not a Socialist.'
Shaw made the odd observation, which I have not seen made anywhere
else, that Chesterton was a typical Frenchman.

He is the son of his mother, and his mother's name is Marie Louise
Grosjean. Who his father was will never matter to anyone who has
once seen G.K.Chesterton, or at least seen as much of him as the
limited range of human vision can take in at once. If ever a Grosjean
lived and wrote his name on the sky by towering before it, that man
is G.K.C. France did not break the mould in which it formed Rabelais.
It got to Campden Hill in the year 1874; and it never turned out
a more complete Frenchman than it did then.

In contrast Shaw saw Belloc, who, of course, was half French, as
neither French nor English, but beside Grosjean Shaw thought he
seemed Irish; anyway 'not English, and therefore for ever incomprehensible to Wells'. It was true that Wells and Belloc later became bitter
enemies, whereas Wells found Chesterton an admirable companion and,
discovering they shared a love for Toy Theatre, invited him to stay
at Easton.

Shaw had ended his article with a desire to dismantle the monster
and free Chesterton from the domination of 'Hilaire Forelegs' for, he
said, in Battersea Park a great force was in danger of being wasted.
Shaw had not released the pressure he had been putting on Chesterton
to write a play. On 1 March he wrote:

What about that play? It is no use trying to answer me in *The New
Age*: the real answer to my article is the play. I have tried fair means:
the *New Age* article was the inauguration of an assault below the
belt. I shall deliberately destroy your credit as an essayist, as a journalist, as a critic, as a Liberal, as everything that offers your laziness
a refuge, until starvation and shame drive you to serious dramatic
participation. I shall repeat my public challenge to you; vaunt my
superiority; insult your corpulence; torture Belloc; if necessary call
on you and steal your wife's affections by intellectual and athletic
displays, until you contribute something to the British drama.

Nothing could save Chesterton now, Shaw said, except a rebirth as a dramatist. He had done his turn and now it was time to call on Chesterton 'to do a man's work'. The letter ended on a cryptic note: 'Lord help you if you ever lose your gift of speech, G.K.C.! Don't forget that the race is only struggling out of its dumbness, and that it is only in moments of inspiration that we get out a sentence. All the rest is padding.' Shaw had to remain frustrated in his efforts, and the only theatrical venture Chesterton worked on was when in company with Wells, who had a 'vigorous and unaffected readiness for a lark', he performed a pantomime about Sidney Webb.

In February Chesterton's second novel, *The Man Who Was Thursday*, was published. In his dedication verse to Bentley Chesterton offered 'a tale of those old fears, even of those emptied hells'. It was safe to tell the tale, he said, now that fortified by 'marriage and a creed' he was able to face up to those times of their youth when there had been a 'sick cloud upon the soul' and 'huge devils hid the stars'.

On its title-page *The Man Who Was Thursday* was described as 'A Nightmare', and it was C.S.Lewis who first pointed out the Kafkaesque quality of the story. Chesterton, like Kafka, Lewis said, 'gives a powerful picture of the loneliness and bewilderment which each one of us encounters in his (apparently) single-handed struggle with the universe'. He thought that Chesterton, by 'attributing a more complicated disguise to the universe, and admitting the exhilaration as well as the terror of the struggle', had got in rather more, and his novel was therefore better balanced than any of Kafka's.

This nightmarish story, which Monsignor Ronald Knox said was 'rather like the *Pilgrim's Progress* in the style of the *Pickwick Papers*', is certainly one of Chesterton's best. Beginning in Saffron Park, a scarcely disguised Bedford Park, where 'a man who stepped into its social atmosphere felt as if he had stepped into a written comedy', the story tells how a Christian poet, Gabriel Syme, who also happens to be a Scotland Yard detective, initially led on by Lucian Gregory, an anarchist poet, infiltrates a supposed anarchist plot to destroy the world. The Central Anarchist Council consists of seven members, each known by the name of one of the days of the week, and Syme is given the name of Thursday. In the course of the nightmare Syme becomes involved with each member of the Council in turn, and he seems to explore an ever-increasing hellishness of both will and intellect. It turns out at the end of each episode that each member of the Council is also

a detective sent out to unmask the plot under the orders of the Police
Chief, of whom Syme had only seen the huge back.

Only the President of the Council, Sunday, remains elusive, and
as the six detectives pursue Sunday in the wildest chase of all, he uses,
in the inconsequential manner of dreams, a cab, a fire-engine, an elephant and finally a balloon, as means of escape. At last, in Sunday's
own back garden, robed in garments denoting the six days of God's
Creation, the six face Sunday, who turns out to be the Police Chief
who had given them their orders; but when he is asked who and what
he is, he replies without moving: 'I am the Sabbath. I am the peace
of God.' The nightmare ends with the poet, Gregory, the only real
anarchist, appearing before them all, since 'when the sons of God came
to present themselves before the Lord . . . Satan came also among them'.
Gregory admits he would destroy the world if he could. He accuses
the seven of having found happiness, but Syme replies:

> 'It is not true that we have never been broken. We have been broken
> upon the wheel. It is not true that we have never descended from
> these thrones. We have descended into hell. We were complaining
> of unforgettable miseries even at the very moment when this man
> entered insolently to accuse us of happiness. I repel the slander;
> we have not been happy. I can answer for every one of the great
> guards of Law whom he has accused. At least –'

> He had turned his eyes so as to see suddenly the great face of
> Sunday, which wore a strange smile.

> 'Have you,' he cried in a dreadful voice, 'have you ever suffered?'

> As he gazed, the great face grew to an awful size, grew larger
> than the colossal mask of Memnon, which had made him scream
> as a child. It grew larger and larger, filling the whole sky; then every-
> thing went black. Only in the blackness before it entirely destroyed
> his brain he seemed to hear a distant voice saying the common-place
> text that he had heard somewhere. 'Can ye drink of the cup that
> I drink of?'

When the 'vision' ended Syme could only remember that he had
'swooned before the face of Sunday', but he could not remember how
he came to be there. 'Gradually and naturally he knew that he had
been walking along a country lane with an easy and conversational companion.' He felt as though he were now in possession of some 'impossible
good news'.

It was as though Chesterton's old dialogue with his diabolist fellow student at the university had at last been resolved. The allegorical meaning of the ending of *The Man Who Was Thursday* seems at first sight obvious enough, but Chesterton years later explained that he had never intended Sunday to be God. The point was, he said, that the whole story was a nightmare of things, not as they are, but as they seemed to be to a young half-pessimist of the 1890s. 'The old ogre who appears brutal but is also cryptically benevolent is not so much God, in the sense of religion or irreligion, but rather Nature as it appears to the pantheist, whose pantheism is struggling out of pessimism.'

The critics were mostly agreed that Chesterton had produced an extraordinary fantasy, behind which, as Frank Harris noted, lurked 'a great, serious mission (for Mr Chesterton, like all clowns, is intensely serious)'. An unsigned review in *The Daily Telegraph*, possibly written by Bentley, said that 'wild as are the incidents of this phantasmagoric farce, the author has charged so much of it with thought that we feel that there is in him no small share of that genius which informs that wisest of all persons, the Shakespearean fool'. Perhaps the reviewer had been one who knew how Chesterton, like the fool, had known the terrors of the storm and the empty loneliness of the heath.

During the summer months of 1908, having Frances's health in mind, the Chestertons rented a house in Rye, the town which Chesterton described as 'a wonderful inland island, crowned with a town as with a citadel, like a hill in a mediaeval picture'. Their house, as it happened, was directly next door to Lamb House, an 'old oak-panelled mansion which had attracted, one might almost say across the Atlantic, the fine aquiline eye of Henry James'. Chesterton remembered how James, who had steeped his sensitive psychology in everything that seemed most antiquatedly and aristocratically English, had cherished his particular house with its rows of family portraits as though they were family ghosts. He spoke in a manner which Chesterton described as 'gracefully groping'.

It seems Wells may have suggested the house to the Chestertons for he did not live far away, and he was a frequent caller on James, and 'would make irreverent darts and dashes through the sombre house and the sacred garden' and drop notes to Chesterton over the garden wall.

On hearing that Chesterton had arrived at the house next door, James made a courtesy call, taking with him his brother William, the philos-

opher. In conversation, Chesterton found Henry James more strict about
the rules of artistic arrangement than he had expected. He complimented
Chesterton on his writing, but expressed surprise that he managed to
write so much. Chesterton suspected him of meaning 'why rather than
how'. In the midst of this rather staid conversation – although William
James had been breezy enough – there had been the most odd sound
like that of 'an impatient fog-horn'. The Chestertons soon realized that
the 'Gilbert! Gilbert!' was no fog-horn but Belloc bellowing for 'bacon
and beer'.

Chesterton had believed Belloc to be in France walking with a friend,
but the pair, having run out of money, had landed back in England,
many days unshaven, and in borrowed clothes, looking like tramps.
Describing the incongruity of the scene, Chesterton many years later
wrote:

> Henry James had a name for being subtle; but I think that situation
> was too subtle for him. I doubt to this day whether he, of all men,
> did not miss the irony of the best comedy in which he ever played
> a part. He left America because he loved Europe, and all that was
> meant by England or France; the gentry, the gallantry, the traditions
> of lineage and locality, the life that had been lived beneath the old
> portraits in oak-panelled rooms. And there, on the other side of the
> tea-table, was Europe, was the old thing that made France and Eng-
> land, the posterity of the English squires and the French soldiers;
> ragged, unshaven, shouting for beer, shameless above all shades of
> poverty and wealth; sprawling, indifferent, secure. And what looked
> across at it was still the Puritan refinement of Boston; and the space
> it looked across was wider than the Atlantic.

On 10 September a collection of Chesterton's articles 'upon current
or rather flying subjects' from the *Illustrated London News* was published
by Methuen under the title *All Things Considered*. The essays were somewhat overshadowed by the great book, *Orthodoxy*, which John Lane
brought out on the twenty-fifth of the same month. Speaking about
his past work at about this time Chesterton had written:

> I have never written a lie because I thought it was funny; but I have
> often taken a rather babyish pleasure in truth because it was a funny
> truth. It is one thing to invent a monster who does not exist; it is
> another thing to discern that the rhinoceros does exist and then to

take pleasure in the fact that it looks as if he didn't. But it is not for this purpose that I introduce the difficult question of the too easy paradox. I introduce it because I wish to make a confession; not the dirty confession of having ever been a sophist, but the ordinary human confession of having been an ass. If ever I glance now at my earliest books and articles I agree with everything that anyone could possibly say against them. I was not insincere, but I certainly was intolerably showy and assertive. I never said what I did not believe; but I certainly strained my voice hideously in saying what I did believe. And I have been punished exactly in the funniest and most fitting style; I have discovered of my truths not that they weren't true but that they were not mine. When I fancied that I stood alone I was really in the ridiculous position of being backed by all Christendom. It may be, Heaven forgive me, that I did try to be original; but I only succeeded in working out a dim copy of Christian traditions. I did exaggerate and make a foolish fuss. I did attempt to found a heresy of my own.

The same thoughts were expressed, and many of the same sentences used, in the introduction to *Orthodoxy*, although Chesterton extended and explained them more fully. 'I did try to found a heresy of my own,' he said, 'and when I had put the last touches to it, I discovered that it was orthodoxy.' He tried to be original; and he had tried to be some ten minutes in advance of the truth and found that he was eighteen hundred years behind it.

Orthodoxy, as I said earlier, was written in answer to the challenge made when, finding himself included in Chesterton's list of modern 'heretics', G. S. Street had commented: 'I will begin to worry about my philosophy when Mr Chesterton has given us his.' In his answer Chesterton argued from one standpoint only, for 'to show that a faith or a philosophy is true from every standpoint would be too big an undertaking even for a much bigger book.'

Chesterton wished to set forth his faith as particularly answering a double spiritual need, 'the need for that mixture of the familiar and the unfamiliar which Christendom had rightly named romance. For the very word 'romance' has in it the mystery and ancient meaning of Rome.' He was writing for those who desired an active and imaginative life, picturesque and full of poetical curiosity, a life such as western man at any rate seems to have desired. 'If any man says that extinction is better than existence or blank existence better than variety and adventure', then he was not one of the ordinary people for whom Chesterton was writing.

It is important to realize that by mentioning 'Rome' Chesterton was not implying that orthodoxy was Roman Catholicism, though he later came to see that to all intents and purposes it was. 'These essays are concerned,' he said, 'only to discuss the actual fact that the central Christian theology (sufficiently summarized in the Apostles' Creed) is the best root of energy and sound ethics.'

Chesterton began with the proposition that although moderns denied the existence of sin, they had not yet denied the existence of a lunatic asylum. 'We all agree still that there is a collapse of the intellect as unmistakable as a falling house. Men may deny Hell, but not, as yet, Hanwell [a lunatic asylum].' To begin with, he followed the same argument he had followed in his correspondence with Blatchford, whose name appeared several times in the chapter, 'The Suicide of Thought'; but he extended his argument against rationalism by making the claim that the modern world was not evil, but in some ways was 'far too good'. The modern world, he argued, was full of 'wild and wasted virtues'. When a religious scheme is shattered, as Christianity was shattered at the Reformation, it is not merely the vices that are let loose.

> The vices are, indeed, let loose, and they wander and do damage. But the virtues are let loose also; and the virtues wander more wildly, and the virtues do more terrible damage. The modern world is full of the old Christian virtues gone mad. The virtues have gone mad because they have been isolated from each other and are wandering alone.

This idea of virtue doing damage is uniquely Chestertonian. He cites Blatchford as a case of someone who had gone mad on 'the merely mystical and almost irrational virtue of charity. He has a strange idea that he will make it easier to forgive sins by saying that there are no sins to forgive.' Chesterton then takes each virtue in turn and shows how, used in isolation, they cause damage. Modesty had settled on the organ of conviction where it was never meant to be.

> A man was meant to be doubtful about himself, but undoubting about the truth; this has been exactly reversed. Nowadays the part of a

man that man does assert is exactly the part he ought not to assert
– himself. The part he doubts is exactly the part he ought not to
doubt – the Divine Reason. Huxley preached a humility content to
learn from Nature. But the new sceptic is so humble that he doubts
if he can ever learn. Thus we should be wrong if we had said hastily
that there is no humility typical of our time; but it so happens that
it is practically a more poisonous humility than the wildest prostrations
of the ascetic. The old humility was a spur that prevented a man
from stopping; not a nail in his boot that prevented him from going
on. For the old humility made a man doubtful about his efforts, which
might make him work harder. But the new humility makes a man
doubtful about his aims, which will make him stop working altogether.

Chesterton then moved on to what he referred to as 'The Ethics
of Elfland', where he set out the philosophy he had 'learnt in the nursery'.
He had always vaguely felt that the infinite varieties and constant repeti-
tions in nature were miracles, in the sense that they were wonderful,
but now he began to think them miracles in the stricter sense that they
were wilful. 'In short; I had always believed that the world involved
magic; now I thought that perhaps it involved a magician.'
He next set out his ultimate attitudes towards life, what he called
'the soils for the seeds of doctrine'.

I felt in my bones; first, that this world does not explain itself. It
may be a miracle with a supernatural explanation; it may be a conjuring
trick, with a natural explanation. But the explanation of the conjuring
trick, if it is to satisfy me, will have to be better than the natural
explanations I have heard. The thing is magic true or false. Second,
I came to feel as if magic must have a meaning, and meaning must
have someone to mean it. There was something personal in the world,
as in a work of art; whatever it meant it meant violently. Third, I
thought this purpose beautiful in its old design, in spite of its defects,
such as dragons. Fourth, that the proper form of thanks to it is some
form of humility and restraint: we should thank God for beer and
Burgundy by not drinking too much of them. We owed, also, an
obedience to whatever made us. And last, and strangest, there had
come into my mind a vague and vast impression that in some way
all good was a remnant to be stored and held sacred out of some
primordial ruin. Man had saved his good as Crusoe saved his goods:
he had saved them from a wreck. All this I felt and the age gave

me no encouragement to feel it. And all this time I had not even thought of Christian theology.

Once he had prepared the ground for 'the seeds of doctrine' Chesterton argued the case for orthodoxy against the extremes of optimism and pessimism, although he could not help thinking that the definition of each given by a little girl was the best: 'An optimist is a man who looks after your eyes, and a pessimist is a man who looks after your feet.' There was even a sort of allegorical truth in it, he said, 'for there might, perhaps, be a profitable distinction drawn between that more dreary thinker who thinks merely of our contact with the earth from moment to moment, and that happier thinker who considers rather our primary power of vision and of choice of road'. Chesterton said that his acceptance of the universe was not optimism, but something more akin to patriotism, a matter of primary loyalty. 'The world is not a lodging-house at Brighton, which we are to leave because it is miserable. It is the fortress of our family, with the flag flying on the turret, and the more miserable it is the less we should leave it.' The point was not that this world was too sad to love or too glad not to love: the point was that when you did love a thing, its gladness was a reason for loving it, and its sadness was a reason for loving it more.

All optimistic thoughts about England and all pessimistic thoughts about her were alike reasons for the English patriot. Similarly, optimism and pessimism were alike arguments for the cosmic patriot.

Men did not love Rome because she was great. She was great because they had loved her.

The evil of the pessimist was not that he chastised gods and men, but he did not love what he chastised; he had not 'this primary and supernatural loyalty to things'. On the other hand, the evil of the optimist was that in his wish to defend the honour of the world he defended the indefensible. He was the 'jingo of the universe who said, "My cosmos, right or wrong"', and whitewashed the world rather than washed it.

Orthodox Christianity steered a course between the two extremes, although it had so often been accused, at one and the same time, of being too optimistic about the universe and of being too pessimistic about the world. Was it, Chesterton wondered, that Christianity had felt just as he had, a need for a first loyalty to things, and then for a ruinous reform of things? To those who argued that Christianity might well have provided answers in the past, that some of her dogmas might have been credible in the twelfth century, but were totally irrelevant in the twentieth, Chesterton replied,

> You might as well say that a certain philosophy can be believed on Mondays, but cannot be believed on Tuesdays. You might as well say of a view of the cosmos that it was suitable to half-past three, but not suitable to half-past four. What a man can believe depends upon his philosophy, not upon the clock or the century. If a man believes in unalterable natural law, he cannot believe any miracle in any age. If a man believes in a will behind law, he can believe any miracle in any age.

Christianity came as the answer to a riddle and not as 'the last truism uttered after a long talk'; and to have survived after being attacked mercilessly on all sides was one of the signs of its supernatural origin. However, to strip Christianity of its armour of dogma, as some suggested, was, Chesterton said, like stripping a man of his 'armour of bones'; and it was the 'thrilling romance of orthodoxy' that it had so defined its doctrine in order that 'men might enjoy general human liberties'. In a passage of exceptional power his chapter, 'The Paradoxes of Christianity', came to a close.

> This is the thrilling romance of orthodoxy. People have fallen into a foolish habit of speaking of orthodoxy as something heavy, humdrum and safe. There never was anything so perilous or so exciting as orthodoxy. It was sanity: and to be sane is more dramatic than to be mad. It was the equilibrium of a man behind madly rushing horses, seeming to stoop this way and to sway that, yet in every attitude having the grace of statuary and the accuracy of arithmetic. The Church in its early days went fierce and fast with any warhorse; yet it is utterly unhistoric to say that she merely went mad along one idea, like a vulgar fanaticism. She swerved to left and right, so as exactly to avoid enormous obstacles. She left on one hand the huge bulk of Arianism, buttressed by all the worldly powers to make Christianity too worldly. The next instant she was swerving to avoid an orientalism, which would have made it too unworldly. The orthodox Church never took the tame course or accepted the conventions; the orthodox church was never respectable. It would have been easier to have accepted

the earthly power of the Arians. It would have been easy, in the Calvinistic seventeenth century, to fall into the bottomless pit of predesti-
nation. It is easy to be a madman: it is easy to be a heretic. It is
always easy to be a modernist; as it is easy to be a snob. To have
fallen into any of those open traps of error and exaggeration which
fashion after fashion and sect after sect set along the historic path
of Christendom – that would indeed have been simple. It is always
simple to fall; there are an infinity of angles at which one falls, only
one at which one stands. To have fallen into any one of the fads
from Gnosticism to Christian Science would indeed have been
obvious and tame. But to have avoided them all has been one whirling
adventure; and in my vision the heavenly chariot flies thundering
through the ages, the dull heresies sprawling and prostrate, the wild
truth reeling but erect.

The arguments about small points of theology that so often aroused
the derision of the Church's enemies – usually those who did not care
even about large points of theology – were essential to keep the balance
right, for, as Chesterton pointed out, it may have been a matter of an
inch in the shift of emphasis, but 'an inch is everything when you are
balancing'.

Many of the sects that had broken away from the main stem of orthodoxy, many of whom were proud to consider themselves branches of
that stem, those that had, as it were, 'fallen off balance' – and even
those who claimed that the stem had tottered to such an extent that
they had to break away in order to restore equilibrium – still survive
today and indeed, Chesterton would have argued, keep people away
from the truth. Many of these still hold to some doctrine; but to those
who seek to hold to no doctrine, except some vague doctrine of the
Inner Light, he had this to say: 'If I were to say that Christianity came
into the world specially to destroy the doctrine of the Inner Light, that
would be an exaggeration, but it would be very much nearer the truth.'
Such people tended to be 'unselfish egoists', he said.

An unselfish egoist is a man who has pride without the excuse of
passion. Of all conceivable forms of enlightenment the worst is what
these people call the Inner Light. Of all horrible religions the most
horrible is the worship of the god within. Any one who knows any
body knows how it would work; any one who knows any one from
the Higher Thought Centre knows how it does work. That Jones

shall worship the god within turns out ultimately to mean that Jones shall worship Jones. Let Jones worship the sun or moon, anything rather than the Inner Light; let Jones worship cats or crocodiles, if he can find any in the street, but not the god within. Christianity came into the world firstly in order to assert with violence that a man had not only to look inwards, but to look outwards, to behold with astonishment and enthusiasm a divine company and a divine captain. The only fun of being a Christian was that a man was not left alone with the Inner Light, but definitely recognised an outer light, fair as the sun, clear as the moon, terrible as an army with banners.

One would not have to look far to see what Chesterton would have said to our more liberal theologians, to those who teach a 'New Theology' that turns out to be nothing but a hotch-potch of the old tired heresies that the Church managed to 'avoid' long ago.

The only thing which is still old-fashioned enough to reject miracles is the New Theology. For some extraordinary reason, there is a fixed notion that it is more liberal to disbelieve in miracles than to believe in them. Why, I cannot imagine, nor can anybody tell me. For some inconceivable cause a 'broad' or 'liberal' clergyman always means a man who wishes at least to diminish the number of miracles; it never means a man who wishes to increase that number. It always means a man who is free to believe that Christ came out of his grave; it never means a man who is free to believe that his own aunt came out of her grave. It is common to find trouble in a parish because the parish priest cannot admit that St Peter walked on the water; yet how rarely do we find trouble in a parish because the clergyman says that his father walked on the Serpentine.

Finally, Chesterton brought his long argument to a close with what is the strongest argument of all, namely, that orthodoxy was the principal source of joy.

The mass of men have been forced to be gay about the little things, but sad about the big ones. Nevertheless (I offer my last dogma defiantly) it is not native to man to be so. Man is more himself, man is more manlike, when joy is the fundamental thing in him, and grief the superficial. Melancholy should be an innocent interlude, a tender and fugitive frame of mind; praise should be the permanent pulsation of the soul. Pessimism is at best an emotional half-holiday; joy is the uproarious labour by which all things live. Yet, according to the apparent estate of man as seen by the pagan or the agnostic, this primary need of human nature can never be fulfilled. Joy ought to be expansive; but for the agnostic it must be contracted, it must cling to one corner of the world. Grief ought to be a concentration; but for the agnostic its desolation is spread through an unthinkable eternity. This is what I call being born upside down. The sceptic may truly be said to be topsy-turvy; for his feet are dancing upwards in idle ecstasies, while his brain is in the abyss. To the modern man the heavens are actually below the earth. The explanation is simple; he is standing on his head; which is a very weak pedestal to stand on.

Chesterton ended by saying that even Christ restrained his joy, because:

there was in that shattering personality a thread that must be called shyness. There was something that He hid from all men when He went up a mountain to pray. There was something that He covered constantly by abrupt silence or impetuous isolation. There was some one thing that was too great for God to show to us when He walked upon our earth; and I have sometimes fancied that it was his mirth.

Chesterton dedicated *Orthodoxy* to his mother, in fitting contrast to the dedication of *Heretics* to his father. Marie Louise in all probability did not appreciate the importance of the book, but she would have felt proud to see it described as 'an antidote to insanity', and as a far more satisfactory bible than Carlyle's *Sartor Resartus*, for 'with equal earnestness and far more genuine humanity' it upheld a far more definite creed. Some years earlier Chesterton had written:

> My mother in whose soul abide
> Perversity and secret pride
> In all she loves: no toils control
> Her humorous mutiny of soul.

It was largely to allay his own perversity and secret pride and to bring order to his own humorous mutiny of soul that he had written his book.

Photographs of Chesterton at this time show him to have been grossly overweight and bloated; but his mother did little to support Frances in her attempt to restrict his diet. Whenever the couple visited Warwick Gardens 'the table groaned with salmon, veal cutlets, cream meringues,

all the things of which Gilbert was most fond, with lashings of Burgundy
and crème de menthe', and she would heap his plate as she had always
done, while Frances looked on, concerned and really unhappy. Another
problem which began to reveal itself at this time was the state of Gilbert's
teeth. Like his mother, he never seems to have visited a dentist, and
his teeth when he smiled were noticeably nicotine-stained and in poor
condition.

Frances did her best to keep some kind of a check on Gilbert, but
like him she took to making jokes about his size. 'I am off to seek
my Mighty Atom,' she was heard to have remarked one day when Gilbert
was late for a meal. It must have been at about this time that an acquaintance described Chesterton as 'so grotesquely fat that he could not dress
himself, he used to appear in his socks at breakfast, eat hugely, and
then go out into the garden with a pad of paper and a packet of cigarettes.
In the course of a couple of hours there would be a ring of cigarettes
on the grass around him.' In fact, Chesterton preferred to smoke 'interminable cigars, his favourite small, black, strong cheroots, which he
always carried in a paper packet'.

The early months of 1909 were busy with numerous lecture engagements, and always in the background there was the thought of moving
away from London. Chesterton had long been aware that a lot of things
that were supposed to be English were simply London, and there is
no evidence to suggest that he was deeply bothered about the prospect
of moving. Unlike Cecil and Ada Jones, for whom the idea of Gilbert
leaving London was 'as though, in the days of Queen Anne, it had
been proposed to transport Dr Johnson to the Cotswolds', Chesterton
had no resentment and was pleased to be able to please Frances in
this way. Nevertheless, Fleet Street was buzzing with rumours, and
for a time it was thought the Chestertons were about to retire to the
Yorkshire Moors. It is possible that such a move was discussed, for
Frances would have enjoyed being close to the Steinthals, and Fr O'Connor was becoming an even closer friend; but it would have been totally
impracticable. In later years, Chesterton recalled that both he and
Frances had known from the earliest days of their marriage that London
would never be their 'real place of abode'. He described how they had
first visited Beaconsfield by taking a train of unknown destination and
arriving in Slough.

and from there [we] set out walking with even less notion of where

we were going. And in that fashion we passed through the large
and quiet cross-roads of a sort of village, and stayed at an inn called
the White Hart. We asked the name of the place and were told that
it was called Beaconsfield (I mean of course that it was called Becons-
field and not Beaconsfield), and we said to each other: 'This is the
sort of place where some day we will make our home.'

So it was that by the summer of 1909 negotiations were under way
for the leasing of Overroads, the small house which at the time was
surrounded by open fields, and which would be their home for the
next thirteen years.

During the third week in August Chesterton's *George Bernard Shaw*
was published by John Lane. In his introduction to the first edition
Chesterton wrote, 'Most people either say that they agree with Bernard
Shaw or that they do not understand him. I am the only person who
understands him, and I do not agree with him.' It was a bold boast,
and a somewhat mean response to all that Shaw had attempted on his
behalf, although it is true Chesterton had not sought his aid. One might
even say that Shaw had become a bore in his efforts to bring about
Chesterton's début in the theatre; but the publication of Chesterton's
book was to make no difference to Shaw's determination in this regard.
When the book was shown him, Shaw insisted on reviewing it himself
for *The Nation*. 'This book is what everybody expected it to be: the
best work of literary art I have yet provoked,' he wrote; but he was
undoubtedly hurt by it. 'Everything about me which Mr Chesterton
had to divine, he divined miraculously. But everything that he could
have ascertained easily by reading my own plain directions on the bottle,
as it were, remains for him a muddled and painful problem solved
by a comically wrong guess.' However, Shaw was only able to take
up Chesterton on points of detail, while Chesterton was not so much
interested in what Shaw wrote as in the processes of thought that lay
behind what he wrote. He was quite convinced that Shaw was hiding
something. 'Shaw is like the Venus de Milo,' he said, 'all that there
is of him is admirable.'

Chesterton saw Shaw as the 'greatest of the modern Puritans and
perhaps the last'. As such, much of what he wrote would of necessity
be error, though he might have been thinking partly of himself when
he wrote, 'The truth is that the very rapidity of such a man's mind
makes him seem slow in getting to the point. It is positively because

he is quick-witted that he is long-winded. A quick eye for ideas may actually make a writer slow in reaching his goal, just as a quick eye for landscape might make a motorist slow in reaching Brighton.'

St John Ervine said the book was 'the best book on Shaw that has been written and will probably be the best that will ever be written'. Certainly, it was generally recognized that Shaw had at last met his match, and Chesterton remained his natural antagonist for the rest of his life. For several months after the book's appearance anything which might link Chesterton with Shaw was news. For instance, the *Cheshire Echo* carried a short column on 27 July 1910, which read:

Yesterday Bernard Shaw was fifty-four. It would be interesting to know how he kept it, or did not keep it, for G.B.S. objects to birthdays. When asked to attend the Stratford Ter-centenary he wrote back: 'I do not keep my own birthday, and I cannot see why I should keep Shakespeare's.' Says G.K.C. in his reply, 'I think that if Mr Shaw had always kept his own birthday he would be better able to understand Shakespeare's birthday and Shakespeare's poetry.' And again, after weighing certain Shaw defects, he says: 'It all comes of that mistake about not keeping his birthday. A man should always be tied to his mother's apron-strings; he should always have a hold on his child-hood, and be ready at intervals to start anew from a childish standpoint. Theologically, the thing is best expressed by saying, "You must be born again." Secularly, it is best expressed by saying, "You must keep your birthday." Even if you will not be born again, at least, remind yourself that you were born once.'

Chesterton had seen in Shaw 'an absence of the red-hot truisms of boyhood'. He was not, he said, 'rooted in the ancient sagacity of infancy', and this was largely because he was a member of an alien minority in Ireland. 'He who has no country can have no real home.' Shaw was a daring pilgrim who had 'set out from the grave to find the cradle. He started from points of view which no one else was clever enough to discover, and he is at last discovering points of view which no one else was ever stupid enough to forget.'

On 23 September another collection of Chesterton's essays was published. This consisted of the best of his *Daily News* articles, and had been given the title of *Tremendous Trifles* by Methuen's literary editor, E.V.Lucas. The collection included several of Chesterton's best known essays: 'A Piece of Chalk', 'What I Found in My Pocket', 'The Toy Theatre', and 'The Diabolist'.

On the following day Chesterton was summoned before a Joint Select Committee of both Houses of Parliament which was inquiring into the working of stage censorship. Shaw was another of the authors invited to give his opinion; but, unlike Shaw, Chesterton said he represented the audience, since he was 'neither a dramatist nor a dramatic critic'. He said he was in favour of censorship but was not in favour of the present Censor, Mr Redford. He was in favour of setting up a licensing authority made up of a jury of 'twelve ordinary men'. 'If you have one ordinary man judging,' he said, 'it is not his ordinariness that appears, but it is his extraordinariness that appears.' The hearing received wide coverage in the national press, and several papers showed photographs of Chesterton arriving for the hearing, quite smartly dressed in a top hat and morning coat, in the company of the Jewish author, Israel Zangwill. Chesterton had come to discuss 'the happiness of the English people', he had come to 'speak for the gallery'.

Always seeing himself as merely one of the crowd, it was sad for him, perhaps, that he was so conspicuous wherever he went. On 12 November Constance Smedley wrote in *T.P.'s Weekly*:

> Fleet Street crowds have been used to the ways of great men since Dr Johnson and Dean Swift trod the paving stones. Chesterton is enveloped in an abstraction so mighty that it neutralises the attention of the passer-by. His huge figure, enveloped in its cloak and shaded by a slouch hat, rolls through the streets unheeding his fellow beings. His eyes stare before him in a troubled dream; his lips move, muttering, composing, arguing. He is an imposing figure; of immense proportions, almost balloon-like with a fine impetuous head which rises over the surrounding crowds; his hair is properly shaggy, his countenance open and frank, wearing indeed a curious childlike unconsciousness in spite of the thought intensity that clouds his brow.

Such was the sight of Mr Chesterton, the 'Sage of Beaconsfield', as he ambled along the street.

II

The Rolling English Road

1909–1911

By the late autumn of 1909 Gilbert and Frances Chesterton were reasonably well settled in their new home at Overroads. Beaconsfield was some twenty-five miles west of London on the Oxford road, but it was well linked to the capital by a regular train service, and Chesterton made frequent journeys just before Christmas to fulfil his lecture engagements. On 17 December he spoke in the lounge of *The Times* Book Club on 'The Romances of the Future', discussing the subject for an hour using as his basis 'notes he had made on the train'. *The Westminster Gazette*, reporting the lecture on the following day, noted that 'G.K.C. has forsworn the town of which he is the doughty champion and now breathes the country air.' The room had been so packed that Chesterton had had some difficulty in squeezing in, and at the end of his talk had 'sat down upon the edge of the rostrum before making an effort to get out'. It was then that two or three ladies sitting near began to compliment him on his books. 'I tried hard to understand your *Orthodoxy*,' said one sweetly.

'You seem to know everything,' said another.

'I know nothing, Madam,' Chesterton replied. 'I am a journalist.'

Needless to say, he had been harsh on most writers of romance dealing with the future, though those who used the future as a playground passed without censure. It was the writer who 'wrote seriously a scientific and dogmatic novel upon the subject, who was always taking a tendency an inch long and extending it to the end of the world' who incurred Chesterton's rebuke. For writers like this, he thought, 'it would be a salutary limitation' if in the construction of their books they had to employ the future tense.

This might bring it home to them that they were taking upon themselves to be the prophets of God. In the old accounts of prophecy there had always been an air of reluctance about the prophet, which was the strongest mark of sincerity; he seemed to be forced into the future to be knocked into the middle of next week.... These modern prophets have that remarkable air of levity which suggests that they go into the middle of next week as to a health resort.

The future was our own unborn actions, he said. We were to make the future, but we were not to prophesy it.

Chesterton's propensity for missing trains meant that he became a familiar figure in the refreshment room at Marylebone Station, with his black bag in which he invariably carried a bottle of wine. He was observed many times 'taking alternate sips of tea and wine between mouthfuls of a penny bun', having asked for a cup of tea and a wine glass. After he had been making the journey for some considerable time, Frances was surprised that he still seemed to have no idea of the timetable. 'Don't you really know the trains to London?' a friend heard her ask, and Chesterton had replied: 'My dear, I couldn't earn our daily bread if I had to study timetables.'

Soon after the move it was announced in the press that Chesterton had been nominated for the National Liberal Club: 'Now that he lives in Buckinghamshire G.K.C. feels he wants a London club.' In the following January his name appeared among the club's 103 new members. Frances was greatly relieved to have made the move: the country air was much better for her health, and as a keen gardener she was looking forward to the spring. Although she often suffered pain in her back, she liked to attend to the flowers herself. Gilbert, on the other hand, knew few of the flowers by name; but Child, the gardener they later employed, was probably exaggerating when he remarked, 'Master, he do like a bit of wallflower. It's the only flower he knows the name of.' Chesterton had always admired the way Frances knew the names of all the wild flowers they saw as they walked through the country. He once wrote a poem to her. 'Twas Eve that named the flowers,' he began, and then continued with a string of floral images that were botanically quite inaccurate.

Chesterton's *Daily News* articles began to reflect something of his life in the country. On 11 December he had written, 'I have now lived for about two months in the country, and have gathered a last rich autumnal fruit of a rural life, which is a strong desire to see London.'

He was, he said, in his more animated moments 'taken for the Village Idiot', and tended to walk with 'a stiffness of gait proper to the oldest inhabitant'. He later varied the theme a little and told his barber, 'I am sure you do not arouse curiosity as I do. When I sit by the wayside, the villagers look and they take me for one of two things. They either take me for the village idiot or for one of Harrods' delivery vans.'

The following May he told his readers: 'Within a stone's throw of my house they are building another house. I am glad they are building it, and I am glad it is within a stone's throw; quite well within it, with a good catapult. Nevertheless, I have not yet cast the first stone at the new house – not being, strictly speaking, guiltless myself in the matter of new houses.' The article had been written as he sat in a garden chair; and the next week he returned to the subject. 'I do not see why I should not go on writing about it,' he said; but it did begin to look as if Cecil and Ada had been right after all, and Chesterton was 'cut off from those deep draughts of stimulative discussion which were so large a part of his mental existence'. He asserted that he had never understood what people meant by domesticity being tame; it seemed to him 'one of the wildest of adventures'.

On 10 January Parliament was dissolved when the House of Lords had declined to pass the Liberal Budget. The General Election commenced on the fourteenth, and for the following two weeks the campaign was carried on 'with tremendous zeal and some bitterness'. Chesterton agreed to canvass for the Liberal candidate for Beaconsfield. Speaking at one of the meetings against the frequent and often silly interruptions from the back of the hall by a gang of Tories which 'only served to display effectively the speaker's powers of repartee and hard-hitting', his manner was typical. 'Conservatism was impossible even for the purpose of conservatives', he said.

What did they mean by being conservatives? They meant that they wanted to keep certain good and valuable things as they were. He should like to be a conservative if he could, because he should like to keep the old English institutions in existence. He liked them, and was fond of them, but they would find that any institution, the boots they wore, their hats, their shirts, however fond they were of them, all had to be constantly revolutionized. If they wanted a white shirt, for instance, they would find it desirable occasionally to have it washed, and even from time to time to replace it. Therefore,

Liberalism meant the principle of laundry, of the washing from time
to time of all the institutions of the State.

Predictably, Chesterton's manner provoked loud laughter and occasional cheers. Unable to resist the temptation, he continued the metaphor. It was no good saying as some people, no doubt, did say: 'Give
me the dear old shirt of my boyhood, and I will wear it still.' He admitted
that there were certain dangers in change, great disasters often happen
to a shirt in sending it to the wash, but still if one wanted a white
shirt it must be sent to the wash. Politics in the main was bosh, he
asserted, something 'even the gentlemen at the back of the room in
their own taking way' would agree with.

Politics exists to a very great extent in people coming to you with
things that don't concern you; for instance, suddenly some fine morning diamonds are discovered in the neighbourhood of, say, Peking.
It is then shortly afterwards discovered that the Emperor of China
is a man of very immoral life, that it is necessary to rush to the rescue
of somebody, probably the Emperor of China's mother-in-law.

At this point Chesterton was interrupted with cries of 'What has this
got to do with Tariff Reform?'
'Oh, I'll tell you about Tariff Reform in a minute. If *you* would tell
me about Tariff Reform it would be more surprising,' he replied. Then,
addressing one of the hecklers, he added: 'My good friend, you only
know four words in the whole of politics, "Tariff Reform" and "Free
Trade", and you don't care a dump about one of the four.'
The meeting caused an uproar, and it is worth recording it at a little
more length because Chesterton revealed how wrong he was about Germany. He thought that Germany was a weak country, and he knew
people who had seen both the German army and navy. Those who
spoke of a 'German scare' had been reading the wrong kind of newspapers. He knew better than to follow the papers, he said, because he
was a journalist – a remark that prompted loud laughter.
The meeting was a triumph for the Liberal side, since every time
Chesterton gave the hecklers an answer they fell back on some other
subject. They were not now judging the immortal soul of William Ewart
Gladstone, Chesterton told them, but whether, if a war with a great
continental power was threatened, it was wise to put into power people
who were notoriously incompetent in a war with a small South African

Gilbert Chesterton at the Slade School of Art, 1892

Gilbert Chesterton and Frances Blogg during their engagement

Gilbert Chesterton and Israel Zangwill leaving a Select
Committee hearing, 1910

Gilbert Chesterton dressed as Dr Johnson

Cecil Chesterton, Lizzie Firmin, Marie Louise Chesterton, Annie
Kidd (née Firmin) and her two children, with Gilbert and Frances
Chesterton at Warwick Gardens, 1911

'Overroads', the Chestertons' first house in Beaconsfield

Hilaire Belloc in Vienna

Hilary Gray

Gilbert, Cecil, Ada and Frances Chesterton

Dorothy Collins and Gilbert Chesterton in California with a young friend, 1931

Overleaf, Gilbert Chesterton

republic. Chesterton went on to summarize his preceding arguments, adding the final one that if it was a question of fighting they should remember that the Liberal policy was to resist the tyranny of the landlords and to restore to the soil a peasantry; and a peasantry could always fight. 'If we are in danger', Chesterton concluded, 'if we are the last of the English, let us at least be free men before we fight.' The meeting ended with loud cheers, and a resolution in favour of the Liberal candidate was carried by a large majority.

The Liberals lost 108 seats in the election, and had a clear majority of only two; but with Irish and Labour support they managed to survive a second election at the end of the same year, and remained in power under Asquith's leadership until 1916.

Belloc had been returned as member for South Salford; but Masterman, who had risen to Cabinet rank in the previous Parliament, lost his seat, partly owing to the bitter attacks made upon his integrity by Belloc and Cecil Chesterton. Cecil had even turned up to heckle Masterman as he addressed the electorate of North West Ham during the build up to polling day. Through their 'League for Clean Government' the two condemned Masterman for having betrayed his Liberal principles after he had become a junior minister in the Cabinet, and in particular for his having voted in favour of the 'Right to Work' Bill in 1908 and then voting against it after he had come to office in 1909. It was a condemnation that Gilbert Chesterton did not share, and indeed he was greatly distressed by it; as far as he was concerned Masterman had been 'entirely misunderstood and underrated'. He had become a politician, said Chesterton, 'from the noblest bitterness on behalf of the poor', and what had been blamed in him 'was the fault of much more ignoble men'. As Christopher Hollis pointed out with regard to this matter, it was almost inevitable that Masterman would have 'somewhat changed his tune on accepting office'. However, neither Belloc nor Cecil Chesterton relinquished their attack, and the two wrote rude words to the tune of 'God rest you, merry gentlemen', which went:

> God rest you, merry gentlemen; let nothing you dismay.
> I fear that Mr Masterman will never go away.
> He's lost his seat in Parliament but draws his weekly pay,
>   Oh, tidings of comfort and joy.

After two unsuccessful attempts to regain a seat in Parliament through by-elections, Masterman was successful in the following December.

The kind of sustained attack on an individual that Belloc and Cecil had perpetrated was, at this time, quite foreign to Gilbert Chesterton. He would always heartily attack an individual's ideas if he disagreed with them, as was seen in the cases of Blatchford and Shaw; but he never attacked the person in the vicious manner of his brother. It would become otherwise after Cecil's trial in 1913, but that was largely out of a sense of loyalty.

The year 1910 also saw two events, though quite unconnected, that would come to take up his time. In April the Marconi Wireless Service was introduced between London and Canada; and on 18 June a great demonstration in favour of womens' suffrage took place, in which ten thousand women from every walk of life processed from the Embankment to the Albert Hall bearing a large banner with the slogan 'From Prison to Citizenship'. Chesterton's comment was typical: 'Ten thousand women marched through the streets of London saying: "We will not be dictated to", and then went off to become stenographers.' In fact, Chesterton had a very low regard for the business of voting for anybody on the grounds that few people took the matter seriously.

The average man votes below himself; he votes with half a mind or a hundredth part of one. A man ought to vote with the whole of himself, as he worships or gets married. A man ought to vote with his head and heart, his soul and stomach, his eye for faces and his ear for music; also (when sufficiently provoked) with his hands and feet. If he has ever seen a fine sunset, the crimson colour of it should creep into his vote. If he has ever heard splendid songs, they should be in his ears when he makes the mystical cross. But as it is, the difficulty with English democracy at all elections is that it is something less than itself. The question is not so much whether only a minority of the electorate votes. The point is that only a minority of the voter votes.

Chesterton believed that women were called to a special place in society.

All we men had grown used to our wives and mothers and grandmothers, and great aunts all pouring a chorus of contempt upon our hobbies of sport, drink and party politics. And now comes Miss Pankhurst, with tears in her eyes, owning that all women were wrong and all men were right; humbly imploring to be admitted into so much as an outer court, from which she may catch a glimpse of those masculine merits which her sisters had so thoughtlessly scorned.

He argued what he considered to be the 'case' against female suffrage at considerable length in his book *What's Wrong with the World*. He saw this demand on the part of women as a public surrender to man. Women could do great and necessary things without the boring business of voting. Somewhat fittingly, it might have seemed, Florence Nightingale died that August at the grand old age of ninety.

Four years earlier, when he had been interviewed by Maude Cherton Braby for the *Tribune*, Chesterton had admitted that women's suffrage was the only topic in the universe to which he had not come to a decision. He thought that if the mass of women wanted it, then it should be given, but he feared that political rights might 'simply give to women the same snappy, scientific civilization of men, make them more pert, more sophisticated, more fond of pretending to knowledge', and this would be simply throwing away their virtues and giving them men's vices instead. Ultimately, the whole matter turned on whether the state consisted of separate individuals or whether, as Comte had put it, it was a collection of people of which the family was a unit. Chesterton was inclined to the latter view, that each family was a nation in itself, and therefore the state duties must be divided between the members of the family: to one the duties of bringing up the children, to the other the fighting and politics. However, if the state consisted of separate individuals, then a woman should be allowed to vote, as she was, of course, in every way equal to a man. The nonsense about woman being man's intellectual inferior, Chesterton would dismiss with his hand, or rather with his foot. The vast majority of men, he said, were guided by women all their lives.

The main objection to universal franchise is that men are possibly more fitted for the business of politics than women, just as women are more fitted for the function of child bearing. All sane men are fond of children, but if they have to look after them for long they would be bored, just as women would be bored if they sat for hours in a stuffy hall talking for hours about Tariff Reform.

Chesterton had something important to say to those who spoke of a woman's work in the home as drudgery, and it was a point he made frequently from the platform.

When domesticity is called drudgery, all the difficulty arises from a double meaning of the word. If drudgery only means dreadfully hard work, I admit that woman drudges in the home, as a man might drudge at the Cathedral at Amiens or drudge behind a gun at Trafalgar. But if it means that the hard work is more heavy because it is trifling, colourless and of small import to the soul, then as I say, I give it up. ... To be Queen Elizabeth within a definite area, deciding sales, banquets, labours and holidays; to be Whitely within a certain area, providing toys, boots, sheets, cakes, and books; to be Aristotle within a certain area, teaching morals, manners, theology, and hygiene; I can understand how this might exhaust the mind, but I cannot imagine how it could narrow it. How can it be a large career to tell other people's children about the Rule of Three, and a small career to tell one's own children about the universe? How can it be broad to be the same thing to everyone, and narrow to be everything to someone? No; a woman's function is laborious, but because it is gigantic, not because it is minute. I will pity Mrs Jones for the hugeness of her task; I will never pity her for its smallness.

On 24 February Chesterton's *The Ball and the Cross* was published. Much of the novel had been serialized in *The Commonwealth* between March 1905 and November 1906 and, appearing now in both America and England, it received wide attention. An unsigned review in the *Pall Mall Gazette* gave a succinct and accurate account of the book's merits.

The theme in Mr Chesterton's new novel is largely the same that he treated in *Orthodoxy*; there he contrasted the cross with its symbolism of four arms stretching away infinitely and the circle with its narrow completeness, and here he develops the contrast. The cross and ball of the title are the cross and ball of St Paul's Cathedral on the dome of which the first scene occurs. When we say that in the last chapter we have a conflagration in a lunatic asylum, and between these two points we come across Tolstoyans, Nietzscheans, eugenists, psychologists, the devil, a fellow madman, the fringe of the smart set, the Channel Isles, Thanet, the police, and the mob, we have said enough to show that the book is eminently characteristic. What is perhaps more important is that the story has far less fireworks and far more good solid work than any of Mr Chesterton's essays in fiction. The central idea and the central figures are admirably conceived and admirably kept in the front; there is far less sidetracking than is usual with Mr Chesterton. The idea is simply that there are two men left in the world keen enough to fight for religion: Turnbull, the red-haired atheist, and Evan MacIan, a highland Catholic. MacIan starts the fight by smashing Turnbull's shop windows, or perhaps we should say that Turnbull starts the fight by putting in his window a blasphemous image that MacIan feels bound to take up. Thenceforth the story is concerned with the effort of the two honest men to fight a duel on the most vital problem in the world, the truth of Christianity.

Of course, the novel had been written some time before *Orthodoxy*, but it was seen by some as a further indication that Chesterton's Christian orthodoxy was, in fact, Catholicism, and it was a short time after the book's appearance that two Catholic priests happened to see Chesterton browsing at the bookstall on Coventry station, after he had lectured to the Anglican Society in the city. On their asking him whether the rumour was true that he was considering becoming a Catholic, he replied, 'It's a matter that is giving me a great deal of agony of mind, and I'd be very grateful if you would pray for me.' The rumour was nothing new, and by the time Chesterton spoke to the two priests it had spread far and wide. In Canada, for instance, the *Toronto Catholic Register* in the same year was speaking of 'Chesterton, the eminent English publicist and the most noteworthy convert to the faith in recent years'.

Chesterton was anxious to do as much as possible locally, and he began to accept invitations to speak at places within easy reach of his home. He agreed to lecture to the WEA at High Wycombe on Education and amused his audience by saying that education was not in itself a good thing, it depended upon what the education was. If they considered success as the result then Fagin in Dickens was a most successful educationalist.

Chesterton's popularity prompted a bizarre episode in Beaconsfield itself. On 11 March the *Daily Star* showed a photograph of Chesterton at his desk with the headline 'Mr Gilbert K. Chesterton to be a parish constable.' When he had been interviewed for the paper Chesterton was unaware that his name had been put forward for what was merely an honorary position, and he thought there must have been a huge mistake. 'It would be a good thing for the criminal,' he quipped. Still, the rumour did not die down, and several other newspapers elaborated on the story. The *Star* carried a cartoon of Chesterton dressed as a constable, wearing a helmet and wielding a truncheon; and the *Westminster Gazette* guessed that if G.B.S. were to try to motor through Beaconsfield above the speed limit G.K.C. would have to 'comprehend' him, and that again was just what he would like to have the opportunity of doing. 'We do not know what the duties may be,' the report continued, 'but we are quite sure that G.K.C. would discharge them with dignity and the weight of parochial authority.' Like the rumour of his conversion, the parish constable story reached Canada, a country where Chesterton has always been popular. The *Montreal Herald* commented: 'The Police Station at Beaconsfield would become the thinking centre of the Empire. The lock-up system would probably be put aside in favour of a new system of street corner conversation. If Mr Chesterton should lock up an offender he would probably try to convince him that he was really being set at liberty.'

Chesterton himself told the story in the *Daily News* on 2 April. The office of Parish Constable, he wrote, breathed of a somewhat breezier age, a 'jolly time when there was no nonsense about wanting to serve your country; no buying of peerages by breeding cattle; no climbing into rich idleness by means of "polite work"'. His article ended with a question: 'What would any six streets in Hoxton or Whitechapel give if they could elect (however indirectly) the policeman who should stand at the street corner?'

In the same month Chesterton travelled north once again to give a series of lectures, taking in numerous places including Manchester, Huddersfield and Hull. On 15 April, dressed as Dr Johnson, he presided over a gathering of IDK members at the Old Cheshire Cheese. The other guests were supposed to represent various members of Johnson's circle, and it was an uproarious evening, as the photograph published in the *Daily Mirror* the following morning testified. Chesterton's Johnson outfit was probably his favourite, although a few months later he appeared at a literary dinner dressed as the Blessed Damozel. Rossetti's words 'leaned across the bar', he said, always fascinated him, but he preferred to see three stars on a bottle than have seven stars in his hair. On that occasion Chesterton's 'irresistibly comic' costume was outmatched only by Hall Caine's 'tender and sympathetic interpretation' of the Lady of the Lake, with a costume that consisted chiefly of bulrushes.

However, the Johnson costume was to appear on numerous occasions; indeed, he had worn it first at a CSU pageant held in Fulham. Mrs

Mills remembered how, tired out after the effort of talking Johnsonese, Chesterton had sat down in someone's doorway as he waited for a cab, and had been quite unaware that a crowd had gathered to stare at him. One of the problems with his Johnson impersonation was what to do with his moustache. Frances would not let him shave it off. 'She says it can be disguised,' he explained dubiously. 'Let us hope so. I daren't go home without it.' There was no such problem about his hair, he said, although he 'knew nothing of a wig'. 'My own hair is so long and beastly,' he said, 'that it looks very like Johnson's wig as it is.' On one occasion, when he was only just recovering from whooping cough, Chesterton attended a Beaconsfield fair in his costume, accompanied by the vicar's wife dressed as Mrs Thrale. In spite of his illness he had been persuaded to keep to his promise for, as Maisie Ward put it, a whooping Dr Johnson was thought to be a greater attraction than no Dr Johnson at all.

Of the real Johnson Chesterton once said, 'He may seem to be hammering at the brain through long nights of noise and thunder; but he can walk into the heart without knocking.' He might have been speaking about himself.

On the evening of 6 May the telephone rang at Overroads. Chesterton, who invariably left all answering to Frances, was called, and tried to make sense of the garbled message that a London editor was giving him down the crackling line. 'I heard something momentous and unintelligible,' he said; 'it might have been the landing of the Germans or the end of the world.' With the snatches of this strangled voice in his ears he went out into the garden. The night was clear, 'a night of startling and blazing stars – stars so fierce and close that they seemed crowding round the roof and tree-tops. White-hot and speechless they seemed striving to speak, like that voice that had been drowned amid the drumming wires.'

The year was one in which Halley's comet might be seen. With such a prospect in mind, Chesterton experienced 'one of the immortal moods out of which legends arise', the kind of mood in which 'men have joined the notion of a comet with the death of a King', and he wrote tenderly of Edward VII in the *Illustrated London News*, and 'the dark and half-superstitious suggestion' that by his death the fate of the country had turned a corner and entered a new epoch.

At the end of the following month, on 28 June, Chesterton's *What's Wrong with the World* was published. The title was not the author's choice, and he was not very happy about the change. What he had intended was to simply ask the question 'What is Wrong?'; but the publishers, Cassell, no doubt with an eye on possible sales, felt that the question should be replaced with an answer. It was a last-minute decision, it seems, since the first edition's jacket and spine had the new title with a question mark, while the title page was not expressed as an interrogative. The matter was put right in all subsequent editions, and for these there was not long to wait; in August the *Westminster Gazette* reported that a sixth edition had become necessary within two months of publication.

Nevertheless, the publisher's decision had been unfair on Chesterton, and it left him open to much unjust criticism. For example, the *Evening Standard* commented: 'We haven't the faintest notion what's wrong with the world, and after reading Mr Chesterton's book – nearly 300 pages – we regretfully come to the conclusion that he doesn't either.' The best plan, the reviewer suggested, was to accept the author's own valuation of himself, and 'laugh at his brilliance, and assume the attitude of an indulgent crowd at a circus'. The book was Chesterton's first, for want of a better word, 'sociological' book. He had stated his creed in *Orthodoxy*, and now he reaffirmed his belief that morality was the fruit of doctrine. The way to find out what is wrong was to first answer the question, 'What is right?' Social science, as far as Chesterton was concerned, was 'by no means always content with the normal human soul'; it had all sorts of fancy souls for sale. To those who talked of social diseases, societies becoming old, and countries dying, Chesterton said that such metaphors were quite useless, there was a gaping absurdity in talking about 'young nations' or 'dying nations', or talking about a sick or healthy society. 'We agree about the evil; it it is about the good that we should tear each other's eyes out,' he said. 'We can all see the national madness; but what is national sanity?'

In one important passage Chesterton saw the modern Englishman, the father of a family, as a man 'who should be perpetually kept out, for one reason after another, from the house in which he had meant his married life to begin'. The man had always desired 'the divinely ordinary things'; but 'just as he is moving in, something goes wrong. Some tyranny, personal or political, suddenly debars him from the home, and he has to take his meals in the front garden.' Extending his metaphor through a series of even greater deprivations, Chesterton sees in a horrific vision the man as eventually 'owned by the State and ruled by public officers in the commonwealth of the sublime future'. Socialism might well be the world's deliverance, he said, 'but it is not the world's desire'.

In *What's Wrong With the World* it is possible to see, not only the emergence of the 'Distributist State', but also the mood of Chesterton's ever-increasing hatred of Calvinism. He was here making his strongest attack so far on the evil of Calvinism, an evil he came to denounce more and more violently over the coming years. The Calvinistic idea that 'if once a man is born it is too late to damn him or save him' Chesterton said was 'the last lie in hell'. In fact, he went so far as to draw for the first time a distinction between the Calvinist and the Christian.

> The difference between Puritanism and Catholicism is not about whether some priestly word or gesture is significant and sacred. It is about whether any word or gesture is significant and sacred. To the Catholic every other daily act is a dramatic dedication to the service of good or of evil. To the Calvinist no act can have that sort of solemnity, because the person doing it has been dedicated from eternity, and is merely filling up his time until the crack of doom. The difference is something subtler than plum-puddings or private theatricals; the difference is that to a Christian of my kind this sort of earthly life is intensely thrilling and precious; to a Calvinist like Mr Shaw it is confessedly automatic and uninteresting. To me these three score years and ten are the battle. To the Fabian Calvinist (by his own confession) they are only a long procession of the victors in laurels and the vanquished in chains. To me earthly life is the drama; to him it is the epilogue. Shavians think about the embryo; Spiritualists about the ghost; Christians about the man. It is as well to have these things clear.

Chesterton had been at pains to emphasize that *What's Wrong With the World* was not intended to be a religious book, and, as Christopher Hollis pointed out, it might well be read 'without the reader being aware that religious influences were playing a part in the development of Chesterton's political and economic interests'. Such readers would have missed an important truth. He had learnt from Belloc what Belloc in his youth had learnt from Cardinal Manning: that all human conflicts ultimately have a theological basis.

On the evening of 4 November Chesterton, accompanied by Frances as was usual at this time, visited the Roman Catholic College of St

Edmund's, Ware. He had agreed to deliver a lecture on Chivalry, and
the occasion had been thought important enough for Monsignor Barnes,
the Catholic chaplain at Cambridge, to bring over a party of undergraduates. Chesterton was in fine form. He told his audience that
chivalry, like everything else in our civilization, could be traced back to
the Roman Empire, and it was from the Romans that the barbarous tribes
of Europe learned to use horses. This was worthy of consideration, he
quipped, for some people said that all good things come from Germany.
The chivalric ideal, Chesterton argued, was the very opposite of the
modern ideal of the superman. The latter was superior to us only in
the way that the rhinoceros was superior to us, his horn was exalted
and he was extremely unlike us, the chief ground for his self-congratula-
tion; but the good knight of Christian legend was humble and magnanimous, he had a spiritual beauty which was denied even to the great
pagan heroes. There was an art in losing a battle, and in the Dark
Ages Europeans had learnt to reverence the man who could lose nobly.
Chesterton hoped that his audience would still preserve the similar reverence in the Dark Ages which were probably in front of them.

This last remark shows how Chesterton had changed his attitude
towards Germany in the short time since he had addressed the political
meeting in January, and at Ware he made several ominous references
to the German threat. However, he could not have seen how close the
new Dark Ages were in front of his young audience, many of whom
would never see the age of thirty.

Chesterton published two more books during November 1910: a book
of essays drawn from his weekly articles, which was entitled *Alarms
and Discursions*, and as a companion to his earlier study of G.F.Watts
in the Popular Library of Art series, a little book on William Blake.
'Although Mr Chesterton's "Blake" appears in a series of books about
art,' complained the reviewer in *The Nation*, 'he has not troubled much
to give any special consideration of Blake as a draughtsman, painter,
or engraver. The immensely important question, for instance, of Blake's
power of design, its amazing successes and its unaccountable failures,
is entirely ignored.' The complaint, if typical of many who failed to
understand Chesterton's purpose, was in this case justified, since Chesterton was far more interested in Blake's character and 'his mental and
spiritual endowment'. He came to the conclusion that Blake had been
mad, but he was mad 'because his visions were true. It was exactly
because he was unnaturally exposed to a hail of forces that were more

than natural that some breaches were made in his mental continuity, some damage was done to his mind. He was, in a far more awful sense than Goldsmith, "an inspired idiot". He was an idiot because he was inspired.' As might have been expected, the book revealed as much about Chesterton as it did about Blake, and the author drew many parallels from his own times, as when, for instance, he said, 'You and I may be a little vague about the relations between Albion and Jerusalem, but Blake is as certain about them as Mr Chamberlain about the relations of Birmingham to the British Empire', or when he spoke of Blake's love of nakedness: 'As the hygienist insists on wearing Jaegar clothes, Blake insisted on wearing no clothes. As the aesthete must wear sandals, he must wear nothing.'

Above all Chesterton saw in Blake's mysticism a chance once again to attack the agnostics, as he did when he spoke of Blake's 'The Lamb'. A true understanding of Blake's use of symbolism made some very odd passages in Blake seem clear.

In the ordinary modern meaning Blake's symbols are not symbols at all. They are not allegories. An allegory nowadays means taking something that does not exist as a symbol of something that does exist. We believe, at least most of us do, that sin does exist. We believe (on highly insufficient grounds) that a dragon does not exist. So we make the unreal dragon an allegory of the real sin. But that is not what Blake meant when he made the lamb the symbol of innocence. He meant that there really is behind the universe an eternal image called the Lamb, of which all living lambs are merely the copies or the approximation. He held that eternal innocence to be an actual and even an awful thing. He would not have seen anything comic, any more than the Christian evangelist saw anything comic, in talking about the Wrath of the Lamb. If there were a lamb in one of Aesop's fables, Aesop would never be so silly as to represent him as angry. But Christianity is more daring than Aesop, and the Wrath of the Lamb is its great paradox. If there is an immortal lamb, a being whose simplicity and freshness are for ever renewed, then it is truly and really a more creepy idea to horrify that being into hostility than to defy the flaming dragon or challenge the darkness or the sea. No old wolf or world-worn lion is so awful as a creature that is always young – a creature that is always newly born. But the main point here is simpler. It is merely that Blake did not mean that meekness was a mere shadow of the everlasting lamb. The distinction is essential to anyone at all concerned for this rooted spirituality which is the only enduring sanity of mankind. The personal is not a mere figure for the impersonal; rather the impersonal is a clumsy term for something more personal than common personality. God is not a symbol of goodness. Goodness is a symbol of God.

Several short extracts from *William Blake* were chosen to be included in *A Chesterton Calendar*, which Kegan Paul published in January 1911. The entry for 28 February read: 'The wise man will follow a star, low and large and fierce in the heavens, but the nearer he comes to it the smaller and smaller it will grow, till he finds it the humble lantern over some little inn or stable. Not till we know the high things shall we know how lowly they are.' The editor had also picked out a typical Chestertonian aphorism from the book for the 12 June entry: 'There is more of the song and music of mankind in a clerk putting on his Sunday clothes than in a fanatic running naked down Cheapside.' *A Chesterton Calendar* showed how eminently quotable Chesterton was. It did not matter whether the entries were very short, a couple of lines or so, or longer passages taken from books where they had formed part of a much more lengthy argument. This was particularly true of several extracts from his *Appreciations and Criticisms of the Works of Charles Dickens*, a collection of all Chesterton's introductions to Dickens' works in the Everyman Library series; and several verses from what was referred to in the calendar as 'Ballad of Alfred', which would appear in the August of that year as 'The Ballad of the White Horse'. The *Chesterton Calendar* was a great success and was followed in 1916 by a second similar collection.

During the early months of 1911 Chesterton was also busy fulfilling his many lecturing engagements. On the evening of 25 January he kept his audience in the Hampstead Town Hall waiting for a quarter of an hour because, as he explained, 'his cab had had to get up Haverstock Hill'. Such excuses had become increasingly necessary, and on several occasions the lecturer had failed to arrive at all. However, he usually managed to placate his audiences with an amusing, if not a convincing, reason for his lateness, as when some years later he told the Knights of the Blessed Sacrament, 'As knights you will understand my not being here at the beginning, for the whole point of knighthood was that the knight should arrive late but not too late. Had St George not been late there would have been no story. Had he been too late, there would have been no princess.'

The Hampstead lecture on 'The Ideals of Bernard Shaw' was typical of many at this time, when clubs and societies that could afford them would ask first Shaw and then Chesterton to speak so that both sides of an argument could be heard. In this instance the lectures had been arranged by the Hampstead clergy and the local Free Church ministers. As the *Christian Commonwealth* reported, 'the élite of Anglicanism were present; together with dear, deaf, old ladies from the front pew of the Baptist Chapel looking a little uncomfortable'. There was also a group of young men and women who were evidently members of the Fabian Society, who 'laughed first at every clever remark and applauded most at every academic reference'. The stance of the two authors had not really altered and the subjects on which they took different sides, although far-reaching, were predictable, with Chesterton still arguing fiercely for orthodoxy against Shaw's materialism. In August 1911, a few months before their first public debate with Belloc acting as chairman, the subject was cremation. Shaw had condemned bodily interment as 'superstitious, slavery, stupidity'. Chesterton's comment was that this was just the view he would have expected Shaw to take, and launched into an eloquent defence of the grave.

The instinct that made Christian men put bodies in the ground was a humane and religious one, because it recognises that the flesh is a sacred thing, and has not lost its sacred character simply because the life has gone out of it. We say of ourselves: 'This temple of life has become unsuitable, and we will leave it, but we will not burn it. It has been a sacred vessel, and it shall not be we that destroy it.' In the same way, the Church in early days cherished her relics feeling that matter is not cast out from God, because for a time it has lost its immediate purpose.

Of course, Chesterton realized that it made no difference to a man whether his body was burnt or not, but he thought it made a great deal of difference to the people he had left behind. He saw the move towards cremation as yet another sign of the paganism of the times.

Chesterton, seeing that so many people attacked the established usages of Christianity, and by so doing threw away much of the joy of living, felt inclined, as he said, to propose that all who disagreed with the Christian tradition should go and do the opposite. The world would be very much jollier if the people who preached polygamy would go away and keep harems and see what happened. But it was very much easier in this matter of cremation to be consistent, and that was why he would support the reversion to real pagan practice. If people thought it a finer idea to destroy the body by burning the thing they have loved, let them do it as the pagans did, and make the destruction magnificent. He put the same idea into one of his best-known poems: 'The Song of the Strange Ascetic'.

> If I had been a Heathen,
>   I'd have piled my pyre on high
> And in a great red whirlwind
>   Gone roaring to the sky.
> But Higgins is a heathen,
>   And a richer man than I;
> And they put him in an oven,
>   Just as if he were a pie.

In February 1911 the Chestertons had travelled north once again, and when Gilbert lectured to the Liverpool Sanitary Association on 'The Romances of the Future' at the Adelphi Hotel Frances was singled out by reporters as 'wearing a long black coat over a blue gown, and a black plumed hat with touches of gold'. She was presented with a bouquet of pink tulips and lilies of the valley. Indeed, her presence was necessary to make certain that Gilbert arrived at the correct places and that he lectured on the advertised subject. It seemed she might not have been present at the Leeds Playgoers' Society meeting when Chesterton lectured on 'The Drama of Ideas' when the lecture had been advertised as 'The Modern Drama'. As was noticed with some disgust, 'a lecture on the drama of today which takes no account whatever of the theatre as a living reality, and ignores the social tendencies and movements at the root of the whole question, cannot be accepted as an illuminating contribution to the discussion'. In contrast, his lecture at Sheffield to an audience of over five hundred people was described as 'entertaining and stimulating, and full of wit and quaint deceits' in which the lecturer 'made jokes at which he himself laughed occasionally and his audience almost continually'.

It was generally admitted by those who heard Chesterton lecture that he had his off days, and there were times when he was downright boring. The tours meant many tiresome train journeys and Chesterton was often worn out, having more and more frequently to drink in order to perk himself up. The result was unpredictable, but on the whole the evening lectures were more lively and successful than afternoon engagements. There were occasions when he gave two lectures on the same day, and this added to his fatigue. Nevertheless, audiences were always pleased to see him, and most were as tolerant as the *Yorkshire Weekly Post* reporter who wrote of one performance: 'As a lecture it was a fiasco, but as an exhibition of Chesterton it was pleasing.' Chesterton himself once remarked, 'I might call myself a lecturer; but then again I fear some of you may have attended my lectures.'

On 22 June 1911 Belloc and Cecil Chesterton, with the help of one or two rich friends, launched the first number of *The Eye-Witness*, the weekly magazine which, although it could not have possibly been foreseen, was destined to play a major part in Gilbert Chesterton's life; and it would hardly be an exaggeration to say that he sacrificed his life for it, or at least for its successor. The idea to publish a magazine that might keep the public informed of corruption in government was largely Belloc's own; his first attempt at such a venture, *The North Street Gazette*, had folded up after only one number in 1908. In the former venture Belloc had collaborated with Maurice Baring, and the magazine had taken its name from Baring's house, No. 6 North Street, where it had been printed on a press they had bought specially for the purpose. *The Eye-Witness* was a much more firmly based venture, the majority of the shares having been purchased by Charles Granville, a staunch supporter of Belloc and Cecil Chesterton, who had been particularly impressed by their book, *The Party System*, which they had written 'to support the tendency now everywhere apparent and finding expression, a tendency to expose and ridicule as it deserves, to destroy and to supplant the system under which Parliament, the governing institution of this country, has been rendered null'.

Like *The North Street Gazette*, whose epigraph had been 'Out, out, brief scandal!', *The Eye-Witness* was intent upon muckraking; but while Belloc remained editor (which was only for a year, since he soon became bored by the office) the tone of the magazine was surprisingly restrained, although it was hard-hitting in the matters of the Mentally Deficient Bill and the National Unemployment and Health Insurance Bill. However, once Cecil Chesterton had become editor in June 1912, and the magazine had been succeeded by *The New Witness*, the ferocity of the editorial comment increased in the events leading up to what became known as the 'Marconi Scandal'.

To begin with Gilbert Chesterton's part in the business was slight. He contributed verse mostly, and an occasional book review. A feature of the early numbers of *The Eye-Witness* was a series of ballades: poems in a form much used by the French troubadours with a refrain, not to be confused with a ballad. Chesterton provided several of these, as did Belloc, Bentley, and Baring, and sometimes the ballades were a combined effort. One or two of Chesterton's ballades, such as 'A Ballade of an Anti-Puritan' and 'A Ballade of Suicide', remain among his best-known poems; the latter, with the refrain 'I think I will not hang myself today', appeared in *The Eye-Witness* on 21 September 1911.

> The gallows in my garden, people say,
> Is new and neat and adequately tall.
> I tie the noose on in a knowing way
> As one that knots his necktie for a ball;
> But just as all the neighbours – on the wall –
> Are drawing a long breath to shout 'Hurray!'
> The strangest whim has seized me.... After all
> I think I will not hang myself today.

The poem ended with:

> ENVOI
> Prince, I can hear the trumpets of Germinal,
> The tumbrils toiling up the terrible way;
> Even today your royal head may fall –
> I think I will not hang myself today.

The Envoi at the end of the ballade form, traditionally addressed to the poet's royal patron, became in the hands of Chesterton and Belloc a means of loading on heavy irony.

In July Cassell had brought out *The Innocence of Father Brown*, a collection of twelve short stories that had previously appeared in either *The Storyteller* or Cassell's own magazine; the first Father Brown story, 'The Blue Cross', which some think to have been the best, had been seen in *The Storyteller* in September 1910. By the middle of the following year the little priest with his bashed umbrella and brown paper parcels was becoming popular; but perhaps the reviewer in *Country Life* was right when he wrote: 'The stories of Father Brown should have been left to their proper place scattered in the pages of a magazine, where their effect, not being cumulative, would have been greater.'

It is ironic that Chesterton is best known today for what he himself considered his least important work. In later years, if Frances informed him that they were running short of money, he would usually reply somewhat wearily, 'Oh well, I suppose I shall have to write another Father Brown story.' The popularity of the stories has, of course, rested on Chesterton's creation of his hero, and Father Brown will always be seen in the happy company of Holmes, Poirot, and Wimsey – although his closest companion would surely have been Miss Marple. Chesterton's dumpy, dishevelled and unassuming little Catholic priest, whose crime detection depended upon psychological insight and an intimate know-ledge of moral and pastoral theology, while in some respects modelled on Fr O'Connor, has a mind recognizable immediately as Chesterton's own. Father Brown comes to the old things with new understanding. He begins, as one reviewer noted, 'by appearing a fool, and ends by reducing to foolishness the wisest round him'. However, as Christopher Hollis pointed out, 'there is no pretence to any detailed lesson in the Father Brown stories'; and he thought they were regarded by Chesterton himself largely as 'pot-boilers'.

The story that aroused the most interest in *The Innocence of Father Brown* was the fifth, 'The Invisible Man'. A millionaire named Isidore Smythe, the inventor of 'Smythe's Silent Service' of automatic figures that do the housework by machinery, while living in his flat at Himalaya Mansions, Hampstead, is bombarded with anonymous letters threaten-ing him with death. On the last fatal day, when Smythe returns to his flat with a new acquaintance, a Mr Angus, he is assured by the com-missionaire and the porter that nobody has been near his apartments; yet when the two men enter the ante-room they discover a scrap of paper lying on the floor, written in red ink, 'still wet', with the message, 'If you have been to see her today I shall kill you. . . .'

The postman turns out to be a disguised criminal who had visited Himalaya Mansions twice within ten minutes, something the porters must have noticed; but, as Father Brown asked: 'Have you ever noticed this – that people never answer what you say? They answer what you mean – or what you think you mean.' Father Brown, of course, unmasks the criminal, 'an ordinary passing postman who had bustled by them unnoticed under the shade of the trees'. '"Nobody ever notices postmen somehow," he said thoughtfully; "yet they have passions like other men, and even carry large bags where a small corpse can be stowed quite easily."' The priest walked under the stars with a murderer, 'and what they said to each other will never be known'.

When he spoke about Father Brown in his autobiography, Chesterton said that he had intended him, rather like the postman, to be featureless.

> When a writer invents a character for the purpose of fiction, especially of light or fanciful fiction, he fits him out with all sorts of features meant to be effective in that setting and against that background. He may have taken a hint from a human being. But he will not hesitate to alter the human being, especially in externals, because he is not thinking of a portrait but of a picture.

The point of Father Brown was that he should appear pointless, he said, 'and one might say that his conspicuous quality was not being conspicuous. His commonplace exterior was meant to contrast with his unsuspected vigilance and intelligence; and that being so, of course, I made his appearance shabby and shapeless, his face round and expressionless, his manners clumsy, and so on.'

Chesterton admitted that he had taken some of Father Brown's inner intellectual qualities from Fr O'Connor, but that was all. In fact, Fr O'Connor was externally quite unlike 'the little Suffolk dumpling from East Anglia', not shabby, but rather neat; not clumsy, but 'very delicate and dextrous'. Chesterton saw Fr O'Connor as a sensitive and quick-witted Irishman, 'with the profound irony and some of the potential irritability of his race'; but in a very real sense he had been the intellectual inspiration of the stories, and 'of much more important things as well'.

Among the 'important things' had been Fr O'Connor's interest and encouragement given in the composition of 'The Ballad of the White Horse', which was published on 31 August. He had felt increasingly that Frances was right, that Chesterton 'should cease to spread and dissipate his gifts on daily papers', and concentrate more on his poetry or, as he put it in a way which would not have appealed to Chesterton, 'begin to print on handmade paper with gilt edges'. Fr O'Connor has told how several passages in the epic ballad were composed as a result of his conversations with the author while the poem was 'on the stocks'.

The inspiration for the ballad of King Alfred had been a true inspiration, in that a short passage of the poem had been given to Chesterton

in a dream one night at Battersea. It was part of Alfred's speech before
the battle of Ethandune:

> People, if you have any prayers,
>   Say prayers for me:
> And lay me under a Christian stone
> In that lost land I thought my own,
> To wait till the holy horn is blown,
>   And all poor men are free.

No poet could ask for more. Here was the theme, the tone, and a complete
stanza; all he had to do was to find the rest!

The finished poem is a ballad epic divided into eight books, in which
Chesterton tells of Alfred's victory over 'the heathen things'. The theme
is the cause Chesterton himself had championed, the cause of Christendom against the forces of pagan darkness that constantly assail it. The
poem contains passages of great excitement, of blood and battle, contrasted with moments of touching simplicity. Perhaps the most beautiful
passage describes how Alfred at the lowest moment in his fortune, in
hiding on the island of Athelney, sees a vision of the Mother of God.
Frances told another priest friend, Dom Ignatius Rice, a Benedictine
monk of Douai Abbey, that the whole poem had been written in a fortnight, and that she had gathered the sheets of paper as her husband
had thrown them on the floor; and that 'when she went through them
all there was scarcely a correction to be made'. This is certainly a wild
exaggeration, for as well as the verses published in *A Chesterton Calendar*
in 1911, a fragment from a 'Ballad of Alfred' had been published in
the *Albany Review* as early as April 1907. Nevertheless, it is likely that
Chesterton had written long passages at a stretch, and, as Maisie Ward
has pointed out, he disclaimed the idea that he took trouble over anything. 'Taking trouble has never been a weakness of mine,' he once
said. The ballad has a spontaneous energy about it such as had not
been achieved since Coleridge wrote 'The Rime of The Ancient
Mariner'.

12

Of Great Limbs Gone to Chaos

1911–1913

During the autumn of 1911 *The Eye-Witness* carried a series of articles on 'The Jewish Question', in which the history of Jewish influence in Europe, and particularly in England, was explored in some depth. Although Gilbert Chesterton had no hand in the articles, he would have agreed with them. In the first article the 'problem' had been stated.

> There exists in the midst of European civilisation a race alien to and different from the Western blood among which it must live. This race is segregated in no artificial manner yet permanently and uniquely survives intact. So far from this segregation being due to stratification or difference of abilities between higher and lower, the Jewish nation is, and has always been, eminent in the highest intellectual employment which European civilisation could find. It has on this account been accepted sometimes as a necessity, sometimes as an advantage, but always in practice as a part of the European scheme. None the less the presence of this alien element has proved sometimes an irritant, always an element of friction, and a social arrangement in which that friction should be reduced to a minimum, and the necessary or, at any rate, normal presence of the small non-European minority in our midst shall be made an innocuous as possible, is a goal practically obtainable and eminently to be desired.

The eight articles, in a style immediately recognizable as that of the editor, trace the history of Jewish finance which, Belloc argued, had achieved three great periods of influence. The last period, which had opened at the time of the French Revolution, was now waning, although 'the whole tone of international finance is still marked with the Jewish mark'. After laying at the door of Jewish financiers 'the South African business for England; the Dreyfus business for France; the Revolutionary business for Russia' in his fourth article, 'The Peril', Belloc continued:

> Now unless the Jewish race is to be absorbed and disappear in the mass of European blood and tradition surrounding it, that contrast and its consequent friction will increase in the near future until their worst fruit shall have ripened: a fruit of oppression, injustice, and enduring hatred.
>
> To avoid that lamentable conclusion three policies are present. The first – and that still most generally held in Western Europe – is to regard the matter as solved; vaguely to suppose the absorption of the alien race as feasible, and its presence for the moment as something at once absurdly separate and yet *not* separate from the life of the community as innocuous. The second policy is that of exclusion. The third policy is to grant the Jew recognition and privilege.
>
> Which of these three shows comprehension of our need and of the Jewish need, and which is the most likely to afford a standing answer to this gravest of modern questions?

In arguing the case for a policy of privilege against the two alternatives of absorption and exclusion Belloc ended on a cryptic note.

> All that is said here by way of conclusion to this series of articles, is no more than a general adumbration of that third large line of policy which the solution of the Jewish problem must take in the near future, now that the first line of absorption has certainly broken down, if we would avoid the second line of persecution.
>
> It sounds fantastic to those who prefer words to things; it cannot be detailed because the crisis is but beginning; but it certainly marks out the road by which, and by which alone, we can avoid in the near future throughout Europe disaster to the Jewish race and shame to our own.
>
> Every modern discussion is alive with it. You cannot speak of the South African business, of the vast religious quarrel in France, of the moral struggle in Italy, of the Young Turks, of Egypt, of India, of the influence of secret societies to-day, of any conceivable matter of real and practical import, without speaking in the same breath of the Jewish people – and alas! not in their noble aspect, the last

defence of which is the inheritance of that ignoble fear of Jewish
financial power, which has tarnished the whole debate.

You cannot avoid a reality so insistent, so pressing, and so enormous. You must meet it, and if you do not meet it with the intention
of recognition and of privilege you will inevitably be driven to meet
it in the long run with the intention of exclusion, injustice, and oppression. All history is there to teach you your lesson, and you have
perhaps thirty years in which to make up your minds.

The interview he had given to the *Jewish Chronicle* in the April of
the same year (see p. 154) showed how much Chesterton had been
influenced by Belloc's ideas; but in some ways, particularly in his strong
argument in favour of a Zionist solution to the problem, he saw further
than Belloc, who had argued for a special recognition of the Jewish
people in society, 'to admit that the Jew is a Jew', and to introduce
laws 'laid down to prevent those explosions and disasters which, in
the absence of such laws, must inevitably take place sooner or later
as the result of an intolerable friction'. The most remarkable, not to
say alarming, thing about both men was the clarity with which they
foresaw the horrific results if their warnings were not heeded. Such
was the situation in the autumn of 1911.

When the sixth of Belloc's articles was printed on 12 October, *The
Eye-Witness* also included Chesterton's historical poem, 'Lepanto'. The
poem was the result of yet another conversation with Fr O'Connor in
the spring of the same year. The two men had taken part in a Ladies'
Debating Society meeting in Leeds, and Chesterton had led the discussion on what was one of the commonplaces of his thought at the time,
namely that 'all wars were religious wars'. In the course of the debate
Fr O'Connor had told of Lepanto, and, to use his own words,

> ...how Philip the Second of Spain had been assembling his Armada
> to invade England, and could only spare two ships to face the hundred
> galleys of the Porte; and how Don John of Austria, the only com-
> mander under whom Genoa would agree with Venice, burst the battle-
> line in a sinking ship, after fighting through all the hours of daylight.
> And the story of the Pope's prayer all that day, and his vison of
> the crisis of the action at three in the afternoon, with his vision of
> the victory about the time of the Angelus.

If Fr O'Connor is correct in thinking that the poem was the direct result of the meeting at Leeds, it is of particular interest since it brings forward by a whole year the event that he described as occurring in the train on their way back to Ilkley.

On the way home I got fierce about what trash [Lepanto] made of English history, and what rubbish we talked and sang of Nelson and Trafalgar. What was at stake at Tragalgar? Only the Industrial Revolution and the Financial Supremacy of the City of London, with child-labour and Gin-Palaces, only one small department of the gilded manure-heap called Modern Progress.

It was during this tirade that Chesterton had interrupted him and told him – for the two were alone in the compartment – that he had made up his mind to be received into the Catholic Chuch, and that he was only waiting for Frances to come with him, as she had led him into the Anglican Church out of Unitarianism. Chesterton said, 'I think I have known intimately by now all the best kinds of Anglicanism, and I find them only a pale imitation.' Fr O'Connor was thrilled but not surprised. 'The surprise always had been at his natural affinity for all those things for which Catholics are persecuted or brow-beaten,' he said. 'I found during those years of intercourse preceding that night that, whatever he believed, he had rejected before I knew him all the slanders, and had unravelled for himself all the misrepresentations.'

How to tell Frances of his decision began to worry Chesterton intensely. He began to drop hints; but the matter did not really come out into the open until his serious illness in the last weeks of 1914, and he was not actually received into the Church for another eight years after that. As will be seen, the years following his intimation to Fr O'Connor were to be years of deep anxiety, until his conscience began to scream so loudly that he eventually made the move alone.

On 18 November 1911 Chesterton travelled to Cambridge to address the 'Heretics', one of the numerous university societies. The meeting was held in a large room in the Guildhall and, it being a Friday evening, the room was packed with a crowd of between eight and nine hundred people. Chesterton was once again answering Shaw, who had spoken earlier at the end of the summer term. He arrived a quarter of an hour late, but he soon made up for it by speaking brilliantly for almost two hours. It was not surprising that in the course of his address he said he thought the claims of the Greek Church and the Anglican Church were less near the truth than those of the Roman Catholic Church.

When he had risen to speak he had been given a loud and prolonged ovation; but the applause was renewed when he said that England was a pagan country, 'a heathen country to be conquered and redeemed'. All the press reports of the occasion noted that Chesterton was at his best, 'the very incarnation of G.K.C.'. As *The Gownsman* noted, 'it was a rare pleasure to observe the agility with which he pounced upon the gist or motive of a question, his scrupulous fairness, his exacerbating aplomb'. However, the writer was less certain about 'the dissipation of endowments of such breadth and profundity in acceptance of the Miraculous, and the palliation of Papal Oppression'; but, he added, 'we must be grateful indeed to a speaker who can occasionally introduce Humour into the Divine'.

An amusing argument took place during the question time, when an undergraduate suggested that Chesterton could not say he knew a thing unless he had scientific proof of it. The questioner would not say 'I know', but only 'I have an intuition.'

Chesterton asked: 'You know you exist?'

The questioner: 'No; I should be very careful to avoid the word "know". I should say, "I have an intuition that I exist."'

Chesterton: 'Then so much the worse for you. I know. I am absolutely certain that I exist, and I should say that that gentleman is quite certain that he exists, and that he is incorrect in saying that he could not be certain of anything of which he had not absolute scientific proof.'

'It is merely a matter of definition,' replied the questioner. 'I use the word in a different sense. I say it is perfectly true that I have an intuition that I exist.'

To laughter and applause, Chesterton replied, 'Cherish it.'

It was in the same November that Frances was involved in negotiations with the Burke's Estate over the purchase of a field behind their house. In the summer months if the weather was hot she and Gilbert had taken to picnicking in the fields. One day, in the company of Mildred d'Avigdor, Frances had taken some rugs and a bag of gooseberries, and Gilbert had read one of the early Father Brown stories. In the middle of the story he had suddenly broken off and looking across at the opposite field, said, 'I would like to build a house in that field.'

'Well, why shouldn't you, when we have the money?' Frances replied.

Chesterton went on to say he wished to build around a certain tree, and when eventually a studio was built in the field the tree was incorporated into the building.

All practical matters, as has been said before, were left entirely to Frances, and all the correspondence from their solicitors, Salter & Lees, was addressed to her. 'Please ask Gilbert to sign where his initials are pencilled,' said one letter, with the postscript added: 'I write to you rather than Gilbert, as I think you see to his business correspondence.'

In the February of the following year another novel, *Manalive*, was published by Thomas Nelson. It had been started many years earlier when Chesterton was still at University College, and he added to it in the Fisher Unwin days, so that the style has all the freshness and uninhibited vitality of *The Napoleon of Notting Hill*. The story tells how Innocent Smith is literally blown, by a wind as fierce as that which blew on the Day of Pentecost, into the dull lives of the residents of Beacon House, a boarding house in Swiss Cottage. Smith is an allegorical being whose message is that life is worth living, 'and innocence the only really glorious adventure in the world, that goodness is the only really romantic thing in existence, and that the only merry man on earth is the hardened and inveterate saint'. As Ronald Knox noticed, Smith represents the innocence and the fresh eyes of childhood investing with excitement and colour the drab surroundings – or so they have seemed hitherto – of half a dozen unsuccessful and disillusioned people. What 'sins' this 'spirit of youth reborn' is capable of committing are sins in appearance only. He is guilty of housebreaking, but it is his own house he has entered; he has committed bigamy, but he has each time married his own wife; and his attempts at murder have managed only to fire life into his victims. The principle Smith represents is set out clearly towards the end of the book: 'he refuses to die while he is still alive'. He has broken the conventions but kept the commandments. Smith's spiritual power was that he distinguished between custom and creed. The idea that Chesterton was attacking in the character of Smith was that, living in an entangled civilization, men had come to think certain things wrong which were not wrong at all.

Innocent Smith had continued far into his middle age a farcical existence that exposed him to so many false charges, 'because he is really happy, because he really is hilarious, because he really is a man and alive'. The reason for Innocent Smith's happiness was simply that he was innocent. He could defy the conventions because he could keep the commandments. If one were able to keep as innocent as a child, Chesterton argued, one could keep as happy as a child, the secret was 'barely and brutally to be good'.

'Like nearly all the author's essays in fiction,' said the unsigned review in *The Eye-Witness* on 21 March, 'it is a sort of doctrinal harlequinade ... still, it is ungracious to look a gift horse in the mouth, and *Manalive* is a gift horse (even if we call it a nightmare) which we shall all enjoy riding.' However, not everyone was happy, and the *British Weekly* reviewer complained that 'a more dreary task than plodding through the novel I have not attempted for a long time'. He felt that Mr Chesterton could afford to be told the truth, and 'the truth is that this book is a total, unredeemed, blank failure. It is the very worst of all Mr Chesterton's novels, and that is saying a great deal. Valueless from every point of view, the book should mark the termination of Mr Chesterton's efforts in this kind.' It was surely a matter of missing the point completely, for the same reviewer admitted that 'as an interpreter of life, sympathetic, passionate, full of understanding, there is no living writer to match him. When he is at work which suits him, Mr Chesterton is unrivalled.' At least, the reviewer had acknowledged the author could on occasion and at his best be himself a man alive.

On 7 March the Liberal Government accepted the tender of the London-based Marconi Wireless Telegraph Company to build wireless stations in strategic places throughout the British Empire in fulfilment of the terms of the Imperial Conference held in the previous year. The plan seemed innocent enough, but the events which led up to the infamous Marconi Scandal took place during the four-month period between the acceptance of the tender and the tabling of the contract in the House of Commons on 19 July. Briefly, the scandal was caused by the unethical trading in Marconi shares by several individuals who had inside knowledge of the company's affairs and therefore a head start over the general public. The managing director of the Marconi Company, Godfrey Isaacs, who was a brother of Rufus Isaacs, the Attorney General, had travelled across to the United States, where he was a director of the American branch of Marconi; there he set up a series of business deals based on his privileged knowledge of affairs in London, and returned home with 500,000 American Marconi shares to distribute. The beneficiaries of these shares, which could not but increase rapidly in value, included, besides Godfrey Isaacs himself, his brother Harry, who soon sold 10,000 of his allocation of 50,000 to Rufus at their original price. Rufus, who had evidently thought it unwise to receive shares from Godfrey direct, then sold 1,000 shares to Lloyd George, the Chancellor of the Exchequer, and a similar number to the Master of Elibank, the Government Chief Whip. This underhand dealing was irregular, to say the least, and at the time no money changed hands. Nor, until 19 April, when the American company authorized their issue, did the shares exist; but when the market in this particular issue opened the price rose from £3 5s. od. to £4 0s. od. on the first day, while the ministers had agreed with Godfrey Isaacs the low price of £2 0s. od. a share.

Thus started the scandal of 'Ministers Gambling in Marconi's'. The repercussions were to affect both Chesterton brothers profoundly, though in different ways, and were this book a biography of Cecil it would be necessary to go into the whole business in very much more detail. However, Gilbert became involved only towards the end of the matter when he gave evidence at his brother's trial. Obviously, the whole business was grist to *The Eye-Witness*'s mill. Cecil Chesterton had succeeded Belloc as editor in the third week of June, though the magazine would not lose the invaluable aid of Belloc's 'pen, his knowledge, and his inspiration'. He set about the task of bringing the ministers to book, and in particular attempting to demolish the reputation and lower the status of both Godfrey and Rufus Isaacs.

Besides contributing his editorial, Cecil Chesterton wrote under the signature of 'Junius' numerous attacks on politicians, and he launched a bitter attack on Rufus Isaacs in the issue of 4 July, which was described by one correspondent the following week as 'little more than vulgar abuse, envenomed by anti-semitism'. Cecil's tone towards all politicians tended towards the contemptuous, and he referred to them scathingly by their surnames – Samuel, Isaacs, and so on – whether they happened to be Jews or not: Lloyd George was just 'George'. On 8 August *The Eye-Witness* asked 'What progress is the Marconi Scandal making? We ask the question merely from curiosity and under no illusion as to the inevitable end of the affair. Everybody knows the record of Isaacs and his father, and his uncle, and in general of the whole family.' The die was cast, and Cecil's prolonged attack on the Isaacs family resulted ultimately in his being sued for criminal libel by Godfrey Isaacs. The preliminary hearing in the magistrates' court was held towards the end of February the following year.

It is now time to see what Gilbert Chesterton had been doing since the publication of *Manalive*. On 12 April he had told a large audience at Church House that the matter with England was that for centuries it had not had a civil war. If England had a civil war the next morning it would be a good thing and, judging by the demeanour of those present, he thought it would be quite possible to have one that night. The meeting or, rather, demonstration had been organized by the Church Socialist League during the miner's strike; Conrad Noel presided and the Countess of Warwick, speaking as a coal owner, said they were 'expressing their intense feeling of gratitude for the magnificent example that had been set them in true comradeship by the miners of the United Kingdom'.

Chesterton said he was not a socialist 'as the term was used by intelligent people, and with regard to how the term was used by unintelligent people he was not interested in it'. According to some people, he said, a socialist was sometimes a kind of saint and sometimes a sort of philanthropist. It was far above him to be a saint and far beneath him to be a philanthropist. Amid loud laughter at this last remark, he admitted that socialism was a definite proposal, and those who said it was unbusinesslike or could not work did it a great wrong. He feared it might work.

After making his comments about a civil war he thought no one would 'accuse him of any lack of revolutionary sentiment'. One thing that had been absolutely abolished by recent events was the legend of the agitator. It was now impossible for any intelligent man to say that the anger of the poor was produced by agitators. Every single leader of the strikers had tried to calm the men. The poor were angry. There was no theory of the civic system of the state which did not support the aim of the striker. Unless the populace very quickly and very forcibly wrenched out of the hands of the rich the power and government of the country, our country would go through one of those long periods of defeat and eclipse which ended either in disappearance or in a slow emergence from a long period of barbarism.

Immediately after the meeting a procession of some six hundred people, led by George Lansbury, MP, carrying a cross, moved towards Lambeth Palace. Here the Rector of Lambeth received a memorial of the occasion in Dr Davidson's absence, since the Archbishop had assured the meeting by letter that 'any communication forwarded to him would receive his attentive consideration'. After the presentation Conrad Noel 'dismissed the procession with the Benediction'.

The meeting was important as being the first occasion on which Chesterton's famous hymn 'O God of Earth and Altar' was sung; the words were printed in the *Christian Commonwealth* three weeks later on 1 May. There must be thousands of people who, knowing no other lines by Chesterton, will know these words, which are usually sung to the traditional English melody arranged by Vaughan Williams, although occasionally to a nineteenth-century tune by R.L.de Pearsall.

O God of earth and altar,
　Bow down and hear our cry,
Our earthly rulers falter,
　Our people drift and die;
The walls of gold entomb us,
　The swords of scorn divide,
Take not thy thunder from us,
　But take away our pride.

From all that terror teaches,
　From lies of tongue and pen,
From all the easy speeches
　That comfort cruel men,
From sale and profanation
　Of honour and the sword,
From sleep and from damnation,
　Deliver us, good Lord.

Tie in a living tether
　The prince and priest and thrall,
Bind all our lives together,
　Smite us and save us all;
In ire and exultation
　Aflame with faith and free,
Lift up a living nation,
　A single sword to thee.

Chesterton could not have had the Countess of Warwick in mind when he told his *Daily News* readers on 8 June:

A revolutionist would say (with perfect truth) that coal-owners know next to nothing about coal-mining. But we are past that point. Coal-owners know next to nothing about coal-owning. They do not develop and defend the nature of their own monopoly with an consistent and courageous policy, however wicked, as did the old aristocrats with the monopoly of land. They have not the virtues or even the vices of tyrants; they have only their powers.

The article was among those included in the collection of essays published as *A Miscellany of Men* by Methuen in the following October,
and it showed once again Chesterton's hatred of the capitalist system.
'The special and solid result of the reign of the employers,' he wrote,
'has been – unemployment. Unemployment not only increasing, but
becoming at last the very point upon which the whole process turns.'

Meanwhile, during that same summer, Belloc was putting together
his notes for his book *The Servile State*, considered by some to be the
most prophetic book of the twentieth century. Chesterton seemed to
have had Belloc's theme in mind when he concluded his *Daily News*
article with:

> If you visit the villages that depend on one of the great squires, you
> will hear praises, often just, of the landlord's good sense or good
> nature; you will hear of whole systems of pensions or of care for
> the sick, like those of a small and separate nation; you will see much
> cleanliness, order, and business habits in the offices and accounts
> of the estate. But if you ask again what has been the upshot, what
> has been the actual result of the reign of landlords, again the answer
> is plain. At the end of the reign of landlords men will not live on
> the land. The practical effect of having landlords is not having tenants.
> The practical effect of having employers is that men are not employed.
> The unrest of the populace is therefore more than a murmur against
> tyranny; it is against a sort of treason. It is the suspicion that even
> at the top of the tree, even in the seats of the mighty, our very success
> is unsuccessful.

Chesterton shared Belloc's argument, set out so clearly in his book,
that the 'servile state' had begun in 'that arrangement of society in which
so considerable a number of families and individuals are constrained
by positive law to labour for the advantage of other individuals as to
stamp the whole community with the mark of such labour'. It is important
to understand that Belloc was not speaking about the collectivist state;
he was not reviving Herbert Spencer's description of socialism as 'the
New Slavery', nor was he applying the term to any tyrannical or interfer-
ing state; as Cecil Chesterton put it in his review of the book, 'to a
state which shuts up public houses or prohibits betting'.

On 17 June Chesterton received an enthusiastic letter from Galsworthy
about 'The Ballad of the White Horse'. 'A really splendid stir and
thrum in it,' Galsworthy wrote, 'and that passage beginning: "'Brothers

at arms,' said Alfred" rouses me to high enthusiasm.' At about that time too the builders had completed work on the studio in the field behind Overroads, and soon the timber and brick building was accommodating the 'enlarged audiences', especially of children of all ages, that came to enjoy Chesterton's toy theatre productions and puppet shows. Another amusement, always popular, was charades, and the studio had a ready supply of costumes for dressing up. On one well-remembered occasion everyone was given a sheet and expected to improvise; Chesterton appeared as the front part of an elephant with a knotted sheet for a trunk. During the same summer of 1912 Fr O'Connor, whose name appears at regular intervals in the Overroads visitors' book, remembered playing the part of Canon Crosskeys in a charade in which Lily Yeats, the poet's sister, also took part. The evening waxed late, he recalled, and no doubt a quantity of wine had been consumed with the supper. When at a quarter to midnight the party broke up and those who were staying at Overroads made their way across the field, the night being particularly dark, the priest offered Chesterton his arm; but Chesterton refused somewhat irritably, which was out of character and done in a manner 'foreign to the friendship'. Perhaps Fr O'Connor had sensed danger, but he was unable to prevent Chesterton from tripping over a tree-pot and falling so heavily on his right side that he broke his arm and had to rest in bed for almost six weeks.

'Gilbert is progressing,' recorded Frances, 'but his arm is more painful now that it is beginning to knit, and the heat is trying. Dr Pocock has managed to get the arm into a splint.' Two photographs taken some weeks afterwards in July showed Chesterton looking very solemn with his arm in a sling. Also very noticeable was the patient's increased weight, which had likely contributed to the seriousness of the fall; not that Chesterton was ever careful about safety, and another episode related by Fr O'Connor showed now carefree he could be. The priest had accompanied Frances down to the shops one bright morning and on their return had 'suddenly seen Gilbert at his largest, on all fours on top of the pergola, peering down through the creepers'. They had left him, so they thought, 'sending articles to hell', as he called his life-long pursuit of journalism. With a cry Fr O'Connor rushed to the rescue, but Frances remained calm and called him back saying, 'Don't worry, I had the pergola very strongly built in anticipation of Gilbert's antics.'

The fact that Chesterton's writing hand was temporarily out of action did not affect his weekly articles, which he was able to dictate to a secretary. It is not certain exactly when Nellie Allport, who 'knew neither shorthand nor typing', and used to take down his dictation in longhand, handed over her duties to Mrs Meredith, but it was probably before the summer of 1912. Mrs Meredith, who lived in Beaconsfield and was a friend of the Solomons, worked for Chesterton until the outbreak of the First World War. She was able to give Maisie Ward an amusing account of her time at Overroads, and said that what amazed her at first was the way Chesterton could produce two articles at once on totally different subjects by dictating one to her while he scribbled away at another himself. Needless to say, 'the dictation came very slowly; but this was so even when he was only dictating'. The accident meant that he could only produce one article at a time! Even when he was well his 'Our Notebook' contribution made every Thursday a rush, since Chesterton would invariably put it off till the last minute. 'We'll do it presently,' he would say, 'but I don't think it would matter much if my worthless words didn't appear this week.' The article usually missed the last post to London and had to be put on a late train to be met by a messenger from the magazine's office, after Frances had made an urgent telephone call and the secretary had dashed to the station on her bicycle. The Thursday agitation is said to have even affected the little dog, Winkle.

By the autumn of 1912 *The Eye-Witness* had run into such serious financial difficulties that it collapsed. Cecil Chesterton acted swiftly and was able to persuade his father to put up sufficient capital to buy the paper, which Cecil 'proposed to carry on under the title of *The New Witness*'. It was, according to Ada Jones, the only occasion Cecil approached his father for monetary backing. Ada herself, who up to that time had only occasionally written for the paper, became a permanent member of the staff, and after a shaky start in the old offices in John Street, Adelphi, the paper's headquarters became 20–21 Essex Street, where the window overlooked the Embankment. There Cecil dictated his 'thunderous leaders and barbed paragraphs', and the 'extraordinary history of the Marconi shares' was further revealed to the public.

Meanwhile a Select Committe of the House of Commons had been appointed in an attempt to get at the truth of the Marconi business. Chesterton was quite convinced that if he had not raised 'a pretty considerable agitation' the Committee would never have been appointed. However, there were other periodicals in the field, and Leo Maxse's *National Review* and the *Morning Post*, as well as the financial press, were loud in their condemnation of the ministers' actions.

Cecil Chesterton was summoned to appear before the Committee on 2 January, and he announced the fact in the columns of his paper. In the same issue he said that the past year 'may, perhaps, be known to history as the Year of Scandals'. It was a year in which 'Samuel, the Postmaster-General, handed over the wireless telegraphy of the Empire to Isaacs' brother under a contract which no one outside the official gang has had the hardihood to defend'. The preceding week he had written:

> It may be worthwhile to ask how it comes about that Mr Wilson of Cadbury's *Daily News* is apparently always in possession of exact information as to the intentions of the Committee in the matter of calling witnesses and the like some time before those intentions have been communicated to the persons affected. It is clearly most improper that a particular journalist, who has constituted himself a sort of Special Excuser to the Front Benches, should be in communication with anyone inside the Committee or in touch with any of its members.

There were several other derogatory references to George Cadbury's 'Cocoa Press' in the same issue, and two weeks later Cecil published his brother's 'A Song of Strange Drinks', one of a series of poems entitled 'Songs of the Simple Life'. The third stanza of the poem was to lead to the abrupt end of Gilbert Chesterton's twelve-year association with the *Daily News*. After praising wine and water, and giving some tolerance to tea, which 'although an Oriental, is a gentleman at least', Chesterton added:

> Cocoa is a cad and coward,
>   Cocoa is a vulgar beast,
> Cocoa is a crawling, cringing,
>   Lying, loathsome swine and clown,
> And may very well be grateful
>   To the fool that takes him down.

'I hate all separations,' said Gardiner in his letter informing him that his services as a weekly journalist would no longer be required. 'This I hate for many reasons, but I will not trouble you with them.' He went on to say how sorry he was that Frances Chesterton had been ill, and gave particular praise to a poem of hers he had seen in the *Westminster Gazette* some weeks before. Gardiner was wrong in thinking

that the *Daily News* columns would be open to Chesterton in the future.
His last article appeared on 1 February, and not until 1928 did the
paper publish anything by him again. Nothing daunted, Chesterton
immediately began negotiations with the socialist paper, the *Daily Herald*,
and his first article, 'The Epitaph of Pierpoint Morgan', appeared on
12 April.

On 28 February, in the company of Belloc, he attended Cecil's preliminary hearing before Sir Albert de Rutzen at Bow Street police court,
at which the defendant was committed for trial. As Belloc informed
Maurice Baring, Cecil's speech created a very powerful impression 'and
Godfrey Isaacs's counsel went about saying so'. Towards the end of
his speech Cecil made a strong defence of *The New Witness*, which
Isaacs's counsel, Mr Muir, had tried to brand as a 'gutter rag'. 'When
any man acquainted with letters,' he said, 'were to make out a list of,
say, the twenty best-known literary men in England to-day, I will undertake to find twelve of them among the contributors to my paper.' He
went on to mention Quiller-Couch, Wells, Shaw, and Belloc by name;
but he might well have added Desmond MacCarthy, E. Nesbit, Katharine
Tynan, J. C. Squire, and Arthur Ransome, besides Maurice Baring and
his own brother, who were all regular contributors at the time, although
some names may not have been as well known as they later became.

The New Witness printed the full text of Cecil's Bow Street speech
on 6 March, and in the same issue Gilbert Chesterton reviewed Bentley's
Trent's Last Case which he described as 'a quite unusually triumphant
detective-story'. A good detective story, he said, is, broadly speaking,
a reversible machine.

> It is a series of points or pegs fitting into certain holes, which must
> be so skilfully made that when folded back the opposite way all the
> pegs fit into the holes as neatly as they did before. The word spelt
> forward must exactly contradict the word spelt backward, but using
> only the same letters, and, unlike some Baconian inscription, they
> must both be correctly spelt. The very fact that one end of the stick
> points to one thing ought to warn the reader that the other end points
> to the opposite. It is a struggle between the writer and reader for
> the possession of the right end of the stick.

Chesterton rightly refused to give any of the story away; to do that
with a mystery story, he said, would be like burning all the copies of
the book.

The following week the paper carried G.S.Street's review of Chesterton's latest book, *The Victorian Age in Literature*. This short volume, commissioned by Williams and Norgate for their Home University Library of Modern Knowledge, had taken the editors rather by surprise, and a short explanation was printed at the beginning of the book to the effect that it was not 'an authoritative history of Victorian literature', but rather 'a free and personal statement of views and impressions about the significance of Victorian literature made by Mr Chesterton at the Editors' express invitation'. As Street pointed out, the book would be useless and mostly unintelligible to anyone not fairly well versed in the writers Chesterton discusses and, as with the Watts and Blake books, the reader learns more about the author than about the writers under discussion; but many of the observations remain in the memory, as when Chesterton said of Macaulay that his greatness 'lay not in his reasoning power, but in his imagination. He had a warm, poetic and sincere enthusiasm for great things as such; an ardour and appetite for great books, great battles, great cities, great men. He felt and used names like trumpets'; an observation immediately recognizable to anyone who has been 'encouraged' to learn Macaulay at school.

In comparing Meredith's novels with Hardy's; Chesterton said,

One of them went upwards through a tangled but living forest to lonely but healthy hills: the other went down to a swamp. Hardy went down to botanise in the swamp, while Meredith climbed towards the sun. Meredith became, at his best, a sort of daintily dressed Walt Whitman: Hardy became a sort of village atheist brooding and blaspheming over the village idiot.

Such observations were those of 'a clever undergraduate', according to the *Times Literary Supplement*, whose reviewer went on to deplore Chesterton's 'obsession with religion'. 'But let no one imagine,' he continued, 'that there is nothing in the book but a series of debating society epigrams and perversities of judgment. There is the other Mr Chesterton in it, whose phrases are none the less brilliant for having the day-light of truth in them.' As an example of this 'other Mr Chesterton' the reviewer mentioned 'the greater issue', in which the author had argued that real fraternity can exist only in the presence of religion. 'Man is merely man when he is seen against the sky. If he is seen against any landscape he is only a man of that land. If he is seen against any house he is only a householder. Only where death and eternity are intensely present can human beings feel their fellowship.' No one would put the book down, said the same reviewer, 'without the sense of having taken a tonic or perhaps of having received a series of impertinently administered electric shocks'.

In the interval between his brother's appearance at Bow Street and the opening of the case of *Rex* v. *Chesterton* in the Central Criminal Court on 27 May, Gilbert Chesterton for a while became more deeply involved in *The New Witness*'s attack on the Isaacses and Samuel. For one thing he had a little more time now that his Saturday article was not needed for the *Daily News*, and *The New Witness* published several longer articles by him as well as his poems; but his action was more prompted by loyalty to his brother, and the strange libel action brought by Sir Rufus Isaacs and Herbert Samuel against the French paper *Le Matin*. However, the paper withdrew its allegations and the case was dropped. As Cecil Chesterton pointed out, compared with *The New Witness*'s continued barrage *Le Matin* had been mild in its reporting of the Marconi business. The matter prompted from Gilbert 'The Song of Cosmopolitan Courage', a satirical poem which he later excluded from his collected poems, although he quoted a few lines from it in his autobiography.

Chesterton really was angry, and his bitterness towards Sir Rufus Isaacs in particular knew few bounds. On 31 March he wrote a letter from Beaconsfield in which he said:

> If ever a human being on this earth most distinctly did not tell people 'what was in his mind' even when he professed to doing it, he is Sir Rufus Isaacs. What was in his mind was the recent memory of shovelling Marconis in and out as a croupier does coins; what was on his lips was a distinct denial proper to an intellectual man who had hardly heard of such things.

In an article, 'The Dawn of Something Else', published in *The New Witness* on 10 March Chesterton renewed his attack.

> The politics of Sir Rufus Isaacs are as wearisome to the flesh as his religion would be a revelation to the soul. It must also be remembered that in the days when theological tests united and divided men clearly, it was much easier to look at an alien thing with the clean curiosity of the artist. Anti-Semitism is a sour fruit – but it is the fruit of Crypto-Semitism.

Cecil's trial lasted for ten days; Godfrey Isaacs won the case, and Chesterton was only fined £100, instead of the three-year prison sentence he was expected to receive. By a strange irony, the judge, Mr Justice Phillimore, was a cousin of John Phillimore, Chesterton's and Belloc's great friend, who held the Chair of Classics at Glasgow University, and whose review of *The Oxford Book of Latin Verse* was published in *The New Witness* the very same week. It was generally felt that Cecil Chesterton had gained a moral victory, and there had been considerable cheering in the court when the verdict was announced.

Gilbert Chesterton had attended each day of the proceedings with Frances beside him, unlike his mother who 'regarded it as a joke that Cecil should be a prisoner on trial', and refused to see him in the dock. Gilbert remained in the courtroom and now and then slipped outside to tell his father and mother what was happening. On the ninth day he was called and questioned on oath, as were Maurice Baring and Conrad Noel, about his brother's character. When he was asked how long he had known 'the accused gentleman', he replied, 'Since he was born, I think'; and when asked what he had to say about him he answered, 'I can only say I rather envy him the dignity of his present position.' Then, after being brought to the point, he added, 'His character is good in my opinion and most other people's opinion.'

Perhaps Cecil's 'present position' was not all Gilbert envied at this time, for Cecil had only recently done what he so far lacked the courage to do without Frances's approval and had been received into the Catholic Church, a decision taken 'swiftly and without any period of doubt', although like all converts he had received a course of instruction. The priest he had chosen had been Fr Bowden of the Brompton Oratory, who three years earlier had performed the same office for Baring. Another ironic aspect of the whole Marconi affair was that some years later Godfrey Isaacs himself was received into the Catholic Church, the kind of twist to a story which, as Belloc once said, would be suppressed on the stage as being too violently improbable, and in fiction 'ridiculed for a clumsy trick'; but in life such a thing is to be found. Belloc himself had been on the Continent, and so had missed the trial, but like many he rejoiced at its unlikely outcome.

Thinking about it all many years later, and long after the war, Gilbert Chesterton pointed out that there had never been anything like *The Eye-Witness* in England, anyway since the days of Cobbett, and 'certainly not within the memory of the oldest men then living'. The charge against

the Marconi ministers was 'that they had received a tip, or were "let
in on the ground floor", as the financial phrase goes, by a Government
contractor whose contract was at the time being considered or accepted
by the Government'. The question at issue, Chesterton argued, was
one of a contract and a tip, and not of 'an ordinary little flutter in
stocks and shares'. Such was the Marconi Affair; but it is important
to distinguish between the Affair and the case. The case, as the judge
emphasized at the trial, had nothing to do with the question of whether
the politicians had dabbled in Marconis. The jury's verdict was not
to answer that political question one way or the other. They were concerned solely with 'whether the individual Godfrey Isaacs, in his career
as a company-promoter previous to the Marconi Case, had been unfairly
described by the individual Cecil Chesterton. The jury were strongly
instructed to find, and did find, that the description of the company-
promoter was wrong.'

It is almost impossible to accept Chesterton's assertion that throughout
the campaign his brother 'while he undoubtedly used all the violent
vocabulary of Cobbett in attacking Godfrey Isaacs and the rest,... had
not in fact the faintest grain of malice, or even irritation'; but even
Mr Justice Phillimore had hinted when he sentenced Cecil that Cecil
might not have considered deeply enough the effects of his actions.

> When I consider the cruelty of some of these charges, the effect I
> daresay not considered but obvious to anybody who did consider
> them, it might have rendered Godfrey Charles Isaacs a beggar and
> driven him from his employment as well as driven him from all fame
> and respect and good name, and when I remember the sending of
> those placards along the front of his place of business in the Strand,
> it is extremely difficult to restrain oneself from sending you to prison.

While all the excitement of Cecil's trial was at its height Chesterton
himself had been threatened with a libel action by Lever Brothers over
a remark he had made in answer to a question during a lecture at
the City Temple, when he had described Port Sunlight as 'corresponding
to a slave compound'. Chesterton had only reiterated Belloc's theory
of servility in the sense of a loss of liberty. In the preparation of a
possible defence he exchanged correspondence with several people
including Shaw, who offered his financial help should it become necessary. 'Though Lever may treat him as well as Pickwick would no doubt
have treated old Weller,' he wrote, 'if he had consented to take charge

of his savings, Lever is master of his employee's fate, and captain of his employee's soul, which is slavery.' Chesterton's attitude was that Lever, whom he referred to as 'Old Sun and Soap-suds', could sue him till he burst. He was not afraid of him.

It was absurd, he said, to have libel actions rather than mere quarrels about controversies. 'It would mean every Capitalist being persecuted for saying that Socialism is robbery and every Socialist for saying property is theft.' As he informed Wells, he was prepared if necessary to conduct his own case and fight it 'purely as a point of the liberty of letters and public speech', and he asked Wells if he would care to come 'to see the fun'. In any event the case never came to court once it had been made clear to Lever Brothers that Chesterton was 'not a scurrilous person making a vulgar and slanderous attack upon their business'.

The withdrawal of the case meant that there was no way of making copy out of the situation, whereas Cecil continued to use the Marconi case for many weeks after the trial had ended, and on 27 June Gilbert Chesterton chaired the first *New Witness* Conference held in the Essex Hall, just off the Strand. The subject of the conference was predictably 'The Meaning of the Marconi Scandal'; the chief speaker was Frank Hugh O'Donnell, and when towards the end of the proceedings Cecil Chesterton got up to speak there was loud applause for the man who had 'belled the cat'.

The first conference proved to be such a success that the large hall had to be taken on 4 July for Mr G.K.Chesterton on 'Why I am not an Official Liberal'. The audience was told that the speaker was 'a sedentary, casual, self-indulgent person, as are most journalists', and as he had the conscience of a journalist he would not say that he was not a liberal, but he would say that the sort of liberalism 'based on a real body of conviction and doctrine' that he stood for was now very hard to find in the Liberal Party. 'I am a Liberal', he said. 'It is the other people who are not Liberals.'

There was ecstatic laughter when after illustrating his point he continued:

My brother has been all sorts of extraordinary things in his time. When I appeared for a brief moment in Court to give what appeared to be an entirely superfluous testimony to his character, Mr Justice Phillimore said, 'What we want to know is, whether his character is respectable?' I consider it the greatest act of self-control of my life that I did not answer what occurred to me to answer at that moment. I felt inclined to say: 'Lord bless me, he was in the Fabian Society.' By a violent effort I refrained from alluding to the fact. We have all gone through many paths and stages in arriving at our present political opinions.

Later that month it was rumoured that Sir Rufus Isaacs was likely to be appointed the new Lord Chief Justice. The rumour was true, and Isaacs was introduced to the Bench and Bar on 22 October. In the meantime the appointment stirred the Chesterton brothers into renewed hostility. 'It will hardly be denied that we want a Lord Chief Justice who shall be free from all taint and suspicion of corruption. Sir Rufus Isaacs is not free from such taint and suspicion,' declared *The New Witness* on 24 July, and in the same issue Gilbert Chesterton produced an article which stated for the first time the absurd idea, which all Chesterton's admirers must regret that he ever countenanced, that 'Jews ought to be allowed to do everything done by everybody else on condition that they wear Arab costume'.

In the course of the article he admitted 'a faint fear that the Jewish race has now more vitality than the English'. However, the purpose was to attack Isaacs.

> I am a Liberal; and I dislike the idea of Jews being excluded from any civic order. By all means let a Jew be Prime Minister. But what a good taste Disraeli might have had in Oriental dress! And what a damnable taste he had in English dress! By all means let a Jew be Lord Chief Justice. I cannot quite grasp why the most discredited Jew should be specially selected for that post; but in this precisely what puzzles me is the existence of so many more worthy Jewish lawyers. By all means let him be Lord Chief Justice; but let him not sit in wig and gown, but in turban and flowing robes.

If the Jew were dressed differently, he argued, we should 'know what he meant; and when we were all quite separate we should begin to understand each other'. His whole argument, such as it was, he had expressed near the beginning of the article when he said, 'Israel will once more come out of captivity on the day when a Jewish tailor has the courage to cut out a gaberdine.' Chesterton admitted that many people would regard his suggestion as a joke; but nevertheless he seemed to have lost his way dangerously in one of his games of charades. The news that *The New Witness* had run into financial difficulties, largely owing to the costs awarded against Cecil Chesterton at his trial, was greeted with some relief by certain members of the Government. On 31 July the editor appealed for support from 'those who have already helped us so abundantly by their generous encouragement and good wishes'. One did not set out to attack the most powerful people in England, suggested the editor, 'without fully counting the cost'. In the same issue there were letters of support from several eminent literary figures, including Shaw who called *The New Witness* 'a very remarkable paper', and hoped that it would be able to continue. 'I do not mind seeing Mr Samuel and Sir Rufus Isaacs and the rest treated as malignant dragons, giants, serpents,' he wrote. *The New Witness* was 'a consciously and purposely romantic paper, the organ of an attempt to revive Romance from the swoon into which it was thrown by the poisoned sting of Cervantes'.

Shaw, who admitted to being 'the great Anti-Romancer of the age', understood as well as anyone the essential difference between the two Chesterton brothers. He knew that Cecil was the harder character, a down-to-earth, hard-hitting pugilist of a journalist who, as Wells put it, in comparison with his brother 'seemed condensed: not quite big enough for a real Chesterton'; while Gilbert was not even sure if he was his own 'Wild Knight', let alone the 'verray parfit, gentil knyght' of Chaucer.

It would have been difficult to imagine Cecil firing off arrows from the upstairs windows of 11 Warwick Gardens, or making wild passes at the shrubbery with a sword, but visitors to Beaconsfield had to be prepared always for such things. It was all so very 'jolly', that ubiquitous word that Wells said Chesterton should be restricted to using only forty times a day; yet the world was growing less 'jolly' daily, as Chesterton could see only too clearly. It was almost impossible to bear: the world in which he had grown up, the pre-Marconi world, had been to him like a toy, and 'a toy is not a trifle, but the very opposite', as he reminded his readers in the summer of 1913. 'The happy age at which we regard the whole universe as a toy is the very age at which we feel most secure of its solidity and permanence.' He had learnt his philosophy in the nursery: the world must be full of wonder, the characters in the toy theatre continued to contend with *their* parade of 'malignant dragons, giants, serpents', the gargoyle faces of his imagination gaped back at him in charcoal against their background of brown paper. He had striven to extend childhood, and others thought him innocent, but he knew he had lost his innocence; he had entered his fortieth year, and his anxiety about his ability to go on fulfilling all his engagements and completing his articles on time weighed ever more heavily. He had found it impossible, it seems, to deliver an article on the disappearance of the hansom cab for *The Observer*: perhaps it would have been too painful. When he returned to Fleet Street now, it was 'not in peace he came'. He wrote:

> A cloven pride was in my heart,
>   And half my love was shame.
> I came to fight in fairy tale,
>   Whose end shall no man know –
> To fight the old Green Dragon
>   Until the Cock shall crow.

The pre-Marconi Fleet Street had disappeared for ever; now the journalists' copy was subjected to more strict editing to suit the policy of the papers' owners. As 'he that dreams and rambles through his own elfin air' might see, the journalists were 'chained to the rich by ruin', and like those earlier inmates of the Fleet prison they were in chains.

Yet he was overstretching himself; he was writing too much, and drinking far too much. Frances, whom he loved more than all the world, was so often ill and depressed, and he found he was little comfort, and he needed even more comfort and reassurance from her, but he was unable to discuss with her that thing which was first in his mind, the decision he had already taken with regard to the Church. Just now it would wound her too deeply and, besides, he knew days when his mind was less certain. The time was drawing near when both mind and body would be unable to carry the burden of all his endeavours. In the summer of 1913 he kept them going by sheer force of will; in fact in just over a year, in the fulfilment of Providence, his mind and body would tell him: 'Enough'.

13

Breakdown

1914

'The trouble with the journalist,' Chesterton wrote in the May of 1913, 'is that he has to work as hard as a millionaire, while he hates work as heartily as a mystic. It is a dangerous trade to be at once lazy and busy.' He would certainly have applied this charge to himself, but he knew his brother to be different, for Cecil had a steely attitude to work. Through his energy *The New Witness* survived its crisis, and by an issue of 5,000 shares at £1 each sufficient capital was raised to carry on as normal. The prospectus filed with the Registrar of Joint Companies showed that in a contract between Cecil and his father at the beginning of the year '40 shares were allotted to Mr Gilbert Keith Chesterton in satisfaction of moneys owing in respect of services to *The New Witness*', and his name appears also as a director of the company. Chesterton's lasting involvement in the paper's finances was to prove over the years an ever-increasing burden on his purse, and a major bone of contention between himself and Frances.

The autumn of 1913 brought with it the fulfilment of Shaw's hopes when Chesterton's first play, *Magic*, 'a fantastic comedy in three acts', opened at Gertrude Kingston's Little Theatre under the direction of Kenelm Foss. The play, which was an immediate success and ran initially for three weeks, was performed together with a one-act farce, *Geminae*, by George Calderon, and a programme of music by a string trio that played, among other things, one of Brahms's Hungarian Dances.

In *Magic* Chesterton once again expounded the main outline of his philosophy, that a belief in 'God and the demons and that Immortal Mystery' is essential to an understanding of reality, and that even those who deny the existence of the supernatural dimension to life are nevertheless bound by it. The play's action centres on a conjuror's power to make an electric lamp, which is normally red, turn blue, and the manner in which he achieves it. Once again Chesterton drew upon the dark period of his life, when as an undergraduate he and Cecil had played with the planchette. Two actors, both well-known in their day, took part in the well-received first production: Franklin Dyall played the Conjuror; and Grace Croft the part of Patricia Carleon, the play's heroine, who believes in good fairies, and seems to have read too much early Yeats.

Besides the two chief characters Chesterton had introduced five others, each representing different aspects of his central argument. Their roles were fairly predictable: the sceptical doctor, the Christian socialist Anglican, Patricia's atheist brother, the Duke at whose mansion the action takes place, and his agent, Hastings. The first audiences were feasted on Chestertonian wit, but the humour of the stage directions was reserved for those who bought copies of the text; comments included 'The Duke is a healthy, hearty man in tweeds, with a rather wandering eye. In the present state of the peerage it is necessary to explain that the Duke, though an ass, is a gentleman.' When the Conjuror declares his love for Patricia, which she is pleased to reciprocate, they are directed to do 'whatever things passionate people do on the stage'.

On the opening night, at the end of the performance, as one member of the audience recalled, Chesterton

> ... came forward, and in a delightful little speech told us he did not believe in his powers as a writer. He did not believe he could write a good play, nor a good article, nor even a picture postcard, perhaps the hardest task of all. But he did believe in his own opinions, and so sure was he that they were right that he wanted his audience to believe them too.

He went on to describe himself as an amateur, and his play, he said, should be judged by amateur standards. Nevertheless, most of the critics gave the author a good reception the following morning in their reviews. Some, as Chesterton would have expected, made fun of the demons. 'Mr Chesterton,' wrote William Archer in *The Star*, 'is an elusive and tricksy – not to say tricky – Puck of Spooks' Hill.' In *The Nation* the editor, H.W.Massingham, adopted much the same tone: 'Only when he resorted to his "spooks" and his "crystals" did he become a bore of the first water.'

Perhaps the greatest praise was given to Chesterton verbally by Forster Bovill, if Bovill had remembered to pass on the message he had received from George Moore, who on 24 November had written:

I followed the comedy of *Magic* from the first line to the last with interest and appreciation, and I am not exaggerating when I say that I think of all modern plays I like it the best. Mr Chesterton wished to express an idea and his construction and his dialogue are the best that he could have chosen for the expression of that idea: therefore, I look upon the play as practically perfect.

Moore found some fault with the Conjuror's love for the girl.

That she should love the magician is well enough, but it materialises him a little too much if he returns that love. I should have preferred her to love him more and he to love her less. But this spot, if it be a spot, is a very small one on a spotless surface of excellence. ... I hope I can rely on you to tell Mr Chesterton how much I appreciated his play as I should like him to know my artistic sympathies.

When one remembers that nine years previously Moore had been one of Chesterton's 'heretics', the praise was magnanimous indeed. In 1904 Chesterton had described Moore as being 'in a perpetual state of temporary honesty. He has admired all the most admirable modern eccentrics until they could stand it no longer.' At the same time, the reasons Moore had given for his decision to leave the Roman Catholic Church had seemed to Chesterton 'the most admirable tribute to that communion which has been written of late years'. It had been not so much the dogma of the other world that had troubled Moore, he said, 'but the dogma of the reality of this world'.

The programme for *Magic* showed not only photographs of the leading members of the cast, but also a full-page picture of the author, taken at the height of Chesterton's podginess and captioned with a quotation from Holbrook Jackson's *Romance and Reality*: 'He sees the wonder, mystery and utility of common everyday things, just as a child does, and he is not afraid of proclaiming his delight to the whole world.'

As I said at the beginning of the book, the childlike sense of wonder that Chesterton was blessed with throughout his life was very much part of his religious sense, and must not be confused with the idea of 'never growing up'; but by 1913 the latter idea had become a commonplace in the phraseology of those who reviewed his work, and so it was not surprising that it appeared in several reviews of *Magic*. 'G.K.C. is like Peter Pan. He has never grown up. He has the heart of a child,' wrote one reviewer. The last sentence, had he been vain enough to acknowledge it, Chesterton would have received as a great compliment, but he would have hotly rejected the first two. Perhaps he had the review in mind when at about the same time he came to put together his article for the *Illustrated London News* of 27 December. 'I have always held that Peter Pan was wrong,' he wrote. 'He admitted it would be a great adventure to die; but it did not seem to occur to him that it would be a great adventure to live. If he had consented to march with the fraternity of his fellow-creatures, he would have found that there were solid experiences and important revelations even in growing up.' The mistake of Peter Pan, Chesterton argued, was the mistake of the new theory of life. 'I might call it Peter Pantheism.'

When that article appeared the Chestertons' home was packed with guests for Christmas. Chesterton himself had been unwell, but on 29 December a large party was held in the studio. The visitor's book gives the names of those who stayed for the night: Frances's mother, Ethel Oldershaw, and her five children; Lucian Oldershaw's sister, who had married a Dr Nash, with their four children; and another family friend, Fanny Keat. Besides those who stayed in the house many others will have been invited in from the neighbourhood; but it is worth noting that Cecil and the Chesterton parents do not appear to have been present, even if they had been invited, for the Overroads house–parties always seemed to have been heavily loaded in the favour of Frances's family, which was understandable in view of the number of children they brought into the home.

In the early weeks of 1914 Chesterton was contributing weekly articles to the *Daily Herald*. Raymond Postgate wrote:

> When he left the *Daily News* for the *Daily Herald* he felt he was regaining his freedom; and for a long time he wrote regular weekly articles of a high merit and great political significance. I still consider that the Socialists would have been well advised to take note of some of his fundamental criticisms, and had he remained with the *Daily Herald* group the course of history might have changed to some extent. What he wrote at this period ranks with the letters of Junius as among the best polemical writing, and deserves reprinting.

The literary worth of the articles remains in doubt, but many of them were collected together in 1917 and published in the United States under the title *Utopia of Usurers*.

Chesterton's regard for the *Daily Herald* was high at the time. On 8 January, the day after he had presided as judge at the mock trial of John Jasper for the murder of Edwin Drood, he published an article in *The New Witness* in which he had written, 'It is to be hoped that we shall see a number of small and trenchant journals, in the manner of the *Daily Herald*, talking about what happens day by day; on which the larger newspapers now never touch, except when they describe the pleasures of the wealthy or the crimes of the needy.' He had worked at his article, he said, 'sitting on a chair made a mile or two away from High Wycombe', and in the intervals between writing it, he had been 'looking out of a window at the beech-woods of Buckingham out of which it was made'. He had been sitting in his study in the new studio, where he now did most of his work.

On 20 January, on hearing that Elodie Belloc was seriously ill, Gilbert and Frances Chesterton travelled down to Sussex for the day to visit her. Chesterton had only recently recovered from a fit of bronchitis himself. It would be the last time they would see Elodie, for she never recovered and died about two weeks later a little before midnight on 2 February, the Feast of the Purification, perhaps better known as Candlemas.

Ada Jones thought that Elodie Belloc was the most attractive woman she had ever known. She had, she said, 'a genius for friendship, and was ungrudging in her loyal service for those she loved'. Certainly her influence on the Chestertons had been profound, on Cecil Chesterton in particular, who 'adored her' and is said to have sought instruction in the Catholic faith largely at her instigation. Ada Jones tended to compare Frances with her unfavourably, and repeated a conversation she had witnessed between Cecil and Elodie soon after the decision to move to Beaconsfield had been taken, which they all thought would deprive Gilbert of his old friends and haunts.

'I'm very sorry for Frances,' Elodie had said, 'It would distress her terribly if she knew how this – this ban hurt him.'

'Why on earth does Gilbert stand it?' Cecil had asked.

'He loves her,' Elodie had replied with eloquent simplicity. '... But really he should beat her. Hilary would beat me if I behaved like that. ... Frances would be much better if Gilbert *could* beat her.'

After his wife's death Belloc was always to be seen dressed in mourning, and the King's Land writing paper was edged with black. He thought it most unlikely that Gilbert Chesterton would ever follow his brother

into the Church, feeling that his attitude towards the faith was one
of mood; and faith was an act, he said, and not a mood. Elodie would
have seen Gilbert's love of the mood as an essential step for him, and
had she lived longer she might well have helped him to make the move
sooner.

Meanwhile, *Magic* was still running at the Little Theatre. Its companion piece, *Geminae*, had been succeeded by *The Impulse of a Night*
by David Ellis and Mrs George Norman; this in turn gave way at the
beginning of March to *The Music Cure*, advertised as 'A Piece of Utter
Nonsense', by Shaw.

On 22 January Chesterton's well-known novel, *The Flying Inn*, was
published by Methuen. The story, set largely in an England given over
to Islamic law, relates how Humphrey Pump, the dispossessed landlord
of the Old Ship, was able to outwit the harsh prohibition laws by moving
his inn sign about the countryside, and so continued to serve his customers.

When reviewing his colleague's book, W.R.Titterton wrote in *The
New Witness* that 'G.K.C. was the first man to show the true importance
of the inn as the centre of social life; he was the first to warn us how
its jolly, casual fellowship was threatened by the manoeuvres of the
Asiatic reformers.' Titterton saw the 'brave English innkeeper' and his
accomplice in the story, the 'brave Irish crusader', Patrick Dalroy, as
'two aspects of the soul of G.K.C.'.

Many people wanted to possess copies of *The Flying Inn*, as did Titterton, because it included many songs, mostly drinking songs, that had
appeared in *The New Witness* during the previous months under the
general heading of 'Songs of the Simple Life'. These included poems
like 'The Rolling English Road' which, many of its admirers will be
surprised to hear, was originally called 'A Song of Temperance Reform'.

The poem was only slightly altered when it appeared in *The Flying
Inn*. Several other well-known songs were also included in the book,
such as the 'Song of Quoodle' (the dog); the 'Song against Grocers',
and 'The Good Rich Man'. So popular did the book become that after
only a month the publishers were advertising a fourth edition. Although
the prose did not come up to the liveliness of *The Napoleon of Notting
Hill* or *Manalive*, it did have some very amusing passages, and one
of the most amusing came in the first chapter, 'A Sermon on Inns',
where an Arab is addressing the passers-by on the front at Pebblewick-
on-Sea, in an attempt to prove that all English inn names have an Islamic
origin.

Passages such as these were described by the *Times Literary Supplement* as 'Mr Chesterton's rollicks and frolics', though behind the rattle of bones and the slapped tambourine the reviewer felt he could 'almost see the beads of perspiration standing on the author's brow'. The story was not funny on the face of it, he continued, and it was dressed up in a vague allegory of Chesterton's favourite ideas

> ... that England is going to the dogs, that the good old religion is dead, that Asiatics are getting too much influence, and that we shall not be ourselves again till the good old English countryside is what it used to be and old-fashioned inns, not tied to breweries, are kept by 'mine hosts' of the 'Tabard' description, and the good old, bluff old, hardy old, sturdy old English spirit, with its mine of country lore and its contempt for books, once more takes the lead to the confusion of aesthetes, politicians, poets, Jews, and sentimentalists.

The reviewer thought that possibly this was right, but doubted whether 'the good old English spirit' would understand.

Surely this was yet another instance of Chesterton's amazing far-sightedness, and 'the good old English spirit' in as much as it still exists today will understand him only too well. This was the 'extremely serious idea' at the back of Chesterton's mind which, thought the reviewer, had 'a depressing influence on the ostensibly irresponsible fun of his fantastic story'.

During the late spring and early summer much of Cecil Chesterton's energy was taken up by the Irish Home Rule issue. The third Home Rule Bill, after being delayed in the House of Lords, became law in the summer of 1914, although Ireland's future remained uncertain. The Prime Minister, Asquith, and King George v were both urging that Ulster should be excluded from Home Rule. *The New Witness* was energetically anti-Unionist, and had no illusions about the mentality of the Orangemen or about 'the social condition of that tiny north-east corner of Ireland which journalists absurdly call "Ulster"'. As the editor put it, 'We know that these men hold very fanatically what we, in common with most Englishmen, Catholic, Protestant or Agnostic, should regard as a very inferior and provincial religion.' The Ulster Protestant, it had been noted in the issue of 2 April,

> ... refuses to accept all modern ideas upon Civil Government. He

stands where the Cromwellian did, or the John Knoxite, or the Hussite
of the Fifteenth Century. 'Dominion is founded in grace.' As Catholics are outside the saving grace of Protestantism, they are incapable
of exercising dominion over Protestants. There is the Ulster trouble
in a nutshell.

On this matter Gilbert Chesterton was in total agreement with his
brother, although he wrote little about Ireland at the time, preferring
to reserve this until later. Instead he dashed off articles on a variety
of subjects which had nothing to do with politics. On 18 June there
appeared an article on 'Asparagus', which began with the arresting sentence: 'At about twenty-one minutes past two to-day I suddenly saw
that asparagus is the secret of aristocracy.' On 9 July there was another
article, 'The Respectability of Bohemians', in which it was only possible
to discern any strain in the relationship between England and Germany
by implication in such comments as 'A man may reasonably dislike
both gin in Camberwell and beer in Munich. But who has ever disliked
beer in Munich more than gin in Camberwell?' The week before war
was declared he wrote: 'In so far as England and Germany are in danger
of quarrelling, it is not through their being different, but similar: with
the same dark energy in the factories, the same dizzy building in the
docks.' At the same time he thought it 'inconceivable that a Liberal
should sympathise more with Germany than with France, as some of
the most powerful seemed to do'.

On 4 August the Germans refused Britain's ultimatum to withdraw
from Belgium, and war was declared. Two days later *The New Witness*
welcomed the war: 'The news comes as an immense relief after the
long strain of waiting,' wrote Cecil. 'Stern as is the struggle ahead
of us, dreadful as are the possibilities which defeat would involve, it
is something to have done with the scheming fear that hung over us
all last week – the fear that we were going to see England lose her
honour.'

Chesterton thought like his brother that the German or, as they called
it, Prussian war was 'a war for the defence of European civilization
against those barbarians to whom (as in the ninth century) a military
victory has given for some forty years a temporary but most mischievous
supremacy'. As the French had been beaten in 1870, they were particularly determined not to be beaten in 1914, but Prussia was so powerful
that all civilized people had to fight her. The war was in Chesterton's

eyes a crusade, and he was as certain that England was right to fight as he had felt sure she had been wrong in fighting the Boers. If Prussia were successful in the war, her victory might destroy the Christian civilization of Europe.

When, at the end of August, Pope Pius X died Chesterton used his *Illustrated London News* column to pay tribute to him.

Chesterton felt a deep sympathy with the pope. Since the shock of the Marconi case he had been working under an almost impossible burden, and his writing at this time began to show the strain. During the build-up to the war it had been much easier to write about such things as asparagus than to concentrate his mind on the complexity of the conflict; but once war was declared he set to work on a series of balanced articles in which he traced the background to what he called 'the universal war of liberation'. 'If the Germans prevail,' he wrote, 'of course there will never be any history any more. There will only be an enormous fable eating up all the facts.' On the other hand, if the English won, he said, they might at least rescue Shakespeare. 'He has been captured by the Germans; arrested as a philosopher, or some such low fellow.' But 'through wall within wall of a labyrinthine fortress of libraries', Chesterton could 'hear him laughing still'.

In October the second collection of Father Brown stories was published as *The Wisdom of Father Brown*, dedicated to Lucian Oldershaw; and in the following month *The Barbarism of Berlin*, a short book based on articles that had appeared in the *Daily Mail*, which as the title suggests attempted to show that the Germans were truly barbarians in that they were hostile to certain necessary human ideas. The 'Prussian', Chesterton argued, was not bound by his own past any more than a man in a dream. 'He avows that when he promised to respect a frontier on Monday, he did not foresee what he calls "the necessity" of not respecting it on Tuesday. In short, he is like a child, who at the end of all reasonable explanations and reminders of admitted arrangements has no answer except "But I *want* to."'

On 25 November Chesterton addressed a large gathering of undergraduates at Oxford. During his speech he was suddenly overcome by a fit of dizziness and had to leave the platform. When he eventually reached home, still feeling decidedly odd, he staggered into his bedroom and collapsed so heavily on to his bed that it broke.

PART THREE

The Everlasting Man

14

A Certain Detachment

1914–1918

Chesterton's illness turned out to be serious. On 25 November Frances wrote to Fr O'Connor: 'It is mostly heart trouble, but there are complications.' The 'complications' are difficult to assess in the absence of any medical records, but Fr O'Connor's comment that the sickness could only be described as 'gout all over' suggests that there was some kind of liver or kidney disorder as a result of excessive drinking. Dr Pocock ordered a complete rest and decided this might be achieved most satisfactorily if the patient lay on a waterbed. Day and night nurses were brought in to cope with the situation, and in the early stages of the illness Chesterton seemed to benefit from the extra attention. As Frances put it, as to his head and brain he seemed 'quite his normal self'. He managed to read and even dictate from his bed, so that it looked as though after a few weeks of physical rest he could recover and be able to carry on as he had done before. It was not to be so.

The body had rebelled against the total lack of consideration its owner had given it: the irregular eating, constant drinking, and a punishing schedule of engagements which meant tiring travelling and late nights, had brought upon it an almost inevitable breakdown; but no one would have predicted that the mind, one of the most capacious, was about to rebel also. On Christmas Eve Chesterton became desperately ill, and muttering, 'I wonder if this bally ship will ever get to the shore', sank into a coma. For the next few days he slipped in and out of consciousness. 'He is often conscious,' Frances informed Fr O'Connor on 29 December, 'and he is so weak – I feel he might ask for you – if so I shall wire. Dr is still hopeful, but I feel in despair.'

Five days later she wrote, 'If you came he would not know you, and this condition may last some time. The brain is dormant, and must be kept so. If he is sufficiently conscious at any moment to understand,

I will ask him to let you come – or will send on my own responsibility. Pray for his soul and mine.'

Frances was particularly worried about Gilbert receiving the last rites, and it appears from her actions that she was well aware of his desire to become a Catholic, and that he would wish to receive the sacrament from a Catholic priest. During his moments of consciousness Chesterton had rambled on about wanting to be buried at Kensal Green, which was, of course, a Catholic cemetery. On 7 January Frances wrote to Fr O'Connor again.

> Gilbert seemed decidedly clearer yesterday, and though not quite so well today the doctor says he has reason to hope the mental trouble is wearing off. His heart is stronger, and he is able to take plenty of nourishment. Under the circumstances therefore I am hoping and praying he may soon be sufficiently himself to tell us what he wants done. I am dreadfully unhappy at not knowing how he would wish me to act. His parents would never forgive me if I acted only on my own authority. I do pray God He will restore him to himself that we may know. I feel in His mercy He will, even if death is the end of it – or the beginning shall I say?

Two days later Frances sent Fr O'Connor a postcard. 'There has been quite distinct improvement and awaking the last three days – we hope the recovery may move much more rapidly now, but we may do nothing to hasten the brain or make any suggestions. He is sleeping a great deal.'

On 12 January the postcard was followed by a letter. 'He is really better I believe and by the mercy of God I dare hope he is to be restored to us. Physically he is stronger, and the brain is beginning to work normally, and soon I trust we shall be able to ask him his wishes with regard to the Church. I am so thankful to think that *we* can get at his desire.'

At the same time as she had been keeping Fr O'Connor informed Frances had kept in constant touch with Warwick Gardens, and with several other people, including Wilfrid and Josephine Ward, the parents of Maisie Ward, Chesterton's biographer. The Wards were a staunchly Catholic family and, realizing from Frances's letters the seriousness of the situation, that Chesterton might well be on his death-bed, and, it seems, being aware of his desire with regard to the Church, Mrs Ward sent Fr O'Connor a telegram stating that Chesterton was *in extremis* and asking him to come south as soon as possible. She arranged to meet the priest at the Ladies' Club, and together they decided that he should go down to Beaconsfield and give Chesterton the last rites on the strength of his declared intention to be received into the Church as soon as Frances could be persuaded to join him. It was no time, they decided, for any delay; the matter could not wait for Frances.

When Fr O'Connor arrived at Overroads Frances refused to allow him into the bedroom. Gilbert's treatment, she explained, was so strict that only she, besides the doctor and nurses, could enter the room. She had only allowed Marie Louise to peep at her son 'from over the bed-rail when it was certain that he slept'. Fr O'Connor explained why he had come, and what he had in mind, and Frances gave a 'long half-amused cry', as the priest recalled later. 'So that is what Gilbert meant by all the dark hints about being buried in Kensal Green, and so on,' she said. 'I couldn't make head or tail. I suppose he wanted to put it to me straightforwardly, but he couldn't bring himself to the crisis. It's just like him.' As her letters showed, she had in fact understood perfectly well what he had meant.

It was a difficult situation for the priest to be in, and he did the only thing possible, which was to depart as he had come. Certainly Frances held nothing against him. However, she was anxious to keep the whole matter a secret, as may be seen from a letter she wrote to Josephine Ward some weeks later.

> I think I would rather you did not tell anyone just yet of what I told you regarding my husband and the Catholic Church. Not that I doubt for a moment that he meant it and knew what he was saying and was relieved at saying it, but I don't want the world at large to be able to say that he came to this decision when he was weak and unlike himself. He will ratify it no doubt when his complete manhood is restored. I know it was not weakness that made him say it, but you will understand my scruples. I know in God's good time he will make his confession of faith – and if death comes near him again I shall know how to act.

Although the periods of lucidity began to increase, Chesterton remained confused for about three months. On 15 March Frances informed Fr O'Connor that things were going satisfactorily 'though very very slowly'. The patient had to be kept very quiet, for he became upset easily, and this affected his heart; but gradually he was beginning to recognize his surroundings. By Easter Eve his mind was definitely clearing, and the previous night he recited the Creed, 'this time in English'.

'I feel I understand something of the significance of the resurrection of the body,' wrote Frances, 'when I see him just consciously laying hold of life again.'

Recovery was on the way, but life would never be quite the same again. For one thing Chesterton had lost several stones in weight, and his friends noticed how his clothes seemed to hang from his shoulders. He had passed through the Valley of the Shadow of Death, and it was as though he had been recalled from the dead to fulfil some great task. He had been allowed to live to see what he felt was the fruit of the sufferings of war, 'a rebirth of England', if his mere presence in an older generation did not prove that England never died. 'Did you think I was going to die?' he had asked Frances as he began to recover.

'I feared it at one time, but now you are to live,' she had replied. The two needed each other more than ever now.

While he had been ill his weekly column in the *Illustrated London News* had been written by a still grief-stricken Belloc; but by late May Chesterton's articles began to appear again. On 10 June he wrote in *The New Witness*:

As I have been physically and socially interned for nearly half a year, I feel a certain detachment which permits me to say things in praise of this paper which its editor might feel more shy in saying. And I think it is time that somebody noted the almost creepy exactitude with which many enormous events of to-day are but the scribbles of *The New Witness* writ large. The very things which we were told that nobody should say are the things everybody is saying.

Among the several instances of the paper's foresight of events Chesterton noted chiefly that it had said, 'The Prussians were barbarians even in peace, long before they proved themselves to be barbarians in war.' The paper had also been right, he said, about the Jews, and it could not be too often repeated that *The New Witness*'s utterance was a warning to Jews, and not merely a warning about Jews.

We asked repeatedly for the co-operation of the Hebrew community itself in finding a way out of a very dangerous position. We strongly advised the Semites to appear as Semites if they wished to avoid an outbreak of Anti-Semitism. We implored the individual alien to take up the word Jew as a compliment to himself, and drop his hysterical habit of only taking it up as an insult from other people. We told them that harm would come, to them especially, if they insisted on belonging both to their own nation and to the nations that were called the Gentiles. By a process that no Englishman and no Jew foresaw, that harm has come.

For in London to-day there is a real Jewish grievance. Having asked to be trusted as Englishmen, they have come to be distrusted as Germans: when, in fact, they are neither one nor the other. Numbers of harmless and homeless Orientals are being hooted and plundered under the delusion that they are gory sea-kings from the North. Some small, sensitive tailor in Whitechapel is made responsible for the quite uncongenial crimes of the Junkers who have dispersed and oppressed him. He is supposed to be concealing a howitzer somewhere about his person; and to exult in the clash of sabres rather than the clash of shears. It is a great shame; but it is partly his own fault, for not reading *The New Witness*. If we had got rid of the whole hypocrisy of not calling a Jew a Jew, we might have prevented the poor man from being hunted from one false name to another.

During his illness Frances had managed to correct the proofs of her husband's collection of poems which was published under the simple title *Poems* by the Catholic publishing house, Burns & Oates, in April 1915. Frances had also had to answer the hundreds of letters which came from well-wishers, and in order to ease the burden she had asked for the help of a young neighbour, Freda Spencer whom, she knew, was 'rather lonely and unhappy at home'. The action was typical, as Frances took a keen interest in local problems and was always anxious to find a solution. Her many acts of kindness, and her deep involvement in Beaconsfield life, are still remembered by older members of the community. Freda Spencer remained part of the Chesterton household for about two years, and became Gilbert's secretary as soon as he resumed work. She recalled that he was 'chaotic and eccentric' with a 'complete blank space in his mind about money, time and space'. While she was taking down his articles prior to typing them, she said, 'You could sometimes write a letter while you were waiting. He would stop almost in the middle of a phrase. He would draw his sword-stick and walk up and down fencing with the cushions.'

Poems had not included the drinking songs from *The Flying Inn*, but these were published separately in August as *Wine, Water and Song*, a little book that became immensely popular and went into fifteen editions before its author's death. However, the collection had included Chesterton's poem 'Antichrist, or the Reunion of Christendom: an Ode', which had been prompted by F.E.Smith's fatuous statement that the Welsh Disestablishment Bill was 'a Bill which had shocked the conscience of every Christian community in Europe'. Smith, who was later raised to the peerage as Lord Birkenhead, had been, with Sir Edward Carson, counsel for the prosecution at Cecil Chesterton's trial. The poem lacks the sting of a satirist like Swift, but it is nevertheless a very fine piece of irony.

> Are they clinging to their crosses,
>   F.E.Smith,
> Where the Breton boat-fleet tosses,
>   Are they, Smith?
> Do they, fasting, trampling, bleeding,
>   Wait the news from this our city?
> Groaning 'That's the Second Reading!'
>   Hissing 'There is still Committee!'
> If the voice of Cecil falters,
>   If McKenna's point has pith,
> Do they tremble for their altars?
>   Do they, Smith?

It was likely to have been this poem Katharine Tynan had in mind when in her review of *Poems* she wrote of a book 'great with personality, a big, a generous, a rich and vital personality. G.K.C. tilts at windmills and windbags: he tears sham and hypocrisies to tatters.' Another point worth noting is the extent to which readers of *Poems* would have gained an entirely false impression of the author's size and facial features from the finely reproduced photograph at the front of the book. Evidently it had been taken when Chesterton was at his flabbiest early in 1914. Yet this puffy ghost of the past had become so fixed in most people's imaginations that when in 1921 Chesterton visited America, the reporters and photographers who crowded round him at New York simply could not believe how small he was compared with what they had expected.

By the late summer of 1915 Chesterton was more or less fully recovered and working normally, although always under the careful eye of Frances, who regulated his diet and saw that he did not overtire himself. After twelve months of fighting, he wrote in *The New Witness*, 'when we say that the war has lasted a year, we miss a very real sense in which it lasted a week. Its nature and place in history were settled in those six days from the fall of Namur to the German flight from Paris.' Like many people at the time he had foreseen how long the conflict might last, but to Chesterton that hardly mattered. 'The middle of this war was the one week after Mons; and the piece of work was not evolutionary but creative. For it was stamped, after a deadly struggle, with the seal of Christendom and not the seal of the "usurpers".'

Whatever happened now would not change the situation, Chesterton argued, since the moral battle had been won, and nothing short of a triumph, now practically impossible, would compensate Germany for what had happened in those 'supreme' six days. Whatever the barbarians did in England, he said, even if 'they restored Westminster Abbey with all the brightness of Berlin' or improved the Temple Church off the face of the earth, or cremated Chaucer when he had been five hundred years buried; even if they undid the work of six centuries, 'they will not undo the work of six days'.

Chesterton followed the course of the war in considerable detail, relying largely on Belloc's weekly articles in *Land and Water*, the magazine he was told he had asked for immediately he came out of his coma. 'Mr Belloc had already begun his well-known series of war-articles, the last of which I had read, or been able to understand, being the new hope from the Marne. When I woke again the real things, the long battles before Ypres were over and the long trench war had begun.' The nurse, thinking that any back number would do since Chesterton had been incapable of reading for so long, gave him a copy at random. His mind, he said, had 'suddenly become perfectly clear', and he asked for all the numbers of the paper that had appeared since the battle of the Marne. If Chesterton's time-scale is correct, it would suggest that his mind had become confused, and he had ceased to be able to take very much in, at an earlier date than his collapse at Oxford the previous November. Certainly Belloc's *Land and Water* articles were excellent, with clear diagrams and numerous maps, and in all very much better than the two volumes of *A General Sketch of the European War*, which he gleaned from them, would lead one to expect. However, it did mean that Chesterton's view of the war was largely seen through Belloc's eyes. Unlike Belloc and Cecil, Chesterton did not visit the

battlefield although, like most men of his age, he was a member of
the Army Reserve until he was pronounced 'permanently and totally
unfit for any form of Military Service' on 25 June 1918.

On 21 October 1915 the *Daily Telegraph* printed a short poem called
'Our Day', which Chesterton had composed especially in aid of the
Red Cross. In this small way he was able to contribute to the war effort,
and the poem (not one of his best), was published on the same day
in a small leaflet and sold to help 'our Sick and Wounded Sailors and
Soldiers at the Front'. He was, as he had joked to the lady who goaded
him, always 'out at the front', but not so far now as before his illness.
Earlier, in September, Chesterton had begun a series of articles under
the general heading of 'At the Sign of the World's End' for *The New
Witness*. These were not about the war, except indirectly, but seemed
more designed to take people's minds off the serious events at the Front,
and were reminiscent of the earlier *Daily News* articles, except that they
show how Chesterton's thoughts were concentrating on the situation
in Ireland.

At about this time *The New Witness* began to print advertisements
for concerts and opera performances on which the name of a young
conductor, Thomas Beecham, seemed to be prominent. Beecham was
a keen supporter of the paper, and was soon made a director of the
company. As a member of the family which owned the pharmaceutical
company of that name, Beecham was in a position to give much-needed
financial support, and it was through him that Ernest Newman became
a regular contributor, with weekly articles on music which added a
new dimension to *The New Witness* and continued for many years.

Chesterton's *The Crimes of England* was published at the end of
November by Cecil Palmer. It was a small, fairly short book, in which
Chesterton set out to show how England had encouraged Prussia in
the past, largely at the expense of Austria; but that her worst crime
was using Prussian mercenary troops in Ireland in 1798. 'When the
Irish say, as some of them so say, that the German mercenary was worse
than the Orangemen, they say as much as the human mouth can utter.
Beyond that there is nothing but the curse of God, which shall be
uttered in an unknown tongue.'

He traced the rise of Prussianism to the Reformation. 'Luther was
hardly a heresiarch for England,' he said, 'though a hobby for Henry
VIII.' But the 'negative Germanism' of the Reformation, and its drag
towards the North, 'its quarantine against Latin culture, was in a sense

the beginning of the business'. England had indeed committed many crimes, Chesterton argued, but now she was awake to her folly.

Christmas at Overroads in 1915 was celebrated with the usual party. As in previous years Ethel brought her children over from Fernley, near Maidenhead. Remembering that the year before he had been unconscious throughout the season, one imagines Chesterton felt pleased to be alive. Writing on 'The Legend of Yule' in the early part of the month, he had said, 'Christian charity is something as special as the smell of onions', and explained that he had chosen that strong comparison because he knew no other phrase strong enough for the fact. There existed a definite and artistic sentiment, which was different from the pagan, or indeed Puritan, sentiment about feasting.

Speaking of Charity, it would seem likely that the Chestertons had invited to the party the family of five children that had recently moved into Boyne House, almost opposite Overroads, and next door but one from the Studio. The second daughter was called Charity, and Chesterton was always pretending he could not tell the difference between her and the eldest daughter, Hilary, calling them 'Chillary' and 'Harrity'. The girls' father, Edward Gray, who was formerly an official of the Bank of Bengal before it merged with the Bank of India, had retired when his wife died giving birth to their youngest child. Hilary, whose birthday was early in January, was fourteen when the family moved to Beaconsfield, and when she left school she became the 'daughter at home', looking after her father and the others during the holidays. The Chestertons became a great support to the family, and Chesterton himself grew particularly fond of Hilary. Although one may be certain his friendships with young girls remained innocent, there is no doubt that they provided a stimulus to his imagination, and he wrote copious letters, composed poems, and played practical jokes for their amusement. In particular he liked to invent a romantic atmosphere for them. For instance, for Freda Spencer he decided that the dashing Spaniard, Julian Alvarez, on the lid of his cigar box, was in love with her, and so he composed verses which he signed 'Julian'.

> Look, girl, upon the pallid wreck you made:
>   Demon, behold your work; let conscience hiss.
> You have reduced a substance to a shade
>   A fairly solid gentleman to This.

When Freda eventually left Overroads for a post at Godolphin House

A cartoon drawn for Hilary Gray by Chesterton

School, Chesterton imagined that the thwarted Julian was still pursuing her. In much the same way he had amused Rhoda Bastable in earlier days, drawing pictures of her possible husband, but neither Rhoda nor Freda received what one day Hilary would receive: a Sherlock Holmes story by the creator of Father Brown, all about herself.

Early in the new year the Society of SS Peter and Paul, publishers to the Church of England, brought out Chesterton's small pamphlet *Divorce Versus Democracy*, which had appeared earlier in *Nash's Magazine*; and in July a similar-looking pamphlet, *Temperance and the Great Alliance*, was issued by the True Temperance Association. These were the only titles Chesterton published in 1916; but he was as busy as ever now writing articles, and working on *A Short History of England*. He dictated this partly to Freda, now nicknamed 'Bicycle Freda' because of her frequent cycle rides down to the station to send Gilbert's articles by train, and partly to another Beaconsfield resident, Mrs Walpole, who helped out when Freda left.

'Will you really take on Gilbert's work?' Frances had asked, greatly relieved. 'He'd like to work with you. He likes someone in sympathy with his ideas.' After only a fortnight's typing practice Mrs Walpole began work, coming to Overroads at all odd hours, which suited her well, as she could fit them in when she was not looking after her young daughter Felicity. Often she would work after Felicity was in bed, or when Chesterton had ambled across to her house with the exhortation: 'Absent thee from Felicity awhile'.

'I didn't care how late I stayed at night,' she told Maisie Ward; and Chesterton would sometimes still be dictating long after midnight, when Frances would call down from upstairs, 'When are you going to let that poor girl get to bed?'

The events in Dublin during the Easter weekend that year received only scant attention from *The New Witness* to begin with. 'Much curiosity was aroused by the Sinn Feiners capturing the Dublin Post Office,' the editor noted; but after some weeks several editorials were devoted to Irish affairs. The 'rebellion' had obviously been fomented by the enemy. 'Everyone knew that there was a rather unbalanced and fanatical minority in Ireland which was opposed to an English Alliance even in defence of all that Irishmen held dear.' A few weeks later, Cecil wrote: 'The "rebellion" organised by a small minority in Ireland is, to all intents and purposes, over, and we may indulge in the hope that we have seen the last blood to be shed in that unfortunate island, though not the last blood shed by Irishmen in her cause.' Cecil made it quite clear that the Irish were fighting side by side with their English comrades in France for the same cause, that of liberty.

At the time Cecil Chesterton was himself making every effort possible to join the fighting himself. He had been given a promise by Ada, whom he always called 'Keith', that she would marry him if he was sent out to the Front. Later in the autumn he was passed fit enough to enlist into the East Surrey Regiment. This had a serious effect on his brother, who had agreed to take over the editorship of *The New Witness* until the fighting was over; in the event it meant he had taken it over for the rest of his life.

The last number of the paper to be edited by Cecil was that of 12 October. The following week he wrote 'An Au Revoir to *The New Witness*'. After informing his readers that he had been passed for service in Class C1 as a private, he went on to thank his brother, 'who, at no little personal sacrifice, has consented to undertake the editorship in my absence, and to allow his name to appear on the front page of the paper'. His brother's succession to the post, he said, would not only add prestige to the paper, but also, and more importantly, it would be a guarantee of continuity in principles.

Fortunately for Gilbert, the staff of the paper would remain the same, centred on Ada Jones, who had run the office while Cecil had been in America early in 1915 during Gilbert's illness. Cecil expressed the wish that his brother's succession should 'offer a splendid chance of improving the position of the paper, getting new subscribers, increased publicity, and ampler financial support'. He hoped the chance would not be missed.

The truth was that Gilbert was quite unsuited to be an editor. For a start, he lived too far away, and kept in touch with the office by telephone, only making the journey up to town once every few weeks. Temperamentally he would have preferred to have written the whole paper himself, for he was never a good organizer; nor did he pretend to be. 'I am the worst editor in the world,' he announced only two months after taking over. He had no more expected to become an editor 'than to be the policeman who stops the traffic in the Strand'. He was a proletarian, he said, and his only claim to respectability was that he had been a proletarian on strike. He faintly hoped that all his faults would be put down to incompetence and not to discourtesy, but he found it difficult to throw off the customary sensation that he was writing for somebody else's paper.

He promised that he would not take himself seriously as either an editor or a contributor. Then, he noted with mock alarm, they wanted to put some sort of picture or drawing or diagram of him in the Christmas Number; he supposed they would, since he could not summon up sufficient seriousness to resist. Then rising to the suggestion, he added: 'There will be given away with the paper a lock of my hair, a fragment of one of my broken bootlaces, a small piece of blotting-paper, which I have really used (and used up), and some of the shavings of a blue pencil actually used in *The New Witness* office.'

Perhaps the best reason why he was bound to do his work badly, he said, was that he found it so interesting. 'In that it is like life itself; nearly the chief trouble of life is that there is nothing dull in it.'

The Christmas Number bore no 'diagram' of the editor, but his editorial written at a most serious phase of the war was one of the best he ever wrote:

Christmas Day forces itself into daily life, like mummers entertained in a house of mourning. We believe the house of mourning will be wise to let the mummers in – if only for a deeper reason, which touches the deepest defect in the philosophy of a false peace. Christmas is not, as the Pacifists do vainly talk, the condemnation of all war. But Christmas is the test of all war. The real test of whether any army on the march has the right to be marching is whether it can rightly pass by any wayside cross and salute but not surrender.

Much of Chesterton's energy in the early months of 1917 was taken up by denouncing the kind of pacificism that was urging some kind of settlement with the enemy. He attacked Bertrand Russell in particular, who, he said, was a Whig of the old school. 'If ever a Whig intellectual can comprehend why a plain man wishes to own, to alter, to love, and to live for the land, I think he will also understand why he wishes to die for it.'

Among those who had died for the land was one whom Gilbert Chesterton knew and loved. On 9 April his old school friend, R.E.Vernède, a lieutenant in the Rifle Brigade, and one of the early members of the JDC, was killed in action. 'Rest is the key-note of his poetry,' Chesterton had written all those years before. The following month *The New Witness* mourned Edward Thomas, who had been an occasional contributor; 'A beautiful and essentially noble figure died for England.'

In Beaconsfield many whom Frances and he knew were killed or reported missing, and there would soon be the added anxiety of his brother being out at the Front.

According to her promise, Ada married Cecil as soon as he was posted to France. He had been drafted from the East Surreys into the Highland Light Infantry, and one of the few photographs of him shows him wearing the uniform of that regiment. The wedding took place in June 1917 in two stages, first a civil ceremony at the Register Office in Covent Garden, followed by a nuptial mass at Corpus Christi, Maiden Lane. All the Chestertons attended, as did Belloc and his sister, Mrs Belloc-Lowndes; and Conrad Noel was among the other guests who assembled at the Cheshire Cheese for the reception, when Gilbert Chesterton was among the speech-makers. Cecil's parents gave the couple £100 as a wedding present, and as Ada recalled with gratitude, 'Marie Louise was inexpressibly dear and sweet to both of us ... and Mister was equally affectionate.' When the bride had arrived at the altar on the arm of her brother, Cecil had leant forward towards her and said: 'I warn you, they'll sprinkle you with Holy Water and you'll say my beastly religion has spoilt your hat. But don't worry, I'll buy you a new one.'

In the issue for 26 July the editor of *The New Witness* commented on the situation emerging in Russia.

> We have always defended the Russian Revolution considered as a Russian Revolution. We do not care how revolutionary it is, so long as it is Russian. But the dangers now developing make it necessary to mark off the unnational element and recognize it as what it is – a clique of Jews. When we say that they are Jews we do not (as some critics seem to fancy) mean that they are rascals. On the contrary, the idealist may be more of a problem than the huckster, when his ideals are not the national or popular ideals. Thus a quarrel has already come between Petrograd Socialism and a peasantry; and the Jew never and nowhere understands the peasant, whether he tries to bleed him with usury or benefit him with Collectivism.

Then, unable to resist an attack on Isaacs, who had been recommended to become Viceroy of India, Chesterton added:

> And if the purely idealistic Jew is a nuisance to the more prosperous peasantries of Europe, what sort of a nuisance is a purely financial Jew, set up to rule the impoverished peasantry of India? for Asia

knows nothing of the more humane side of the Jew in history; nothing of the better Jews in arts and sciences, of Heine or Mendelssohn or Ricardo. There the Jew is a money-lender, and nothing else. It is a crucial case of what is called Anti-Semitism being really a liberation of the mind. If we could open our minds to take in India as we open our eyes to take in an Indian elephant, we should instantly see the idiocy of enthroning so preposterous a prince in the howdah. As it is, we give up a distant population to disaster, simply because we mean to make the best of the worst Jews by never seeing anything beyond Bayswater – and not too much even there.

In the same month that the Russian Revolution came to its crisis the publishers Chatto & Windus were advertising a second impression of Chesterton's *A Short History of England*. The book was highly subjective and often inaccurate as to facts – usually silly inaccuracies such as saying that Shakespeare had died rather than was born on St George's Day – but, as I have pointed out before, such things did not bother Chesterton in the least. In spite of its obvious defects Shaw hailed the book as 'something like a history of England at last', and praised the author for 'knowing the epochs', and for being able 'to tell you when the temple became a den of thieves'.

For the professional historian, however, the book was hardly worth comment. Professor Pollard, writing in the *Times Literary Supplement*, said that it would be vain to review the book as a History of England when it was interesting 'only as an expression of Mr Chesterton's mentality and as an illustration of the whimsical visions of the past which appear to the agitated and the agitators'. The book was a spirited attempt to capture for Catholicism the 'patriotic passion generated by the War', he said.

Chesterton's intention had been to write a history on behalf of the people, to cut through the rigmarole of Whig history that had attempted to justify the theft of the people's inheritance. He had argued that since the failure of the Peasants' Revolt, which, he said, was the 'real turning point in history', the people had been steadily robbed, and the steady run-down towards the Servile State had been the inevitable result. If men would now do what the mediaeval men did, 'beginning, by guilds and small independent groups, gradually to restore the personal property of the poor and the personal freedom of the family', in short, to become distributors, there might be some hope. The individual was under attack from all directions.

Towards the end of March the following year Chesterton came strongly to the defence of the family in a series of articles on 'The Superstition of Divorce', a subject that he would attack mercilessly until the end of his life. He saw divorce as another fad which, if the true nature of marriage were not understood might become a major force of destruction to the family. In this matter it is easy to see that Chesterton was right. A secularist like Sir Arthur Conan Doyle, he argued, said there was only a 'theological' opposition to divorce, and that it is entirely founded on certain texts in the Bible about marriages. 'This is exactly as if he said that a belief in the brotherhood of men was only founded on certain texts of the Bible, about all men being the children of Adam and Eve'; but yet millions of people all over the world thought marriage to be static 'without having ever clapped eyes on any text'.

Chesterton set out his argument in considerable detail. A vow was a violent and unique thing; though there had been many besides the marriage vow; vows of chivalry, vows of poverty, vows of celibacy, pagan as well as Christian. But modern habit, he said, had rather fallen out of the habit; and men missed the type for the lack of parallels. The shortest way of putting the problem was to ask whether being free included being free to bind oneself. For the vow was a tryst with oneself. The articles formed the first part of Chesterton's book *The Superstition of Divorce*, which was published two years later in 1920.

On 11 April Chesterton addressed the inaugural meeting of the New Witness League at Essex Hall. He expressed regret that his brother was unable to be present; Cecil had been brought back from France wounded and had recuperated in Scotland, but was 'amongst those who have volunteered immediately for the Front'. The aims of the League, Chesterton said, were fivefold:

1. To support the prosecution of the War to a victorious issue.
2. To reform the present state of political corruption.
3. To secure the restoration of those personal liberties abrogated during the War by the repeal of servile and oppressive acts of Parliament.
4. To secure the rights of small nationalities.
5. To build up an organization for the dissemination of propaganda on these points, and to secure the fullest publicity for the exposure of political corruption.

At the end of the meeting Chesterton was elected President of the League, which one can see was the forerunner of the Distributist League, which followed later. Meetings were held at regular intervals, when there would be either a debate or a talk of some sort, always with much lively questioning afterwards. The gatherings were usually of the 'jolly' sort; for instance, on 4 June Chesterton proposed the motion 'That this meeting condemns the extension of State Control as threatening further interference with the liberty of the citizen', a debate at which Belloc, Eccles and Haynes spoke, which had been advertised as an 'Important Meeting: In Defence of People's Drink', to be held at the Venetian Room of the Holborn Restaurant.

On 26 July *The New Witness* announced: 'The Allies have won the race. This does not mean that they have already won the War.' Cecil, back in France, was carrying on in spite of recurring ill health, as he would do until the Armistice. On 15 November his brother wrote in his editorial: 'The Prussian devil is defeated.' Cecil had by this time reported sick, but in spite of this he was made to endure the twelve-mile march from Ypres in the pouring rain. The result was that he collapsed and was taken to the field hospital at Wimereux, from where he wrote his wife a letter in which 'an underlying note of pain and disappointment' gave her 'a queer foreboding', which deepened as time went on.

Ada decided she would have to go to France as quickly as possible; in fact, a telegram asking her to come had been sent some weeks before, but had been misdirected. Arranging transport proved difficult at such short notice, but through Maurice Baring's influence it was made available. When, after a distressing journey, she reached the hospital Cecil was already nearing the end, although he talked and laughed and declared he felt better. The next day, however, he took a turn for the worse. 'It's goodbye, Kiddy darling,' he said, smiling. Realizing that he was now dying, and that the news would soon be flashed around Fleet Street, Ada asked the nurse to wire a message through to Gilbert at Beaconsfield. Chesterton was quite unable to face the situation, and left it to Frances to inform his parents. Ada's description of her husband's death is particularly beautiful.

Cecil looked up and smiled. Life was all round him and me: only in the brave face that still kept courage was it ebbing little by little, until it passed beyond the last faint breath.

Suddenly the consciousness came down on me that all our hopes and dreams, light-hearted plans, ambitious undertakings had gone.

The future – our future – had ended. I should never hear him speak again. I should never feel his touch, or watch the light in his eyes when unexpectedly he saw me.

I could not think. The blank was so intolerable, the pain so limitless, I could not stay inside the hut. I had to get into the open; but the sky and the sea and the earth in their vast aloofness were frightening. I could find nothing to lay hold of.

I think I was on the borderline of endurance when suddenly, without conscious wish or will, the long slope of the cliff side, curving out and down to the channel far below, held my eyes. It was a carpet of sea lavendar, grey-blue and pink. The sheer fact of the small proud flowers brought a dim sense of security. In a world of torture they remained serene. Right up to the door of that grim squatting hut, soaked in the blood of sons, husbands and lovers, beauty had laid a tender touch. Before time was, perhaps, sea lavender had cloaked the shores in merciful rejection of man's cruelty to man.

I gripped at self-control and went back to my husband. He looked happy and quite peacefully at rest . . . .

I have always loathed and hated officialdom. In State offices it is bleak and barren, and in human relationships it is lifeless and callous. The hostel hurt like frost on an open wound, and I left it the next morning inexpressibly thankful for escape. At the little shop in the Square, where I bought the black hat and gloves convention demanded, Madame gave me a warm sympathy which helped on my journey to the Cemetery. There I found Cecil's special nurse waiting, and together we listened to the burial service and watched the coffin lowered into the narrow grave that, like hundreds of others, lined the hills. The Last Post echoed across the sea . . . .

On 13 December Gilbert wrote in his editorial:

It is already known that the late Editor of *The New Witness* has died in France of the effects of the last days of the fighting. He lived long enough to march to victory which was for him a supreme vision of liberty and the light. The work which he put first he did before he died. The work which he put second, but very near to the other, he left for us to do. There are many of us who will abandon many other things, and recognise no greater duty than to do it.

In the same issue Belloc spoke of Cecil's courage.

His courage was heroic, native, positive, and equal: always at the highest potentiality of courage. He never in his life checked an action or a word from consideration of personal caution, and that is more than can be said of any other man of his time.

In his grief Gilbert Chesterton wrote what may only be described as an article of hatred, which he printed as his 'At the Sign of the World's End' contribution in the same issue. He called it 'An Open Letter to Lord Reading'. 'It would be irrational to ask you for sympathy,' he wrote; 'but I am sincerely moved to offer it. You are far more unhappy; for your brother is still alive.'

15

The Editor Travels

1918–1920

Chesterton lived with his brother's death for the rest of his life. 'I never conceived myself here save as carrying on, amid a sort of social chaos, the name and general principles I shared with my brother, till he should return to manage his paper as he alone could manage it.' He had seen himself as a stop-gap, and now the gap would never be filled 'till God restores all the noble ruin that we name the world'. He felt he must either accept the duty of editorship entirely, or abandon it entirely. Frances, quite understandably, and for very good reasons, favoured the latter course; but since he felt a deep loyalty to his brother and, as he put it, 'every instinct and nerve of intelligence' had told him that this was a time when it must not be abandoned, he decided he must accept the challenge. He would have to accept a comparison that must be a contrast, he said, and it was a crushing contrast, since he could never be as good as his brother; but he would see if he could be better than himself. Politics, he admitted, had never been his province, 'either in the highest or lowest sense'. He was not among those who knew from the very beginning the most sensational secrets of politics, nor was he one who knew their 'mostly darkly disguised details' as well as some of his colleagues knew them.

After Cecil's death Ada Chesterton felt she could not continue at the office, anyway for the time being; but Chesterton was fortunate in keeping the same office staff, led by Titterton, who became assistant editor in Ada's place; and the mainstay of Essex Street, Miss Dunham, whom Cecil had nicknamed 'Bunny' because of her protruding teeth. So it was that G.K.Chesterton remained editor of a weekly paper for almost the next eighteen years. From now on it must be assumed that every week he was responsible for his editorial, several items of comment, and usually another article, besides his 'Our Notebook' contribution to the *Illustrated London News*. What was remarkable was the fact that he found the time to do so much more besides. How he did it all Titterton just did not know; still less did he know how Chesterton always managed to appear at ease and happy for a chat.

'The secret of his prodigious output', Titterton imagined, 'was that he had made up his mind about things, and his mind was as clear as crystal, his power of reason as powerful as a Rolls-Royce. He knew just what he wanted to say upon any subject that he tackled.'

Besides all that he had to do at home, after the war Chesterton became something of a traveller. He had already begun in a small way by visiting Ireland in the early autumn of 1918 at the invitation of Yeats, who was organizing a series of lectures at the Abbey Theatre in Dublin, and had arranged for both Shaw and Chesterton to speak, though on different occasions. The Arts Club held a dinner in Chesterton's honour which Yeats, as Chairman of the meeting, had been invited to attend, but refused 'on the grounds that G.K.C. had never been a "garreteer" and was therefore unknown, as Goethe would have said, to the Heavenly Powers'. Chesterton made a speech to the assembled company, and had barely come to the end when the door swung open and Yeats strode in, and 'in answer to greeting cheers made a passionate speech, the event of the evening'. Yeats dined with Chesterton the following night, and introduced 'the genial Catholic sophist' to the 'unencomistic Protestant philosopher', John Eglinton, thus, as his biographer put it, 'exposing his own vehement imagination to fire from two sides at once'. Yeats, of course, remembered Chesterton from the Bedford Park days, and he admitted to liking him, though he had less time for Chesterton's poetry. The last two stanzas of 'The Rolling English Road' he thought 'sentimental and rather disgusting'.

Chesterton set down his own impressions of Ireland in a series of articles that were printed in his own paper during the weeks leading up to the Armistice; these were added to and published as *Irish Impressions* in November 1919. This unique book, which went into only one edition, would be very well worth reprinting today, for Chesterton, in spite of his obvious Catholic leanings, gives a very balanced view of the causes of the conflict which is sadly still with us in the late 1980s.

To begin with Chesterton felt that St George's Channel had been wrongly named, since it would seem more natural to call it St Patrick's Channel because that great missionary 'did almost certainly cross that unquiet sea and look up at those mysterious mountains'.

The Englishman had always considered himself superior to the Irishman, and since the Reformation this had been accentuated. The discovery of most Englishmen arriving in Ireland, Chesterton said, 'will be like touching the trees of a faded tapestry, and finding the forest alive and full of birds. It will be as if, on some dry urn or dreary column, figures which had already begun to crumble magically began to move and dance.' This was because Englishmen believed in Irish decay 'even when they were large-minded enough to lament it. It might be said that those who were most penitent because the thing was murdered, were most convinced that it was killed.'

For Chesterton, however, the sight of things sustaining, and a beauty that nourishes and does not merely charm, was 'a premonition of practicality in the miracle of modern Ireland'. It was a miracle more marvellous than the resurrection of the dead. It was 'the resurrection of the body'.

The Irish Question had never been discussed in England, Chesterton said; only Home Rule had been discussed, but few Englishmen understood what the Irish meant by Home. It was anyway impossible for Englishmen to rule Irishmen, since merchants cannot rule peasants. 'It is not so much that we have dealt benefits to England and blows to Ireland. It is that our benefits to England would be blows to Ireland.'

The irony was that it was primarily Sinn Fein, the extreme nationalist party, which had failed to realize that Ireland was a nation.

At least it failed in nationalism exactly so far as it failed to intervene in the war of the nations against Prussian imperialism. For its argument involved, unconsciously, the proposition that Ireland is not a nation; that Ireland is a tribe or a settlement, or a chance sprinkling of aborigines. If the Irish were savages oppressed by the British Empire, they might well be indifferent to the fate of the British Empire; but as they were civilised men, they could not be indifferent to the fate of civilisation.

Chesterton aired his thoughts on many aspects of the relationship between two great countries, and in the last chapter he wrote about the serious matter of 'Belfast and the Religious Problem'. Chesterton saw Protestant Ulster as 'reeking in superstition'. He had been told of a mother warning her children to keep away from a certain pond, or similar place of danger, by saying: 'Don't go there; there are wee popes there'. A country where that could be said 'is like Elfland as compared with England', he judged, though he was charmed 'in the fancy of a pool full of these peculiar elves, like so many efts, each with his tiny triple crowns or crossed keys complete'. The difference between an industrial centre like Manchester and Belfast was that, however Nonconformist a Mancunian might be, he would hardly be likely to see a puddle as a breeding ground for Archbishops of Canterbury, for 'little goblins in gaiters and aprons'.

Besides this mythology the Irish commercial province had also retained theology, and wherever men are still theological, Chesterton said, there was still some chance of their being logical; 'and in this the Calvinist Ulsterman may be more of a Catholic Irishman than is commonly realised, especially by himself'.

Attacks and apologies abounded about the matter of Belfast bigotry; but bigotry was by no means the worst thing in Belfast, Chesterton argued. In some ways he thought it the best thing, since it was all part of the dream from which the Calvinist might suddenly wake. The more remarkable fault of the society had indeed a religious root; 'for nearly everything in history has a religious root, and especially nearly everything in Irish history'. The more prominent and practical evil was ultimately the theology itself, but not the habit of being theological. It was the creed, but not the faith.

In so far as the Ulster Protestant really has a faith, he is really a fine fellow; though perhaps not quite so fine a fellow as he thinks himself. And that is the chasm; and can be most shortly stated as I have often stated it in such debates: by saying that the Protestant generally says, 'I am a good Protestant', while the Catholic always says, 'I am a bad Catholic'.

The old tradition of Christendom was that the highest form of faith was doubt. It was the doubt of a man about his soul. The Calvinistic certainty of salvation and the 'election of the few' was the root cause of what Chesterton called 'Protestant pride'. As far as those ideas prevailed, he saw that Belfast and Berlin had given battle for the same thing: 'Berlin gave battle to the older civilisation of Europe; and Belfast gave battle to the older civilisation of Ireland.' 'There is a religious question; and it will not have an irreligious answer. It will not be met by the limitation of Christian faith, but rather by the extension of Christian charity.'

There seemed to be a fashionable fallacy, Chesterton said, to the effect that religious equality was something to be done and done with, that we might go on to the real matter of political equality. In philosophy it was the flat contrary that was true. Political equality was something to be done and done with, that we might go on to the much more real matter of religion.

As Chesterton left Ireland there came better news from France, though Dublin was 'full of the awful tragedy of the *Leinster*'. With all the emotions of an exile, he felt his own land was secure. Somehow, he said, the bad and good news together turned his mind more and more towards England, 'and all the inner humour and insular geniality which even the Irish may some day be allowed to understand'.

The Wicklow hills receded in a rainy and broken sunlight as he took the boat home. One sentiment about Ireland clung to him, one sentiment he could not transfer to England. As he looked at those rainy hills he knew at least that he was looking, perhaps for the last time, on something rooted in the Christian faith.

> There at least the Christian ideal was something more than an ideal; it was in a special sense real. It was so real that it appeared even in statistics. It was so self-evident as to be seen even by sociologists. It was a land where our religion had made even its vision visible. It had made even its unpopular virtues popular. It must be, in the times to come, a final testing-place, of whether a people that will take that name seriously, and even solidly, is fated to suffer or to succeed.
>
> As the long line of the mountain coast unfolded before me I had an optical illusion; it may be that many have had it before. As new lengths of coast and lines of heights were unfolded, I had the fancy that the whole land was not receding but advancing, like something spreading out its arms to the world. A chance shred of sunshine rested, like a riven banner, on the hill which I believe is called in Irish the Mountain of the Golden Spears; and I could have imagined that the spear and the banner were coming on. And in that flash I remembered that the men of this island had once gone forth, not with the torches of conquerors or destroyers, but as missionaries in the very midnight of the Dark Ages; like a multitude of moving candles, that were the light of the world.

As he said, Chesterton saw Ireland as a 'testing-place', but there was another great testing-place, as both he and Belloc saw clearly: Poland. In his editorial for 25 April, written 'on the day after Easter Sunday', he said, 'The only thing really important in Mr George's speech last week was the thing that was not there. He did not dare to say a single serious thing about Poland.' Just as his brother had insisted on doing, Chesterton always referred to the Prime Minister simply as Mr George. The fact that Lloyd George had chosen Lord Reading to accompany him to Versailles only increased Chesterton's derisive attitude towards him. If Poland were to be deprived of her port, 'the one place that should have been held, and the one place that is being surrendered', Chesterton said, it would not be given up by English public opinion, but by what for him was the cause of all ills. As he wrote on 20 June, 'At the time of writing there is no final news to tell us whether the German Jews have dictated the desertion of the cause of Poland, that is, of the cause of England.' He poured derision on the fact that 'Mr George had called Germany a great and friendly country'. It is true that Lloyd George had been privately unwilling 'to squeeze Germany until the pips squeak', and Chesterton firmly supported the policy of Clemenceau, who spoke for the French at Versailles – that the Germans should be made to pay a sum of money in reparation – but Poland was of paramount importance.

> We know that a flood threatens the West from the meeting of two streams, the revenge of Germany and the anarchy of Russia; and we know that the West has only one possible dyke against such a flood, which is not the mere existence, but the might and majesty of Poland. We know that without some such Christian and chivalric shield on that side, we shall have half of Europe and perhaps half of Asia on our backs.

The missed opportunity over Poland would mean that 'after another cycle of terror and torment and abominable butchery' we would one day have to come back to the place where we started, 'a place where we might, in perfect peace and perfect safety, stand firm today'.

In the autumn of 1919, it was suggested that Chesterton should take Frances abroad with him to a warmer climate, as she had been suffering increased pain in her back. Almost certainly it was Bentley who, through his position on the *Daily Telegraph*, commissioned Gilbert Chesterton to write a series of articles on the Holy Land. The idea was appealing, for since Allenby's successful entry into Jerusalem the Cross had replaced the Crescent, and the campaign was being referred to as 'The Last Crusade'. If permission could be obtained from the military authorities, Chesterton agreed to go. Fortunately Maurice Baring had a close

friend on Allenby's staff, and wrote off immediately. The General himself replied, saying he would be delighted to welcome the Chestertons
in Jerusalem, and that every possible facility would be afforded for easy
travel in Palestine.

Christmas was celebrated at Overroads as usual, and on 29 December
Gilbert and Frances Chesterton set off for France. As he came out
of his garden in the season of Christmas, he said, he began to walk
backwards through history to the place from which Christmas came.
'The modern man is more like a traveller who has forgotten the name
of his destination, and has to go back whence he came, even to find
out where he is going.'

After a fairly good crossing, they found there was 'an awful confusion
at Boulogne' as they took their train to Paris. Frances kept a detailed
account of the whole journey, with the result that the four months they
were away from England between December 1919 and April 1920 is
the only period of Chesterton's life which was completely documented
until Dorothy Collins became his secretary in 1926. From Paris they
took a sleeper to Rome; at the Italian border Chesterton had to pay
20 lire for his box of cigars. On New Year's Day they toured the city,
visiting the Forum in the morning and the Colosseum in the afternoon.
The same evening they departed for Brindisi, where they found they
would have to wait a day longer than expected for the boat to Alexandria.
From the evening of 3 January until the early morning of the 7th the
Chestertons were at sea; Frances was seasick for the first two days.
In Alexandria they visited the Catholic Cathedral of St Catherine, where
Christmas was still being celebrated, and there was one of the most
beautiful cribs Frances had ever seen.

Chesterton's articles for the *Daily Telegraph* were, as he said, 'notes
taken on the spot', a series of random thoughts interspersed with descrip-
tions of the places he visited, and there is no sense of an itinerary;
however, from Frances we learn that they went by train to Cairo

... across the Nile Delta, flat as flat, with fields of cotton, or beans,
or sugar cane – little Arab mud huts all the way – here and there
a small mosque – and by the road that runs beside the railway, an
unending procession of camels, mules, donkeys, goats, sheep, oxen,
and buffaloes, men, women and children. Every scene like some picture familiar from childhood from some illustrated Bible. The palm
trees and date trees are the only things that rise any height above

the ground. Then we saw the Nile, and to our surprise, in the distance the Pyramids!

In Cairo, where they remained for several days, Chesterton gave a series of lectures to military audiences, where Frances was often the only woman present. In the mornings he would stay in his hotel room to write his articles and letters, and in the afternoons go sightseeing with Frances, returning to lecture in the evenings. Throughout their journey they found themselves bumping into people they knew, or the relations of people they knew, at home. For instance, in Cairo they found Captain Penfold, whose home was in Beaconsfield. On 18 January, wearing a cassock and surplice, Chesterton gave an address after Evensong at the Bishop's Chapel, which, according to Frances, 'was very good'.

On the journey to Jerusalem, which they began on the 20th, Chesterton delivered lectures wherever they stopped on the route, at Ismailia, Suez and Jaffa. When they reached Jerusalem on the 26th, it was pouring with rain and bitterly cold, and they were driven to their hotel in a Red Cross ambulance. The Grand New Hotel, where they had a bedroom and a sitting room, was to be their base until 30 March.

While they were in Jerusalem the Chestertons were treated as special guests, and as soon as they arrived at the hotel they were greeted by Fr Waggett, the Political Officer, who had been appointed to look after them. His name appears frequently in Frances's diary, when he came to escort them to some important function or to accompany them on a sightseeing tour. It is obvious too from the diary that one of Chesterton's reasons for coming to Palestine was to stimulate discussion on the problem of Zionism, and besides visiting the Holy Places he tried to visit as many leading Zionists as possible. On 31 January he had been entertained to lunch at the home of Dr and Mrs Eder; the doctor was President of the Zionist Commission, and the Chestertons found him 'a very interesting man'. It was through the Eders that they later met 'the famous Zionist' Dr Weizmann, who told Chesterton that he did not think Palestine could ever be a single and simple national territory quite in the sense of France, but he did not see why it should not be a commonwealth of cantons after the manner of Switzerland. Some of these could be Jewish cantons, others Arab cantons, and so on according to the type of the population. This idea, Chesterton saw clearly, involved the abandonment of the solidarity of Palestine, and tolerated the idea of groups of Jews being separated from each other by populations of a different type.

Chesterton set out this argument in an article for the *Daily Telegraph*, in which he had written: 'The greatest of the real difficulties of Zionism is that it has to take place in Zion.' It was hardly surprising that after coming to the end of the great man's dispatch the editor decided he could not publish it. Taking Dr Weizmann at his word, Chesterton had written:

It seems possible that there might be not only Jewish cantons in Palestine but Jewish cantons outside Palestine. Jewish colonies in suitable and selected places in adjacent parts or in many other parts of the world. They might be affiliated to some official centre in Palestine, or even in Jerusalem, where there would naturally be at least some great religious head-quarters of the scattered race and religion. ... I think it is sophistry to say, as do some Anti-Semites, that the Jews have no more right there than the Jebusites. If there are Jebusites they are Jebusites without knowing it. I think it sufficiently answered in the fine phrase of an English priest, in many ways more Anti-Semitic than I: 'The people that remembers has a right.' The very worst of the Jews, as well as the very best, do in some sense remember.

There, for the first time, as far as I have been able to discover, Chesterton admitted his anti-semitism, and it appears on almost the last page of his book *The New Jerusalem*, which was published in November 1920.

Chesterton said that a Jewish territorial scheme might be really attempted, if the Jews were in agreement. 'It seems possible,' he said, 'that by some such extension of the definition of Zionism we might ultimately overcome even the greatest difficulty of Zionism, the difficulty of re-settling a sufficient number of so large a race on so small a land.' He was not in favour of such a scheme being administered by England alone, but by 'a general suzerainty of Christendom', and he felt this, he said, not from any desire to restrain English power, 'but rather from a desire to defend it'. He thought it a wiser course for France and England to hold Syria and Palestine together rather than separately. However, with the failure of Zionism 'would fall the last and best attempt at a rationalistic theory of the Jew'. We should be left facing a mystery which no other rationalism has ever come so near to providing within rational cause and cure.

Chesterton had been particularly anxious to visit some of the Judean Colonies; these were agricultural settlements or, as they are now better known, kibbutzim, which had been already established by the Jews, and encouraged by the Zionist Commission. There were some sixty in all, mostly situated about fifty miles north of the city. On 10 March Dr Pool, of the Zionist Committee, drove the Chestertons through mountainous country and on to the plain towards the two most important colonies at Rishon and Robobart, on the Jaffa road. 'The plain is a fertile part of the land, though a lot has been reclaimed by sheer hard labour,' Frances wrote. Near Rishon, however, the land was so sandy that the car would not plough through, and they were obliged to walk. The chauffeur, who was, according to Dr Pool, a reclaimed Apache, was none the less 'a wonderful driver', though the whole journey had been 'not an unmixed joy, for the road is quite broken up in many places and we had violent shakings and nerve-racking escapes'.

At Rishon they saw the great vats and cellars which stored the vast quantity of wine produced, much of it for export; and oranges, almonds and olives were growing. 'After sampling the wine (very strong), we drove on to Robobart where we first had lunch at a little restaurant. The food very charming – sort of fish rissoles – poached eggs – sour cream and potatoes – very brown bread – sort of cheese, coffee and oranges – but all very nice,' Frances recorded. They then went off to see Mr Isenberg, one of the chief Colonists, and the Father of the Community. The settlement itself was rather as Frances imagined an early American township might have been like, 'or Dutch, perhaps'. Many of the Jews they met had come out of Russia.

At Robobart, Gilbert and she were given 'more strong drink', and they walked about the Colony; Frances was glad to be able to pick oranges and lemons herself. On the way home they called at the Jewish Camp Battalion, the 1st Judeans, and were entertained to tea in the officer's mess by 'a nice Jewish Colonel'. The journey back to Jerusalem was varied by many halts as the tyres had to be often attended to, but it was very interesting to see the Arab tents pitched for the night, with the camels and donkeys outside. At the entrance to the mountain pass they passed an old inn, 'dating from the Crusaders, or probably earlier, where man and beast halt for the night'. Once it had turned dark the headlights had proved to be a problem, since they continually gave out, but all arrived back eventually at about 8.30 'very tired but after a very wonderful day'.

While the Chestertons were in Jerusalem it had snowed for the first time for ten years. The snow was some two feet deep and for several days they were unable to leave their hotel; at the same time Frances suffered from severe headaches and spent much of the time in bed. Chesterton became agitated when Frances was ill, which was caused chiefly by genuine concern, but there was always the feeling that she could not devote herself entirely to his own needs. During the spell of snow he wrote that 'The tradition about the December snow was not quite so false as suggested.' It was not a mere local illusion for the Englishman to picture the Holy Child in a snowstorm, as it would be 'for the Londoner to picture him in a London fog. There can be snow in Jerusalem, and there might be snow in Bethlehem; and when we penetrate to the idea behind the image, we find it is not only possible but probable.'

Frances recorded that the Yorkshire Regiment, no doubt used to such conditions at home, had cut paths through the snow, and had been busy distributing food to the poor people. At the same time military orders had been issued to compel people to open their shops as usual. After about a week the snow began to melt, causing freak flooding, and the streets were so slushy that the Chestertons had to buy themselves pairs of galoshes. Such was the 'warmer climate' that was to do Frances so much good. However, the cold weather did not last for long, and Frances was soon writing: 'Jerusalem herself again, warm and sunny like a lovely May day.'

During their stay, although they visited all the Holy Places and often went to shrines in the care of Catholics, there is no doubt that in as far as they practised their religion it was Anglican. They attended services at St George's Cathedral, and at the Place of the Nativity they said together the collect for Christmas Day. Fr Waggett and Canon Waddy, the Head of the English College, saw much of them, and Chesterton gave talks to primarily Anglican audiences; but, although Frances was happy enough, Chesterton was even more aware that his heart and mind were no longer at peace in the Church of England. As he informed Maurice Baring in a letter, his train of thought, 'which really was one of thought and not fugitive emotion, came to an explosion in the Church of the Ecce Homo in Jerusalem'. He also indicated to Baring that there was something important that he wished to discuss with him, 'because of certain things that have been touched on between us in former times'.

Before they left Jerusalem the Chestertons gave a party in their rooms for all those to whom they owed hospitality, for throughout their stay they had seldom had to eat alone. On 26 March the *Jerusalem News* announced that 'Mr and Mrs Gilbert Chesterton's At Home at the Grand New Hotel was their farewell party to Jerusalem. Their multitude of friends will be sorry to know that they leave for England on Thursday next. They will travel by way of Rome.'

Chesterton's 'train of thought' described to Baring what had happened on Palm Sunday. In the morning Frances and he had attended the 10 o'clock service at Christchurch, the soldier's church, where the Bishop of Jerusalem had preached. It was a very wet and cold day, but after lunch they decided to go to Benediction at the Ecce Homo Church, where 'the music was very beautiful'. Two days later they began their journey home, returning the way they had come, although they only passed through Cairo this time, going on to Alexandria the same day and arriving there after travelling all night exactly twenty-four hours after leaving Jerusalem. On the boat they found themselves in the company of Dr and Mrs Eder and, to Chesterton's horror, Herbert Samuel, who had been in Jerusalem at the same time. On one occasion there Chesterton 'was a little embarrassed' to find Samuel sitting opposite him at a dinner where he had to make a speech. Even had he wished to, he could not possibly have made any reference to Marconi, and might have found some difficulty in informing his audience that he was writing articles for the *Telegraph*.

The boat reached Brindisi at 7 o'clock in the morning on Easter Day. The Chestertons found their hotel, and after taking breakfast decided to go to Mass. In that church, surrounded by Catholic things – statues, candles, rosaries, vestments and the steadily rising mist of incense – Chesterton realized that it was not those things that made up Catholicism: those things the Anglo-Catholics had in abundance, almost to a fault. It was not 'fasts, relics, penances or the Pope'; those things did not make up the Catholic life; but if men needed an image, 'single, coloured, and clear in outline, an image to be called up instantly in the imagination, when what is Catholic is to be distinguished from what claims to be Christian or even in one sense is Christian', Chesterton saw it or, rather, saw her there, in that little seaside church on Easter Day.

Now I can scarcely remember a time when the image of Our Lady did not stand up in my mind quite definitely, at the mention or the thought of all these things. I was quite distant from these things, and then doubtful about these things; and then disputing with the world for them, and with myself against them; for that is the condition before conversion. But whether the figure was distant, or was dark and mysterious, or was a scandal to my contemporaries, or was a challenge to myself – I never doubted that this figure was the figure of the Faith; that she embodied, as a complete human being still only human, all that this Thing had to say to humanity. The instant I remembered the Catholic Church, I remembered her; when I tried to forget the Catholic Church, I tried to forget her; when I finally saw what was nobler than my fate, the freest and the hardest of all my acts of freedom, it was in front of a gilded and very gaudy little image of her in the port of Brindisi, that I promised the thing that I would do, if I returned to my own land.

16

What I Saw in America

1920–1922

When the Chestertons arrived back in England in the middle of April, it was obvious that unless something was done quickly *The New Witness* was heading for financial disaster. The paper had been running at an ever-increasing loss, and the circulation figures had begun to drop, largely owing to the anti-Jewish bias of many of its articles; although this was more because of their manner rather than the editorial policy, which continued to be a strong support for the aims of Zionism and a welcome to the proposal to make Palestine the home of the Jews.

While he was away Chesterton had asked Ada to oversee things at the office, and to write the editorials, which had led to a certain amount of friction between Titterton and Ada. Although Chesterton had faith enough in Titterton's ability as a journalist, he no longer entirely trusted his judgement, since Titterton had commissioned a series of articles on Wells by Edwin Pugh, which had annoyed Wells to the extent of his threatening legal action. In fact, the articles were not so unfair on Wells, but the wrangle was resolved only through his affection for Chesterton. 'I can't quarrel with you,' he said, once he realized that it had been none of Chesterton's doing. Chesterton, however, informed E.S.P. Haynes, 'I think that one man largely responsible for it is Wells himself. He has printed things even about me which I could easily quarrel over, if I had been so quarrelsome. He has printed things about my brother far more unpardonable than anything Pugh could say.'

So tired was he after his travelling that for a while he felt he just could not 'pick up the threads'. 'I cannot look at *The New Witness* or the *Illustrated London News*', he told Baring. He was relieved that Belloc, who had once again taken over the 'Our Notebook' column, was prepared to continue for a few weeks. However, it did not turn out to be very long before he was busily at work for both papers.

By June it had become clear why Herbert Samuel had been out in Jerusalem, for he was appointed British Commissioner in Palestine. Chesterton wrote that the appointment was a typical example of the muddle-headedness that pervaded modern politics.

At long last the admission has been made that a Jew is not alone a synonym for a member of an odd religion and it is conceded that there is something to be said for the Zionist's point of view and our own contention that the Jews should have territory to which they officially belong. Palestine having been selected as the place which the Jew could regard as his home, as distinct from countries which he has invaded, it might have been thought that the British Empire in taking the experiment under its protection would have affirmed the distinction and have chosen an Englishman, the whole point of the experiment being that the Jews were to develop as a separate entity. As it is the muddle has been perpetuated, Great Britain as the protector of a Jewish State, pledged to see fair play between the mixed races of Palestine, despatches a Jew who claims to be an Englishman. The Press commends the appointment as highly suitable, deliberately ignoring the fact that the nomination of Herbert Samuel as British representative destroys the significance of the attempt to give his race a nationality.

Two months later the situation at *The New Witness* office became so serious that on 13 August Chesterton begged his readers for financial support if the paper was to continue. 'It would in many ways be a good thing for me if it were to stop,' he wrote; 'for I am both busy and unbusiness-like, and the paper has suffered from both defects; but I do quite seriously and even impartially believe that it would be bad for England.'

The outcome of the appeal was that just over £1,000 had been raised by Christmas, of which amount a little over half had been donated by Chesterton himself, and his mother had also given £100. It was a desperate situation as twice the sum was really necessary to ensure the paper's future, but the small boost in funds meant that some outstanding debts might be met, and the paper could continue for the time being. Fortunately there was a chance of the editor himself earning more money, as a lecture tour of the United States had been arranged for the early months of 1921.

On 17 December Chesterton wrote in his editorial: 'England today has no foreign policy; she has only foreign politicians. There are many powerful and wealthy elements watching English politics in the interests of essentially alien things; but nobody is really watching European politics in the interests of English things, least of all English credit or English prestige.' The English people, 'the secret people', those whom Cobbett had championed, were once again being betrayed; the great nation that had faced and conquered the menace of Prussianism was now being represented abroad by men who could not possibly put England first. Was it for this that the young warrior, so lately buried in Westminster, had died? The laying to rest of the Unknown Warrior, Chesterton said, 'was one of the few modern conceptions that are worthy to outlast the modern world'. The occasion was, Chesterton said, 'an excellent time for confessing the sins of Capitalism and the modern capitalist state'.

As though all Chesterton's problems with the paper had not been enough to cope with, 1920 proved also to be a very difficult year for Frances. Although the Middle Eastern journey had given her much to think about, by the summer her arthritis was worse than ever, and she was referred to a specialist; however, he could find no evidence of infection of the joints, and the pain seemed to him to be of nervous origin, 'and the difficulty she has in raising her arm probably due to the same cause'.

During the following two years Frances was under constant medical surveillance, and the doctors all felt she was doing far too much. As one doctor wrote: 'I am sure Mrs Chesterton can, and should, be made much better than she is, but it is a tough job and will need all our united efforts. But how far it is possible for her to live at home and get well, I do not know.'

In spite of her continual pain Frances carried on with great courage, and after an extensive course of treatment, she was pronounced as 'better in many ways' by the end of the year. For one thing, she was sleeping better now, and looked 'less drawn and haggard', and she was able to wear a support belt which helped her considerably. During the summer she had been able to help at the bazaar held at Burnham Hall to raise much-needed funds for the Beaconsfield Convalescent Home, an occasion at which Chesterton, dressed as Old King Cole, had run a tobacco stall, and sold parodies on the nursery rhyme in the style of five different poets, including Yeats. The parodies were later published in *The New Witness* just before Christmas with a note that the Home would be glad to receive and acknowledge subscriptions.

Readers of the parodies will probably have been less familiar with the style of Walt Whitman than with that of Tennyson, Browning and Swinburne; but here, perhaps with his forthcoming tour of America in mind, when America was in the throes of Prohibition, Chesterton excelled himself.

Me clairvoyant,
Me conscious of you, old camerado.
Needing no telescope, lorgnette, field-glass, opera-glass, myopic
    pince-nez,
Me piercing two thousand years with eye naked and not ashamed;
The crown cannot hide you from me;
Musty old feudal-heraldic trappings cannot hide you from me,
I perceive that you drink
(I am drinking with you. I am as drunk as you are).
I see you are inhaling tobacco, puffing, smoking, spitting
(I do not object to your spitting),
You prophetic of American largeness,
You anticipating the broad masculine manners of These States;
I see in you also there are movements, tremors, tears, desires for
    the melodious,
I salute your three violinists, endlessly making vibrations,
Rigid, relentless, capable of going on for ever;
They play my accompaniment; but I shall take no notice of any
    accompaniment;
I myself am a complete orchestra.
So long.

In the autumn of 1920 Chesterton had published a collection of essays, *The Uses of Diversity*; and also *The New Jerusalem*, which consisted of his *Daily Telegraph* articles, and the article the editor had largely cut. The fame of Chesterton's views on Zionism was to prove a mixed blessing when he arrived in America at the beginning of the following year.

The transatlantic liner, the *Kaiserin Augusta Victoria*, left Liverpool on New Year's Day 1921 with, among those on board, 'the World Famous Literary Genius and his wife', as the American press had reported. 'I did not know I was the wife of a great man until I came to America,' Frances was to say. It had never bothered her before.

After calling in at Queenstown to take Irish passengers aboard, the vessel headed into the Atlantic to meet 'fresh gales and rough seas' and, on 8 January, two days before arriving at New York, decidedly 'squally' weather. As I mentioned earlier, the American reporters just could not believe what they saw, for Chesterton was so much thinner than everyone had expected. It was thought that 'he must have lost weight on the voyage'. However, they found the mind and repartee of the 'brilliant epigrammist' came up to their expectation. When asked why he had come, Chesterton answered: 'It would be absurd for a man to go to his grave without seeing America. I'm all for the Statue of Liberty.' He told the reporters that it was a pity to see a people who had started out with the Declaration of Independence end up with Prohibition. He considered the Prohibition to be utter nonsense: 'Our Lord turned water into wine, not into ginger beer.' While the liner had come up the bay, he said, he had felt the urge 'to take all the liquor on board and pour it out to the Statue in a final libation'.

In New York the Chestertons' hotel was the Biltmore. After spending a few days resting from the voyage, Chesterton began his lectures at the Times Square Theatre. Lee Keedick, the organizer of the series, had been well forewarned of the lectures' titles; but one may imagine the audiences were bemused by them. Subjects such as 'The Ignorance of the Educated', 'The Perils of Health', and 'Shall We Abolish the Inevitable?' were familiar phrases in England wherever Chesterton's name appeared on a billboard, but in America they were an arresting novelty.

Chesterton was an instant success, but the tour soon began to tire him out, as he often delivered two lectures in a day. It was not long before a reporter noted: 'Mr Chesterton is fading fast; his looks are more disordered than ever.' The fact was that the constant attention of the press became a pest to both Frances and him. Women reporters crowded outside their room hoping for an interview. Eventually, Frances took to going out first to reconnoitre, to see if the coast was clear, or to fend off reporters, before Gilbert could come out. On one occasion Chesterton remarked to a crowd of staring onlookers, 'I am only human.'

From New York they moved to Boston. 'Chesterton's figure is quite imposing when he stands up, though not so abundantly Johnsonian as his pictures lead one to expect,' wrote one reporter. 'He has cascades of grey hair above a pinkly beaming face, a rather straggly blond moustache, and eyes that seem to be taking up infinity in a serious way.'

The Americans were amused by the falsetto laugh and prominent teeth, but they found his general aspect 'rather Rooseveltian'. In dress he resembled 'a thrifty long-shoreman in his Sunday-go-meeting clothes'. Chesterton might well have taken this last statement as a compliment; he told the Bostonians that his sympathies lay with the working classes in the form of 'democratic Bolshevism', under which all property would be distributed and controlled by everyone. He protested against any socialist system of governmental regulation of property, declaring that 'While a group of capitalists have brought evils, it would be no better to have property controlled by another group who would be governmental officials.'

He said he did not think he would travel any farther west than Chicago since, having seen both Jerusalem and Chicago, he thought he would have touched on the extremes of civilization.

On the subject of Ireland Chesterton said that had Home Rule been granted twenty years earlier, the Irish Question would have been settled. 'England has done many outrageous things to Ireland,' he said, 'but I think the Irish, starting out with a rightful cause, have gone far toward making it wrong by their conduct.'

Ireland was the subject of the first article Chesterton sent home, which *The New Witness* published on 18 February. 'It is a commonplace that the Englishman has been stupid in his relations with the Irish, but he has been far more stupid in his relations with the Americans on the subject of the Irish. His propaganda has been worse than its practice; and his defence more ill-considered than the most defensible things that it was intended to defend,' he wrote. Coming to America had put one thing clearly into perspective: it was stupid for England to think that in dealing with Ireland it was dealing with a small nationality, 'when she is really dealing with a very large nationality. She is dealing with a nationality that often threatens, even numerically, to dominate all the other nationalities of the United States. The Irish are not decaying; they are not unpractical; they are scarcely even scattered; they are not even poor. They are the most powerful and practical world-combination with whom we can decide to be friends or foes.'

In the same way that America was nearer to Ireland in spirit than England was, so it was closer to Europe. This was no new idea, and Chesterton had expressed it several years earlier when America had entered the war, but it was something the English hardly realized.

The tour took in many cities, as far south-west as Nashville, and north across the border into Canada. Chesterton himself enjoyed it for the most part, though he suffered from lumbago much of the time, and he was anxious that Frances was finding the travelling so tiring and that she did not become used to the attention they received wherever they went. 'The real truth is', she told one reporter, 'that I care more for my dog, donkey and garden in the little English village where we live than for all the publicity in the world.' Describing their life together, she said, 'Gilbert and I have the good fortune to be congenial, and our life is unostentatious, to say the least. I'm afraid that as an ideal adorer I should fail miserably – in the first place, we are both just normal people. Of course my husband is intelligent, and I admire intelligence, but life is too short to put one's husband on a pedestal, and then it would prove unutterably boring.'

Frances went on to say that she did all the work for Gilbert, looking after the correspondence and, worst of all, reading stupid letters from feminine admirers, 'who are splendid in their capacity for hero worship'. She said that when she had first come to America it had shocked her to realize the 'remarkable way' people had regarded her position, and when people had asked her what it was like to be married to a famous man, she had become angry and 'quite incoherent'. A man's work was the least important thing. 'Thank Heaven,' she said, 'my husband is thoroughly normal and unaffected; he doesn't care for popularity any more than I do, and we are just terribly homesick for our home in England.' However, she realized the people were very kind, and they were always so appreciative. 'While my husband is going on a lecture tour, I am organizing a campaign for the emancipation of the wives of famous men.'

Chesterton was full of praise for his audiences.

I find Americans a literary revelation, but they take my work absolutely too seriously, though they make the best audience to lecture to in the world. In England a lecture is a most dry affair. It is not a national sport. Here the good people are most appreciative of the individual's effort, whether that individual be Charlie Chaplin, Mr Dempsey, or myself.

Among those who were impressed was the poet John Crowe Ransom, who described Chesterton as one of the best lecturers he had ever heard.

Wherever he went Chesterton tried to enter into the spirit of the place; for instance, at Oklahoma City he enthused: 'I am fearfully interested in oil, I should dote on beholding a gusher.' At Albany, where there was a trolleybus strike, he said, 'I am always unalterably on the side of labour.'

Chesterton was being paid a thousand dollars for each lecture, and his audiences tended to be large, in spite of organized Jewish opposition in some places. At Omaha Chesterton told reporters he had felt 'a kind of trail of wailing rabbis all across the continent', and said that he understood that one of their own rabbis had advised every 'lover of his fellow man' to stay away from the lecture. It did not worry him in the least, he said, because he liked a small audience. 'Just picture to yourself,' he chuckled, 'a few misanthropes sitting several chairs apart, scowling into space, and all the humanitarians staying at home. Wouldn't it be funny now.'

Chesterton had been alluding to the fact that *The New Jerusalem* had been denounced in two New York synagogues. The bitterest attack had come from Dr Samuel Schulmann, of the Temple bel-Fifth Avenue and Seventy-Sixth Street synagogue, who had spoken of 'a brilliant book, disfigured by a constitutional Jew-bating which in its disgracefulness is simply disheartening. It is one of those books which, because of the magnificent powers of the writer, do the most harm, for it is thoroughly vitiated by an unreasoning and immoral persecution of the Jew.'

What Dr Schulmann said was entirely justified. He went on:

The worst kind of Jew-baiting is not that of the mob, but that of the false literary prophet of the age, which subtly attempts to instil poison into the minds of those who may become leaders of the mob; it is therefore a humiliating, even if a necessary task, to dissect this latest attempt of the well-known Anti-Semite. It is necessary because as Jews and as Americans, we must protest against the attempt to transplant to our country the artificially fostered animosity against the Jew which flourishes in Europe.

Chesterton, of his own volition, undertakes to bless, if not the Jews, the Zionists, and ends by cursing them. He professes to agree with the Zionists and yet, in every line of his description of what he saw in Palestine, he bristles with suspicion, with insults, with threats, and with opposition to the Zionist's efforts. His is a book thoroughly false, and its falsity is all the more dangerous because of its attractiveness. It is false because it is pure reactionary romanticism.

Chesterton's comment on being told of the rabbis' attacks was: 'If they have read all the chapters on the Jews and think it fanaticism, then all the fanaticism is on their side.'

Chesterton always said that his policy towards the Jews was not guided by malice, but rather by serious concern for what he saw as a serious problem, and that, to use his own words, it would have been more accurate to call him Semitic, in an active sense. It was plain that Cecil Chesterton, and other *New Witness* people, as Frances Chesterton put it, could not 'see the jewel inside for the dirty pocket handkerchief in which it is wrapped'; yet somehow Gilbert Chesterton, in spite of his absurd personal vendetta against Lord Reading, still seemed to plead innocence. But in one of his notebooks from the war period, where he jotted down odd thoughts as they had occurred to him from day to day, there are entries which show without any doubt that Chesterton did indeed have a bitter scorn for the Jews. He wrote: 'In modern Europe, Jews are not traitors, but traitors are Jews', a phrase that was mild in comparison with what was also there. 'The Jews are fleas, but they are not all practically parasites. There are performing fleas.' Now it is true that these phrases were written after the Marconi business, when Chesterton's anger was aroused against certain individual Jews, and he obviously had not intended such jottings to be seen by anyone but himself; but they do indicate something of the way he was thinking, even if the statement about the fleas was meant to be a joke.

As I said earlier, his attitude towards the Jews was a serious blemish on Chesterton's character, for which, in as much as he was motivated by malice, he has certainly had to pay dearly. When towards the end of his life he learnt of the atrocities of Hitler towards the Jews, he wrote:

In our early days Hilaire Belloc and myself were accused of being uncompromising Anti-Semites. Today, although I still think there is a Jewish problem, I am appalled by the Hitlerite atrocities. They have absolutely no reason or logic behind them. It is quite obviously the expedient of a man who has been driven to seeking a scapegoat, and has found with relief the most famous scapegoat in European history, the Jewish people. I am quite ready to believe now that Belloc and I will die defending the last Jew in Europe.

As Dr Schulmann might have said, it was a little late to say it, but for the state of Chesterton's soul it was a good thing that he did.

In Canada Chesterton spoke in Montreal and Toronto, and also in Ottawa where Frances and he stayed with his uncle and aunt, Mr and Mrs W.Chesterton, in Waverley Street. The Canadians were anxious to learn how he had fared under Prohibition, and asked him whether he thought England would ever be 'dry'. He replied, chuckling,

> I believe not, and trust not. The idea that the English governing class would ever do without its glass of champagne is so drastic and absurd that no sane man in England will ever entertain it. And we don't want a 'dry' law for the poor that is 'wet' for the rich. If there were some way of legalising prohibition by which the governing class could be assured of its glass of champagne, then I say there might be some hope of our getting liquor restrictions similar to what they have on this side.

Meanwhile in *The New Witness* was the news that the appeal had risen to a figure of £1,214 10s. 5d. and the accountant's notification that 'The Net Sales of *The New Witness*, after deducting all unsold and free copies, for the six months ending December 31, 1920, amounted to 25,191 copies, an average of 933 for each of the 27 issues comprised in the half year.' As was pointed out at the same time, perhaps somewhat hopefully, the circulation figures did not take into account those groups who were unable individually to afford a shilling a week, but who clubbed together small amounts to take out a subscription so that the paper might pass from hand to hand, securing increased publicity. There was also, it was noticed, 'a growing number of subscribers in America and the Colonies'. All this may have been a boost for the morale of the office, but it in no way altered the fact that in spite of the moderate success of the appeal the paper's future was shaky.

The Chestertons left New York in the *Aquitania*, travelling on C deck, on 10 April. The Americans had been sad to see their 'medieval Santa Claus in "civies"' depart; but Chesterton, realizing that Frances had had enough, was content to leave. On the next occasion his American hosts would prevail upon him to stay for longer, and he would accept. Frances was pleased to see the shoreline sink below the horizon. For much of the time, if not feeling physically ill, she had felt homesick, and tended to talk mostly of home. As one interviewer reported, 'Mrs Chesterton keeps chickens, a whole flock of them of which she is very proud', and it was noticed how she had suddenly brightened up when she heard from Kathleen Chesshire, now the secretary, who was holding the fort at Overroads, that the crocuses there were in bloom. In Boston Frances had consulted an eminent specialist, Dr Osgood, who sent back to England 'a most lugubrious report on her condition'. It was hardly a good time, Chesterton must have thought, to worry Frances further about religion.

As he had told Fr O'Connor in a letter written on the previous Christmas Eve, 'Frances has not been well, and though I think she is better, I have to do things in a considerate way, if you understand me. I feel it is only right to consult with my Anglo-Catholic friends; but I have at present a feeling it will be something like a farewell.'

He felt that he owed his friends an explanation, though not necessarily a justification. He had made his position quite clear in a letter he had written to Baring during the summer. He wished to be certain he was 'inside' the Church. 'I used to think', he wrote, 'one could be an Anglo-Catholic and really inside it; but if that was (to use an excellent phrase of your own) only a Porch, I do not think I want a Porch, and certainly not a Porch standing some way from the building. A Porch looks silly, standing all by itself in a field.' That he might cause Frances even more pain was the chief of what he called 'the real ties and complications and difficulties, difficulties that seemed almost duties'.

It was difficult, if not impossible, to be honest about his conversion without appearing to denigrate the Anglo-Catholic position, and this must inevitably hurt several people he loved. Nevertheless, the fact that there was something 'insufficient' about the Anglo-Catholic position was clearly in his mind. During the war he had written in one of his notebooks: 'Catholicism necessarily feels for Protestantism not the superiority a man feels over sticks and straws, but that he feels over clippings of his hair and nails. She feels Protestantism not merely as something insufficient, but something that would never have been even *that*, but for herself.' However much he argued the matter out in his own mind, he could not help but see the Anglo-Catholic position, as Newman had done before him, as essentially a protest.

So it was that on their return from America there was much to be decided. It was known that the lease on Overroads would expire early in the summer of the following year, and would not be renewed. The work on extending the Studio into a dwelling was already under way, but it would be predominantly Frances who would have to make all the decisions.

During that summer Chesterton attended to *The New Witness*, and besides producing the editorials continued to entertain his readers with his impressions of America. He told them that 'Old England might still be traced in Old Dixie'. He told them that when he had gone to America he had had some notion of not discussing Prohibition; but he had soon found out that 'Well-to-do Americans were only too delighted to discuss it over nuts and wine.' He did not say whether he had eaten all the nuts himself, as Fr O'Connor once saw him eat a whole bowl of them in an absent-minded way. On 22 July Chesterton wrote, 'There is nothing that an American likes so much as to have a secret society and to make no secret of it.' While he had been in America, he said, he had carried two walking sticks 'like a Japanese nobleman with two swords'. On second thoughts he had thought the simile too stately, and said he had borne more resemblance 'to a cripple with two crutches or a highly ineffectual version of the devil on two sticks'.

On 14 July Chesterton had again dressed up for charity; but this time there was a difference, for he played the part of Theseus in a production of *A Midsummer Night's Dream* to raise money for the dual purposes of providing a new engine for the Beaconsfield Fire Brigade, and building an extension on to the Church School. The part of Puck was taken by the Chestertons' friend Margaret Halford. It is interesting that Mrs Halford was Jewish, and she confessed to feeling, as she later told Maisie Ward, 'a certain restraint' when she first met Chesterton at a function at the Studio. However, she had found it 'quite impossible to maintain that feeling. The benevolence and love in the air were unmistakeable and irresistible.' It was through their very close friendship that Chesterton became the President of the Players' Club of Beaconsfield.

By the middle of October the papers were, as Chesterton said, 'full of headlines about the Church Congress'. In his editorial on 21 October he commented on Lord Dawson's statement that 'Christian morality need no longer restrain us in the matter of "birth control"', and as many newspapers had rallied behind it, saying that if the Church was to live, it must 'move with the times', or, as some put it, 'must move with the world'. Chesterton said he had much more time for men who recognized Christian morals as Christian, and denied them as such, than he had for those who called themselves Christians and then set about 'brazenly betraying the Christian's vital point of honour'. It was one tiresome, tireless, all-destroying and indestructible piece of nonsense to say that all things should be judged by whether they are suited to our industrial cities. Nothing could be more false to history, he argued, than the statement that, if the Church is to live, it must move with the times.

We do not want, as the newspapers say, a Church that will move with the world. We want a Church that will move the world. We want one that will move it away from any of the things towards which it is now moving; for instance, the Servile State. It is by that test that history will really judge, of any Church, whether it is the real Church or no.

At about this time Chesterton had addressed what turned out to be 'a large Anglo-Catholic Congress at the Albert Hall'. Knowing that his own position was becoming increasingly untenable, he had decided to try to get out of it, but had been held to his promise. He felt he could therefore only speak very briefly, and keep his subject very general, speaking about social ethics rather than theology, as he described in another letter to Baring, adding:

To those to whom I cannot give my spiritual biography, I can say that the insecurity I felt in Anglicanism was typified in the Lambeth Conference. I am at least sure that much turns on that Conference, if not for me, for large numbers of those people at the Albert Hall. A young Anglo-Catholic curate has just told me that the crowd there cheered all references to the Pope, and laughed at every mention of the Archbishop of Canterbury. It's a queer state of things. I am concerned most however, about somebody I value more than the Arch-bishop of Canterbury; Frances, to whom I owe much of my own faith, and to whom therefore (as far as I can see my way) I also owe every decent chance for the controversial defence of her faith. If her side can convince me, they have a right to do so; if not, I shall go hot and strong to convince her. I put it clumsily, but there is a point in my mind. Logically, therefore, I must await answers from

Waggett and Gore [the bishop], as well as Knox and McNabb; and talk the whole thing over with her, and then act as I believe.

Beginning in the 'Special Christmas Number' of *The New Witness* on 9 December, Chesterton turned his attention for several weeks to the subject of Marxian socialism. 'It is true that nobody makes a new earth without first making a new heaven', he wrote, and this was no more especially true when the heaven is full of gods or angels than when the heaven is empty of everything but ether and stardust. It was quite as true when the heaven was only an abyss or bottomless pit of space; it was quite as true, Chesterton argued, when the heaven was rather like hell.

In the same issue of the paper Chesterton had made fun of the Chief Constable of Blackpool who had 'issued a statement declaring that carol-singing in the streets by children is illegal and morally and physically injurious. He appeals to the public to discourage the practice.' Chesterton wrote:

> God rest you merry gentlemen,
> Let nothing you dismay;
> The Herald Angels cannot sing;
> The cops arrest them on the wing,
> And warn them of the docketing
> Of anything they say . . .

That Christmas, judging by the letters and poems Chesterton wrote for Hilary Gray, there appears to have been some larking about with Chesterton singing carols beneath Hilary's room at Boyne House. He wrote:

> It was the Carol of a friend
> That roused you from your bed.
> It was my voice that reached your ears,
> Your boot that reached my head.

It may have been a joke, or perhaps Hilary had responded by flinging a boot out of the window, for Chesterton's next letter began:

Dear Boot-Slinger,
Many thanks for your kind enquiries; the injury was not severe, but it is thought that the head had been in a weak state for some

time. What gives me a greater shock than any boot is the discovery that you have a first name, carefully suppressed, beginning with E.

Horrible thoughts stir within me ... But it cannot be ... the Importance of Being ... or rather the importance of Not Being ... above all, the Importance of concealing it when one is ....

'Ernest Hilary Gray' sounds terribly compact and convincing. True, Ernest is commonly a boy's name; but so, very often, is Hilary. One of my best friends is commonly addressed by it. Or could it be Ernestine?

What would an avalanche of all Mr Grover's shop be, as compared with blows like these?

The letter ended by wishing her a happy Christmas. Hilary's first name was, in fact, Evelyn. Had Chesterton known this all the time? It seems fairly obvious that Chesterton, however naïvely, had a 'crush' on Hilary, and this may well be why her name has never been mentioned before by anyone in connection with him. Her sister has said that Hilary was 'very much G.K.C.'s favourite' among what he called 'the Gray Minstrelsy'. She was intelligent, vivacious, very musical, religious, and in every way attractive, and both she and Chesterton would have gained from the friendship. There would have been no more to it than that.

There was great fun too over the 'rivalry' between the Grays' West Highland terrier Jock, and the Chestertons' Winkle, who was half Cairn, half Aberdonian, and the successor of the more famous Quoodle. Chesterton used to write out large notices with slogans and comments on the state of the 'conflict', such as: 'LATEST NEWS FROM THE FRONT (GARDEN)' with the newsflash 'PRESIDENT WINKLE FIRM: "I WILL NOT BE MUZZLED." Reports indicate that President Winkle remains firmly attached to his fourteen points. He is at his post and tied entirely to his old position: and there seems some probability of Marshal Jock following his lead.' The same notice reported the 'Murder of Princess Hilary. Princess Hilary informs us that the report of her death by martyrdom is still unconfirmed. Her doubts on the point have caused considerable embarrassment to the Church authorities, who had somewhat hastily canonised her as a second St Hilary.'

Another notice announced 'BEACONSFIELD PEACE CONFERENCE' and 'THE PERIL OF PAN-GRAYISM. Mr and Mrs Chesterton are firm for the freedom of the Cs. They regard the proposal to internationalise the Studio and use it as a Free Port as quite impracticable, and a mere

The Case of The Vanishing Car.

Girl's Extraordinary Career of Crime —

(Extract from the reminiscences of Dr Watson, of Baker Street.)

" The mystery is utterly beyond comprehension."

" Beyond your comprehension, doubtless, my dear Watson" said Holmes in his most genial manner " I myself have already solved it."

Sherlock Holmes was leaning back in his chair in the old familiar attitude, his eyes fixed on the ceiling, as he proceeded to tick off on his long lean fingers the points of the mystery of the Car in Grove Road.

" The problem begins, of course, with the discrepancy between the statements of M^r & Mrs Chesterton. The lady has sworn repeatedly, & with the utmost violence, that early on Saturday she saw Mr Gray & his eldest daughter leaving home in a magnificent motor car with every appearance of departing finally on a long journey; & in the company of an unknown gentleman, whose mysterious personality, could we discover it, is undoubtedly the clue to this strange & sinister affair. The man Chesterton, however, stubbornly asserts that some time afterwards, he saw Miss Hilary Gray alone & cycling swiftly through the town, & that she made in passing the strange & significant remark that the weather was windy. Generally, of course, in case of a conflict of testimony between this man & his wife, a sagacious critic would find it easy to believe his wife. The man is a journalist, naturally indifferent to truth; while the wife's firm & even forcible language shows she is in every way acquainted with the nature of an oath. But I have been able, by my own methods, Watson, to some extent to corroborate his story;

pretence to cover aggression. Remember the Jock Atrocities.'

No mention seems to have been made of the Chestertons' donkey, or the Grays' goat, Pauline, nor indeed of the Chestertons' cat, Perky. One day, as the maid, Mary Rushton, remembered, Perky climbed up on the breakfast table after the kippers. She was going to throw the kippers away, but Chesterton said, 'I don't mind eating after Perky.'

Early in 1922 Chesterton wrote to Fr Ronald Knox:

> My father is the very best man I ever knew of that generation that never understood the new need for a spiritual authority; and lives almost perfectly by the sort of religion men had when rationalism was rational. I think he was always subconsciously prepared for the next generation having less theology than he has; and is rather puzzled at its having more. But I think he understood my brother's conversion better than my mother did; she is more difficult, and of course I cannot bother her just now.

Chesterton had begun the letter with the news that his father was 'very ill', but no one in the family realized how close to death Edward Chesterton was. He had developed what Ada described as 'an obstinate cold', and though there seemed 'nothing sinister or alarming in his symptoms, the condition increased the nervous apprehensions and he decided to go to bed'. For some weeks he had tended to stay in bed during the daytime and come downstairs in his pyjamas, and he 'grew quite cheerful over buttered toast and cress sandwiches'. After a while he left his bedroom less often, so much so that the doctor, obviously thinking there was no real cause for alarm, suggested a change of air. Although she loathed being away from London, Marie Louise was in favour of the idea; but Edward lacked the energy to move. Still the doctor thought there was 'no cause for fear'; Mr Chesterton's heart was in good shape, it had never been stronger in fact. But soon the family noticed that he seemed morose and went into long periods of silence. Eventually, when he seemed no better, 'specialists were called in and different diets prescribed'. After several weeks the patient seemed no better, and he tended to remain in bed for longer periods, and, as Ada Chesterton recalled, 'Little by little his mental keenness was overclouded, and he drifted into lassitude and inertia; so that when at last he went out, the end was not wholly a surprise.' His father's illness had lasted for several months, and Frances had to force Gilbert to make the weekend journey to Kensington to see him. However, when

the end came it proved to be a very difficult time, as the Chestertons
had moved into the new house before it was completed, and during
the move Frances had been so unwell herself that Gilbert had had
to attend to everything.

Edward Chesterton was buried in the Chesterton grave at Brompton,
and everyone 'came back to Warwick Gardens for a hospitable tea,
with the little lady presiding'. Marie Louise wished to do nothing about
her husband's study and belongings, and particularly the mass of papers
and large albums of press cuttings in which he had meticulously followed
the careers of his two brilliant sons; all remained untouched until her
own death in 1933. 'My father died on Monday,' Chesterton told Fr
Knox, 'and since then I have been doing the little I can for my mother;
but even that little involves a great deal of business – the least valuable
sort of help.'

Mr Ed had lived long enough to see the publication of Gilbert's
book *Eugenics and Other Evils*, which Cassell brought out towards the
end of February; but had he read it he would have realized that it
was one of Gilbert's less successful books. The prose seemed laboured
in comparison with what he had written before and, indeed, with what
he would write later.

Reviewing the book for *The Nation* Shaw said it might just as well
have been called 'Obstetrics and Other Evils, or Dietetics or Esthetics
or Peripatetics or Optics or Mathematics and Other Evils'. It was a
graver, harder book than its forerunners but, he added, 'A criticism
of Mr Chesterton is in the nature of a bulletin as to the mental condition
of a prophet.'

The misuse of science was all part of what Chesterton called the
'Eclipse of Liberty'. A year earlier he had written, 'Science can mean
anything, even the denial of science; as can be seen in the title Christian
Science. But though a modern fad can do without the elements of a
science, it cannot do without the terminology, not, above all, without
the title. The thing must be an instrument and not a tool; still less
a weapon like the wizard's lance.' The word 'science' had come to
have a 'meaningless mystery and power', and as it increased in confusion
it increased in control. Chesterton saw that great evils could be perpetrated in the name of science, and once again he was not mistaken.

In the summer of 1922 the Studio was still in the process of becoming
Top Meadow, the house designed by 'local talent and Mrs G.K.'s own
ideas', in which Gilbert and she lived for the rest of their lives. When

Ada visited Top Meadow that year she found the effect confusing. To begin with,

> ... the stage, on which amateur talent used to shine, some feet above the auditorium – or should I say floor level? – had been made into a dining-room. It was reached from the small front hall by a narrow passage and you entered, so to speak, by the doorless wings direct on to the dining-table, almost flush with the proscenium curtains. The place was heated by anthracite stove backstage, which could not be kept at a pressure sufficient to warm the whole, as those with their backs almost against it would have been slowly roasted ....
>
> Beyond the stage, and at the lower level, the auditorium stretched through a hinterland to Gilbert's cubby-hole. In the front of the hinterland there was an open brick fireplace with space for a small low chair on either side, where Frances would sit for hours, watching the logs crumble into fiery particles. The huge room, open to the passage, was terribly draughty and the logs burned for most of the year; but inside the fireplace all was warm and cosy.

Ada also remembered how small tables filled with knick-knacks were ranged in the corner near the stage, and at Christmas Gilbert's toy theatre stood on one and a Nativity crib on another. 'Beyond the small tables were those of a larger size holding books and flowering plants and – unexpectedly – a bust of G.K. Oases of easy chairs and Chesterfields culminated in a desert of carpet, while high up near the vaulted roof a toy musician's gallery appeared – where no musicians played.'

Above the stage and the studio there were no rooms, but a new wing had been added, with the kitchens and garage on the ground floor, and above, led to by 'a tolerably wide staircase', there was a narrow corridor

> ... from which opened little monkish cells gratefully provided with gas stoves, and running hot and cold water .... The queerness of the elevation culminated in an unusually tiny W.C., quite incommensurate with Gilbert's outsize. The poor darling had to contort himself unbelievably to get round the narrow door which opened inwards. His stumbling efforts and protest noises were audible all over the house and were so funny that I choked with suppressed laughter and wished that he could share the joke.

According to Ada, Frances 'never turned a hair during these Homeric combats', and it had never seemed to strike her that Top Meadow was 'utterly lopsided in design – one half being framed for a giant and the other for a gnome. The battles between an irresistible force and an immovable object went on for years, until more ample accommodation was built on, together with a man's size bathroom and proportionate bedroom.'

So it was from Top Meadow, Beaconsfield, that Chesterton wrote to Fr O'Connor:

> I ought to have written to you long before in reply to your kind letter; but indeed I do not answer it now in order to agree with you about Ireland or disagree with you about France; if indeed we do disagree about anything. I write with a more personal motive; do you happen to have a holiday about the end of next week or thereabouts and would it be possible for you to come south and see our new house – or old studio? This sounds a very abrupt invitation; but I write in great haste, and am troubled about many things. I want to talk to you about them; especially the most serious ones, religious and concerned with my own rather difficult position. Most of the difficulty has been my own fault, but not all; some of my difficulties would commonly be called duties; though I ought perhaps to have learned sooner to regard them as lesser duties. I mean that a Pagan or Protestant or Agnostic might even have excused me; but I have grown less and less of a Pagan or Protestant, and can no longer excuse myself. There are lots of things for which I never did excuse myself; but I am thinking now of particular points that might really be casuistical. Anyhow, you are the person that Frances and I think of with most affection, of all who could help in such a matter. Could you let me know if any time such as I name, or after, could give us the joy of seeing you?

On 17 July, Fr Knox wrote: 'I'm awfully glad to hear that you've sent for Father O'Connor and that you think he's likely to be available. I must say that, in the story, Father Brown's powers of neglecting his parish always seemed to me even more admirable than Dr Watson's powers of neglecting his practice; so I hope this trait was drawn from life.'

17

My Name is Lazarus

1922–1925

Frances had reached the point (as Gilbert was to tell Fr Knox) 'where Rome acted both as the positive and the negative magnet; a touch would turn her either way; almost (against her will) to hatred, but with the right touch', Chesterton said, she would have a faith far beyond his reach. He had waited patiently for Frances to join him, so that they might be received together. 'I cannot bear to leave her, even psychologically, if it be possible by tact and sympathy to take her with me,' he had told Baring some time earlier. Frances's life, he said, had been in many ways 'a very heroic tragedy', and they had faced many difficult times together. However, the time had come when he could wait no longer. He had chosen Fr O'Connor, he told Knox, because his would be 'a touch that does not startle', because Frances knew him, and was fond of him, and the only thing she had asked was to send for him.

When Fr O'Connor arrived at Top Meadow on Wednesday 26 July, he spent the evening listening to Chesterton's 'difficulties'; and the following morning accompaniend Frances to the village, as he had often done before, and told her quite directly that the only thing holding Gilbert back from being received into the Church was the effect it might have on her. Her reply was immediate. 'Oh! I shall be infinitely relieved. You cannot imagine how it fidgets Gilbert to have anything on his mind. The last three months have been exceptionally trying. I should be only too glad to come with him, if God in His mercy would show the way clear enough to me to justify such a step.'

After lunch the priest was able to reassure Chesterton that Frances was 'happy' about the situation, and 'to make sure there were no snags to a prosperous passage', he gave him the Penny Catechism to read through. As Fr O'Connor recalled, 'It was a sight for men and angels all Friday to see him wandering in and out of the house with his fingers in the leaves of the little book, resting it on his forearm whilst he pondered with his head on one side.'

The idea that Chesterton might be received into the Church at the Benedictine abbey at Douai was rejected in favour of the local church, which at the time was a room in the Railway Hotel, a dance room 'fitted up with Sir Philip Rose's Chapel fixtures'; but the Head Master of Douai, Dom Ignatius Rice, a great admirer of Chesterton, agreed that even if the ceremony could not take place in 'the Abbey's sacred shade', he would at least be present wherever it was.

After luncheon at Top Meadow on Sunday 30 July Chesterton and Fr O'Connor set off for the hotel. Chesterton was carrying the stick given to him in America by the Knights of Columbus. What we know of the reception ceremony is largely from an account of it given by Dom Ignatius to Maisie Ward's husband, Frank Sheed. Fr O'Connor, who actually conducted the ceremony, said very little, except that Frances was in tears which, he felt sure, 'were not all grieving'.

According to Dom Ignatius, Chesterton had taken a last look at the catechism, 'pulling faces and making noises as he used to do when reading', and when they reached the hotel, Fr O'Connor suddenly asked Chesterton if he had remembered to bring the Ritual. 'G.K. plunged his hand in his pocket, pulled out a threepenny shocker with complete absence of embarrassment, and went on searching till at last he found the prayer book.'

Chesterton made his first confession to Fr O'Connor, while Frances went outside with Dom Ignatius. She was overcome by emotion, and wept as she sat on the yokel's bench in the bar of the inn. However, the two returned to the Chapel for the service. 'After the baptism the two priests came out and left Gilbert and Frances inside. Dom Ignatius went back for something he had forgotten and he saw them coming down the aisle. She was still weeping, and Gilbert had his arm round her comforting her.'

According to Dom Ignatius, Chesterton wrote the sonnet on his conversion that day. 'He was in brilliant form for the rest of the day, quoting poetry and jesting in the highest spirits.' If it is true that Chesterton wrote his sonnet that day, he certainly had received a rich gift, for it was one of the best poems he wrote.

> After one moment when I bowed my head
> And the whole world turned over and came upright,

And I came out where the old road shone white,
I walked the ways and heard what all men said,
Forests of tongues, like autumm leaves unshed,
Being not unlovable but strange and light;
Old riddles and new creeds, not in despite
But softly, as men smile about the dead.

The sages have a hundred maps to give
That trace their crawling cosmos like a tree,
They rattle reason out through many a sieve
That stores the sand and lets the gold go free:
And all these things are less than dust to me
Because my name is Lazarus and I live.

Writing about his conversion in his autobiography, or, as Maisie Ward called it, 'completion', Chesterton said,

When people ask me, or indeed anybody else, 'Why did you join the Church of Rome?' the first essential answer, if it is partly an elliptical answer, is 'To get rid of my sins.' For there is no other religious system that does *really* profess to get rid of people's sins. It is confirmed by logic, which to many seems startling, by which the Church deduces that sin confessed and adequately repented is actually abolished; and that the sinner does really begin again as if he had never sinned.

This brought him back, he said, to those visions or fancies of childhood, the

...indescribable and indestructible certitude in the soul, that those first years of innocence were the beginning of something worthy, perhaps more worthy than any of the things that actually followed them ... the strange daylight, which was something more than the light of common day, that still seems in my memory to shine on those steep roads down from Campden Hill, from which one could see the Crystal Palace from afar.

When a Catholic comes from confession,

...he does truly, by definition, step out again into that dawn of his own beginning and look with new eyes across the world to a Crystal Palace that is really of crystal. He believes that in that dim corner, and in that brief ritual, God has really re-made him in His own image. He is now a new experiment of the Creator. He is as much a new experiment as he was when he was really five years old. He stands, as I said, in the white light at the worthy beginning of the life of a man. The accumulations of time can no longer terrify. He may be grey and gouty; but he is only five minutes old.

However, Chesterton was careful to emphasize that the Sacrament of Penance indeed gives a new life, and reconciles a man to all living, but

> ... it does not do it as the optimists and the hedonists and the heathen preachers of happiness do it. The gift is given at a price, and is conditioned by a confession. In other words, the name of the price is Truth, which may also be called Reality; but it is facing the reality about onself. When the process is only applied to other people, it is called Realism.

In spite of his joy at 'restoring his innocence', Chesterton never became a regular visitor to the confessional. According to Dom Ignatius 'he did not go to confession very often, but when he did you could hear him all over the church'. Nevertheless, as Chesterton said himself, he had found the one denomination that dared to go down with him into the depths of himself. His morbidities, mental as well as moral, and his besetting sin of ingratitude, a sin largely of the imagination, could only be pierced, he said, 'by that conception of confession which is the end of mere solitude and secrecy'.

It would not be long before he would say, 'I cannot explain why I am a Catholic; because now that I am a Catholic I cannot imagine myself as anything else.'

The first person to learn of his new situation beyond the small group who had witnessed the ceremony was his mother.

> I write this (with the worst pen in South Bucks) to tell you something before I write about it to anyone else; something about which we shall probably be in the position of the two bosom friends at Oxford, who 'never differed except in opinion'. You have always been so wise in not judging people by their opinions, but rather the opinions by the people. It is in one sense a long story by this time; but I have come to the same conclusion that Cecil did about needs of the modern world in religion and right dealing, and I am now a Catholic in the same sense as he, long having claimed the name in its Anglo-

Catholic sense. I am not going to make a foolish fuss of reassuring you about things I am sure you never doubted; these things do not hurt any relations between people as fond of each other as we are; any more than they ever made any difference to the love between Cecil and ourselves. But there are two things I should like to tell you, in case you do not realise them through some other impression. I have thought about you, and all that I owe to you and my father, not only in the way of affection, but of the ideals of honour and freedom and charity and all other good things you always taught me: and I am not conscious of the smallest break or difference in those ideals; but only a new and necessary way of fighting for them. I think, as Cecil did, that the fight for the family and the free citizen and everything decent must now be waged by the one fighting form of Christianity. The other is that I have thought this out for myself and not in a hurry of feeling. It is months since I saw my Catholic friends and years since I talked to them about it. I believe it is the truth.

The last part of the letter was strictly accurate only as far as Belloc and Baring were concerned, but it was those two particularly that Chesterton regarded as his 'Catholic friends'. Both men wrote to the new convert once they received the news. Belloc, writing on 1 August, spoke mostly about himself, but in the course of the letter told Chesterton that 'The Catholic Church is the natural home of the human spirit. The odd perspective picture of life which looks like a meaningless puzzle at first, seen from that one standpoint takes on a complete order and meaning.'

In fact, as it came out some weeks later, Belloc had made some attempt to prevent Fr O'Connor from ever going down to Beaconsfield, on the grounds that Chesterton 'would never be a Catholic'; but he had obviously thought better of it, for when the priest arrived at Westminster Cathedral to meet Belloc, who had sent for him by telegram, he had waited for an hour, but Belloc had failed to turn up.

Baring told Chesterton that he had, curiously enough, felt it had happened before he saw the news in the newspaper. 'I felt that your ship had arrived at its port,' he wrote.

As soon as the news was known letters and messages of congratulation came in from all over the world, as Fr O'Connor put it, 'all voiced tranquil joy'. Not all, in fact; when Shaw heard the news, he asked whether Chesterton had been drunk. 'My dear G.K.C.,'' he wrote, 'This is going too far.'

On 1 September Chesterton wrote in *The New Witness*: 'Distributism is in a special sense democratic. It is democratic because it can in some sense begin from below. Believing in voluntary action it can call for volunteers; and collectivism cannot call for volunteers.' The fact was that the paper simply could not continue without some radical alteration in its staffing. As Chesterton told Ada, there was very little money left and 'he could see no possibility of raising more'. The result would be ultimately that *The New Witness* would have to close down in favour of another paper, which could be run more cheaply and depend on much voluntary support from both contributors and subscribers. In the event *The New Witness* struggled on until the beginning of May the following year.

While all this worry over the paper was on his mind, Chesterton's impressions of America were published in book form as *What I Saw in America*. Most of the book consisted of the articles seen already in *The New Witness*, but Chesterton had added quite a lot more. For instance, his readers learned what he had thought of Broadway: 'What a glorious garden of wonders this would be, to any one who was lucky enough to be unable to read.'

The following month another book of verse, *The Ballad of St Barbara and Other Verses*, was published by Cecil Palmer. It was dedicated to Frances 'In Memoriam Palestine'. The title poem had a double thread: 'The Battle of the Marne (or more precisely, the Battle of St Gond) and the legend of St Barbara, the patron Saint of Artillery and those in danger of sudden death, supposed to be told by a Breton soldier to his Norman mate, as a symbol of the triumph of martyrdom over the powers of darkness'. The poem, which was, of course, written in time of war, had more appeal when it first appeared that it does today, where it seems one of Chesterton's least successful pieces; but the book contained many finer poems, including the well-known 'The Trinkets' – a poem about the Virgin Mary, likely to stick in the gullet of anyone out of sympathy with the subject. It had a simplicity charming to those who were in sympathy, and was in the same spirit as a story Chesterton had heard while he was in Ireland.

When I was on the wild coast of Donegal, an old unhappy woman who had starved through the famines and the evictions was telling a lady the tales of those times, and she mentioned quite naturally one that might have come straight out of times so mystical that we should call them mythical, that some travellers had met a poor wandering woman with a baby in those great grey rocky wastes, and asked her who she was. And she answered, 'I am the Mother of God, and this is Himself, and He is the boy you will all be wanting at the last.'

In November 1922 a collection of short stories which had appeared in *Cassell's Magazine* and *The Storyteller* was published as *The Man Who Knew Too Much*. 'It is to Mr Chesterton's credit that he can write a detective story that would be rejected by every one of the cheaper magazines,' noted *The Observer*. 'There is hardly a tale in which the Jew, or the scientist, or the plutocrat, or the antiquarian, or the politician does not offer his head to be hit.' The stories were linked together through the character of Horne Fisher, a gaunt aristocratic detective who, though Chesterton may possibly have modelled him on Baring, does not match Father Brown in interest.

Whether Baring had been in Chesterton's mind in the creation of Horne Fisher or not, he remained a close friend at this time, even if only by letter. In their correspondence, however, it was invariably Chesterton who was behind. On 14 February 1923 he wrote a letter in which, six months after the event, he outlined some of the reasons why he had become a Catholic.

To begin with, I am shy of giving one of my deepest reasons because it is hard to put it without offence, and I am sure it is the wrong method to offend the wavering Anglo-Catholic. But I believe one of my strongest motives was mixed up with the idea of honour. I feel there is something mean about not making complete confession and restitution after a historic error and slander....

The larger version of this is that England has really got into so wrong a state, with its plutocracy and neglected populace and materialistic and servile morality, that it must take a sharp turn that will be a sensational turn. No *evolution* into Catholicism will have that moral effect. Christianity is the religion of repentance; it stands against modern fatalism and pessimistic futurism mainly in saying that a man can go back. If we do decidedly go back it will show that religion is alive. For the rest, I do not say much about the details of continuity and succession, because the truth is they did not much affect me.

What I see is that we cannot complain of England suffering from being Protestant and at the same time claim that she has always been Catholic. That there has always been a High Church Party is true; that there has always been an Anglo-Catholic Party may be true, but I am not so sure of it.... But there is one matter arising from that which I do think important. Even the High Church Party, even the Anglo-Catholic Party only confronts a particular heresy called Protestantism upon particular points. It defends ritual rightly or even sacramentalism rightly, because these are the things the Puritans attacked. If it is not the heresy of an age, at least it is only the anti-heresy of an age. But since I have been a Catholic, I am conscious of being in a much vaster arsenal, full of arms against countless other potential enemies. The Church, as the Church and not merely as ordinary opinion, has something to say to philosophies which the merely High Church has never had occasion to think about. If the next movement is the very reverse of Protestantism, the Church will have something to say about it; or rather has already something to say about it. You might unite all High Churchmen on the High Church quarrel, but what authority is to unite them when the devil declares his next war on the world?

Another quality that impresses me is the power of being decisive first and being proved right afterwards. This is exactly the quality a supernatural power would have; and I know nothing else in modern religion that has it. For instance, there was a time when I should have thought psychical enquiry the most reasonable thing in the world, and rather favourable to religion. I was afterwards convinced, by experience and not merely faith, that Spiritualism is a practical poison. Don't people see that *when* that is found in experience, a prodigious prestige accrues to the authority which, long before the experiment, did not pretend to enquire but simply said, 'Drop it.' We feel that the authority did not discover; it knew. There are a hundred other things of which that story is true, in my own experience. But the High Churchman has the perfect right to be a Spiritualistic enquirer; only he has not a right to claim that his authority knew beforehand the truth about spiritualistic enquiry.

Of course there are a hundred things more to say; indeed the greatest argument for Catholicism is exactly what makes it so hard to argue for it. It is the scale and multiplicity of the forms of truth and help that it has to offer. And perhaps, after all, the only thing that you and I can really say with profit is exactly what you yourself suggested; that we are men who have talked to a good many men about a good many things, and seen something of the world and the philosophies of the world and that we have not the shadow of a doubt about what was the wisest act of our lives.

Two weeks before this letter was written Chesterton had alerted his readers to the possibility of 'a new *New Witness*'. The decline of the paper, he said, had started after the Great War and had been

> ...crippled by the death of the only man who could really do it. It lost the one great controversialist against corruption who was materially, mentally and morally on the spot. It passed, by the tragic extension on an interregnum, to an amateur who could only help it in one way by not helping it in another, and was so placed that he could not at once contribute and control.

It was now time to fight for the Distributist cause. What was once true of socialism was now true of Distributism. 'Every other thinking man I meet is conscious of the collapse of industrialism, and the need to recover thrift and freedom,' he said. Once again the appeal for money went out.

> I do think it possible that men with a little money to spare might club together in support of such potential success, when they would not do it for our present avowed failure. I mean that they might subscribe enough to put the paper on the ordinary basis of paying people reasonably to write and direct it, with some hope that they would not lose and might well gain. The very atmosphere of the new adventure would be quite different from the inevitable and trailing tragedy of the old one.

For several weeks *The New Witness* printed a full page advertising the 'new adventure' of a 'sixpenny weekly' with an application form for subscribers. Then on 2 February it was announced that the new paper would in fact be called *G.K.C.'s Weekly*. The following week Chesterton wrote:

> In this day and hour I haul down my flag, I surrender my sword, I give up a fight I have maintained against odds for very long. No; I do not mean the fight to maintain the *New Witness*, though that was a fight against impossible odds and has gone on for years. I

mean a more horrid but hidden conflict, of which the world knew nothing; the savage but secret war I have waged against a proposal to call a paper by the name of *G.K.C.'s Weekly*. When the title was first suggested my feeling was one of wild terror, which gradually softened into disgust.

At the suggestion that his objection was sheer embarrassment, Chesterton replied that if he were called upon to dance in tights on a tight-rope stretched from the cross of St Paul's to the Strand churches, his first feeling would not be embarrassment. Yet, he said, he had come to see the case for the proposal, and that not merely to please the crowd of friends who had pressed it upon him. It was, as the acrobatic feat might have been, 'a mere business matter of advertisement'. He could not really deny, though he would very much have liked to, that the name would probably be better known than any new name that could easily be taken.

It may be my business to think only for the paper; and I set my teeth, or grind my teeth, and do it. If I may be allowed to relieve my feelings by saying that I execrate, abominate and anathematise the new name, that I renounce and abjure it, that I blast it with lightnings and curse it with bell, book and candle, I will then admit that it is certainly the best name we can take.

There was certainly little room for 'vanity touching this vulgar notoriety', as he put it. On 9 March Chesterton's interests were directed towards home. 'A certain scheme of town-planning had been suggested for our little town in Buckinghamshire,' he said. He argued that any town plan must be a plan for a particular town and not 'any new plan for any old town'. He would far rather that 'the town of Beaconsfield were burned to the ground and rebuilt by the Confucians as a circle of Chinese pagodas, or by the Red Indians as a circle of painted wigwams, than that it should be laid out in the manner of what is now called a model village, with all the parvenue aesthetics and priggish philanthropy of a Garden City'. It is ironic that Beaconsfield is well known today for its model village, in the real sense.

On 13 April, in his editorial headed 'Sanity and Semitism', Chesterton said that those responsible for *The New Witness* were the first to attack the Jews, but now that the Jews were being attacked on all sides they might yet be the last to defend them. 'With Beaverbrook himself denouncing Jews, with Rothermere himself denouncing financiers, it would seem at first as if there were little more for us to say.' Newspapers that had been talking nothing but nonsense about Bolshevists, he said, were not likely to begin talking sense about Jews.

Correspondence had begun about the same time about the name of the new paper. Some suggested that it should be called *The Distributist Weekly*, but, as Chesterton pointed out, Distributism was only one application, though the chief application, of the philosophy of the new paper. 'The truth is, of course, that the philosophy is a religion,' he said. 'But a religious title would be still more misleading in modern times; it always implies a tract issued by a sect and not a truth inhering in a system.'

Shaw had suggested that *Chesterton's* would be a better title 'on the analogy of *Cobbett's [Political] Register*, but Chesterton stuck to the title chosen, for the time being anyway.

The new paper, however, will have to be mine, in a sense in which this one has never been mine, even in operation, let alone in origin. It has never been possible for me to be the real and responsible editor of *The New Witness*; for the simple reason that there would have been no *New Witness* to edit if I had not been working at other things. It is a paradox; but it is the last paradox of the kind that I shall contribute to the paper. Unless I am in the position to be a real and responsible editor of my own paper, I shall not start any paper at all. *The New Witness* could be temporarily edited by G.K.Chesterton, in the absence of its real editor, even when that absence was no longer temporarily but tragically final; and the family name means no more than the continuity of a tradition. But *G.K.C's Weekly* has got to be conducted by G.K.C., whether G.K.C. likes it or not.

The last number of *The New Witness* appeared on 4 May. Among those whose valedictory letters were published was one from Wells.

I love G.K.C., and I hate the Catholicism of Belloc and Rome so that I sit by your bedside, the Phoenix death-bed from which *G.K.C.'s Weekly* is to be born, with very mingled feelings. Now if it was only Rothermere's last squeak how happily we might rejoice together. You've been a decent wrong-headed old paper, full of good writing. If Catholicism is still to run about the world giving tongue, it can have no better spokesman than G.K.C. But I grudge Catholicism, G.K.C.

And Belloc wrote: 'It is twelve years since Mr Cecil Chesterton and I founded the paper as *The Eye-Witness* (a title which Mr Gilbert Chesterton suggested), and during that astonishing long life – attack has never, I think, been so long sustained.'

In September Methuen brought out yet another book of Chesterton's essays under the title *Fancies Versus Fads*, a typically Chestertonian one which, like the others, had been provided by the firm's literary editor, E.V.Lucas. The collection was a varied assortment of articles originally seen in the *London Mercury*, *The New Witness* and the *Illustrated London News*. Once again attacking the sentimentalism of divorce, Chesterton said, 'Divorce is a thing which the newspapers now not only advertise, but advocate, almost as if it were a pleasure in itself. It may be, indeed, that all the flowers and festivities will now be transferred from the fashionable wedding to the fashionable divorce.' In another essay he wondered 'how long liberated woman will endure the invidious ban which excludes her from being a hangman. Or rather, to speak with more exactitude, a hangwoman.' Generally speaking there was nothing particularly exciting about the essays, and it might well have seemed to anyone considering Chesterton's career at the time that he had begun to lose his touch. Then in the following month came a surprise, for some of the old power had returned in his *St Francis of Assisi*, the first book written since his conversion.

It was not the first time he had written about the saint for, it may be remembered, Francis had been one of Chesterton's *Twelve Types* in 1906, when he had said of him, 'If you had taken him to the loneliest star that the madness of the astronomer can conceive, he would have only beheld in it the features of a new friend.' Returning to Francis after over twenty years, and now sharing in that sacramental life which Francis experienced, Chesterton wrote one of his most tranquil books. As the *New York Times* reviewer noticed, here was 'a more restrained and less paradoxical Chesterton', writing of a saint who was a Troubadour, and so a Lover. Francis was a lover of God and he was really and truly a lover of men; possibly a much rarer mystical vocation. 'A lover of men is very nearly the opposite of a philanthropist; indeed the pedantry of the Greek word carries something like a satire on itself. A philanthropist may be said to love anthropoids. But as St Francis did not love humanity but men, so he did not love Christianity but Christ.'

Chesterton never wrote with more calm assurance than here. In a passage near the beginning of the book, in the chapter 'Francis the Fighter', he was at his best. Francis had fallen sick after fighting for Assisi against the neighbouring town of Perugia, but he still thought of himself as destined for a military career until the whole course of his life was changed, and he came face to face with 'the great and good debt that cannot be paid'.

High in the dark house of Assisi Francesco Bernadone slept and dreamed of arms. There came to him in the darkness a vision splendid with swords, patterned after the cross in the Crusading fashion, of spears and shields and helmets hung in a high armoury, all bearing the sacred sign. When he awoke he accepted the dream as a trumpet bidding him to the battlefield, and rushed out to take horse and arms. He delighted in all the exercises of chivalry; and was evidently an accomplished cavalier and fighting man by the tests of the tournament and the camp. He would doubtless at any time have preferred a Christian sort of chivalry; but it seems clear that he was also in a mood which thirsted for glory, though in him that glory would always have been identical with honour. He was not without some vision of that wreath of laurel which Caesar has left for all the Latins. As he rode out to war the great gate in the deep wall of Assisi resounded with his last boast, 'I shall come back a great prince.'

A little way along his road his sickness rose again and threw him. It seems highly probable, in the light of his impetuous temper, that he had ridden away long before he was fit to move. And in the darkness of this second and far more desolating interruption, he seems to have had another dream in which a voice said to him, 'You have mistaken the meaning of the vision. Return to your own town.' And Francis trailed back to Assisi, a very dismal and disappointed and perhaps even derided figure, with nothing to do but to wait for what should happen next. It was his first descent into a dark ravine that is called the valley of humiliation, which seemed to him very rocky and desolate, but in which he was afterwards to find many flowers.

But he was not only disappointed and humiliated; he was also very much puzzled and bewildered. He still firmly believed that his two dreams must have meant something; and he could not imagine what they could possibly mean. It was while he was drifting, one may even say mooning, about the streets of Assisi and the fields outside the city wall, that an incident occurred to him which has not always been immediately connected with the business of the dreams, but which seems to me the obvious culmination of them. He was riding listlessly in some wayside place, apparently in the open country, when he saw a figure coming along the road towards him and halted; for he saw it was a leper. And he knew instantly that his courage was challenged, not as the world challenges, but as one would challenge who knew the secrets of the heart of a man. What he saw advancing was not the banner and spears of Perugia, from which it never occurred to him to shrink; not the armies that fought for the crown of Sicily, of which he had always thought as a courageous man thinks of mere vulgar danger. Francis Bernadone saw his fear coming along the road towards him; the fear that comes from within and not without; though it stood white and horrible in the sunlight. For once in the long rush of his life his soul stood still. Then he sprang from his horse, knowing nothing between stillness and swiftness, and rushed on the leper and threw his arms round him. It was the beginning of a long vocation of ministry among many lepers, for whom he did many services; to this man he gave what money he could and mounted and rode on. We do not know how far he rode, or with what sense of things around him; but it is said that when he looked back, he could see no figure on the road.

18

This Single Adventure

1925–1927

Now that he was free from his editorial commitment for a while, Chesterton had the chance to write with much deeper concentration for, apart from his *Illustrated London News* column, which still went off with the same rush every Thursday, there was less general anxiety. During the two years leading up to the launching of *G.K.'s Weekly*, as the new paper was eventually called, Chesterton wrote *The Everlasting Man*, the book which is generally considered to have been his masterpiece. As Evelyn Waugh said of it, 'In that book all his random thoughts are concentrated and refined; all his aberrations made straight.' Waugh saw it as a great popular book, 'one of the few really great popular books of the century; the triumphant assertion that a book can be both great and popular. And it needs no elucidation. It is brilliantly clear. It met a temporary need and survives as a permanent monument.'

The Everlasting Man was an answer to the rationalist thesis of Wells and others that man was merely an animal who had evolved from a primitive form of life, and thus was not a special creation of God. In the first part of the book, which Chesterton titled 'On the Creature called Man', he elaborated on his old insistence that there was no evidence that man had evolved as the evolutionists claimed, and that the difference between man and the beasts was a difference of kind and not of degree. All that was positively known of the cave-man was that he hunted, fought and drew pictures; and art, Chesterton said, was the signature of man. Nevertheless, if Wells and the other rationalists insisted on considering man as merely an animal, then Chesterton would try it as an experiment; but in fact the task proved harder than if man were considered as an angel.

The human story began in the cave-man's cave, so in the second

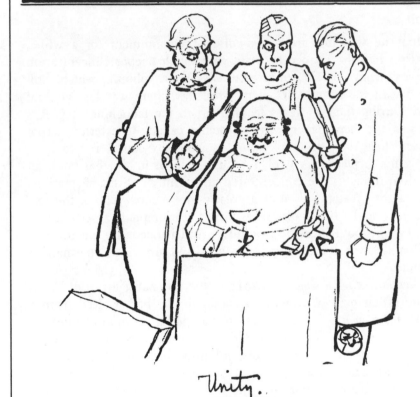

One of Chesterton's cover illustrations for *GK's Weekly*

part of the book, 'The God in the Cave', Chesterton drew a touching parallel.

The second half of human history, which was like a new creation of the world, also begins in a cave. There is even a shadow of such a fancy in the fact that animals were again present; for it was a cave used as a stable by the mountaineers of the uplands about Bethlehem; who still drive their cattle into such holes and caverns at night. It was here that a homeless couple had crept underground with the cattle when the doors of the crowded caravanserai had been shut in their faces; and it was here beneath the very feet of the passers-by, in a cellar under the very floor of the world, that Jesus Christ was born. But in that second creation there was indeed something symbolical in the roots of the primeval rock or the horns of the prehistoric herd. God also was a Cave-Man, and had also traced strange shapes of creatures, curiously coloured, upon the wall of the world; but the pictures that he made had come to life.

A mass of legend and literature, which increases and will never end, had repeated and rung the changes on that single paradox, Chesterton said; 'that the hands that had made the sun and stars were too small to reach the huge heads of the cattle. Upon this paradox, we might almost say upon this jest, all the literature of our faith is founded.'

Just as it was impossible, Chesterton discovered, to consider man as merely a beast, so was it impossible to consider Christ as merely a man. The 'human Christ' Chesterton saw as a made-up figure, 'a piece of artificial selection like the merely evolutionary man'. The Church that Christ founded, he said, although it had begun at a particular moment in history, was always alive; it was not a survival, 'as though the Druids had managed somehow to survive somewhere for two thousand years'. No, the Faith was always new, and even a threat. It was as though the Church grew younger as the world grew old; and this, said Chesterton,

...is the last proof of the miracle. Had it merely appeared and disappeared, it might possibly have been remembered or explained as the last leap of the age of illusion, the ultimate myth of the ultimate mood, in which the mind struck the sky and broke. But the mind did not break. It is the one mind that remains unbroken in the break-up of the world. If it were an error, it seems as if the error could hardly have lasted a day. If it were a mere ecstasy, it would seem that such an ecstasy could not endure for an hour. It has endured for nearly two thousand years; and the world within it has been more lucid, more level-headed, more reasonable in its hopes, more healthy in its instincts, more humorous and cheerful in the face of fate and death, than all the world outside. For it was the soul of Christendom that came forth from the incredible Christ; and the soul of it was common sense. Though we dared not look on His face we could look on His fruits; and by His fruits we should know Him. The fruits are solid and the fruitfulness is much more than a metaphor; and nowhere in this sad world are boys happier in apple-trees or men in more equal chorus singing as they tread the vine, than under the fixed flash of this instant and intolerant enlightenment; the lightning made eternal as the light.

By the time *The Everlasting Man* was published in September, *G.K.'s Weekly* had been running for four months. The new paper was much slimmer than *The New Witness*, and it had eight pages of advertisements. The first number had appeared on 21 March.

Besides an editorial on the subject of Bolshevism, Chesterton had written several items in 'Notes of the Week', and a lengthy article entitled 'How I tried to boom this paper'. Among the other items was a short 'moral tale' by Belloc, and the first of three instalments of Walter de la Mare's story, 'The Thief'. Chesterton had hoped for a poem from de la Mare, and had written to ask him for one on 4 March.

> Will you forgive me if I ask you to assist in what amounts to a conspiracy to suggest that I have something to do with real literature? I have let myself in for editing a weekly paper: like the *New Statesman* or the *Nation* only quite different.
>
> The first number has to be ready by the thirteenth, which is earlier than I thought; but I cannot abandon the wild hope I entertained of publishing something of yours to give a creative touch to its critical and I fear, often controversial pages. Its social tendency is the version that Belloc and I have given of Three Acres and a Cow; but I do want the cow occasionally to jump over the moon. And who can make her do that but you?

The de la Mares soon came to live at Hill House, Taplow, close to Beaconsfield so that the Chestertons saw something of them at this time, although the two men do not seem to have ever been on Christian name terms. However, Frances and de la Mare shared the same passion for miniature ornaments, and sometimes exchanged items for 'the little cupboard'.

From the outset it looked as though the new paper would have to struggle for survival as its predecessor had done; but Chesterton put a brave face on things, pretending that the new venture was being a success. Frances, however, shared all his problems, and knew how he tended to hide his deepest feelings. 'Why did you call beloved, in the night and I so near? The merest lift of breath had brought me to your arms,' she wrote. 'Had you aghast seen evil unashamed, naked and cruel?' By the beginning of the year, while in Bath, she had consulted a specialist, who had warned her to live 'very quietly and rest as much as possible'. Such a thing was difficult at Top Meadow for, although the Chestertons always had domestic help, Frances always had to be at Gilbert's beck and call just in case he needed her. In the second week of January 1926, the doctor said that little could be done to help her back. Some weeks earlier she had gone into a home for a complete rest. 'How you ever got her into a Home for a decent spell ... I cannot imagine, and therefore can only congratulate you,' wrote one specialist to Frances's doctor. 'Mrs Chesterton ought to go away for several months, to Biskra,' he advised. 'Do not let her go to Egypt if you can possibly help it, but I am sure you are right to urge her to go somewhere.'

Since Dr Pocock had left Beaconsfield in 1919, the Chestertons had been patients of Dr Bakewell, who lived in the High Street, and the many letters that have survived from specialist to doctor and vice versa show with what care Frances was attended.

In June 1926 Gilbert and Frances celebrated their silver wedding. On the 20th of that month Frances wrote to Fr O'Connor, 'I want now, as soon as I can see a few days clear before me, to place myself under instruction to enter the Church.' She did not wish to be instructed at Beaconsfield, she said; she did not want to be 'the talk of Beaconsfield'. It was not true that she was only following Gilbert. 'It isn't true and I've had a hard fight not to let my love for him lead me to the truth.' She was, she said, very tired and very worried, and many things were difficult for her, her health included. It made 'strenuous attention a bit of a strain'.

About a month later she wrote again to thank Fr O'Connor for the set of spoons he had sent them as a silver wedding present; among other things, she said she would now visit Fr Walker, the parish priest. Things were very difficult; her nephew was ill and she had to spend much time with her sister. Gilbert was so involved with the paper, and she hoped he would soon give it up. In a further letter she said, 'I feel the paper must go, it is too much for Gilbert (four days work always) and consequently too much for me who have to attend to everything else.' Trying to settle an income tax dispute, she said, had nearly brought her to tears.

However, although she did not know it, help was on the way, for it was in 1926 that Dorothy Collins came to Top Meadow, and like some guardian angel stood by the Chestertons for the rest of their lives. Unlike the other secretaries, who were for the most part quite untrained for the task, Dorothy was a professional secretary of some nine years' experience, and since 1922 had been Secretary and Accountant at the Educational Training College at Lincoln. When she came into the Chestertons' life she was thirty-two years old. Not only was she able to take down shorthand and type at considerable speed, but she could also drive, which revolutionized Chesterton's life. As Maisie Ward has said, she 'drove them both to London for engagements and through England and Europe for holidays or lecture tours'. If anyone telephoned from then on, they were likely to be told, 'Would you ring again when Dorothy comes in. I'm not quite sure. She keeps the engagement book.'

It was two months before Dorothy arrived that the fortunes of *G.K.'s Weekly* took a slight turn for the better. Since the autumn of 1925 the chances of raising the circulation figures above 5,000 seemed slight, and Chesterton had decided to publish one of his novels in weekly instalments, in an attempt to keep up sales. This was *The Return of Don Quixote*, the first instalment of which appeared on 12 December. It continued until the beginning of November the following year and came to an abrupt halt in the middle of Chapter XIV, because of a necessary reduction in the paper's size. The remainder of the story was summarized in the next issue. There is little doubt that *G.K.'s Weekly* would have foundered had it not become the official mouthpiece of the Distributist League, which had been inaugurated in September. After the founding of the League the paper's sales increased rapidly, although this may have been as much to do with the reduction of the price from sixpence to twopence as with any enthusiasm for Distributism.

Distributism has been mentioned on several occasions already in the course of this book; but from 1926 onwards it was Chesterton's constant concern. Quite simply, Distributism meant a system by which as many people as possible were owners of property and their means of livelihood. In a Distributist state the wage system based upon employers and employees would be replaced by an economy of owners. It had its roots in the great encyclical letter of Pope Leo XIII, *Rerum Novarum*, which had been sent out to the whole Church in 1891. The Pope had offered an alternative to both the capitalist system and the emerging socialism, which was unjust because, to use the Pope's own words, 'every man has, by nature, the right to possess property as his own'. It was 'within man's right to possess things, not merely for temporary and momentary use, as other living things do, but to hold them in stable and permanent possession'. Man, the Pope said, precedes the state. 'Prior to the formation of any state, man possesses the right to provide for the sustenance of his body.'

Another important aspect of *Rerum Novarum* which had a direct bearing on Distributism was the Pope's recognition that the present trouble had been largely brought about by the destruction of the old working men's guilds, since nothing had replaced them. 'Hence by degrees it has come to pass that working men have been surrendered, isolated and helpless, to the hard-heartedness of employers and the greed of unchecked competition.'

As far as the Distributists were concerned, there was no time to lose. 'For us Catholics,' wrote Fr Vincent McNabb, 'the Distributist State is not something we discuss, but something we have to propagate and institute. No advance in social thought or social action is possible if we are seeking to prove ourselves as a theory what we should be trying to realise in fact.'

Chesterton was elected President of the League at the inaugural meeting, held at Essex Hall on 17 September, and so from that time until his death ten years later he was the figurehead of a sundry band of enthusiasts, which included such names as Captain West, who became the Secretary, as well as Maurice Reckett, the Treasurer, whose name is particularly prominent in the annals of the League, and who was the prime mover in much that happened in the future. The influence the Distributist movement had on the generation of young men who had grown up during the war, but had been too young to have taken part in the fighting, cannot be overestimated. 'The greatest thing you have done is to give a gospel of faith and courage to a whole generation

of young men,' one of his disciples told Chesterton. Certainly for those
who had not attended a university, to have come in contact with minds
like those of Belloc, Chesterton and McNabb was as good as any 'further
education'. It was not only what they heard in lectures or debate, but
also the social gatherings after the meetings when everyone would gravi-
tate to the bar of the Devereux, the meeting place of the Central Branch
of the League. The atmosphere here was summed up, in somewhat
imaginative terms, by one member: 'with our pint pots banging on the
tables – Father McNabb, Commander Shove, Titterton, Gleeson, Hesel-
tine, and the rest – shouting texts of St Thomas at each other, calling
on the people of England for the overthrow of their taskmasters, and
a return to the religion of their forefathers'.

It was not long before branches of the League had been established
in many parts of the country. 'Of course we owe everything to the League,' Chesterton wrote, 'which in Manchester, Liverpool, Glasgow,
Croydon, Chatham, Worthing, Chorley, Cambridge, Oxford, Bath and
London has made the newsagents aware of the paper.' By 27 November
the sales of the paper had risen to over 8,000 copies per week. Understandably, Chesterton felt greatly encouraged. The financial side of things
might not be all that much better than in the past, but the paper's
influence was growing hourly. He felt he was following in the footsteps
of Cobbett, who had kept his *Register* going through many a crisis. In
fact, Chesterton's own short life of Cobbett had been well received
in the previous autumn, and hailed as 'a most successful effort in sympathetic interpretation'. It was true that some readers would have appreciated a little more about Cobbett's life, but no book, noted *The Observer*,

> ...will give the student of history so clear a view of what Cobbett
> wanted, what he meant, and why he said the things he did. In Mr
> Chesterton's view – and he will find a good many people to agree
> with him – Cobbett stood for England: England unindustrialised,
> self-sufficient, relying on a basis of agriculture and sound commerce
> for her prosperity, with no desire for inflation.

In Chesterton's view, Cobbett was 'as English as any Englishman
who ever lived', but at the same time he had a quality that was not
English. 'He was extremely provocative. He was as provocative as an
Irishman.' Cobbett had refused to leave people alone, and refused
emphatically to let sleeping dogs lie. It was not surprising that at the
end he had the whole pack in full cry after him, which only gave him

a further opportunity for turning on them and telling them they were all 'curs and mongrels, not to mention mad dogs'.

It was this quality that Chesterton had so admired in his own brother who, like Cobbett, had had a 'wonderful lack of fear'. The combination in Cobbett of the deepest English humours and the love and understanding of England, he said,

> ...with this quality which is rare in England, the aggressive and challenging quality, is a sort of coincidence or contradiction which gave his whole value in our politics and history. It was exactly because he was English in everything else, and not English in this, that he did serve England, and very nearly saved England. He very nearly saved her from that oppression by oblivion, that absent-minded cruelty of the mere capitalist, which has now brought upon her such accumulated and appalling problems in the industrial world.

In 19 June 1926, in the days after the General Strike, Chesterton wrote an article on 'The New Heresy', which he said would 'simply be an attack on morality; and especially on sexual morality'. This would come, he argued, '*not* from a few Socialists surviving from the Fabian Society; but from the living exultant energy of the rich resolved to enjoy themselves at last, with neither Popery nor Puritanism nor Socialism to hold them back'. Unlike the thin theory of collectivism which never had any real roots in human nature, the roots of this new heresy were deep in nature itself. It was a heresy 'whose flower is lust of the flesh and the lust of the eye and the pride of life'. A man who could not see this could not see the signs of the times, or, as Chesterton put it, 'the sky-signs in the street', that were the new sort of signs in heaven. 'The madness of tomorrow is not in Moscow, but much more in Manhattan – most of what was in Broadway is already in Piccadilly.'

The new heresy would be convenienced by the aids of artificial means of birth control and of divorce, Chesterton said; but the idea that abortion might ever become legal in some circumstances had not become an issue at the time, although he wrote later that birth control or infanticide or heaven knows what might be found in the 'ultimate paradise of prigs'. Hedonism, he said, with its own heathen logic, would go on to its own heathen end. As far as birth control was concerned it was 'the prevention of birth in order to escape control'.

The religious tradition to which he belonged was sometimes charged with being behind the times; but the only sense in which this was true was that 'human ministers are naturally found dealing with the last heresy rather than the next one'.

Chesterton discussed such subjects under the general title of 'Straws in the Wind', which in *G.K.'s Weekly* had replaced the earlier 'At the Sign of the World's End' articles of *The New Witness*. Many of these found their way into books later, and *The Outline of Sanity*, which came out in the December that year, consisted of such articles. However, several titles were published in the same year. In June *The Incredulity of Father Brown* had shown 'the old ingenuity of construction, the same credible impossibilities, the same thrill and the same magic' as the earlier Father Brown books. The *Yorkshire Post* reviewer thought the supremacy of Sherlock Holmes was threatened. 'Holmes might have the attractive eccentricities, but he never talked mystical philosphy to the attentive Watson. But Father Brown can expound the cosmos at the same moment that he explains a murder.'

By far the most important moment of the year came on 1 November, All Saints' Day, when Frances was received into the Church, bringing to a happy end a long period of anxiety. The decision gave her renewed courage to bear her pain and her many problems, and over the next two years she seemed to those who knew her almost a different woman. Maisie Ward has said there never was a happier Catholic than Frances; and the specialist noticed a remarkable difference in her condition. 'How immensely she has improved from a general point of view,' he told Dr Bakewell, but she would never be entirely free from pain.

Both Gilbert and she had been deeply saddened by the death of their good friend J.S.Phillimore, and Chesterton dedicated his small book of poems, *The Queen of Seven Swords*, which came out just before Christmas, to one who went before him

> ... on all roads,
> On bridges broad enough to spread
> Between the learned and the dunce,
> Between the living and the dead.

This little book has always stood on its own, and the twenty-four poems it contained did not all find their way into Chesterton's *Collected Poems*, which Herbert Palmer published in the summer of 1927. The best of these was 'The Return of Eve', one of Chesterton's many poems about

Our Lady, in which the Jesuit, C.C.Martindale, thought that Francis Thompson had been 'out-passed'.

Now that Frances had joined him in the Church, Chesterton wrote more about conversion, something which, he said 'was more personal and less corporate than communion; and involves isolated feeling as an introduction to collective feelings'. Just as he had argued in *The Everlasting Man* that Christianity was different in kind from all other religions, because of the Doctrine of the Incarnation, so in *The Catholic Church and Conversion*, he argued that the Catholic Church was different in kind from all the other denominations.

> The first fallacy about the Catholic Church is the idea that it is a church. I mean that it is a church in the sense in which the Noncomformist newspapers talk about The Churches. I do not intend any expression of contempt about The Churches; nor is it an expression of contempt to say that it would be more convenient to call them the sects. This is true in a much deeper and more sympathetic sense than may at first appear; but to begin with, it is certainly true in a perfectly plain and historical sense, which has nothing to do with sympathy at all. Thus, for instance, I have much more sympathy for small nationalities than I have for small sects. But it is simply a historical fact that the Roman Empire was the Empire and that it was not a small nationality. And it is simply a historical fact that the Roman Church is the Church and is not a sect....
> ...the Catholic Church stands alone. It does not merely belong to a class of human religions. Considered quite coldly and impartially, as by a man from the moon, it is much more sui generis than that. It is, if the critic chooses to think so, the ruin of an attempt at a Universal Religion which was bound to fail. But calling the wreckers to break up a ship does not turn the ship into one of its own timbers; and cutting Poland up into three pieces does not make Poland the same as Posen.

Poland was very much in Chesterton's mind at the time, and at the end of April, he travelled with Frances and Dorothy to Warsaw via Berlin as a guest of the PEN. They settled at the Hotel Europyski on the evening of the 28th after a lively welcome at the station from 'at least a hundred people'. There were pressmen and photographers, and the Premier, Marshal Piłsudski, had sent several officers as his representatives, one of whom had made 'the most beautiful speech in

French'. Wherever the Chestertons went they were treated with cour-
teous enthusiasm, and the attention from the press compared favourably
with that of the American press. However, Frances found some of the
meals particularly long. 'I found it a little embarrasing to have to eat
hot kidneys and mushrooms standing about with hundreds of guests,
and this was only the preliminary to a long dinner that followed and
refreshments that apparently continued until 2 o'clock in the morning,'
she informed Marie Louise. Gilbert, for his part, enjoyed it all immensely, and he had been surprised to find how well the Poles knew his
work. As Frances recorded, 'The speeches were really perfectly marvellous and delivered in English quite colloquial and very witty and showing
a detailed knowledge of Gilbert's works which no Englishman of my
acquaintance possesses. Gilbert made an excellent, in fact, a very eloquent speech in reply which drew forth thunders of applause.'

The Chestertons were shown much of the city, and they were there
for the National Festival on 3 May, which commemorated the founding
of the Polish Constitution of 1791, 'which was never put into being,
owing to the scandalous partition of Poland, until 1921 when the Poles
celebrated their great Polonia Restituta'. They were entertained to tea
by the officers of the famous cavalry regiment, the Chevaux-Légers,
and attended the reception given by the President of the Republic at
the Royal Palace.

> Everybody in Warsaw was there, at least, so I was told and I think
> it must be true, because the crowd was enormous. It was an extraordin-
> ary sight; the old Royal Palace filled with lights and colour which
> the Poles for the first time were able to claim as their own Palace.
> One Polish lady said to me, 'It is like a dream that we Poles should
> be able to use our own beautiful Palace ourselves. Until now no Pole
> was allowed in the Palace except under escort; and even now, though
> it is still beautiful, the Russians have taken away and the Germans
> have destroyed all the things, such as pictures and decorations and
> furniture that we valued so much.'

As they had been in Palestine, the Chestertons were unlucky with
the weather; in Warsaw the conditions were 'very like England on a
nasty day of east wind'. The Hotel Europyski had no central heating,
but the Chestertons were given a small electric fire, which only warmed
a corner of their immense room. However, one boon, as Frances told
her mother-in-law, was that Dorothy Collins was so efficient, and could

take down dictation so easily, that Frances was able to write much longer letters than usual. 'I find Dorothy Collins the greatest possible help, and she is excellent with foreigners and manages to do a great deal for both of us,' she wrote.

The fact that Dorothy was so reliable took a great load off Frances's shoulders, since she felt able to rest and yet know that Gilbert was in good hands.

In the evening Gilbert and the energetic Dorothy Collins went off to have supper in the very famous wine-cellar of the Fukier family which dates from 1610. There apparently they drank Tokay and Mute (I think that is Mead) and there was a great deal of singing and national songs, both the peasant ones and the military ones and at the end, I am told, a sort of 'He's a jolly good fellow' which is called 'Live for a hundred years' in honour of Gilbert.

There was no doubt the Poles regarded Chesterton as their great champion. At Kraków, where a special performance of *Acropolis* was given in his honour, the manager of the theatre had come in front of the curtain to thank him in the name of the citizens of Kraków for his defence of Poland 'now and in the past'.

The same sense of gratitude had been evident in Warsaw, but the visit was also a sightseeing tour, and the Chestertons visited Poznań, the old German Posen, a very pleasant place that had retained 'all the German cleanliness and thoroughness which is not so conspicuous perhaps in other parts of Poland'; Lwów, 'a busy and at present not a particularly interesting place'; and Vilnius, just over the border in Lithuania, and where most of the inhabitants belonged to the Ruthenian or old Uniat Church, rather like the Greek Orthodox Church but in communion with Rome.

Chesterton's love for Poland had been constant, and now for the first time he had visited the land which was, he said, like Ireland, one of the 'things in the world that are at once intensely loved and intensely hated'. The reason in both cases was the people's great devotion to the Faith, that Faith that both he and Frances, and later Dorothy Collins, could share with those people; a faith that England had also once shared and tragically lost. When the cavalry officer had welcomed him at Warsaw Station on behalf of Marshal Piłsudski he had used a phrase which was typical of the Polish people, the sort of phrase, Chesterton said, 'which inspires one half of the world and infuriates the other'. He had said that he could not call Chesterton the chief friend of Poland, because the chief friend of Poland was God.

This visit to Poland was, in fact, overdue, for the invitation had been extended and the acceptance tendered a year earlier; but then Chesterton had felt that Frances was not fit enough to travel. It had been a disappointment to both of them, so much so that when in the late summer an American journalist had come to Top Meadow for an interview Chesterton had played a game of imagining himself in Poland. 'Why not interview me as though I were in Poland?' he had suggested. It was then decided which part of Poland he was in, some place 'a long way off from a railroad'.

After expressing his sympathy for the Polish people and the Polish situation, he had said:

> People accuse Poland of lacking strength. It may be true. If a man has his legs carried off by one person, his trunk by another, and his head by a third, he is rather apt to be lacking in strength, no matter how strong his natural constitution may be. In fact, it would be cause for comment if the full amount of strength were to be his under such conditions. Poland is like that man. Frederick the Great, Maria Theresa, and Catherine of Russia are those who dismembered him. The rest of the world stands accuser, not of them but of their victim. But the patriotism of Poland is something vital and remarkable. She is one of the countries that produces real statesmen. When it comes to a clash between public and private interests, we need only look to the example of Paderewski to see which call is the louder. They are a wonderful people and deserve to have their own restored to them.

While he was actually in Poland, Chesterton was asked to inscribe something in the Polish PEN Club album, and he had written, 'If Poland had not been born again, all the Christian nations would have died.' It was a statement true at the time, but one which seems equally true today. The importance of Poland in the struggle to save European civilization was seen clearly by both Chesterton and Belloc. 'The Test is Poland,' wrote Belloc. 'The determination to save Poland, which is a determination not only to defeat Prussia but to oust the vile and murderous Communism of Moscow, is the moral condition of victory. If we waver we are lost.'

The Chestertons returned to England in the middle of June, after spending a week in Belgium 'to recover from our fatigues'. Chesterton agreed to lecture on his Polish visit at the Essex Hall. It was turned into an important occasion, with the Archbishop of Westminster and many members of the Polish Embassy, including the Minister, in the audience. The title of the lecture had been advertised as 'What Poland is'; but this, Chesterton said, was a lie, since he did not for a moment profess to be able to say what Poland is. 'I should be very sorry if any brilliant Pole asked me what England is. I think it was Aristotle who said you cannot define a living thing, least of all such a living thing as Poland, one of the most living things in the world, because nothing can be so living as a thing which has risen from the dead.'

The impression that any ordinary Englishman gained from going to Poland, Chesterton said, was that he was going into a sane, well-ordered, humorous, well-balanced form of society, where the people joked with him, talked to him and treated him exactly as they did in this country or any other civilized country. It must be remembered, Chesterton emphasized, that all this had been built up since 1921 'on waste and destruction and a basis of nothingness, and if you do not join with me in saluting and admiring the Polish name I cannot understand your lack of enthusiasm for great things, and I gravely fear the future of your own country'.

After Chesterton had sat down, the Professor of English from the University of Kraków, Roman Dyloski, who according to Chesterton knew all about Polish literature and more about English literature than he did, spoke about Chesterton's visit to his country. He said that Mr Chesterton's visit had not only made the Poles admire England – they had always done that – he had made them very sincerely love her and he was glad that Mr Chesterton had realized that they had a sense of humour. 'They had always had to stand before Europe in a lachrymose attitude, telling the world of their woes. Even during the terrible times when Poland was divided they had produced several humorous writers.' He went on to say that the Polish inheritance of Catholicism had bound them to the centre of the ideas of civilised Europe and the fact that they had remained united to Rome was a factor to be reckoned with.

19

The Thing

1927–1933

If Chesterton's resolve had needed strengthening, his visit to Poland strengthened it. For the remaining nine years of his life he was to devote all his energy to promoting the Distributist ideal and defending the Catholic faith. 'It is not given for goods or gear but for the Thing,' he wrote. He was now of the Thing, and the Thing was not an idea, a body of opinion. It was not a thing, or one of the things; it was the Thing. The Church was, as he said, outside all of us; it was outside everything that men talked about; it was outside the Cardinals and the Pope. They belonged to it, but it did not belong to them. 'If we all fell dead suddenly,' he said, 'the Church would still somehow exist in God.' The Church was not an organization like the Athenaeum Club, that would cease to exist if it lost all its members. All this he had understood long ago, and yet still it was true, as he had said in *What's Wrong with the World*: the Christian ideal had not been tried and found wanting. It had been found difficult and never tried. He knew also that it was impossible to love a thing without wanting to fight for it, although for Chesterton there would always be more of defence than of attack. As Belloc said of him, 'He wounded none, but thus also he failed to provide weapons wherewith one may wound and kill folly. Now without wounding and killing, there is no battle; and thus in this life no victory; but also no peril to the soul through hatred.' It was true: Chesterton lacked that 'acerbity or "bite"' which gave such power to his brother's and Belloc's writing; and this preserved him, as Belloc said, from enmities. 'He had no enemies; and in a society such as ours in Modern England, a society which above all demands comfort and ease, this gave him a universality of appeal but furnished no occasion for attack.'

If he would not floor the Church's enemies he would, nevertheless, in the prophetic sense 'speak out', and always with such graceful humour that he seemed not to give offence however firmly he proclaimed the truth against the forces of scepticism and agnosticism that were threatening to engulf the modern world. Chesterton's connection with the Faith, Belloc said, was the most important aspect of his literary life. In the last years he published two books of essays, *The Thing*, and *The Well and the Shadows*, and his last biographical work, on St Thomas Aquinas; three books where the effect of the Faith on his writing is most evident. In the pages of *G.K.'s Weekly*, on the debating platform and the lecture hall he continued to explain Distributism, although it always remained with him an idea, and he did not enter into the activities of those members of the League who were anxious to put that idea into practice by establishing agricultural communities. In this, Douglas Woodruff thought Chesterton was right: 'He knew his limitations but I do not think he had the least idea of discouraging anybody else.'

At times the meetings of the League disintegrated into wrangles between individual members on such topics as whether machinery should be permitted in the Distributist State. 'The matter of machinery is one to which no doubt you will be giving your official attention before very long, and I do not wish to anticipate,' wrote Eric Gill from Wales. Although Chesterton was not a particularly close friend of Gill he had shown considerable interest in the original community at Ditchling, something he had been introduced to by Fr Vincent McNabb, and in 1925 he had asked Gill to become art editor of *G.K.'s Weekly*. 'You've got to accept my "doctrine" as the "doctrine of *G.K.'s Weekly*" in matters of art,' Gill had informed the editor in his letter of acceptance, 'just as I accept yours in other matters. If you say this is a bit thick – rather a tall order – well, I *know* what I am saying is what is in harmony with your propaganda just as I know that both are in harmony with the Faith.'

The arguments over small points of detail in a state that did not even exist are reminiscent of the difficulties Coleridge had with Southey over the question of whether servants should be allowed in the Pantisocratic State, and although Chesterton might not have entered into such discussions except in an amused way, all was in keeping with what Douglas Woodruff said of him, that he was always 'rather a St Paul's schoolboy, enjoying the discovery of the truth and its proclamation but not expecting to move the powers-that-be'. In fact, Chesterton was often absent from the League meetings, but when he was there he would sit at a table scribbling or drawing on sheets of paper left there specially in the hope that they would remain lying there when he had moved into the bar.

It had seemed like a charade from the past when, one Friday evening in the last week of October 1927, Chesterton debated with Shaw at the Kingsway Hall, with Belloc in the chair, on the question 'Do We Agree?' According to Shaw, Chesterton had suggested the subject. The debate, or, as Chesterton termed it, the enquiry, was something of a *cause célèbre* since it was the first important debate to be broadcast. For this reason the doors of the hall had been closed dead on time, with the result that frustrated latecomers caused a disturbance at the door with cries of 'Stop the debate!' The sound of splintering glass distracted everyone's attention as Belloc introduced the speakers, both of whom were on splendid form.

Shaw said that it may not be generally known that Mr Chesterton and he were two madmen. 'Instead of doing honest and respectable work and behaving ourselves as ordinary citizens, we go about the world, possessed by a strange gift of tongues uttering all sorts of extraordinary opinions for no reason whatever.' The chief matter of the debate, he went on to say, was the distribution of wealth. 'I have watched Mr Chesterton with extraordinary interest and great pleasure; and having Mr Chesterton agreeing with me is a great personal pleasure, because I am very fond of Mr Chesterton,' he said. Chesterton had rejected socialism 'probably because it was a very stupid word', but he had by an independent path arrived at the same position as Shaw had done.

In his reply Chesterton said that up to a point he agreed entirely with Shaw, although there had been a time when he agreed with him absolutely. Like Shaw, he said, he had begun by being a socialist, and 'barring some slight difference of age we were in the same position. We grew in beauty side by side.' Distributists were perfectly sensible and sane people, and they had always realized that there were institutions in the state to which it was very difficult to apply the principle of individual property. At the same time Distributists were not anarchists, and accepted that the state must issue laws; but these should correspond 'with the common conscience of mankind'.

Distributism aimed to restore a right balance, and it did not expect to produce a perfect arrangement. Chesterton said,

> I do not think that a community arranged on the principles of Distributism and on nothing else would be a perfect community. All admit

that the society that we propose is more a matter of proportion and arrangement than a perfectly clear system in which all production is pooled and the result given out in wages.

But what I say is this: let us, so far as is possible in the complicated affairs of humanity, put into the hands of the Commons the control of the means of production – and real control. The man who owns a piece of land controls it in a direct and real sense. He really owns the means of production.

Early in the same autumn the fourth collection of Father Brown stories was published under the title *The Secret of Father Brown*, and dedicated to Fr O'Connor, 'whose truth is stranger than fiction, with a gratitude greater than the world'. The ingenuity of the earlier stories was lacking, and a sinister element, as one reviewer noted, had superseded the element of fun.

This book was closely followed by Chesterton's second play, *The Judgement of Dr Johnson*, which came out at the end of October in the 'Reader's Theatre Series' issued by Sheed & Ward. This three-act comedy was eventually produced for the stage in 1932 by the Arts Theatre Club in London. James Agate reported that the play was 'absolute Chesterton and by so much the less Johnson'. Certainly it failed to fulfil the promise of *Magic*, although as an argument it was entertaining enough. Agate said,

Whenever the play was true to Dr Johnson we found ourselves a little irked, shall I say, by Mr Chesterton; whenever Mr Chesterton had got himself characteristically under way we wondered why he should interrupt that majestic progress to drag in Johnson. The story is a poor one, and perhaps nothing in the play is of any real value except those parts of it which give expression to the author's mind.

It was the old problem once again.

The fact was that Chesterton was again writing too much, and out of necessity since, as Frances had feared, *G.K.'s Weekly* was proving to be a continual drain on the Chestertons' resources. It was inevitable that for the most part Chesterton's style had become laboured, and he too easily fell into the trap of self-imitation, so that only occasionally did the old vibrancy appear.

At the same time his work was coming under the critical eye of a younger generation of writers who had little patience with his expansive,

circumlocutory manner. When in November 1927 he brought out a
life of Stevenson, a companion volume to his *William Cobbett*, T.S.Eliot,
who reviewed it for the *Nation and Athenaeum*, admitted that he had
always found Chesterton's style 'exasperating to the last point of endurance'. The book was, he said, diffuse, dissipated, though not at all
stupid, yet 'Mr Chesterton wastes a good deal of time.'

Eliot was also impatient on another score. 'We are not all so completely
immersed in ignorance, prejudice and heresy as Mr Chesterton
assumes,' he complained. 'He seems always to assume that what his
reader has previously believed is exactly the opposite of what Mr Chesterton knows to be true.'

However, he was full of praise for Chesterton's appreciation of Stevenson's style, and the way he had stopped 'to expound a Roman Catholic
point of view towards *Dr Jekyll and Mr Hyde*'.

Eliot's review had ended with the wry comment that Stevenson was
an author well enough established to survive Chesterton's approval.
The same might well be said of Chesterton with regard to Eliot. Nevertheless, two years later Eliot was seeking a meeting. 'I should like extremely to come to see you one day. I do not expect to have the leisure,
or the brain power, before July,' he wrote from Chester Terrace in
1929. 'May I mention that I have much sympathy with your political
and social views, as well as (with obvious reservations) your religious
views? And that your study of Dickens was always a delight to me.'
Chesterton's attitude to Eliot may be summed up in some lines he wrote
for his last broadcast a few months before he died, which made reference
to the last lines of 'The Hollow Men'.

> Some sneer; some snigger, some simper;
> In the youth where we laughed, and sang.
> And *they* may end with a whimper
> But *we* will end with a bang.

The list of Chesterton's works advertised in the Stevenson book
included two more 'Intimate Biographies' of Savonarola and Napoleon,
neither of which materialized, although it was announced that they were
in preparation. What was in preparation and partly written at the time
was the autobiography, which was not published until after Chesterton's
death. Apart from his short story 'The Sword of Wood', written much
earlier in 1913, which came out in a limited edition, the only Chesterton

title to appear in 1928 was the collection of essays, *Generally Speaking*, yet another gleaning from the *Illustrated London News*.

The event of that year was probably the row that developed over the fate of *G.K.'s Weekly*. The paper's affairs had reached a crisis, and it seems that a deficit of £1,000 had been kept hidden from the editor in the hope that increased advertising might reduce it. It had been feared that Chesterton might concur with Frances's wish to close the office down for, as she told Fr O'Connor, Gilbert was 'dissipating his energies', and thrusting his own work more and more into the background. However, Chesterton's solution to the problem came as a surprise. He allowed Titterton to resign and replaced him as assistant editor with a young man, Edward Macdonald, while at the same time following the advice of a group of young Distributists, who were members of the Central Branch of the League. The paper emerged from the crisis, if anything, in a much stronger position; but as Desmond Gleeson put it, 'The young men from Central Branch with their awareness that finance mattered must have seemed something a little alien to the Bohemian spirit of Chesterton.'

During the summer the Chestertons spent a few weeks resting at Lyme Regis, as they had done for the past two years. Dorothy drove them down to Dorset and they stayed at the Three Cups Hotel as before. On their first visit they had intended to spend only two nights but had remained for two weeks, during which they had met the children of the Nicholl family, to whom they very soon became 'Auntlet and Unclet'. The five girls and a boy were the children of a widow who lived in the town. They became what Maisie Ward has called the Chestertons' 'last family'. Like the Grays, who had moved away from Beaconsfield when Edward Gray had died in 1924, the Nicholl girls became the recipients of poems, letters, and innumerable drawings. So close did the relationship become that the family eventually moved to Christmas Cottage in the same road as Top Meadow; their home became a favourite refuge during Chesterton's last years. Clare Nicholl, the eldest daughter, wrote:

Our friendship with G.K. was the daily bread of life: he made one feel at home in the world and he himself was like a huge comfortable house with great windows opening on vistas and letting in the daylight. Of all the things he said to us there is one remark that we remember with more happiness and gratitude than all the rest. He came in one evening and told us, 'I have just finished writing my Memoirs. None of you are mentioned in my Memoirs: I had to bring in most of my friends, but it delighted me not to have to bring in *all* my friends – it is jolly to have friends who are just one's own property.' A house when it is thrown open to the public is apt to look and feel like a museum rather than a home and therefore recorded stories about G.K. as we saw him and knew him take on the character of 'exhibits', divorced from the personality which made him alive, stripped of the casual intimacy which is the heart of friendship. For us he belongs (it is impossible to think of him in the past tense) not to the limelight, but to the firelight.

In the months before his death Chesterton would frequently wander along to Christmas Cottage and sit by the fire chatting to the girls until the early hours of the morning. According to Dorothy Collins, Frances 'liked to think of him enjoying himself with them. Her best self felt that way. But other times it was too hard.'

The following year the Chestertons, accompanied, as always now, by Dorothy, travelled to Rome, where for almost three months they stayed at the Hotel Hassler, a little hotel 'at the top of the flight of steps that leads down to the Piazza di Spagna', from where there was a magnificent view of the city. Chesterton recorded many impressions of his stay, during which he had met both Mussolini and Pope Pius XI, and these were published as *The Resurrection of Rome* in the autumn of 1930.

While he was in Rome *The Thing* was brought out in London by Sheed & Ward. The book consisted of thirty-five essays which had been published either in magazines or in the Catholic newspaper, *The Universe*. Belloc thought this the best of all Chesterton's books, since it was 'by far the most profound and the most clear'. For his part, he said, he would make it a test of any man's critical sense. 'If the book was read by the generation just rising,' he wrote in 1940, 'that will mean that England is beginning to think. If it is forgotten, that will mean that thought is failing, for nowhere has there been more thorough thinking or clearer exposition in our time.'

While he admitted that 'an excerpt never does justice to a writer', Belloc cited a short passage from the essay 'Why I am a Catholic' which concluded:

It is enough to say that those who know the Catholic practice find it not only right when everything else is wrong; making the Confessional the very throne of candour where the world outside talks nonsense about it as a sort of conspiracy; upholding humility when everybody is praising pride; charged with sentimental charity when the world is loud and loose with vulgar sentimentalism – as it is today. At the place where the roads meet there is no doubt of the convergence. A man may think of all sorts of things, most of them honest and many of them true, about the right way to turn in the maze at Hampton Court. But he does not think he is in the centre; he knows.

On 19 September 1930 the Chestertons, accompanied by Dorothy, set sail from Liverpool for Canada on board the White Star Line's SS *Doric*. Fortunately the liner was by no means full and, as Frances informed Marie Louise, this meant more comfort and space. 'We have a delightful suite on board (paid for by Gilbert's University People) – a bedroom with two beds, a sitting room and a bath room, and Dorothy's room is quite near. We are fed like fighting cocks – as is always the way on these great liners,' she wrote.

'Gilbert's University People' were at the University of Notre Dame, Indiana, a Catholic university, at which Chesterton had been invited to give a series of lectures over a period of six weeks on Victorian history and literature. The fact that the lectures would all be at the same place had attracted Chesterton, as the thought of another lecture tour like the one in 1921 did not appeal to him. In the event the tour turned out to be far more taxing than the first since, as soon as it was known that Chesterton would be in America, Lee Keedick, the leading American lecture agent, hurried over to England in an attempt to persuade him to agree to a short lecture tour, as he was more popular than ever in the States. Chesterton was hesitant, but Keedick assured him the load would be light, and with the plight of *G.K.'s Weekly* uppermost in his mind Chesterton realized that the extra money would be very useful. Everything would be made as easy as possible, and only a few engagements would be arranged, Keedick emphasized. However, he failed to keep his word.

The *Doric* encountered rough seas almost the whole way: on the Sunday when the Chestertons had risen particularly early to attend the 7 o'clock Mass, the service came to an abrupt end about a quarter of the way through because the priest had to rush out to be sick. 'A great disappointment to the nuns who are on board,' Frances wrote.

Besides dictating articles to Dorothy, Chesterton amused himself by arranging a treasure hunt, with clues in rhyming verse, and joining in all the parties and games on board. The Purser, 'a rather remarkable man, very full of good animal spirits and very amusing', had asked Chesterton to act as chairman at the ship's Grand Concert, which he had readily agreed to do; and in the meantime Frances and he had great amusement joining in the horse-racing games. Chesterton's horse was 'Anecdote', whose pedigree was 'by Memory out of Repertoire', and Frances had drawn 'Safety Match', which was a winning horse. 'The excitement was quite thrilling,' she told her mother-in-law. 'This morning I was photographed with my horse. The horses you understand are wooden ones on stands with numbers and jockeys complete and they are made to move by the numbers thrown by the dice like the children's game of Race Horses we used to play.'

On the night of the 27th, after the concert at which Chesterton had made an 'excellent chairman', he went on to make an admirable speech appealing for funds for sailors' charities. The speech was 'a little serious, and humorous too'. The night ended with national songs of America, Canada, Scotland, Ireland and England, and the Chestertons did not retire to their cabin until after 1 o'clock in the morning, which for Frances was hardly 'a Christian hour'.

The journey gave both of them a rest, and Frances was pleased that Gilbert was enjoying himself. The excitement of seeing an iceberg off the coast of Newfoundland, the aurora borealis, and a school of 'spouting whales', which the Captain assured her were porpoises, were all experiences they would treasure.

The stop at Quebec was very short, but a friend suddenly arrived and the Chestertons were whisked around the city in a motor car. Gilbert was particularly pleased to see the Wolfe Monument, and the Montcalm one besides. Then from Quebec the *Doric* continued its journey to Toronto. At both Toronto and Montreal Chesterton lectured to audiences of between four and five thousand people.

When they eventually reached Notre Dame, Chesterton was shown to the lecturer's quarters, and Frances and Dorothy were shown to the Infirmary looked after by nuns, as no women were allowed in college. The following day Frances decided that they must find lodgings where they could all three be together, as Gilbert could not be on his own for six weeks without her special attention. The two women went off to sort the matter out, while Chesterton was made welcome by the university staff, particularly by the President, Fr O'Donnell, with whom the Chestertons had dined the previous evening.

The lodgings Frances and Dorothy found were with a family called Bixler, who lived at South Bend. Frances told Marie Louise:

> There is a grandfather, a husband and wife and two small children – kindness itself, but so utterly unlike people of the same position at home. Here we have the true democracy at work and we shall all lead the family life I can see. Miss Collins is already nursing the baby and Gilbert is conversing with the grandfather about the Civil War and Lincoln, while I must help Mrs Bixler to clear the table.

Frances made a particular friend of little Delphine who was four years old, although, as Dorothy observed,

> Delphine seldom went to bed till midnight and got up in the morning when she felt inclined and danced about all the morning in her pyjamas and dressing-gown. Mrs Chesterton sometimes took her for a walk but she was worn out before they had walked half-a-mile.
> Knowing Mrs Chesterton's love of children, you can imagine how happy she was during our six weeks stay at South Bend.

During those six weeks Chesterton lectured to the students in the evenings, and at the weekends travelled off to lecture elsewhere, but always within easy reach of Notre Dame. In this way he visited Milwaukee, Detroit and Chicago. On 15 November, however, the travelling began in earnest when they left Indiana for Cincinnati. They were sad to leave. 'Every thing and everyone had been so nice and the lectures so successful and Gilbert is beloved by the students,' Frances wrote. When they arrived at Cincinnati they discovered that they had been given the royal suite where Queen Marie of Roumania had stayed. Dorothy recalled:

> The Union Jack was flying, and the entrance hall was decorated with Union Jacks and a large illuminated sign saying 'Welcome G.K.Chesterton'.
> As soon as we had unpacked the manager appeared with one of the staff with a huge cake made as an exact reproduction of Mr Chesterton's latest book, *The Resurrection of Rome*. We could never have

eaten it had not the Chesterton Club turned up in force that evening and they made short work of it.

The Club had added to the Chesterton's luggage by presenting their hero with a large etching, so large that two taxis were now always necessary, but later, after they had lugged the thing as far as New York, in one of the many taxis Chesterton sat on it and smashed the glass.

By the time Christmas came Chesterton had lectured in Pittsburgh, and in Buffalo, where he received an honorary degree, 'one of the many degrees he collected in America'. Travelling from New York, he had spoken at Cleveland, Ohio, and at Albany, Syracuse and Philadelphia. At Albany he told the Americans they worshipped the ideal of energy without knowing its object.

> The people are too eager to build up: they spend their energy in building up something that will be taken down in a few years. It had grown to be almost a religion with the people here.
>
> It is a very subtle thing. I don't know where it came from. It is the outgrowth of history, of the exhilarating climate and the pioneer spirit, I suppose. The Puritans came here full of ideals of religion as if a new light shone.
>
> That passionate energy for religion with which they came to this country passed away and the people have thrown their tremendous energy into business. It is the worship of activity for its own sake. They worship it without an objective. In England the rich classes that worship laziness are as bad. Neither is sound. It is a false religion.

As far as the Puritans were concerned, Chesterton was of the opinion that the English should have instituted a special Thanksgiving Day to celebrate the fact that the Pilgrim Fathers had left.

Christmas and the New Year were spent in New York. Rather than come straight home, Chesterton had agreed to continue his tour in the South and, for the first time, to visit the West Coast. It was to prove a mixed blessing. So it was that on 6 January the lecturing began again. While they were at Chattanooga difficulties arose when Frances suddenly began to feel ill. At first it did not seem too serious, and Chesterton left her in the charge of Dorothy while he continued to travel; but Frances ran a very high temperature and after six days, nursed by Dorothy and the hotel doctor, she seemed little better. It became necessary to take her to hospital, where she had a private room and two private nurses. Two specialists were called in and for four days, as Dorothy recorded, 'it was quite doubtful whether she would get better'. It was just as well that Chesterton was earning some money, although things had not gone too well for him either. He had lost his tickets, his money and most of his clothes, and arrived back in Chattanooga 'looking as if he had not undressed for a week'. He was quite adamant that he could not endure to go anywhere alone again. Many lectures in the South had to be hastily cancelled, which meant that according to the terms of his contract he would have to pay Keedick £100 for each cancellation. The result was that Frances, who was now well on the way to recovery, decided that Dorothy should accompany Gilbert to the West Coast and try to salvage what was left of the tour. She would follow, she said, as soon as she could. It was essential that Chesterton should begin lecturing on 12 February, so he and Dorothy set off immediately. After travelling for three days and nights they managed to reach Los Angeles by the 10th. For the next week, wrote Dorothy, 'we rushed up and down the Californian coast and Mr Chesterton gave a lecture at a different place every night'.

Frances arrived on 17 February accompanied by one of her nurses. Thinking the hotel to be unsuitable for a happy convalescence, Dorothy managed to find a small Spanish hotel in the Californian hills only a few miles outside the city, where Frances remained in improving health for five weeks. In the meantime Dorothy steered Chesterton to San Francisco, to Seattle, to Portland, Oregon, and in Canada to Vancouver and Victoria, British Columbia, for more lectures.

The Spanish hotel was situated close to Hollywood, which Chesterton described as 'a remarkable place. It is like an explosion under an old English pantomime. Bits of Pierrot are joined with a tress or two of Columbine .... A Punch and Judy nose is stuck upon a beautiful face.' However, he was pleased when some producers, who had got wind of his presence, were 'very anxious to get hold of some Father Brown stories for filming'. Frances told Marie Louise, 'It would be splendid financially ... and a great help, as naturally my illness has been a bit expensive. Everything out here is about 4 times as much as in England.'

On 23 March all four of them left California. After dropping the nurse off at Kansas City, the Chestertons and Dorothy eventually reached New York on the 29th. Here another series of lectures began, so it was hardly surprising, as Dorothy recorded, that Chesterton 'got very behindhand with his work for the papers'. One thing is quite certain:

without her, the whole American visit would have been a fiasco, and
the Chestertons could hardly have survived. It was the fulfilment of
Frances's hope. As she had written to Dorothy a little over a year earlier,
'And you have brought a long dead hope to birth that I should hold
a daughter by the hand.'

Chesterton arrived back in England exhausted. It was necessary to
make certain that he did not do too much, and Dorothy set about cutting
down his lecture schedule to a manageable size. Nevertheless, by the
second week in May he was speaking to the City Literary Institute on
Mary Queen of Scots, and the following evening attending the Detection
Club Dinner at L'Escargot Bienvenu, in Greek Street. On the 21st he
was at the Oxford Union proposing the motion 'That the Law is an
Ass'.

However, Dorothy was having some success. On 1 July Ronald Knox
wrote from Oxford:

> Now it seems your secretary refuses to let you lecture for the next
> few months, because you've got so bored with it in America.
> It is so maddening, after five years of being told you wouldn't
> come because you were lecturing too much, to be told now that you
> won't come because you're lecturing too little. I shall begin to believe
> you have a down on me, or Newman, or something.

But both Frances and Dorothy were right; Chesterton was again
attempting too much, and towards the end of the summer he was in
a state of collapse. Maurice Baring wrote:

> I am so sorry Gilbert has been so unwell. Every man of his age
> and mine seems to be unwell at the moment. Tell him that although
> he does not write to me he sometimes does better: he sends me a
> wave and a smile in his articles in the *Illustrated London News* by
> sometimes mentioning things we have talked about or something I
> have written about him . . . . It is like getting a message on the wireless.

On 22 October yet another book of *Illustrated London News* articles
was published by Methuen under the title *All is Grist*; it was the only
book Chesterton published that year. At Christmas he gave a fifteen-
minute broadcast to America on the subject of Dickens and Christmas,
and in the Christmas Number of *G.K.'s Weekly*, which showed a cartoon
of Chesterton milking a cow in place of the usual editorial, he wrote:

Much has been said of the convivial Christmas of Dickens. He has been blamed for sentiment; he has been praised with sentimentality. But we must always remember that, whatever his weaknesses, they never did weaken his fixed idea of waging war on the wickedness of the world. He did not mean by Christmas charity that everybody at Dingley Dell must believe that everything was right at Dotheboys Hall. He did not mean by the benevolence of Mr Pickwick that nobody must think ill of Mr Pecksniff; or that because it was well to trust in Charity it was wicked to trust in Chancery. This old Radical common sense went with his old Tory conviviality; and both came from a religious tradition dying even in his day. Since men have ceased to keep the home fires burning, they have also ceased to keep the watch fires burning; and have thrown the same cold water of comfortable scepticism on the hearths of hospitality and the beacons of defence. With the vanishing of that vigilance or militant loyalty there vanishes every vestige of the first conception of Christmas; the dignity of the outcast; the danger of the innocent. Gush and good fellowship and cheap idealism will never rise to the stature of these mysteries; those content with them will never realise why myrrh was laid before a Mother rejoicing; or why her very name is Bitterness, whose title is Cause of Our Joy.

However tired or turgid Chesterton's prose became in his last years, he seemed always able to achieve sublimity at Christmastide.

In the spring of the following year, Chesterton published two books: *Sidelights on New London and Newer York*, in which he gave his impressions of his American tour; and *Chaucer*.

'When this book on Chaucer came into my hands,' wrote Desmond MacCarthy, 'I realised that there was no author in English literature, after Dickens, who was a better subject for Mr Chesterton; no other with whom he would find himself more instantly at home, and in criticising whom this sense of proportion would be more illuminating.' In no way was MacCarthy disappointed, for, as his son-in-law Lord David Cecil said, Chesterton had brought out more forcibly than anyone had before the scale of Chaucer's genius.

The idea that Chesterton should write about Chaucer at all had been that of Richard de la Mare, the son of the poet, who had been anxious to promote a series of essays for Faber and Faber under the general heading of 'The Poets on the Poets'. This idea developed into a 'critical biography'; although Chesterton had no ambition to be considered as a biographer. He wrote:

> The present writer is prayerfully conscious that he was never meant to be a biographer, not having that eye for detail which can trace a tenable theory among many doubts. On the other hand, if unlearned in the more recondite documents, he has in his time studied about one thousand detective-stories, and is often struck by the resemblance between the ingenuity of their authors and the ingenuity of the learned biographers.

In his chapter on Chaucer's religion Chesterton argued against the claim that Chaucer was really a Lollard, and therefore an honorary 'Protestant' in advance of his time, so that his work had always been 'safe reading' in any Protestant school or home.

> Some critics have vaguely suspected Chaucer of being a Lollard, through a simple ignorance of what is meant by being a Catholic. I am aware that there is a Victorian convention, according to which a literary study shou'd not refer to religion, except when there is an opportunity of passing a sneer at it. But nobody can make head or tail of the fourteenth century without understanding what is meant by being a Catholic; and therefore by being a heretic. A man does not come an inch nearer to being a heretic by being a hundred times a critic. Nor does he do so because his criticisms resemble those of critics who are also heretics. He only becomes a heretic at the precise moment when he prefers his criticism to his Catholicism. That is, at the instant of separation in which he thinks the view peculiar to himself more valuable than the creed that unites him to his fellows. At any given moment the Catholic Church is full of people sympathizing with social movements or moral ideas, which may happen to have representatives outside the Church. For the Church is not a movement or a mood or a direction, but the balance of many movements and moods; and the membership of it consists of accepting the ultimate arbitrament which strikes the balance between them, not in refusing to admit any of them into the balance at all.

Chesterton went on to say that the Lollard was 'the most sympathetic of all the heretics', in that he was the most Catholic and the least Protestant.

On 18 June the Chestertons crossed over from Holyhead to attend the Eucharistic Congress in Dublin. As they drove from the quay through the streets of the city towards the Viceregal Lodge, where they were official guests, Chesterton was recognized by some of the crowd who shouted out: 'God bless him. Three cheers for G.K.' It was something that Frances found both 'exciting and embarrassing', but she was pleased to find they had been given such spacious rooms at the Lodge, and that among the other house guests would be John MacCormack, the tenor, whom they had met in California, and Shane Leslie.

On the 21st the Irish hierarchy gave a garden party at Blackrock for some thirty thousand people. Cardinal Bourne spotted the Chestertons and was 'very gracious' to them both, as Frances told her mother, whom she had left in a nursing home in Beaconsfield.

The great occasion was the Pontifical High Mass in Phoenix Park the following Sunday. John MacCormack sang at the service, and Gilbert Chesterton had hired the scarlet robe, green hood and black velvet cap of a Doctor of Letters of the National University of Ireland, 'an honorary degree given some time ago'.

His many impressions of the Congress were written up for *The Universe*. These, together with an essay on 'The Mission of Ireland' which appeared in a magazine called *Studies*, formed the basis of his book *Christendom in Dublin*, which Sheed and Ward published in the following November. The book was very short but, ten years after the event, it gave Chesterton yet another opportunity to speak of his conversion. He wrote:

No man could be received into the Catholic Church if he were converted by a clang of trumpets or an old Celt bell. I myself should utterly distrust my own conversion, if it had only taken place at the moment of supreme exaltation in Phoenix Park. A man who finds his way to Catholicism, out of the tangle of modern culture and complexity, must think harder than he has ever thought in his life. He must often deal as grimly with dry abstractions as if he were reading mathematics with the hope of being Senior Wrangler. He must often face the dull and repulsive aspects of duty, as if he were facing the dreariest drudgery in the world. He must realise all the sides upon which the religion may seem sordid or humdrum or humiliating or harsh. He must feel all the counter-attractions of Paganism at least enough to know how attractive are those attractions. But, above all,

he must think; above all, he must preserve his intellectual independence, above all, he must use his reason. . . .

I say that *when* you are convinced, when you are rationally convinced, when you have come to the end of the long road of reason,
when you have seen through the tangled arguments of the time, when
you have found the answer to them – *then* you will find yourself
suddenly in the morning of the world. Then you will find yourself
among facts and not arguments, but facts as marvellous as fables;
facts like those which the pagans pictured as a land of giants or an
age of heroes; you will have returned to the age of the Epic; and
the epoch of things achieved.

By the beginning of September Chesterton had again collapsed. Dorothy, who was in the south of France partly on holiday, and partly
to arrange accommodation for the Chestertons in the future, wrote to
Frances from Carcassonne on 15 September: 'It seems almost inevitable
that he should have these attacks at stated intervals. I suppose it is
Nature's warning to him that he is not made of cast-iron and that he
must be careful.' Three days later she wrote again, this time from Avignon: 'Is the doctor going to be very severe about the future regime
for him? He is generally so good after he has been ill for a little while.
I do hope he will be careful. It would be so awful if he got properly
ill again. I always wonder that he does not. What a good thing we
were really firm about autumn and winter engagements.'

This letter crossed with one from Frances to say that Chesterton
was better, though the problem had been that he was drinking again
to keep going. Dorothy wrote back immediately: 'I am glad he is really
better, but sorry to hear that your feelings do not entirely coincide with
the doctor's opinions. What is worrying you now? I can't help feeling
that possibly his nervousness is bound to react on you and you may
worry in sympathy with him when there is not any cause. It will do
you both a lot of good to get away.'

Dorothy's letter had gone on to reveal what had worried her for
some time, and Frances's had obviously brought the matter up. Dorothy
wrote:

I am glad he feels that I am moderately reasonable, because so often
I feel he would be much happier with someone who was more hapha-
zard about the work and did not bother him about dates, and getting
letters answered, and so on. It could be done on those lines I realise

quite well, and I often wonder if I try to drive it too much along a road instead of letting it wander in the woods. He is more than patient with me, whatever he thinks. Please give him my love.

It was an important time for Dorothy too. By now she had realized she would have to remain with the Chestertons indefinitely, not that she minded that; but she had also made the decision to follow them into the Catholic Church, and so she had asked the priest for instruction. In the autumn she drove Gilbert and Frances to France, and they stayed at Avignon, Nîmes and Perignon.

As I mentioned earlier Dorothy had become the daughter Frances had thought she would never have. The intensity of that emotion may have seemed at times a difficulty. Another anxiety at the time was the health of both Gilbert and Frances's mothers. Mrs Blogg, after living for a while with the Oldershaws, during part of which time Ethel had been helped out by Clare Nicholl, was now at The Yews, a nursing home within easy reach of Top Meadow. Marie Louise was still at Warwick Gardens, but she was also failing in health, and Ada had noticed on occasions how quiet she was. 'I am only tired,' she had been assured. 'I'll let you know when I'm going to die, my darling girl.' Ada had remained particularly close to her mother-in-law, and every Sunday evening had been spent at No. 11. Mrs Chesterton was looked after by the maid Thirza, who had been with her for years. Each year she had spent much time at the Queen's Hotel in Brighton, where she had always been made welcome, and she had enjoyed pottering round 'the old streets of the Regency period'. Ada had often accompanied her there, and Gilbert too enjoyed spending a day or two with her, usually alone, since the seaside air was bad for Frances's rheumatism.

It was probably on one such visit that Malcolm Muggeridge caught sight of him. 'The only time I ever saw him in the flesh he was seated outside The Ship Hotel at Brighton shortly before he died. His canvas chair looked preposterously small, as did a yellow-covered thriller he was reading. It was a windy day, and I half-expected him to be carried away. Though so huge, he seemed to have no substance : more a balloon than an elephant.'

Marie Louise had kept in almost daily contact with Gilbert and Frances by letter, and while Frances had been in Dublin she had written either to her or to her own mother every day, asking that the letters might be passed between them. Although she had never followed Gilbert's career with the same attention to detail as her husband had done, Marie Louise was always aware in general terms of what was going on.

She was forthright in any comments she did make and, if it does not seem an absurd remark in this particular case, she was ready to cut Gilbert down to size. When James Gunn's famous triple portrait, now in the National Portrait Gallery, showing Gilbert with Belloc and Maurice Baring, was completed, she said that she could not see what all the fuss was about: 'I fail to see anything remarkable in what is merely a picture of two fat men and one thin man.'

However, as Ada had noticed, despite her courage and vivacity, 'the pulse of this great little woman's life was flagging', and on a quiet day, when her elder son was fifty-nine years old, with a smile on her face, and a last tender look in her eye, with those dearest to her beside her bed, Marie Louise Chesterton died.

20

Te, Lucis Ante Terminum

1933–1936

At about the time Marie Louise had died in Kensington, Frances's mother, Blanche Blogg, who at the end was almost totally blind, had died in Beaconsfield. For Frances her mother's death meant an easing of tension, as she had visited the nursing home every day. She had therefore been unable to accompany Chesterton on his visits to Warwick Gardens – although she was present when Marie Louise died.

The Kensington house was once more up to let, for it seems the Chestertons had always rented from the Phillimore Estate. Everything was cleared out and, as I mentioned earlier, it was only through Dorothy Collins's timely arrival that any of Edward Chesterton's papers were saved from the dustmen. In his mother's will Chesterton had been left sufficient money to leave legacies of his own to all his nephews and nieces, and to donate a sum towards the building of a Catholic church in Beaconsfield, a building which was completed only after his death, and as a memorial to him.

In March 1933 yet another book of essays collected from the *Illustrated London News* articles was published by Methuen as *All I Survey*. At about the same time his *G.K.'s Weekly* editorials became more and more aware of the threat of what Chesterton called Hitlerism, although Chesterton found irony in some of Hitler's policies. 'It is typical of a complex situation in Germany,' he wrote, 'that the Hitler Government should announce, with all the trumpets of the Kremlin, a series of economic measures not at first sight unlike the measures one might call Distributist.' However, it was only at 'first sight' that the similarity existed. 'The centralised State is introducing what might be called Distributist measures with an eye to an Empire founded upon the theory of Race.' Distributism was being forced on the German People 'by the mass methods of the Communist'.

Chesterton went on to say that it was not beyond the bounds of possibility that the last results of Hitlerism would be the salvation of Germany, only because the measures now introduced would be caught up and transformed by those Germans who understood the spirit in which they should be enforced. 'But the very fact that Hitler introduced measures nominally Distributist,' he said, 'generally interlarded though they are with a hotch-potch of Communist and Junker philosophies, may bring saner measures of the same inspiration into being in other countries dying of industrialism. The real Distributism is the only practical politics.'

It should not be deduced from this that Chesterton nursed any admiration for Hitler, as he most certainly did for Mussolini. Ada Chesterton said, 'He seemed to have a growing admiration for Mussolini, and for the alterations the Duce had made in the national administration.' Nevertheless, it would be absurd to call Chesterton a Fascist, as some people did at the time, who suspected that *G.K.'s Weekly* was receiving Fascist funds. Sir Oswald Mosley seemed to Chesterton to be a bit of a joke. 'It is almost as difficult to discover what he and his party do actually propose to do, as if he were already a real Prime Minister, at the head of a national Government in the hour of National Peril,' he said. But at the same time he saw something more sinister in the policies of the British Fascists, those 'who know not Mosley'. He had read some of their pamphlets. 'The writers seem to be rather British Hitlerites than British Fascists, and even then more Hitlerite than British,' he commented. For instance, they even wrote in a sort of semi-German, which certainly did not recall 'the repose of the Roman marble or even the classic dance of the Italian diction'. He would hardly be likely to call out 'Hail Belloc!' – 'Hail Eric Gill!' – 'Hail Father Vincent McNabb!' were he ever to become the Distributist dictator England needed. He wrote in his paper on 16 November in the same year: 'The only tolerable English Dictator would be a Distributist Dictator. He might meet our case; because our country is centuries behind the rest of the world in Distributism.' As to Lord Beaverbrook's objection 'that the Empire would not understand a Dictator', Chesterton said he would cheerfully risk that, 'if there were a Dictator who did understand England'.

He had noticed that the British Fascists were 'furiously anti-Semite' and wrote:

I have been called an Anti-Semite myself and even mistaken for a furious one; and I know all about it, and all that there really is to be said for it. It is true that a non-Christian culture, embedded for ages in what has always been a Christian culture, acts as an irritant and to some extent as a parasite, because it trades and schemes but does not plough or produce. But what seems to be amusing about those particular British Fascists is their complete ignorance of the whole British tradition and attitude in the matter. They talk as if Fascists were bound to be Tories; as if Tories were bound to support the claims of aristocrats; and to all this they add the uncomfortable necessity of being Anti-Semites. Well, every step of this is all wrong; Mussolini is almost the opposite of an English Tory; he does not in the least depend on any aristocracy; and if we are going to depend on the English aristocracy (and I agree that we might do worse) one thing is absolutely certain; and that is we cannot be Anti-Semites.

The autumn of 1933 saw the publication of Chesterton's *St Thomas Aquinas*, which was dedicated to Dorothy, 'without whose help the author would have been more than normally helpless'. The book has been generally recognized as an amazing achievement. Dom Étienne Gilson, the great Benedictine Thomist scholar, wrote:

I consider it as being without comparison the best book ever written on St Thomas. Nothing short of genius can account for such an achievement. Everybody will no doubt admit that it is a 'clever' book, but few readers who have spent twenty or thirty years in studying St Thomas Aquinas, and who, perhaps, have themselves published two or three volumes on the subject, can fail to perceive that the so-called 'wit' of Chesterton has put their scholarship to shame. He has guessed all that they had tried to demonstrate, and he has said all that which they were more or less clumsily attempting to express in academic formulas.

It was Chesterton's belief that the schism in the Church in the sixteenth century was really a belated revolt of the thirteenth-century pessimists: 'It was a backwash of the old Augustinian Puritanism against the Aristolelian liberality.' St Thomas had 'defended the great view of his youth, for freedom and for the poor', and in so doing had 'turned back the whole backward movement of his time'. What Chesterton called 'the

Aristotelian Revolution' had been led by the originality of Aquinas, but this had not meant a break in philosophical history.

In so far as there were ever a break in philosophical history, it was not before St Thomas, or at the beginning of medieval history; it was after St Thomas and at the beginning of modern history. The great intellectual tradition that comes down to us from Pythagoras and Plato was never interrupted or lost through such trifles as the sack of Rome, the triumph of Attila or all the barbarian invasions of the Dark Ages. It was only lost after the introduction of printing, the discovery of America, the founding of the Royal Society and all the enlightenment of the Renaissance and the modern world. It was there, if anywhere, that there was lost or impatiently snapped the long thin delicate thread that had descended from distant antiquity; the thread of that unusual human hobby, the habit of thinking.

What had made the Aristotelian Revolution really revolutionary, Chesterton argued, was the fact that it was really religious, that the revolt was largely a revolt of the most Christian elements in Christendom.

St Thomas, every bit as much as St Francis, felt subconsciously that the hold of his people was slipping on the solid Catholic doctrine and discipline, worn smooth by more than a thousand years of routine; and that the Faith needed to be shown under a new light and dealt with from another angle. But he had no motive except the desire to make it popular for the salvation of the people. It was true, broadly speaking, that for some time past it had been too Platonist to be popular. It needed something like the shrewd and homely touch of Aristotle, to turn it again into a religion of common sense. Both the motive and the method are illustrated in the war of Aquinas against the Augustinians.

The fact that Thomism was the philosophy of common sense was itself a matter of common sense, Chesterton argued. In *G.K.'s Weekly* on 2 November that year he wrote: 'A society is in decay, final or transitional, when common sense has really become uncommon.' Since the modern world began in the sixteenth century, he had said in *St Thomas Aquinas*, nobody's system of philosophy had really corresponded to everybody's sense of reality; to what, if left to themselves, common men would call common sense. Each philosophy had started with a paradox:

... a peculiar point of view demanding the sacrifice of what they would call a sane point of view. That is the one thing common to Hobbes and Hegel, to Kant and Bergson, to Berkeley and William James. A man had to believe something that no normal man would believe, if it were suddenly propounded to his simplicity; as that law is above right, or right is outside reason, or things are only as we think them, or everything is relative to reality that is not there. The modern philosopher claims, like a sort of confidence man, that if once we will grant him this, the rest will be easy; he will straighten out the world if he is allowed to give this one twist to the mind.

Against all this hotch-potch of philosophies the philosophy of St Thomas Aquinas

... stands founded on the universal common conviction that eggs are eggs. The Hegelian may say that an egg is really a hen, because it is a part of an endless process of Becoming; the Berkeleian may hold that poached eggs only exist as a dream exists; since it is quite easy to call the dream the cause of the eggs as the eggs is the cause of the dream; the Pragmatist may believe that we get the best out of scrambled eggs by forgetting that they ever were eggs, and only remembering the scramble. But no pupil of St Thomas needs to addle his brains in order adequately to addle his eggs; to put his head at any peculiar angle in looking at eggs, or squinting at eggs, or winking the other eye in order to see a new simplification of eggs. The Thomist stands in the broad daylight of the brotherhood of men, in their common consciousness that eggs are not hens or dreams or mere practical assumptions; but things attested by the Authority of the Senses, which is from God.

Yet the Augustinian tradition was to be avenged when Luther came out of his cell, and 'the Pope was yet to learn how quarrelsome a monk could be'. However, Chesterton felt he must be just to the huge human figures who were in fact the hinges of history. However strong, and rightly strong, was his own controversial conviction, it must never mislead him into thinking that something trivial had transformed the world.

So it is with the great Augustinian monk, who avenged all the ascetic Augustinians of the Middle Ages; and whose broad and burly figure has been big enough to block out for four centuries the distant human mountain of Aquinas. It is not, as the moderns delight to say, a question of theology. The Protestant theology of Martin Luther was a thing that no modern Protestant would be seen dead in a field with; or if the phrase be too flippant, would be specially anxious to touch with a barge-pole. That Protestantism was pessimism; it was nothing but bare insistence on the hopelessness of all human virtue, as an attempt to escape hell. That Lutheranism is now quite unreal; more modern phases of Lutheranism are rather more unreal; but Luther was not unreal. He was one of those great elemental barbarians, to whom it is indeed given to change the world. To compare those two figures bulking so big in history, in any philosophical sense, would of course be futile and unfair. On a great map like the mind of Aquinas, the mind of Luther would be almost invisible. But it is not altogether untrue to say, as so many journalists have said without caring whether it was true or untrue, that Luther opened an epoch; and began the modern world.

He was the first man who ever consciously used his consciousness; or what was later called his Personality. He had as a fact a rather strong personality. Aquinas had an even stronger personality; he had a massive and magnetic presence; he had an intellect that could act like a huge system of artillery spread over the whole world; he had that instantaneous presence of mind in debate, which alone really deserves the name of wit. But it never occurred to him to use anything exept his wits, in defence of a truth distinct from himself. It never occurred to Aquinas to use Aquinas as a weapon. There is not a trace of his ever using his personal advantages, of birth or body or brain or breeding, in debate with anybody. In short, be belonged to an age of intellectual unconsciousness, to an age of intellectual innocence, which was very intellectual. Now Luther did begin the modern mood of depending on things not merely intellectual. It is not a question of praise or blame; it matters little whether we say that he was a strong personality, or that he was a bit of a big bully. When he quoted a Scripture text, inserting a word that is not in Scripture, he was content to shout back at all hecklers: 'Tell them that Dr Martin Luther will have it so!' That is what we now call Personality. A little later it was called Psychology. After that it was called Advertisement or Salesmanship. But we are not arguing about advantages or disadvantages. It is due to this great Augustinian pessimist to say, not only that he did triumph at last over the Angel of the Schools, but that he did in a very real sense make the modern world. He destroyed Reason; and substituted Suggestion.

Chesterton concluded his book by saying that it had been suggested that the great Reformer had publicly burned the *Summa Theologica* and the rest of the works of Aquinas, and with the bonfire of such books his own book might well come to an end.

Chesterton saw the Thomist philosophy as 'a working and even a fighting system'. It was full of hope and promise, and he shared with St Thomas the certainty that the mind had the power to take hold of reality, and that those who doubted this power lost every other hold on reality and were forced to yield to men 'who know that they can know'. At the same time he was also certain that there was no reality without religion. In one of his last books, *The Well and the Shallows*, he argued that the mind had returned, that man had taken to himself again his own weapons; will and worship and reason and the vision of the plan in things; and he was once more 'in the morning of the world'. Strange words for a world that would soon be plunged into the darkness of war.

Towards the end of his life a new experience opened up for Chesterton for, seemingly with very little effort, he became a popular broadcaster. Ostensibly his broadcasts were book reviews, but the books under consideration tended to become excuses for Chesterton to reminisce or go off at a tangent on one or other of his favourite topics. His manner at the microphone was totally relaxed and confidential, and he seemed to know instinctively the first rule for every broadcaster, that he was only ever speaking to one person. After his first home broadcast at the beginning of November 1932 he had received a letter from Broadcasting House telling him that the building was ringing with his praises. 'You bring us something very rare to the microphone,' the letter had said. Had he lived longer, as Edward MacDonald suggested, 'G.K.C. in another year or so would have become the dominating voice from Broadcasting House.'

However, 1934 was to be a difficult year for Chesterton's health. In the early part of the year he suffered from jaundice, though he was just well enough for Dorothy to drive him out to Florence to deliver a long-promised lecture in May. Later in the year Dorothy accompanied Frances and him to Rome, which he had been anxious to visit during the Holy Year, and as a kind of thanksgiving for his reception into the Order of St Gregory the Great, an honour also bestowed upon Belloc at the same time, 'in recognition of the services' which they had rendered to the Church by their writings. The two new knights were dubbed by Cardinal Bourne at a ceremony held on 22 May.

The intention had been to continue south from Rome and journey on to Sicily and from there to the Holy Land; but at Syracuse Chesterton collapsed, and had to rest for five weeks with 'inflammation of the nerves of the neck and shoulders'. To continue with the journey now seemed out of the question, and the three eventually returned home via Malta, where Chesterton was too ill to dine at Admiralty House, as he had been expected to do.

On 11 October the five hundredth edition of *G.K.'s Weekly* was published. It included a cartoon of Chesterton as St George by Thomas Derrick who wrote:

> I had sort of vowed never again to insult the editor in a picture; partly because although he has often made humorous reference to his own appearance, for all I know, he may not like it when other people do it, especially on the cover of his own paper. I dare not proceed without his consent. It might seem a little strange for him to be shown as a sort of St George; even a comic St George.

He had enclosed a sketch of the proposed cartoon, in which Chesterton is wielding a pen rather than a sword and is seated on a charger. In the final version the pen is replaced by a sword and the horse has disappeared altogether. On 1 October Chesterton replied to the letter:

> As long as you do not make me an idealised St George, which I am sure not even your genius could do, I do not mind what you do. It is only too jolly of you to do anything. What I mean is, I should welcome it so long as it *is* a caricature; and does make fun of me; and, therefore, not make too much of me – except in the obvious physical sense.

By the following March, plans were well in advance for the Chestertons to attend the Catholic Education Congress in Australia in the autumn. A passage had been booked on the RMS *Narkunda* which would arrive in Freemantle on 8 September.

In the same month the last of the Father Brown books was published as *The Scandal of Father Brown*. Many of Chesterton's admirers will have been disappointed by this final offering, and it is sad to have to relate that after the eight stories in the book Chesterton only wrote one more Father Brown story, which was considered so bad that *The Storyteller* refused to publish it, a fact Dorothy Collins was able to conceal from the author.

Reviewing *The Scandal of Father Brown* in *The London Mercury* Winifred Holtby said that all tricks become a little tedious in time – those of the soft as well as those of the hard heart. The souls and hearts and consciences of men were so important to Chesterton, she said, that he preferred to leave the crime out altogether.

To find slightly warmer conditions for Frances, Dorothy drove the Chestertons around the Continent in the spring, visiting France, Spain, and Italy, and returning home via Switzerland and Belgium. Such trips, though tiring in many ways, were a great joy to them all; but they meant much organization, and the preparation of articles for the papers in advance, which put an added pressure on Chesterton's mind. Later, in the summer, the fact that he had taken what he called 'a short holiday' resulted in an internal row at the office about the paper's handling of the Italian campaign in Abyssinia. 'Nobody could accuse the paper of holding a brief for Imperialism – certainly not for the kind of Imperialistic adventure on which Italy is at present engaged in Abyssinia,' he had written on 18 July, and had continued:

> To do Italy justice, her obvious intention to bring Abyssinia under her rule, is not inspired by a spirit of crude exploitation. Apart from that spirit of self-dramatisation which causes the Fascist to see himself as the heir of imperial Rome, the chief motive seems to be to acquire an outlet for emigration – Italy wants colonies, not plantations. But the idea that a country simply because its population is growing has the right to take possession of another nation's territory, is nothing less than an assertion of the doctrine of force in its ugliest form – a form which reduces men to the level of locusts.

However, he went on to say that England was not in a position to administer a moral rebuke, since she was at present in possession of an Empire far bigger than Italy could ever hope to attain, most of which had been acquired by methods 'which the most hard-boiled Fascist would repudiate with disgust'. England had no right to be self-righteous regarding the aggressions of her less-experienced neighbours.

In *G.K.'s Weekly* on 29 August Chesterton apologized or, rather, explained why he had not dealt with Abyssinia at length. His holiday, he said, was 'a thing at this time of the year not uncommon'. In fact it seems that he was not at all well, and had had to rest. In two articles in successive weeks he set out his ideas on the Abyssinian business. All his moral instincts, he said, were against Imperialism; he thought it was bad for the soul. 'I think it hardens the heart and therefore ultimately softens the head, with the running sore and weakness of pride. In so far as there has been some savour in Fascism, I think it is false as all the other older, more admitted, and generally less honest forms of Imperialism.'

Fascism, whether fighting in Abyssinia or forcing its way into Westminster, he said, was a new force with which he did not agree in principle; but he did respect it in comparison with things which are in practice much more unprincipled. Above all, he disagreed with Fascism; not because it had struck out a new path, but because it was travelling only too lamely in the old one.

It was unfair then, Chesterton argued, to deprecate Mussolini as a melodramatic stage tyrant when he was doing for his country what other countries have done; and none more than those called Liberal countries: English parliaments, and American or French republics. However, neither Fascism or Socialism was 'a substitute for the completion of the common man'.

At the same time Chesterton was engaged in a long wrangle with the Cambridge mediaeval scholar at St John's College, Dr G.G. Coulton, a bitter anti-Catholic with whom Chesterton, Belloc, and Knox had all had to contend at different times. It was one of the sadnesses of Chesterton's last days that they were taken up with this stupid quarrel. Dorothy Collins tried as best she could to fob Coulton off. 'I am very sorry to hear of Mr Chesterton's indisposition,' he wrote on 28 January. In the middle of May he was informed that Mr Chesterton was motoring in France, and hoped to reach home at the end of the month.

This last journey abroad was a visit to the Grotto at Lourdes, and the various shrines at Lisieux of St Teresa in the hope that somehow there would be an improvement in Chesterton's health. By this time his condition had become chronic: his body was retaining fluid, and he suffered permanently from catarrh.

On his return home there was little change in his condition, and on 10 June Dorothy wrote to Coulton:

I am sure you will be sorry to hear that Mr Chesterton is very ill.

He is being nursed at home by two nurses and so far we have been able to keep his illness out of the papers, but I do not expect to be able to do so much longer, as all his work has stopped. The specialist who saw him on Monday said he will not be able to work for some months, and then only on one or two of his weekly articles if he is feeling strong enough. He is suffering from cardiac weakness and complications. He was about three quarters of the way through the essay he was writing for you, but had not finished it as he was waiting to go to the British Museum for some research work. He has not been well enough for any extra exertion for some months, although he has tried to keep going. We had hoped to see a great improvement as a result of his visit to France, so this relapse is very disappointing.

By this time Chesterton was drifting in and out of consciousness. Although his relatives and closest friends were aware of the seriousness of the situation, Frances continued to keep the news from the public. If Gilbert *was* dying, it was a family affair, and her attitude now was consistent with her protective attitude in the past. Whatever Gilbert's 'genius' might mean to the world at large was a small matter compared with the more important consideration of his goodness, and the kind of husband he was. Among those she had informed was Fr O'Connor, who had promised to offer his Sunday Mass for Gilbert's recovery.

On 12 June, a Friday, Monsignor Smith, the parish priest, called at Top Meadow to anoint Chesterton with chrism, and Chesterton was conscious enough to receive what turned out to be his last Communion. On the same afternoon Fr Vincent McNabb travelled down from St Dominic's Priory in London. Standing beside the bed, where Chesterton lay unconscious, he intoned the Salve Regina, as was the custom in his order for a dying priest. No doubt he felt that Chesterton's championing of St Thomas Aquinas, perhaps the greatest Dominican of all, had entitled him to the rite. Then, seeing Chesterton's pen on the little table beside the bed, he picked it up and blessed it, and set off back to London.

The following day Frances kept a constant vigil in the room, so that she was present when Chesterton regained consciousness. For a while he seemed more alert than he had been for several days, which is not uncommon just before death. Turning to Frances, he said: 'Hallo, my darling.' Then seeing that Dorothy was also standing near, he said 'Hallo, my dear.' These were his last words, and he soon lost consciousness again. His laborious breathing continued through the night; he died on the following morning a little after 10 o'clock. It was 14 June, and the Sunday in the Octave of Corpus Christi.

The day of the funeral was sunny and hot. A large crowd packed into the little Catholic Church of St Teresa's, Beaconsfield, and overflowed into the porch. Most of Chesterton's close family and friends were present, and Belloc, who had left Sussex at 6 o'clock in the morning, was there with his daughter Eleanor and her husband. After the Mass the funeral moved to the Catholic cemetery in Candlemas Lane, where Chesterton's body was laid to rest in the grave that today is Frances's also, for she survived him by only two years.

Although many people wandered back to Top Meadow after the funeral, Frances had made no preparation for them, and shut herself in her bedroom. Noticing that Belloc was missing from the group, several of the company set off to look for him. He was eventually tracked down to the Railway Hotel, leaning against the door weeping, a pint pot untasted in his hand.

> People, if you have any prayers
>   Say prayers for me:
> And lay me under a Christian stone
> In that lost land I thought my own,
> To wait till the holy horn is blown,
>   And all poor men are free.

REFERENCES

The Following Abbreviations are used:

G.K.Chesterton papers in the keeping of Miss Dorothy Collins TMC
G.K.Chesterton by Maisie Ward (1945) MW
Autobiography by G.K.Chesterton (1936) A
The Eye Witness EW
The New Witness NW
Gilbert Keith Chesterton GKC
Frances Chesteron FC
Marie Louise Chesterton MLC
Collected Poems CP

1.   *Starry Streets that Point to God*
p. 6   'Gilbert's father had . . . them back in the car.' Dorothy
          Collins to the author
p. 7   'a fine-looking old man . . . toasts and sentiments.' A, p. 11
          'Do not forget . . . upon the occasion.' TMC
          'Neither do you suppose . . . in our latter days.' ibid.
p. 8   'It might have stood . . . did so successfully.' A, p. 41
p. 9   'The country people call . . . on their minds.' A, p. 40
p. 10   'I do not remember . . . horse and killed.' A, p. 36
p. 11   'God had given . . . slowly-tempered mind.' *Cecil Chesterton*
          by Brocard Sewell (1975), p. 1
p. 12   'The setting of the home . . . and deep chairs.' *The Chestertons*
          by Mrs Cecil Chesterton (1941), p. 19
          'It attached rather too much . . . pick up a title.' A, p. 15
          'What my parents . . . for miles around.' ibid.
p. 13   'I do not allege . . . into a Christian.' A, p. 9
          'The Rev. Stopford Brooke . . . *The First Clerihews* OUP
          (1982), p. 50
          'What was wonderful . . . miraculous world.' A, p. 38

p. 14   'The things I believed ... common sense.' *Orthodoxy*, p. 85
           'The very first thing ... verging on a swagger.' A, p. 31
           'I am concerned with ... the mere facts.' *Orthodoxy*, p. 87

p. 15   'One of my first memories ... without metaphor.' A, pp. 34–35
           'Aunt Marie ... chicken she got.' MW, p. 17

p. 16   'First; my life unfolded ...

p. 17   or at least being brought up.' A, pp 51–53

2.   *Fide et Literis*

p. 20   'He sat at the back ... what he had seen.' MW, p. 25

p. 21   'Boyhood is the most ... I was doing it.' A, p. 59

p. 22   'He was never angry ... in the background.' *Res Paulinae*
           (1911), pp 118–119

p. 23   'Wished his memory' et seq. *Those Days* by E.C. Bentley (1940),
           p. 46

p. 26   'The dragon is ... pavillion of the King.' *The Debater* vols I–II,
           pp 4–6

p. 27   JDC songs, see TMC

p. 28   'Those early Christians ... my brother's keeper.'
           'On the grim and crowded ... passing to the guillotine.' *The
           Debater* vols I–II, p. 26

3.   *How to be a Lunatic*

p. 31   'A foreign town ... talk too much.' *G.K. Chesterton* by Dudley
           Barker (1973), p. 45

p. 33   'I am enjoying myself ...

p. 34   one sandy nursery.' GKC to E.C. Bentley, 1893, TMC
           'Sir Humphrey Davy ...' *The First Clerihews*, p. 7

p. 35   'The Spanish people think Cervantes ...' ibid., p. 43

p. 36   'I am able to boast myself ... been well brought up.' A,
           pp 99–100

p. 37   'seated on the "throne" ... dazzling apparition.' *Augustus John*
               by Michael Holroyd (1974), see pp 37 ff.

           'I am not proud of ...

p. 38   about this world.' A, pp 81–82

           'The wife of the politician ...
                   Orriblerevelationsinighlife.' A, p. 82–83

p. 39   'There is something truly menacing ...

p. 40   blind spiritual suicide.' A, pp 92–93

p. 41   'It was not in that direction ... the toils of writing.'
         G. K. Chesterton: A Criticism by Cecil Chesterton (1908), p. 16

p. 42   'Chesterton's Notebooks TMC, cf MW, pp 56–64
         'It was strange ...' et seq. *Tremendous Trifles*, pp 225–231

p. 44   'My heart is full ... Your loving mother.' MLC to GKC, May
         1895, TMC
         'Being twenty-one ...

p. 45   end of the service.' MW, pp 54–55

4.   *Vision in Bedford Park*

p. 47   'Redway says ... worried somehow ....' MW, p. 67

p. 48   'It is by this event ... may be dated.' *Those Days*, p. 68
         'Other work has a repetition ... what I've just finished.' MW,
         p. 67

p. 51   'She had a sort of hungry appetite ... she practised a religion.'
         A, p. 152

p. 52   'It was described ... were quite indisputable.' *The Man Who
         was Thursday*, pp 9–10

p. 54   'First a Straw Hat ... in Whitman's poems.' MW, pp 85–86

p. 55   'Little as you may ...

p. 56   foot upon one's neck.' *G.K. Chesterton* by Dudley Barker,
                                                          pp 81–83
         'I wish you both ... happiness with you.' Margaret Heaton
         to GKC, July 1898, TMC

p. 57   'I am going to tell ... true in your case.' MW, pp 81–83
         'Do not be frightened ...

p. 58   Gilbert' MW, pp 81–83

5.   *Pride and a Little Scratching Pen*

p. 59   'I am clean ... is singularly exemplary.' MW, p. 98

p. 60   'So glad that you ... very dry.' *Return to Chesterton* by Maisie
         Ward (1952), pp 39–40

p. 63   'I am black ...

p. 64   than her who is silent.' MW, p. 99

p. 65   'I do not know ... triumphant, dead.' MW, p. 104
         'But when she fell ... in my ear.' TMC

p. 68   'Diego Rodriguez de Silva Velasquez ... virtue of
         inconsistency.' the *Bookman*, December 1899
         'I think there was a spiritual ...

p. 69   do not exist at all.' A, p. 92
          'When paganism ... it dies eternally.' the *Bookman*, December 1899
p. 70   'My father is again ... not stop at all.' MW, p. 105
p. 71   'what looked like an uncultivated ... could be no doubt.'
          Return to Chesterton, pp 51–52
p. 72   'Mr MacGregor, dressed to look ... and everybody else's.'
          ibid., p. 28
p. 75   'Chesterton was a natural romantic ... impatient of reality.'
          The Life of Hilaire Belloc by Robert Speaight (1957), pp 148–149

6.   *The Wild Knight*
p. 76   'In the autumn ... "Who is G.K.C.?" *G.K. Chesterton:*
          A Criticism, p. 30
p. 78   'The main note, then ... able to move Mr. Chesterton.' *Black*
          and White, 23 March 1901
p. 79   'Many thanks for ... marriage make him see people.' Kipling
          to Brindley Johnson, 28 November 1900
p. 80   'Mr Chesterton is ... divines and desires.' *The Speaker*,
          29 December 1900
p. 81   'I could quote ... than his very best.' *The Star* 5 January 1900
p. 83   'The little sardines in the tin ... will the oiliness.' TMC
          'Africa has always ...
p. 84   Ex Africa semper aliquid novi.' TMC
          'Nothing in the whole psychology ... as an intellectual song.'
          the *Daily News*, 19 April 1901
          'I have delayed this letter ...
p. 85   thing at a time.' MW, p. 129
          'I have, as I say, ... becoming the fashion.' MW, pp131–132
          'I make all these ... understood what I meant.' ibid.
p. 86   'A strange idea ... essential symbol of life.' the *Defendent*,
          pp 43–49
          For Belloc on Chesterton vid. *On the Place of Gilbert Chesterton*
          in English Letters, (Sheed and Ward, 1940)
p. 87   'It means that when ... whether it is orthodox.' the *Daily News*,
          October 1911
          'The fact that Thomism ...
p. 88   would call common sense.' *St Thomas Aquinas*, pp 171–172
          'In whatever manner ... in which he excelled.' *On the Place*
          of Gilbert Chesterton in English Letters, p. 39

p. 88   'A Denunciation of Patriotism' was reprinted in the *Defendant*, pp 165–172

p. 92   'It was like meeting ... under the sign.' A, p. 36. I stopped at that ... figure of the White Horse.' ibid., p. 37
'shrank from his touch and screamed when he embraced her.' vid. *The Chestertons*, pp 170–172

PART II

7. *Under a Dragon Moon*

p. 97   'that his brutality ... enjoyed one.' *The Chestertons*, p. 171

p. 98   'Oh when the bitter ... each other's face.' TMC
'Of all human institutions ... kindly habit.' *Return to Chesterton*, p. 83
'dreamy old bachelor notion ... are not one spirit.' ibid., p. 82
'Never again ... and we are one.' TMC

p. 99   'Frances and Gilbert ...

p. 101   gamely as he can.' *Father Brown on Chesterton* by Monsignor John O'Connor (1937), p. 45
'one of the most delightful ... these decadent days.' the *Whitehall Review*, 27 February 1902
For reviews of Chesterton's books vid. *G. K. Chesterton: The Critical Judgements Part I 1900–1937*, edited by D. J. Conlon, Antwerp Studies in English Literature

p. 102   'on the occasions ... home or abroad.' *G. K. Chesterton: A Centenary Appraisal*, p. 157
For Chesterton on Noel vid. A., pp 159–163

p. 103   'According to Dr Clifford ... that man *has* a Maker.' *Arthur James Balfour* by Blanche E. C. Dugdale (1939), p. 248

p. 104   'No nation has ever ...

p. 105   of the battle-field!' *Prophets, Priests and Kings* by A. G. Gardiner, pp 98–105
'I can conceive him ... his jolly laughter.' ibid., pp 331–340
'a well-read and sympathetic editor.' A, p. 124

p. 106   'We were poor ...' et seq. *Return to Chesterton*, p. 66 ff.

p. 107   'When he was in Battersea ... savagery or hate!' *Return to Chesterton*, pp 90–91

p. 108   'Men like Savanarola ... of youth and hope.' *Twelve Types*, p. 168
The *New Age*, 6 November 1902
The *Bookman*, February 1903

p. 109   'I have seldom ... like to meet.' Beerbohm to GKC, 4 May 1902
'Max's queer ... humility' MW, p. 135
For Chesterton on Beerbohm vid. A, pp 97–98

p. 110   The *Atheneum*, 13 June 1903
The *Bookman*, July 1903
The only difference ...

p. 111   ... of anything else.' *Robert Browning*, p.17
'but a herd of bulls ... lay waste the world.' *Orthodoxy*, p. 182

7.   *Enter Father Brown*

p. 113   'If you wanted ... by no means robbed.' *The Chestertons*, p. 47
p. 114   'Upon this place ... between you and me.' TMC
'I like you ... as I think.' Fr O'C to GKC, 9 February 1903
p. 115   'Somebody gave me ... of the Spanish Inquisition.' A, pp 324–325
vid. *Father Brown on Chesterton*, pp 4–5
cf. A, pp 327–328
p. 117   GKC Blatchford controversy cf. MW, pp 173–176
p. 126   The *Bystander*, 27 April 1904
p. 127   'I do not think ... sympathy and insight.' the *Sphere*, 9 April 1904
'There is no more remarkable ... mildewed and unmeaning.' *G. F. Watts*, p. 3
'Now Watts, with all his ...
p. 128   through Watt's "Cain".' ibid., pp 130–134
'There is nothing ... things in general.' ibid., p. 168
p. 129   'He considers himself ... paint the town red.' *Father Brown on Chesterton*, p. 61
'One of the proudest days ...' et seq. MW, p. 147–150
p. 130   'For Chesterton and Swinburne, see A, pp 281–284
p. 131   'He would with a soft ... through the whole.' *One Thing and Another* by Hilaire Belloc, pp 172–174
p. 132   'Some people have declared ... they do not drink.' *British Weekly*, 16 February 1905

p. 133   Chesterton and Meredith A, pp 279–280
The Mind of Chesterton, by Christopher Hollis (1970), p. 61
'Suppose that a great . . .
p. 134   discuss in the dark.' *Heretics*, pp 23–24
'Nobody,' Chesterton said . . . than we.' ibid., p. 36
p. 135   'Progress is not . . . ages of faith.' ibid., p. 37
Chesterton on Shaw. ibid., pp 54–67
'The only simplicity . . . grape-nuts on principle.' ibid., p. 136
p. 136   'Blasphemy is an artistic . . . of some exhaustion.' *Heretics*, p. 20

8.   *The Dust-Heaps of Humanity*
p. 138   'This is a great day . . . little Bellocs.' *The Life of Hilaire Belloc*
by Robert Speaight, p. 207
'antagonised a good many . . . members.' *Cecil Chesterton* by
Brocard Sewell, p. 21
'careless of the feelings . . . disapproved of.' ibid.
'I wrote to him . . . in literature.' 'A Generous Opponent' (the
Mark Twain Quarterly, No. 9, Spring 1937)
vid. *Shaw and Chesterton: The Metaphysical Jesters* by
William B. Furlong (1970), pp 4–9
p. 141   'I remember, I remember . . .
p. 142   I was a monkey.' CP, pp 27–28
p. 143   'There is something slow . . .' et seq. *The Everlasting Man*,
pp 20–21
p. 144   'fearful of the effect . . . he consented.' *The Chestertons*, p. 71
p. 146   'He was . . . wits in other books.' *Charles Dickens*, pp 14–15
'a sort of twins of the spirit.' ibid., p. 109
'Dickens . . . it is incredible.' ibid., p. 17
p. 147   'Dickens was not like . . . what people wanted.' ibid., p. 295
the *Throne*, 8 September 1906
'It is not . . . substance called Mr Chesterton.' the *Bookman*,
October 1906
'From my own knowledge of her . . .' et seq. Kate Perugini
to GKC, TMC, cf. MW, p. 158
p. 148   'the clash between enthusiasm . . . to be baseless.' MW, p. 158
p. 151   'touches his high-water mark.' *G. K. Chesterton: A Criticism*, p. 239
The Secret People, CP, pp 173–176
'were committed to accepting the principle of Socialism.' *Cecil
Chesterton* by Brocard Sewell, p. 23

p. 152   'His lectures are without number . . . or his income.' et seq.
          G. K. Chesterton: A Criticism, p. 257, ff
p. 154   the *Jewish Chronicle*, 28 April 1911

10.   *The Romance of Orthodoxy*
p. 160   'I am the Sabbath . . .' et seq. *The Man Who was Thursday*,
          p. 322, ff
p. 161   'The old ogre . . . out of pessimism.' A, p. 102, the *Daily
          Telegraph*, 4 March 1906
          For Chesterton and Henry James. cf. A, pp 218–220
p. 162   'Henry James had a name . . . wider than the Atlantic.' A,
          pp 221–222
          'I have never written a lie . . .
p. 163   a heresy of my own.' TMC
          'I did not try . . . it was orthodoxy.' *Orthodoxy*, p. 17
          'I will begin to worry . . . given us his.' ibid., p. 11, ff
p. 164   'We all agree still . . . Hanwell.' ibid., p. 23, *The Suicide of
          Thought*, ibid., pp 50–78
p. 165   *The Ethics of Elfland*, ibid., pp 79–116
p. 166   'An optimist is a man . . . after your feet.' ibid., pp 117–118
          'The world is not a lodging-house . . . we should leave it.'
          ibid., p. 119
p. 167   'You might as well say . . . in any age.' ibid., pp 133–134
          'This is the thrilling . . .
p. 168   truth reeling but erect.' ibid., pp 183–185
p. 169   'If I were to say . . . much nearer the truth.' ibid., pp 135–137
          'The only thing which . . . on the Serpentine.' ibid., pp 232–233
          'The mass of men have . . .
p. 170   it was his mirth.' ibid., pp 294–297
          'My mother . . . mutiny of soul.' TMC
          'The table groaned . . .
p. 171   crème de menthe.' *The Chestertons*, p. 73
p. 172   'This book is what everybody . . . have yet provoked.' the
          Nation, 25 August 1909
          'Shaw is like the Venus de Milo . . . admirable.' *George Bernard
          Shaw*, p. 23
          'The truth is that . . .
                                        reaching Brighton.' ibid., pp 7–8

11. *The Rolling English Road*
p. 175   the *Westminster Gazette*, 18 December 1909
p. 176   'Master, he do . . . the name of.' *Return to Chesterton*, p. 111
p. 179   'somewhat changed . . . office.' *The Mind of Chesterton*, p. 125
p. 180   'The average man votes . . . of the voter votes.' *Tremendous Trifles*, p. 235
p. 182   'When domesticity . . . pity her for her smallness.' *What's Wrong with the World*, pp 132–133
p. 186   'We haven't the faintest . . . he doesn't either.' the *Evening Standard*, 28 June 1910
         'We agree about the evil . . . other's eyes out.' *What's Wrong with the World*, p. 6
         'We can all see . . . national sanity?' ibid., p. 7
p. 187   'The difference . . . these things clear.' ibid., p. 184
         'without the reader . . . economic interests.' *The Mind of Chesterton*, p. 118
p. 188   'Although Mr Chesterton's "Blake" . . . is entirely ignored.' the *Nation*, p. 118, 17 December 1910
         'because his visions were true . . . he was inspired.' *William Blake*, p. 94
         'You and I may be . . . the British Empire.' ibid., p. 132
p. 189   'As the Hygienist insists . . . must wear nothing.' ibid., p. 174
p. 190   'In the ordinary modern . . . symbol of God.' ibid., pp 141–142
p. 191   'As the élite of Anglicanism . . . a little uncomfortable.' *Christian Commonwealth*, 25 June 1911
p. 192   'The Song of the Strange Ascetic.' CP, pp 216–217
p. 194   'A Ballade of Suicide' CP, pp 193–194
         'The stories of Father Brown . . .
              would have been greater.' *Country Life*, 23 September 1911
p. 195   'there is no pretence . . . stories.' *The Mind of Chesterton*, pp 179–183
         '"Nobody ever notices . . . never be known.' *The Innocence of Father Brown*, p. 146
p. 196   'When a writer invents . . . but of a picture.' A, p. 322
         For Chesterton on Father Brown, see A, pp 322–323
p. 197   'The Ballad of the White Horse' CP, pp 221–316

12. *Of Great Limbs Gone to Chaos*
p. 198   'There exists in the midst . . . to be desired.' EW, 7 September 1911

p. 198   'the whole tone ... the Jewish mark.' EW, 21 September 1911

p. 199   'Now unless ... of modern questions?' EW, 28 September 1911
'All that is said here ...

p. 200   make up your minds.' EW, 26 October 1911
'Lepanto' CP. pp 114–121, vid., *Father Brown on Chesterton*,
pp 84–85

p. 204   the *British Weekly*, 29 February 1912

p. 207   'O God of Earth and Altar ....' CP, pp 146–147
'A revolutionist would say ... only their powers.' *A Miscellany
of Men*, pp 217–218

p. 208   'If you visit ... success is unsuccessful.' ibid., pp 219–220

p. 211   'A Song of Strange Drinks' NW, 23 January 1913 reprinted as
'The Song of Right and Wrong' CP, pp 217–218

p. 212   'It is a series ... end of the stick.' NW, 6 March 1913
Chesterton on Macauley, vid., *The Victorian Age in Literature*,
pp 28–36

p. 213   'One of them went ... the village idiot.' ibid., p. 143
'A clever undergraduate ....' ff. the *Times Literary Supplement*,
20 February 1913

p. 214   'If ever a human ... such things.' NW, 3 April 1913
'The politics of ... Crypto-Semitism.' NW, 10 April 1913

p. 216   'When I consider ... sending you to prison.' *Rex v Chesterton*,
p. 590
'Though Lever may treat ...

p. 217   which is slavery.' MW, p. 319

p. 220   'A cloven pride ... Cock shall crow.' 'When I came back to
Fleet Street' CP, pp 185–186

13.   *Breakdown*

p. 221   'The trouble with the journalist ... lazy and busy.' NW, 15 May
1913

p. 222   'Mr Chesterton ... Puck of Spook's Hill.' The *Star*,
8 November 1913
'Only when he resorted ... the first water.' the *Nation*,
15 November 1913
'in a perpetual state ... no longer.' *Heretics*, p. 128

p. 223   'G.K.C. is like Peter Pan ... of a child.' *Ladies' Pictorial*,
15 November 1913

p. 224   'When he left . . . and deserves reprinting.' *Return to Chesterton*, p. 137

p. 225   Ada Chesterton on Elodie Belloc, vid., *The Chestertons*, p. 76

p. 226   'G.K.C. was the first man . . . Asiatic reformers.' NW, 29 January 1914

p. 227   The *Times Literary Supplement*, 22 January 1914

p. 229   'He avows that . . . I *want* to.' *The Barbarism of Berlin*, pp 40–41

PART III

14. *A Certain Detachment*

p. 233   For Chesterton's illness, vid., *Father Brown on Chesterton*, pp 98–102

p. 237   Freda Spencer, vid., *Return to Chesterton*, pp 138–146

p. 238   'Are they clinging . . . Do they Smith?' 'Antichrist, or the Reunion of Christendom: an Ode', CP, pp 152–154
         'great with personality . . . to tatters.' NW, 27 May 1915

p. 239   'When we say . . . work of six days.' NW, 5 August 1915

p. 240   'when the Irish say . . . an unknown tongue.' *The Crimes of England*, p. 54

p. 241   'Christian charity . . . smell of onions.' NW, 9 December 1915
         'Look, girl . . . to This.' *Return to Chesterton*, p. 140

p. 243   For Mrs Walpole, see ibid., p. 146
         'Much curiosity was aroused . . . Post Office.' NW, 27 July 1916
         'The "rebellion" organised . . .

p. 244   in her cause.' NW, 11 May 1916
         'I am the worst editor in the world.' NW, 7 December 1916

p. 245   'Christmas Day forces itself . . . but not surrender.' NW, 14 December 1916
         'The Whiggism of Bertram Russell' NW, 11 January 1917

p. 246   For Cecil Chesterton's marriage, see *The Chestertons*, pp 201–204

p. 247   For the Shaw review, see the *Observer*, 4 November 1917
         'Only as an expression . . . and the agitators.' The *Times Literary Supplement*, 22 November 1917

p. 249   For the death of Cecil Chesterton, see *The Chestertons*, pp 237–240

15.   *The Editor Travels*
p. 253   For Yeats and Chesterton, see *W. B. Yeats* by Joseph Hone,
         p. 315
         'did almost certainly cross that . . . mysterious mountains.' *Irish
         Impressions*, p. 3
p. 254   'will be like touching trees . . . to move and dance.' ibid., p. 14
         'even when they were . . . it was killed.' ibid., p. 15
         'a premonition of . . . modern Ireland.' ibid., p. 15
         'It is not so much . . . blows to Ireland.' ibid., p. 35
         'At least it failed . . . civilisation.' ibid., p. 157
         For 'Belfast and the Irish Problem', see ibid., pp 209–243
p. 257   For the Jerusalem visit, see Frances Chesterton's Diary, IMC
p. 260   'It seems possible . . . in some sense remember.' The New
         Jerusalem, pp 297–298
p. 263   'Now I can scarcely . . .
p. 264   to my own land.' *The Well and the Shadows*, pp 176–177

16.   *What I saw in America*
p. 267   'was one of the few . . . the modern world.' NW, 19 November
         1920
p. 268   For the American tour, see TMC
p. 275   'Frances has not been well . . . something like a farewell.' *Father
         Brown on Chesterton*, p. 125
         'I used to think . . . in a field.' MW, p. 384
p. 278   For the information on Hilary Gray I am indebted to the Gray
         family
p. 281   For the death of Edward Chesterton, see *The Chestertons*,
         pp 263–265
p. 282   'My father died . . . sort of help.' MW, p. 393
p. 284   For a description of Top Meadow, see *The Chestertons*,
         pp 254–257
         'I ought to have written . . . joy of seeing you.' *Father Brown
                                             on Chesterton*, pp 126–127

17.   *My name is Lazarus*
p. 285   'where Rome acted . . .' et seq. MW, p. 395
         'Oh! I shall be . . . such a step.' *Father Brown on Chesterton*, p. 129
         'It was a sight . . .

p. 286   head on one side.' ibid., p. 129
'After the baptism . . . comforting her.' MW, p. 396
'After one moment . . .

p. 287   and I live.' CP, p. 387
'When people ask me . . . never sinned.' et seq. A, pp 329–330

p. 288   'I write this . . .

p. 289   it is the truth.' NW, pp 396–397

p. 290   'What a glorious garden . . . unable to read.' *What I Saw in America*, p. 33
'When I was on the wild coast . . .
                    wanting at the last.' *Irish Impressions*, pp 201–202
The *Observer*, 19 November 1922

p. 291   'G.K.C. to Maurice Baring, 14 February 1923, TMC, Also see MW, pp 389–391

p. 293   For 'A new *New Witness*', see NW, 12 January 1923

p. 295   'The new paper . . . it or not.' NW, 20 April 1923

p. 296   'Divorce is a thing . . . fashionable divorce.' *Fancies Versus Fads*, p. 124
'how long liberated women . . . hangwoman.' ibid., p. 46
'A more restrained . . . Chesterton.' *New York Times*, 2 March 1924
'A lover of men . . .

p. 297   but Christ.' *St. Francis of Assisi*, p. 14
'High in the dark house . . .

p. 298   no figure on the road.' ibid., pp 58–61

18.   *This Single Adventure*

p. 299   'In that book . . . a permanent monument.' *National Review*, 22 April 1961

p. 301   'The second half of human history . . . our faith is founded', *The Everlasting Man*, p. 191

p. 304   For Distributism, see *Return to Chesterton*, pp 208–232

p. 306   'will give the student . . . desire for inflation.' the *Observer*, 13 December 1925

p. 307   'with this quality . . . industrial world.' *William Cobbett*, p. 225

p. 308   'Holmes might have . . . he explains a murder.' the *Yorkshire Post*, 23 June 1926

p. 309   'The first fallacy . . . the same as Posen.' *The Catholic Church and Conversion*, pp 75–76

p. 309   For the Polish Visit, see Letters of FC to MLC, TMC

p. 312   'The determination to save ... waver we are lost.' *One Thing and Another* by Hilaire Belloc, pp 206–208

p. 313   'What Poland is', *Pologne Litteraire*, No 25. 1927

19.   *The Thing*

p. 314   'He wounded none ... the soul through hatred.' *The Place of Gilbert Chesterton in English Letters*, p. 81
          'He had no enemies ... occasion for attack.' ibid., p. 80
          'He knew his limitations ... anybody else.' *Return to Chesterton*, p. 229

p. 315   'You've got to accept ... with the Faith.' TMC

p. 318   For Eliot on Chesterton, see the *Nation and Athenaeum*, 31 December 1927
          'Some sneer; some snigger ... with a bang.' the *Listener*, 18 March 1936

p. 319   'The young men ... spirit of Chesterton.' *Return to Chesterton*, p. 220
          For the Nicholls family, see ibid., pp 160–178

p. 321   'Second American Tour. Letters from FC to MLC and Notes by Dorothy Collins, TMC

p. 327   'When this book on Chaucer ... more illuminating.' the *Sunday Times*, 18 April 1932

p. 328   'The present writer is prayerfully ... learned biographers.' *Chaucer*, p. 98
          'Some critics have vaguely ... the balance at all.' ibid., pp 249–250

p. 329   'Details of the Irish visit are taken from Letters of FC to MLC and to her mother Blanche Blogg, TMC

p. 330   'No man could be received ... things achieved.' *Christendom in Dublin*, pp 56–58

p. 331   'I am only tired ... my darling girl.' *The Chestertons*, p. 289
          'The only time I ever saw ... than an elephant.' the *New Statesman*, 23 August 1963

20.   *Te, Lucis ante terminum*

p. 333   'It is typical of a complex ... et seq., *G.K's Weekly*, 8 June 1933

p. 334   'It is almost as difficult ... et seq., *G.K's Weekly*, 17 August 1933

p. 335   'It was a backwash of . . . Aristotelian liberality.' *St. Thomas Aquinas*, p. x
'defended the great vow . . . and for the poor.' ibid., p. 84
'turned back . . . of his time.' ibid.

p. 336   'In so far as there was ever . . . the habit of thinking.' ibid., pp 90–91
'St Thomas every bit as much . . . against the Augustinians.' ibid., pp 93–94

p. 337   '. . . a perculiar point of view . . . which is from God.' ibid., p. 175
'So it is with the great . . .

p. 339   substituted Suggestion.' ibid., pp 233–235
p. 344   'People, if you have prayers . . . poor men are free.' CP, p. 271

Selected Works by
G.K. Chesterton

1900   *Greybeards at Play*, R.Brimley Johnson
       The Wild Knight and Other Poems, Grant Richards
1901   *The Defendant*, Dent (1914)
1902   *G.F. Watts*, Duckworth
       Twelve Types, A.L.Humphreys
1903   *Robert Browning*, English Men of Letters Series, Macmillan
1904   *The Napoleon of Notting Hill*, John Lane
1905   *The Club of Queer Trades*, Harper Bros
       Heretics, John Lane
1906   *Charles Dickens*, Methuen
1908   *The Man Who Was Thursday*, Arrowsmith
       Orthodoxy, John Lane
       All Things Considered, Methuen
1909   *George Bernard Shaw*, John Lane
       The Ball and the Cross, Wells Gardner
       Tremendous Trifles, Methuen
       Defence of Nonsense
1910   *Thackeray*, Masters of Literature Series, Bell
       What's Wrong with the World? Cassell
       William Blake, Popular Library of Art, Duckworth
       Alarms and Discursions, Methuen
       Five Types, A. L. Humphreys
1911   *The Innocence of Father Brown*, Cassell
       Criticisms and Appreciations of Charles Dickens, Dent (1935)
       The Ballad of the White Horse, Methuen
1912   *Manalive*, Nelson
       A Miscellany of Men, Methuen
       The Victorian Age in Literature, Home University Library, Dent
       Simplicity of Tolstoy, A.L.Humphreys

1913   *Magic: A Fantastic Comedy*, Martin Secker
1914   *The Wisdom of Father Brown*, Cassell
        The Flying Inn, Methuen
        The Barbarism of Berlin, Cassell
1915   *Poems*, Burns, Oates & Washbourne
        Wine, Water and Song, Methuen
        The Crimes of England, Palmer & Hayward
        Letters to an Old Garibaldian, Methuen
1917   *A Short History of England*, Chatto & Windus
        The Utopia of Usurers, Boni & Liveright, New York
1919   *Irish Impressions*, Collins
1920   *The Uses of Diversity*, Methuen
        The New Jerusalem, Hodder & Stoughton
        The Superstition of Divorce, Chatto & Windus
1922   *Eugenics and Other Evils*, Cassell
        The Man Who Knew Too Much, Cassell
        What I Saw in America, Hodder & Stoughton
        The Ballad of St Barbara, Cecil Palmer, in *Collected Poems*
1923   *Fancies versus Fads*, Methuen
        St Francis of Assisi, People's Library, Hodder & Stoughton
1924   *The End of the Roman Road*, Classic Press
1925   *The Everlasting Man*, Hodder & Stoughton
        Tales of the Long Bow, Cassell
        William Cobbett, Hodder & Stoughton
        The Superstitions of the Sceptic, W. Heffer & Sons
1926   *The Incredulity of Father Brown*, Cassell
        The Outline of Sanity, Methuen
        The Queen of Seven Swords, Sheed & Ward
        The Catholic Church and Conversion, Burns, Oates & Washbourne
1927   *Collected Poems*, Cecil Palmer
        The Return of Don Quixote, Chatto & Windus
        Robert Louis Stevenson, Hodder & Stoughton
        The Secret of Father Brown, Cassell
        The Judgment of Dr Johnson, Sheed & Ward
        Gloria in Profundis, Ariel Poems Series, Faber & Faber
1928   *Generally Speaking*, Methuen
        The Sword of Wood, Elkin Mathews
1929   *The Poet and the Lunatics*, Cassell
        The Father Brown Stories, Cassell

1929   *Ubi Ecclesia*, Ariel Poems Series, Faber & Faber
        The Thing, Sheed & Ward
        G.K.C. as M.C., edited by J.P. de Fonseka, Methuen
        The Turkey and the Turk, Pepler
1930   *The Grave of Arthur*, Ariel Poems Series, Faber & Faber
        Come to Think of It, Methuen
        The Four Faultless Felons, Cassell
        The Resurrection of Rome, Hodder & Stoughton
1931   *All is Grist*, Methuen
1932   *Chaucer*, Faber & Faber
        Sidelights on New London and Newer York, Sheed & Ward
        Christendom in Dublin, Sheed & Ward
1933   *All I Survey*, Methuen
        St Thomas Aquinas, People's Library, Hodder & Stoughton
1934   *Avowals and Denials*, Methuen
1935   *The Scandal of Father Brown*, Cassell
        The Well and the Shallows, Sheed & Ward
1936   *As I was Saying*, Methuen
        Autobiography, Hutchinson
        Chesterton Omnibus, Methuen
1937   *Paradoxes of Mr Pond*, Cassell
        The Man Who Was Chesterton, collected by Raymond Bond, Dodd
            Mead, USA
1938   *The Coloured Lands*, Sheed & Ward
1940   *The End of the Armistice*, Sheed & Ward
1950   *The Common Man*, Sheed and Ward
1952   *The Surprise*, Sheed and Ward
1953   *A Handful of Authors*, Sheed and Ward
1955   *The Glass Walking-Stick*, Methuen
1958   *Lunacy and Letters*, Sheed and Ward
1964   *The Spice of Life*, Darwen Finlayson
1971   *Chesterton on Shakespeare*, Darwen Finlayson
1975   *The Apostle and the Wild Duck*, Paul Elek
1985   *The Bodley Head G.K. Chesterton*, selected and with an Introduc-
            tion by P.J. Kavanagh, The Bodley Head

Index